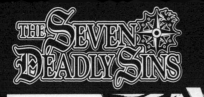

THE SEVEN DEADLY SINS

nakaba suzuki presents

39

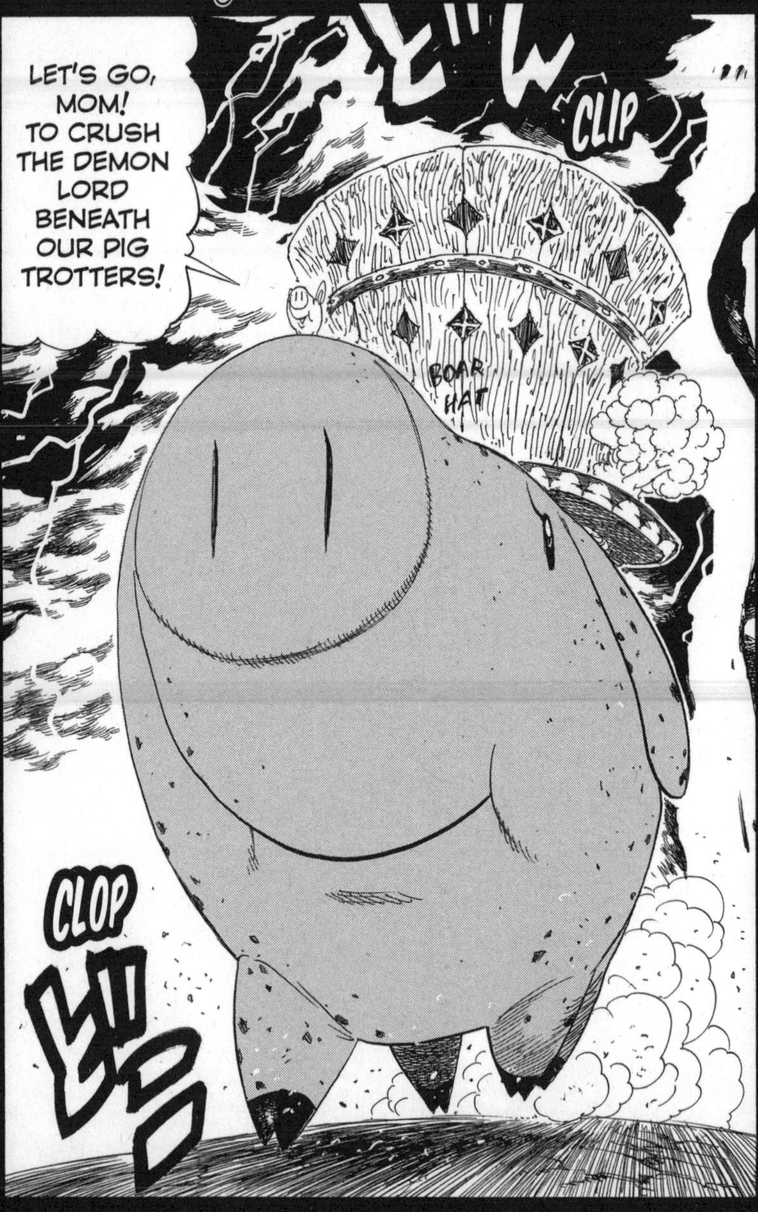
CLIP
LET'S GO, MOM! TO CRUSH THE DEMON LORD BENEATH OUR PIG TROTTERS!
BOAR HAT
CLOP

CONTENTS

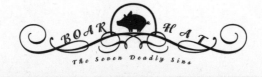

BOAR HAT

The Seven Deadly Sins

THE SEVEN DEADLY SINS

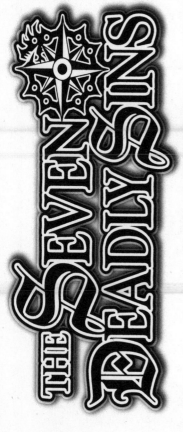

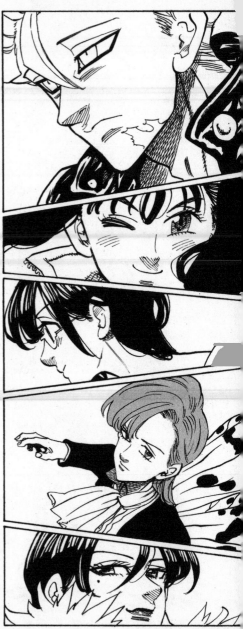

Chapter 321 - The Light

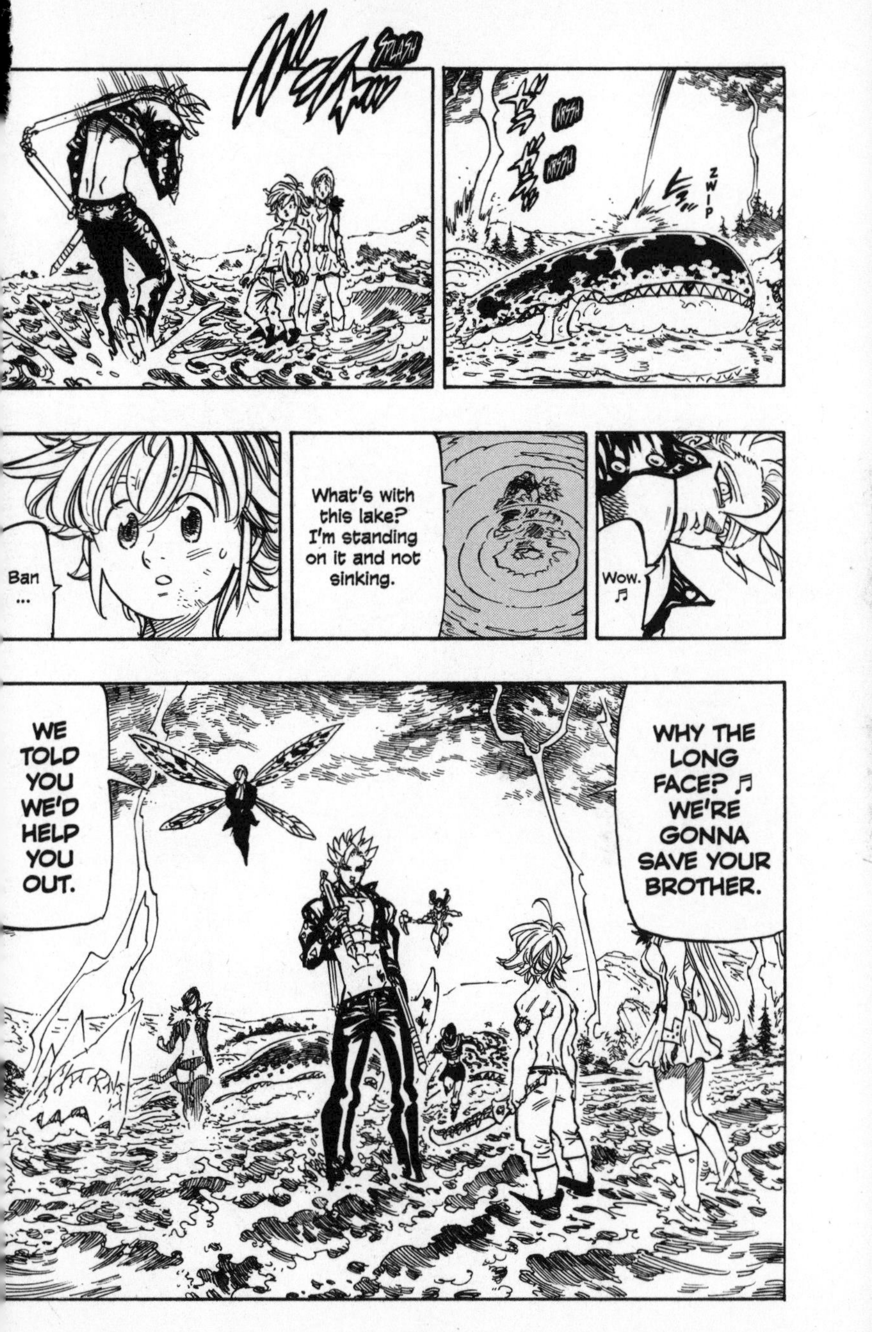
KRSSH
KRSSH
ZWIP
SPLASH
Wow. ♬
What's with this lake? I'm standing on it and not sinking.
Ban ...
WHY THE LONG FACE? ♬ WE'RE GONNA SAVE YOUR BROTHER.
WE TOLD YOU WE'D HELP YOU OUT.

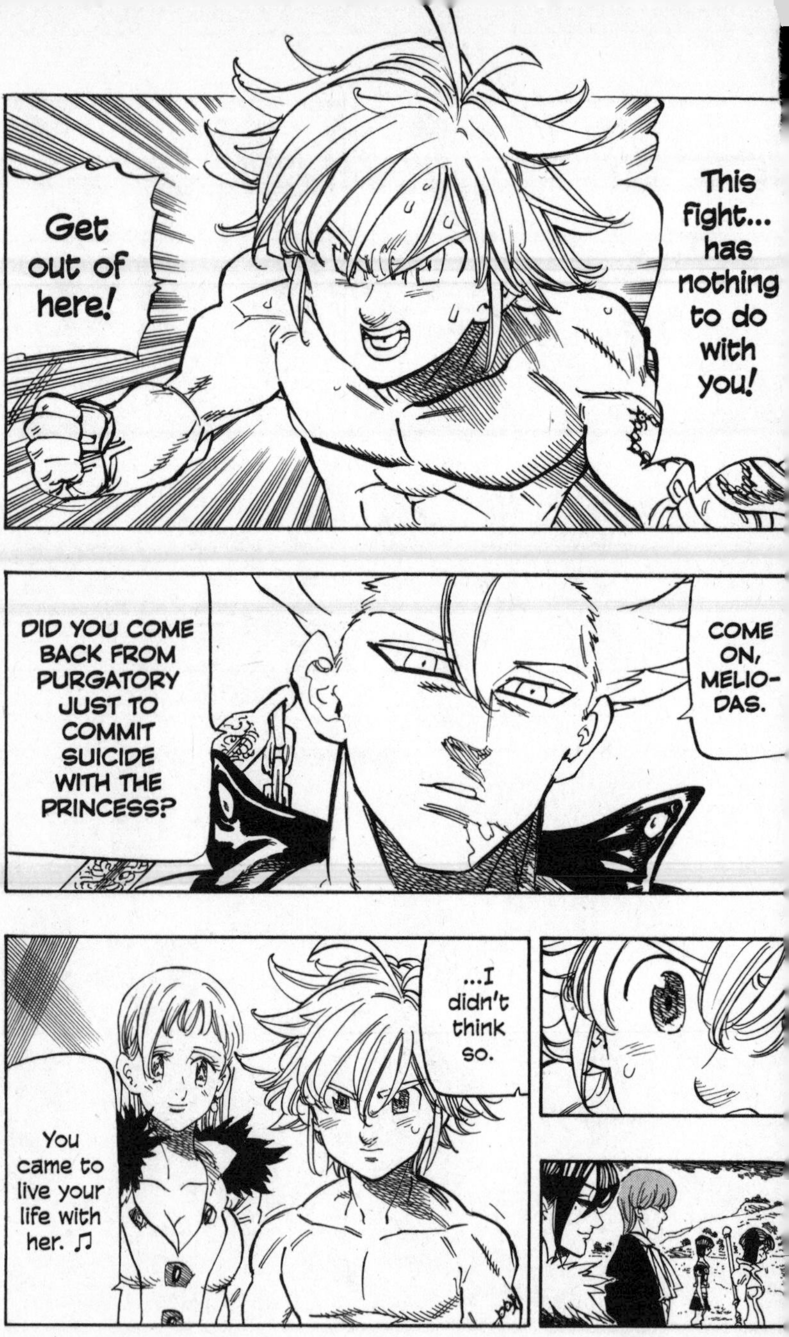
This fight... has nothing to do with you!
Get out of here!
COME ON, MELIO-DAS.
DID YOU COME BACK FROM PURGATORY JUST TO COMMIT SUICIDE WITH THE PRINCESS?
...I didn't think so.
You came to live your life with her. ♫

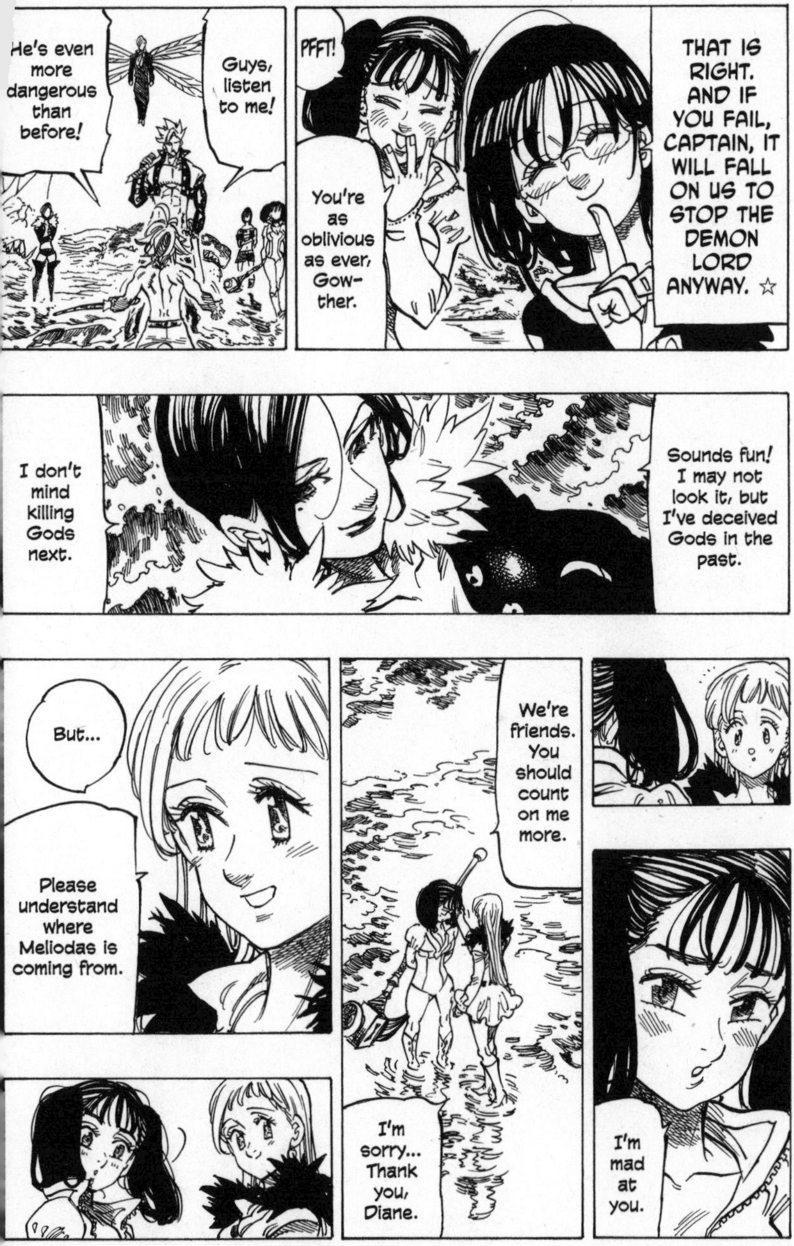
THAT IS RIGHT. AND IF YOU FAIL, CAPTAIN, IT WILL FALL ON US TO STOP THE DEMON LORD ANYWAY. ☆
PFFT!
You're as oblivious as ever, Gow-ther.
Guys, listen to me!
He's even more dangerous than before!
Sounds fun! I may not look it, but I've deceived Gods in the past.
I don't mind killing Gods next.
I'm mad at you.
We're friends. You should count on me more.
I'm sorry... Thank you, Diane.
But...
Please understand where Meliodas is coming from.

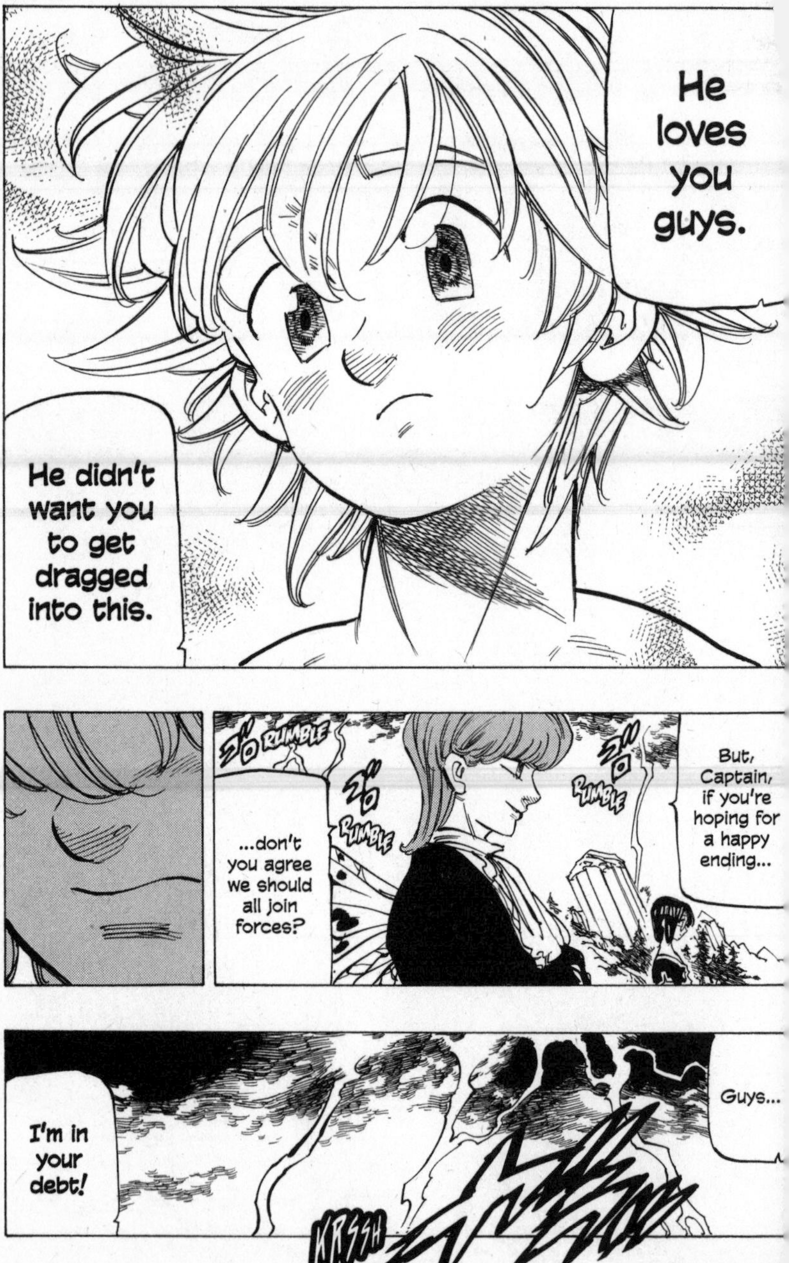
He loves you guys.
He didn't want you to get dragged into this.
But, Captain, if you're hoping for a happy ending...
RUMBLE
RUMBLE
RUMBLE
...don't you agree we should all join forces?
Guys...
I'm in your debt!
KRSSH

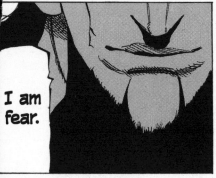

I am fear.

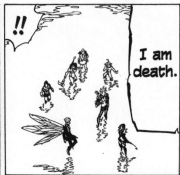

!!

I am death.

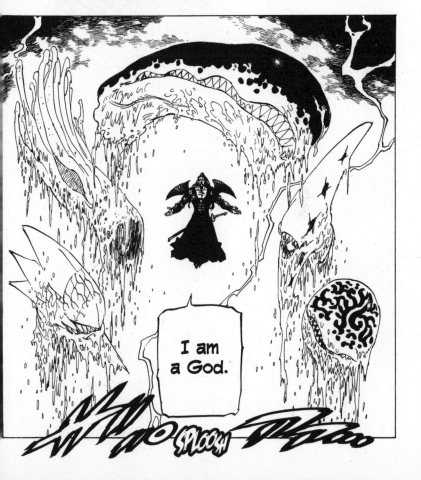

I am a God.

SPLOOSH

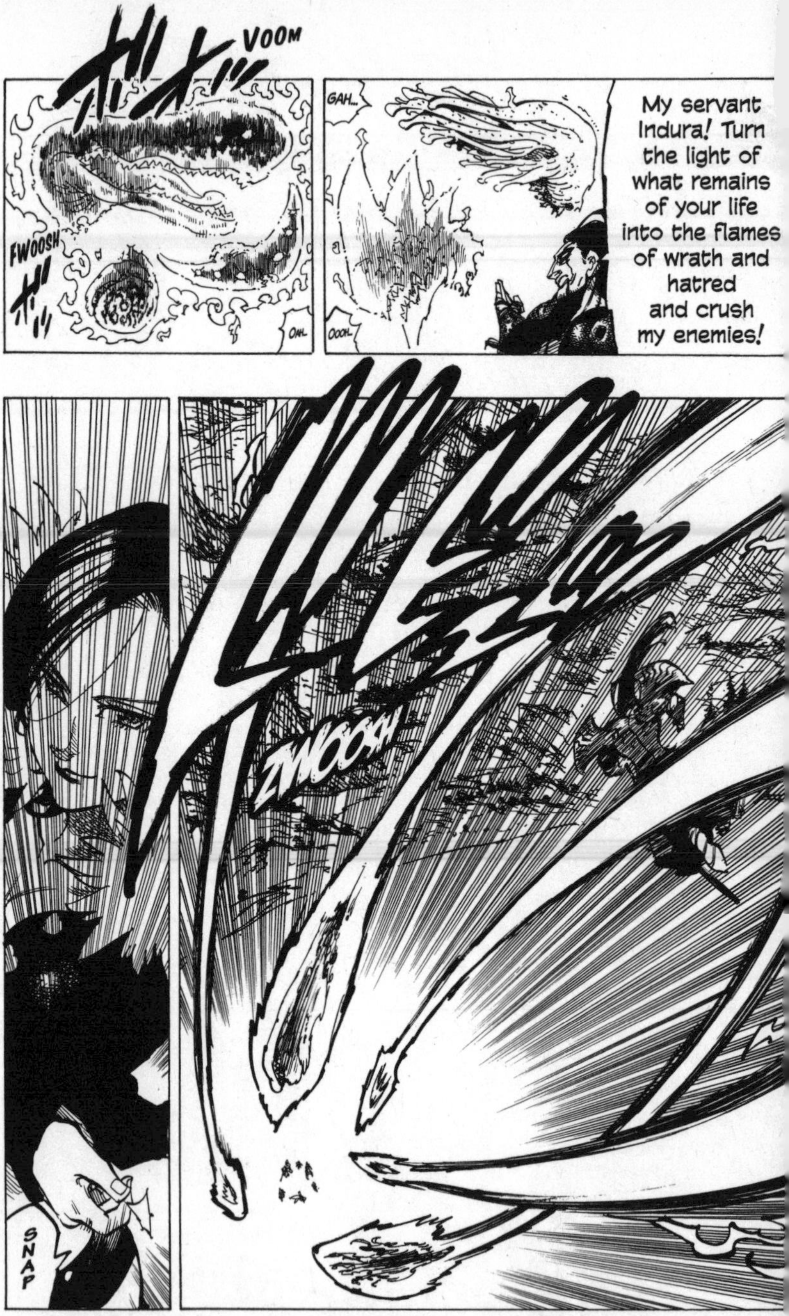
GAH...
My servant Indura! Turn the light of what remains of your life into the flames of wrath and hatred and crush my enemies!
OOOH...
VOOM
FWOOSH
OAH
ZWOOSH
SNAP

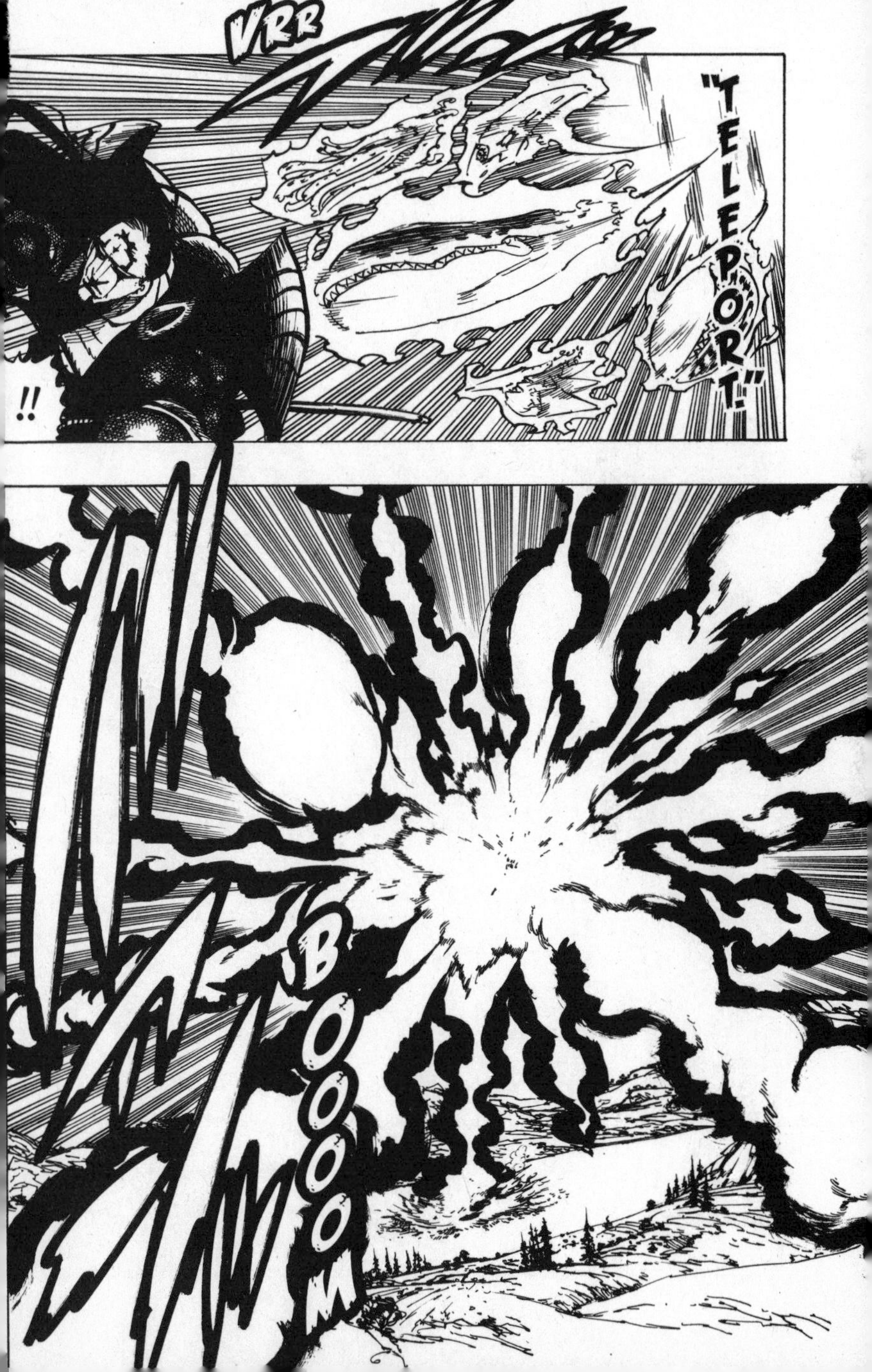
"TELEPORT."
VRR
!!
BOOOOOM

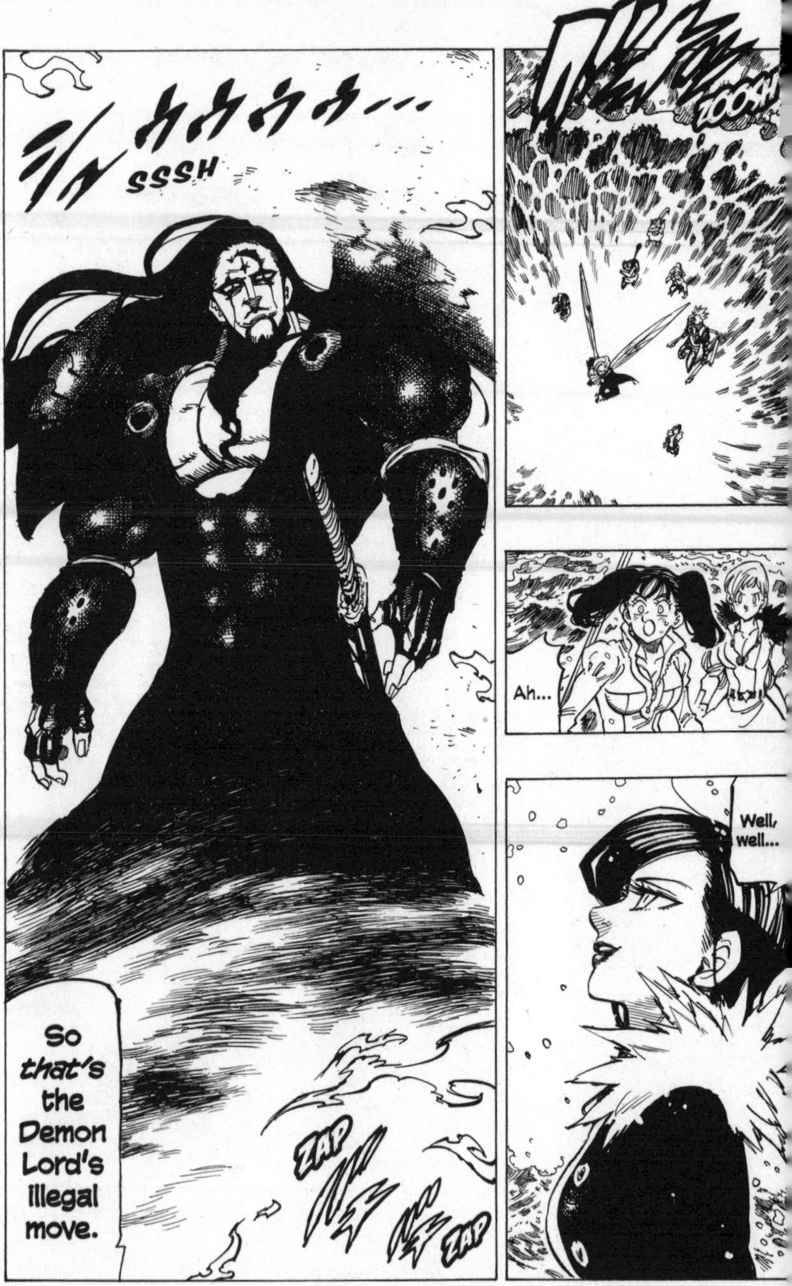
ZOOAH
Ah...
Well, well...
SSSH
So *that's* the Demon Lord's illegal move.
ZAP
ZAP

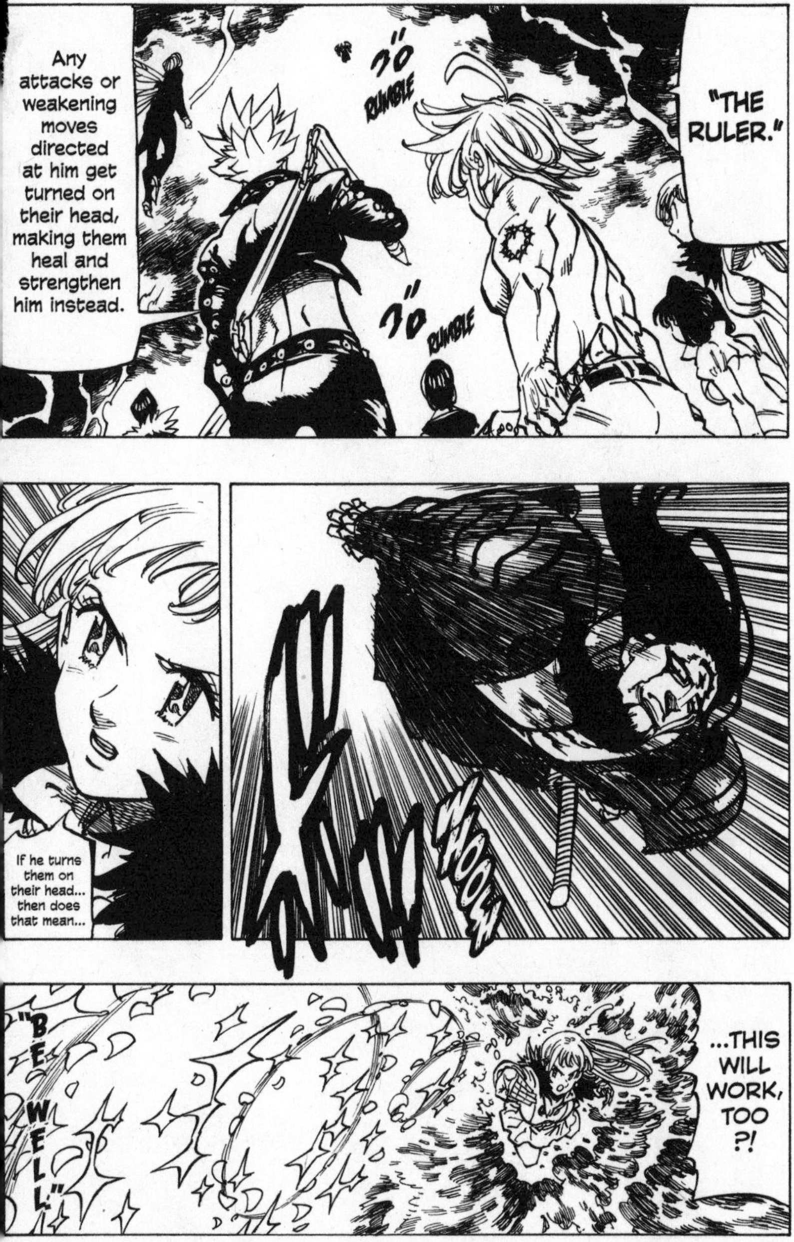
"THE RULER."
RUMBLE
Any attacks or weakening moves directed at him get turned on their head, making them heal and strengthen him instead.
RUMBLE
WHOOM
If he turns them on their head... then does that mean...
...THIS WILL WORK, TOO?!
"BE WELL"

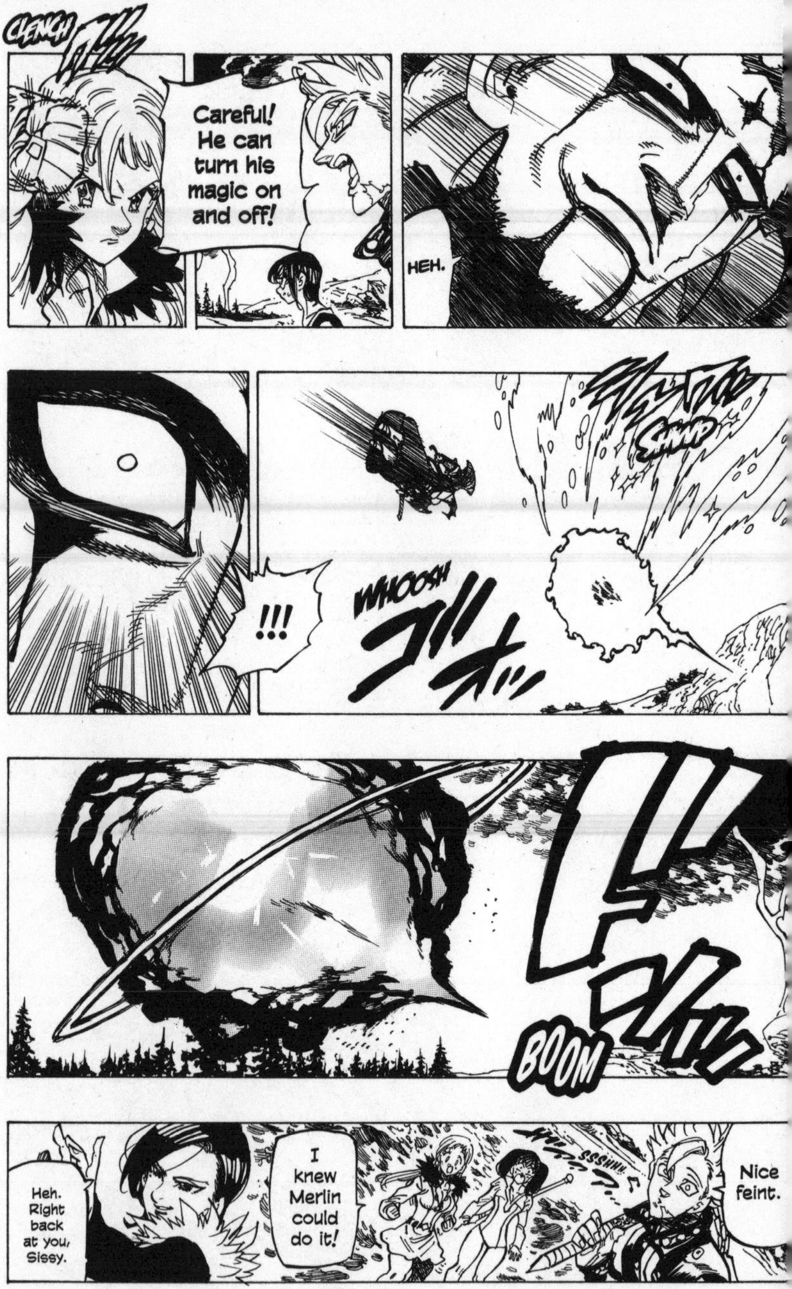
HEH.
Careful! He can turn his magic on and off!
CLENCH
SHWP
WHOOSH
!!!
BOOM
Nice feint.
I knew Merlin could do it!
Heh. Right back at you, Sissy.

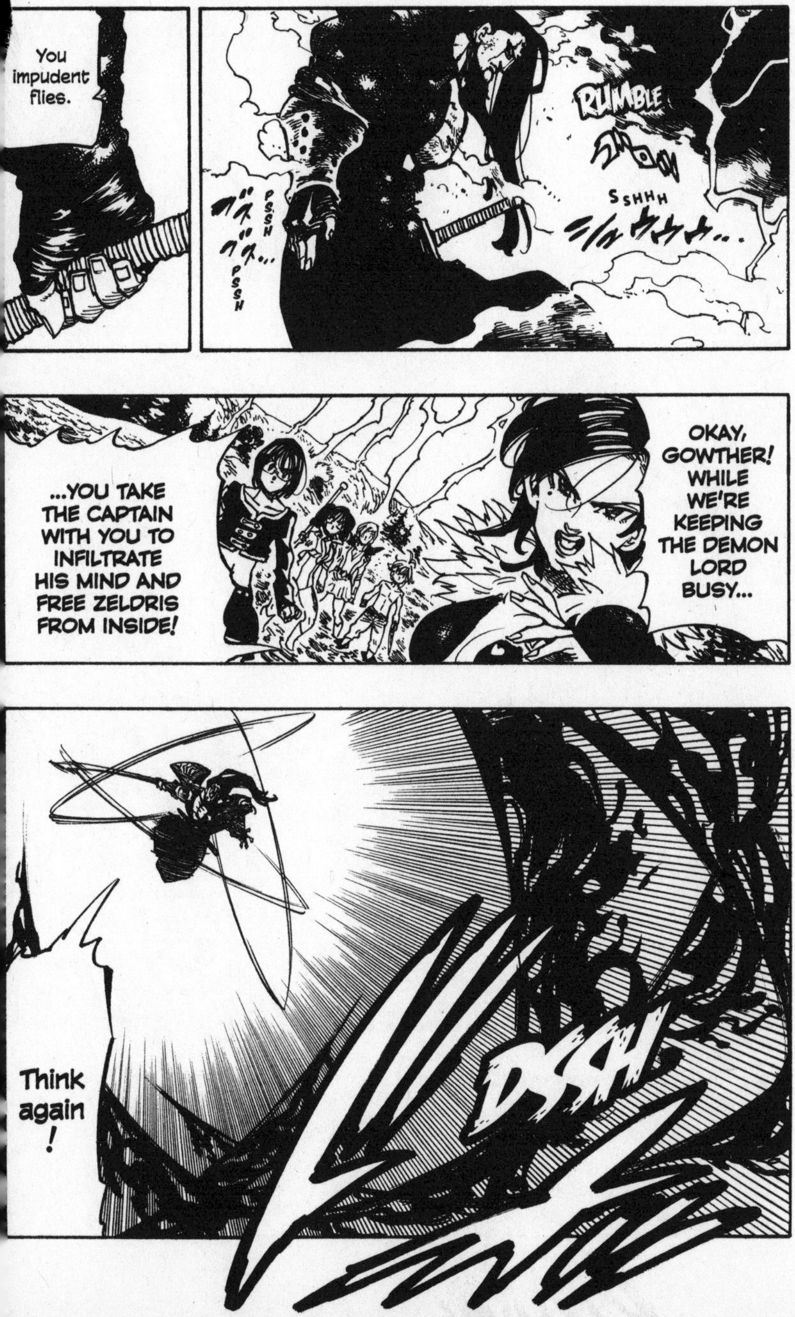
RUMBLE
SSHHH
PSSH
PSSH
You impudent flies.
OKAY, GOWTHER! WHILE WE'RE KEEPING THE DEMON LORD BUSY...
...YOU TAKE THE CAPTAIN WITH YOU TO INFILTRATE HIS MIND AND FREE ZELDRIS FROM INSIDE!
DSH
Think again!

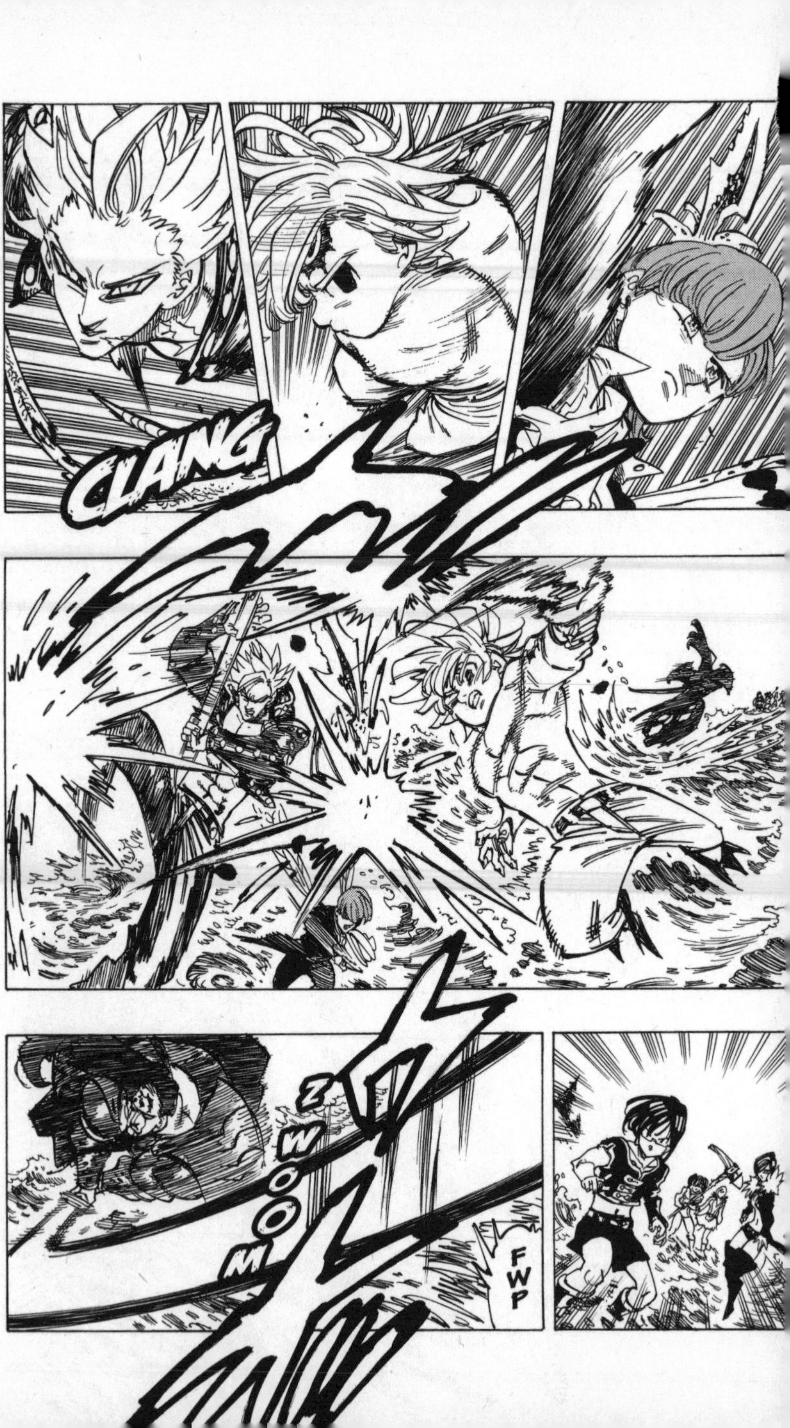
CLANG
FWP
ZWOOOM

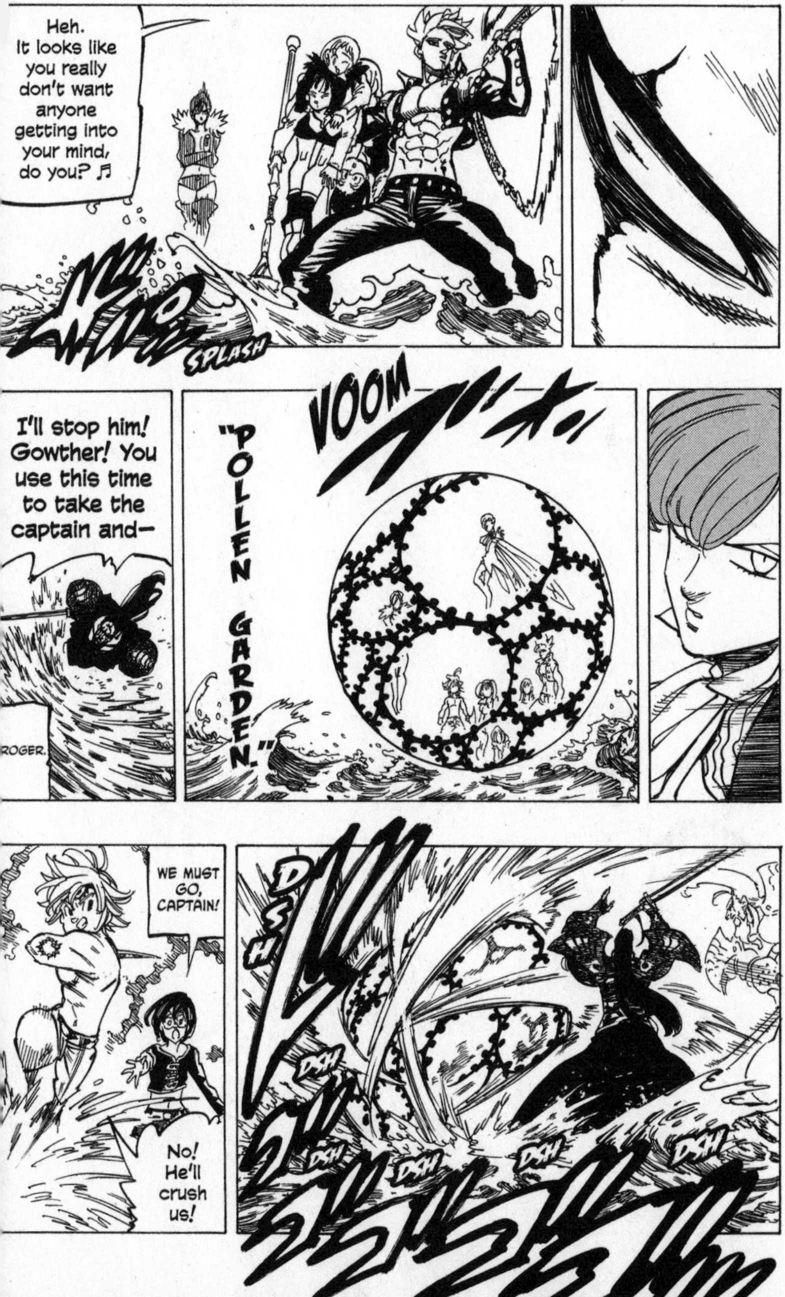
Heh. It looks like you really don't want anyone getting into your mind, do you? ♬
SPLASH
VOOM
"POLLEN GARDEN."
I'll stop him! Gowther! You use this time to take the captain and—
ROGER.
DSH
DSH
DSH
DSH
DSH
DSH
WE MUST GO, CAPTAIN!
No! He'll crush us!

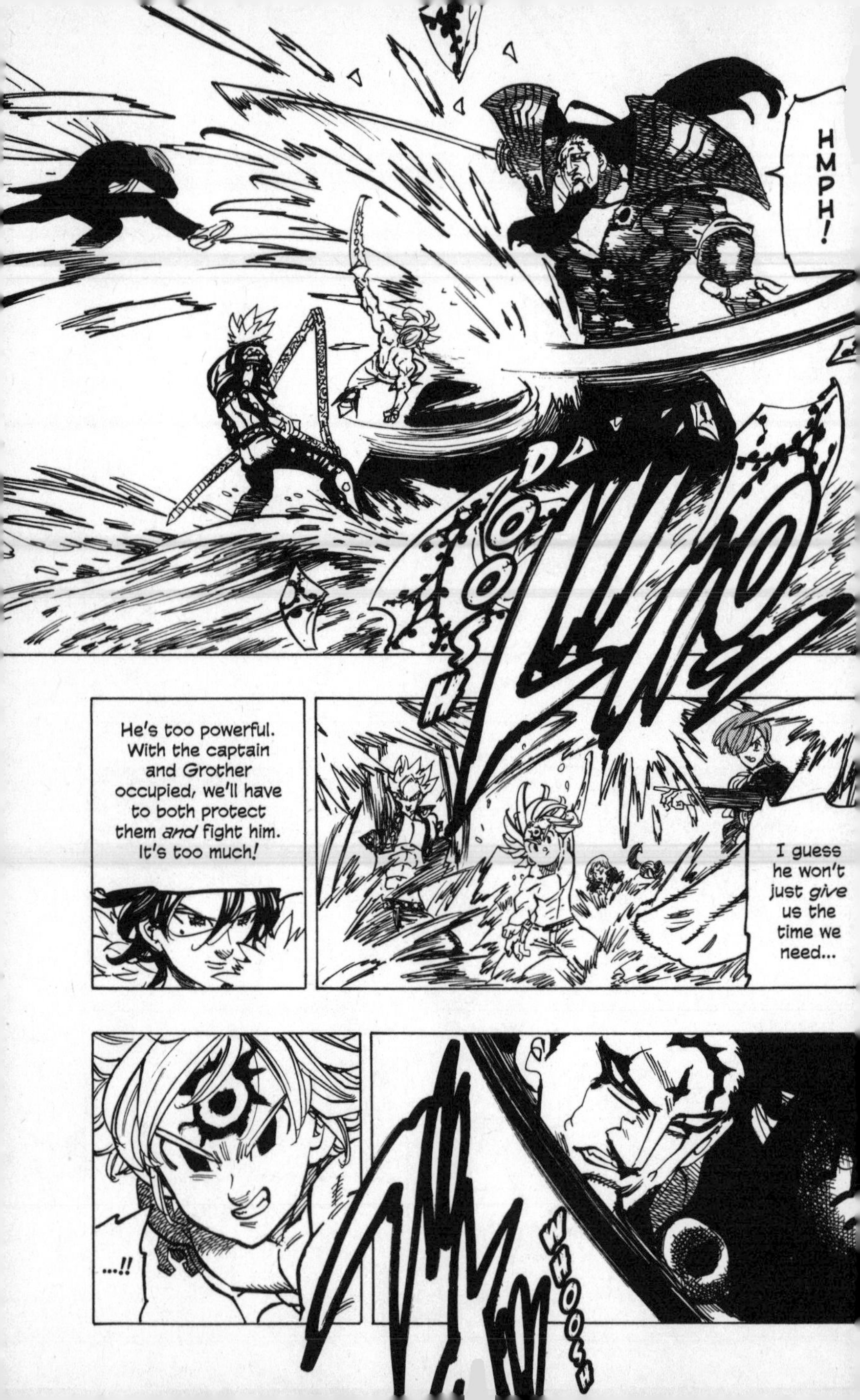
HMPH!
DOOOSH
I guess he won't just *give* us the time we need...
He's too powerful. With the captain and Grother occupied, we'll have to both protect them *and* fight him. It's too much!
WHOOOSH
...!!

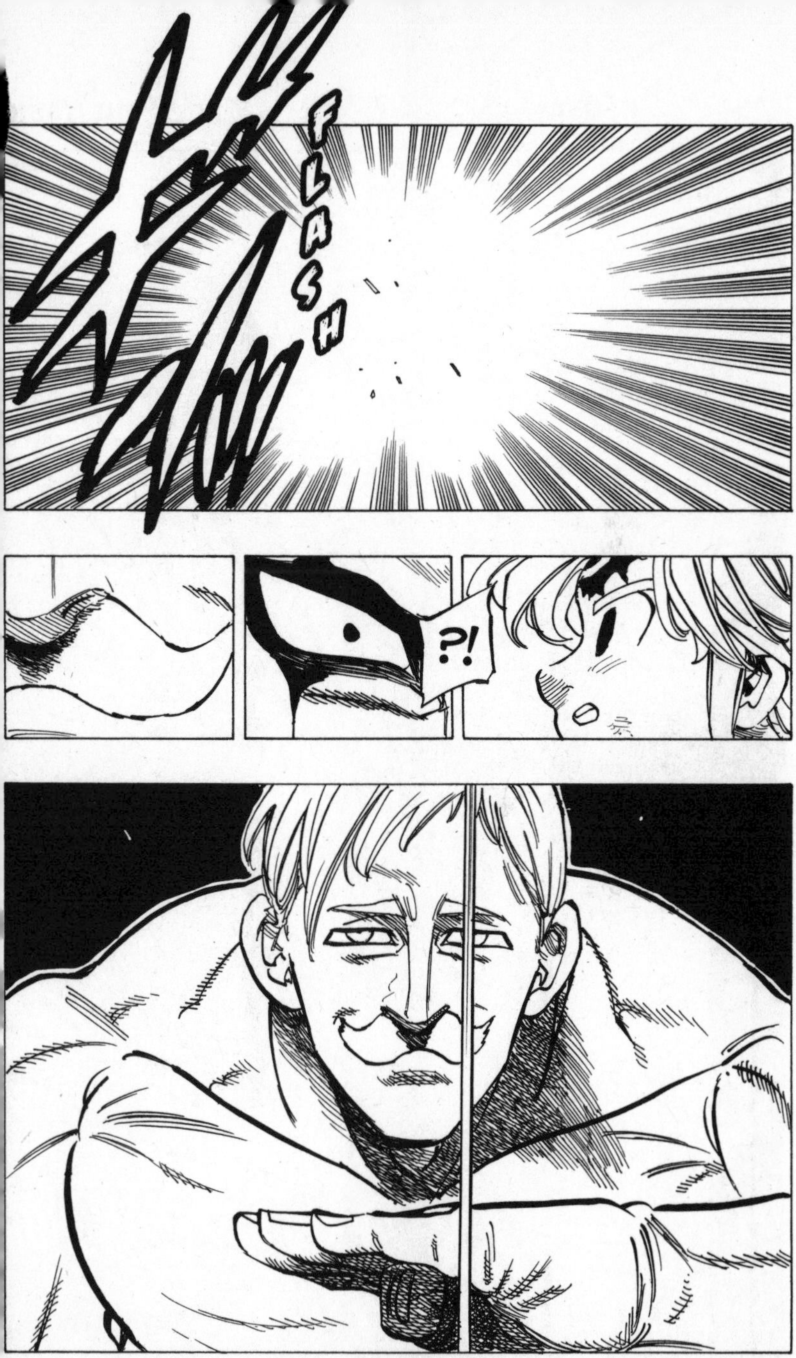
FLASH
?!

Chapter 322 - The Voice Calling Your Name

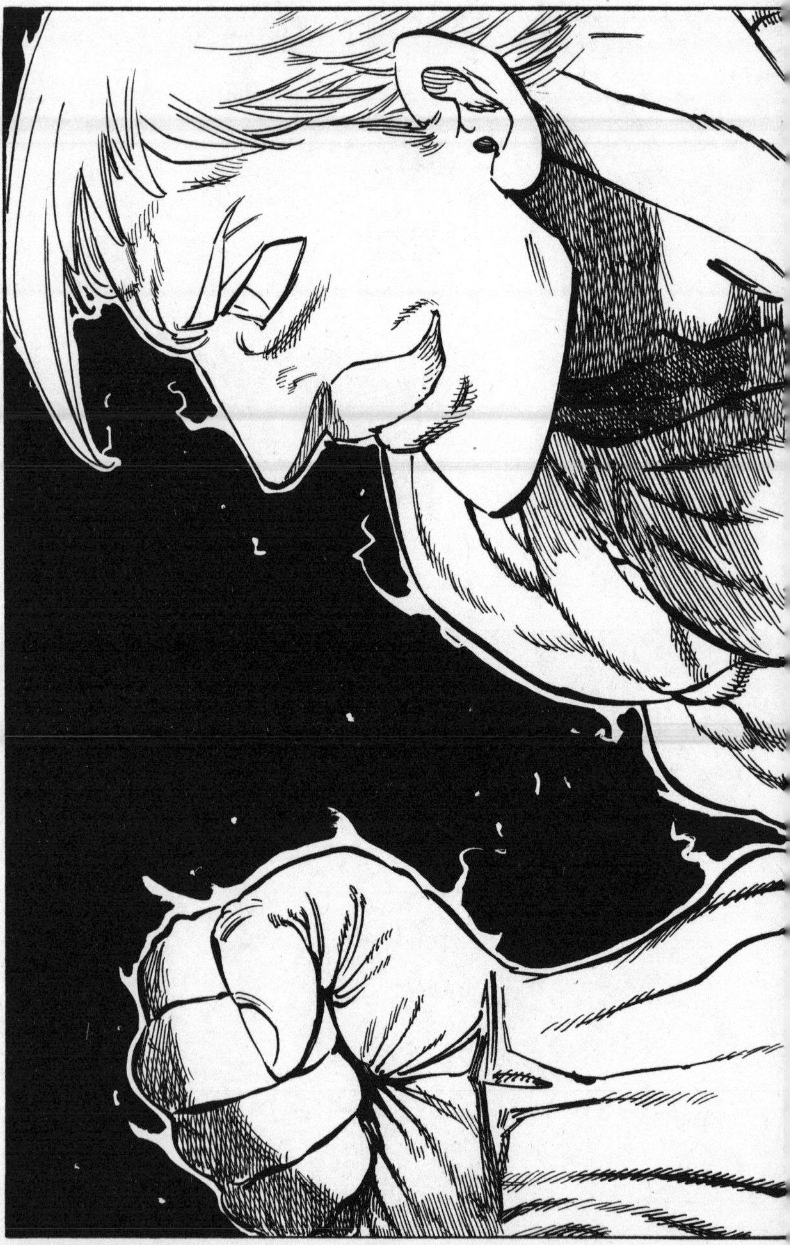

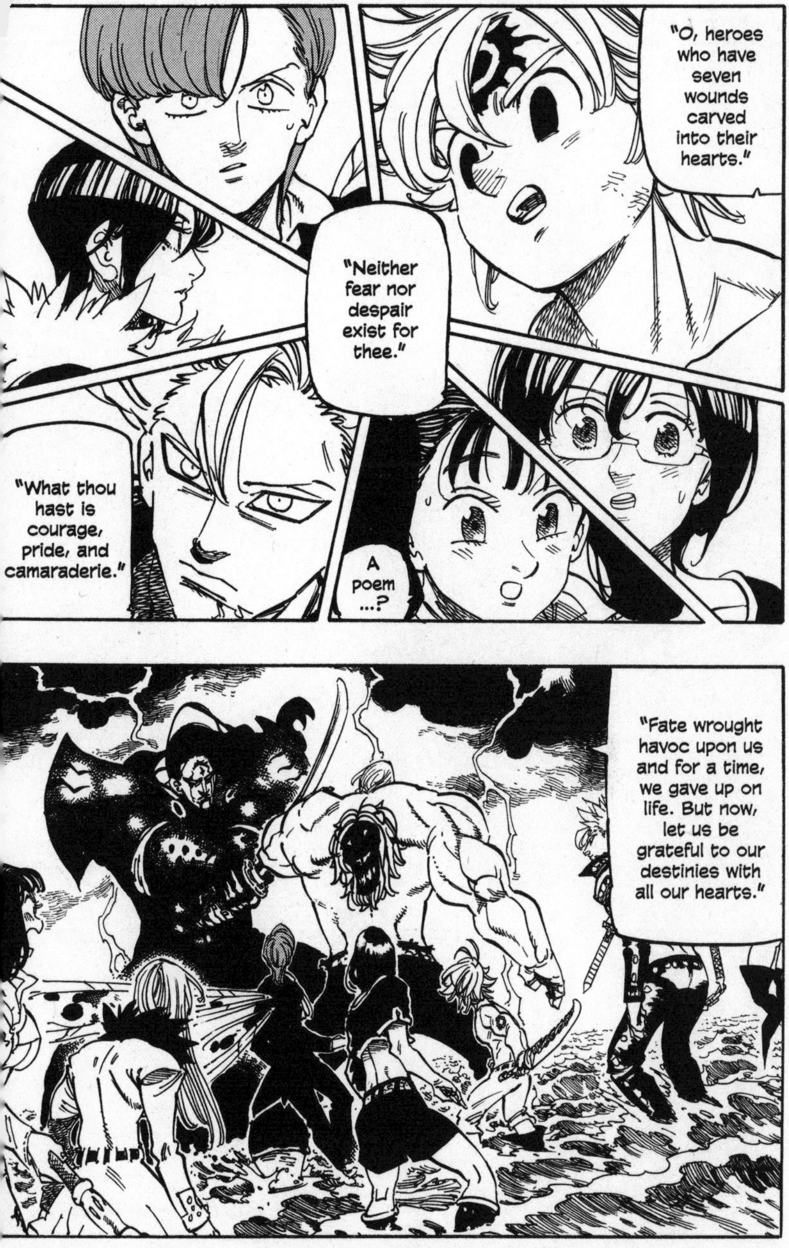
"O, heroes who have seven wounds carved into their hearts."
"Neither fear nor despair exist for thee."
A poem ...?
"What thou hast is courage, pride, and camaraderie."
"Fate wrought havoc upon us and for a time, we gave up on life. But now, let us be grateful to our destinies with all our hearts."

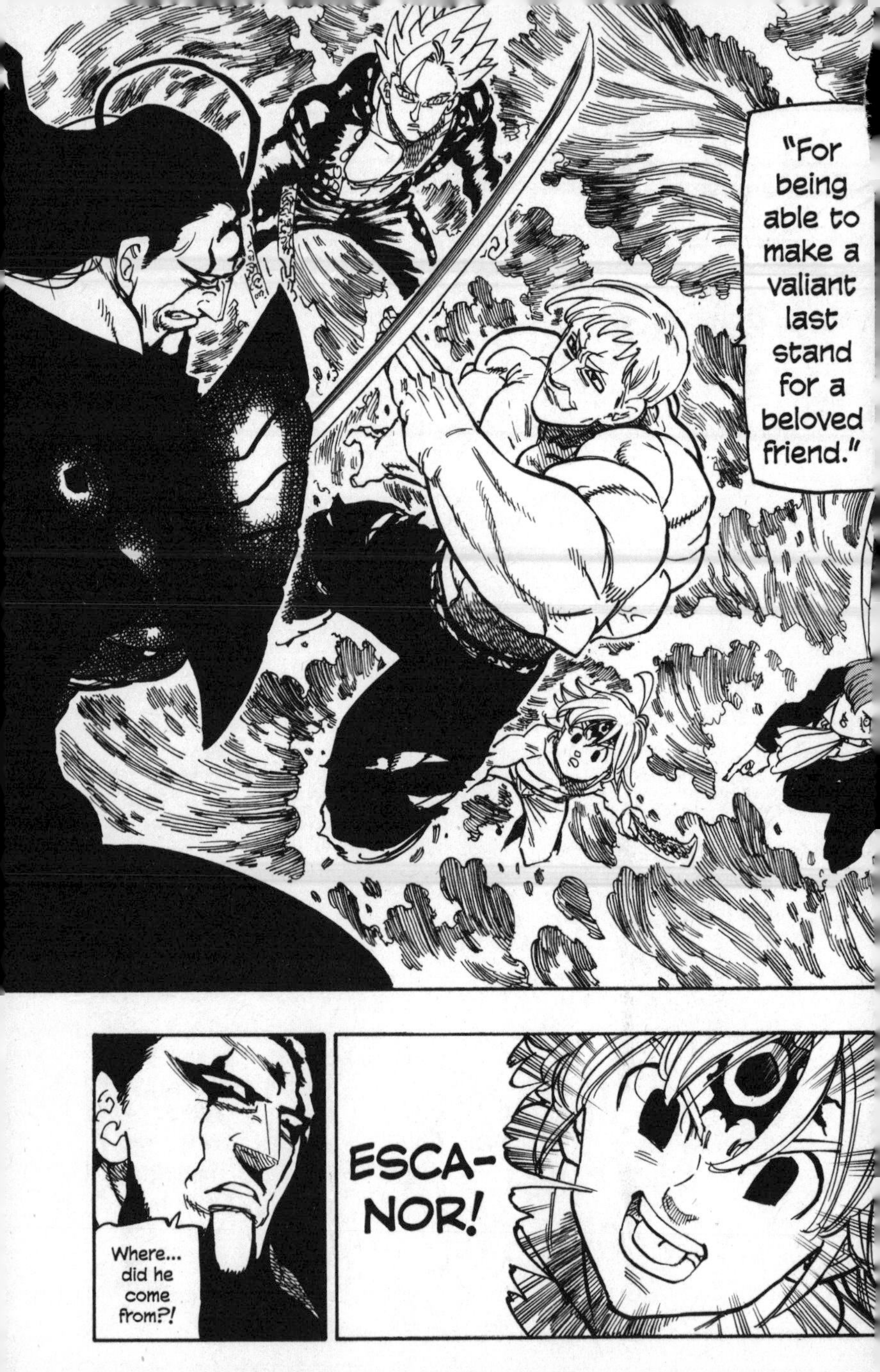
"For being able to make a valiant last stand for a beloved friend."
ESCA-NOR!
Where... did he come from?!

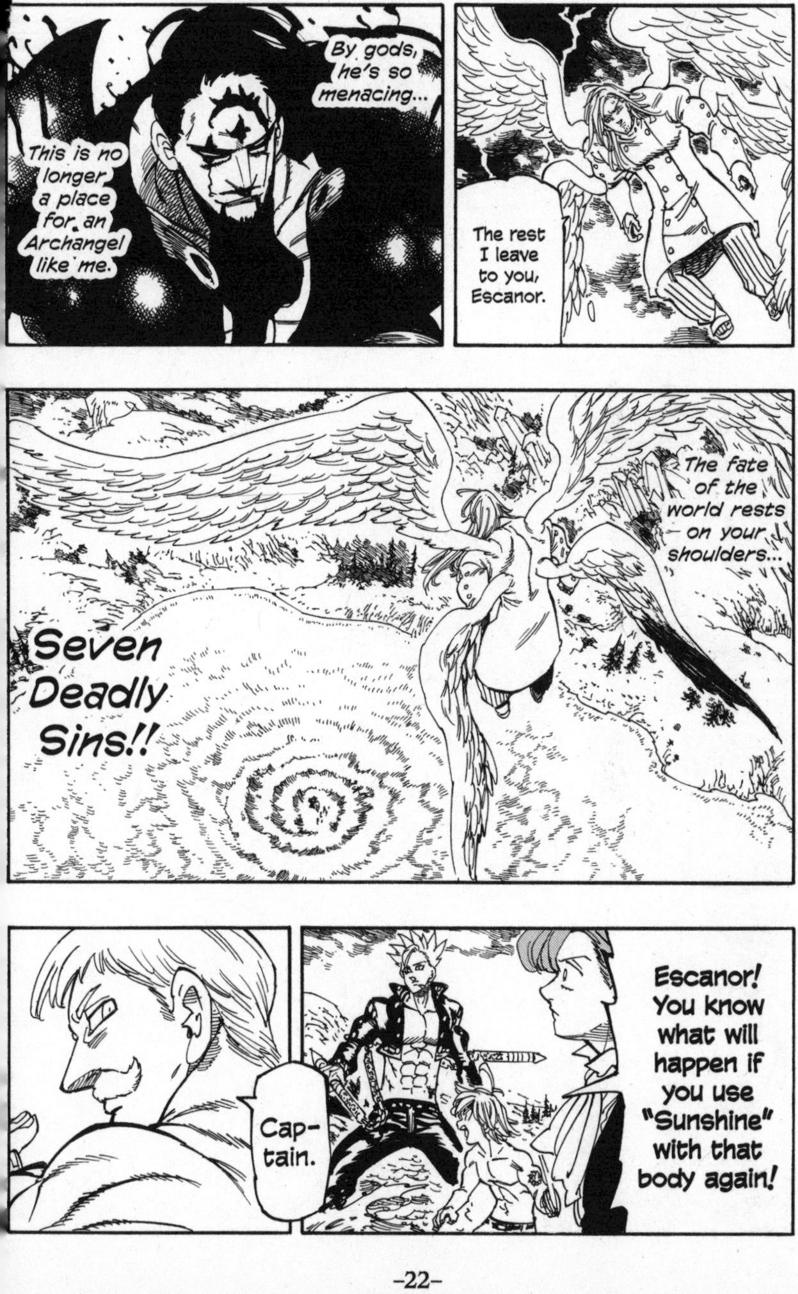
The rest I leave to you, Escanor.
By gods, he's so menacing...
This is no longer a place for an Archangel like me.
The fate of the world rests on your shoulders...
Seven Deadly Sins!!
Escanor! You know what will happen if you use "Sunshine" with that body again!
Cap-tain.

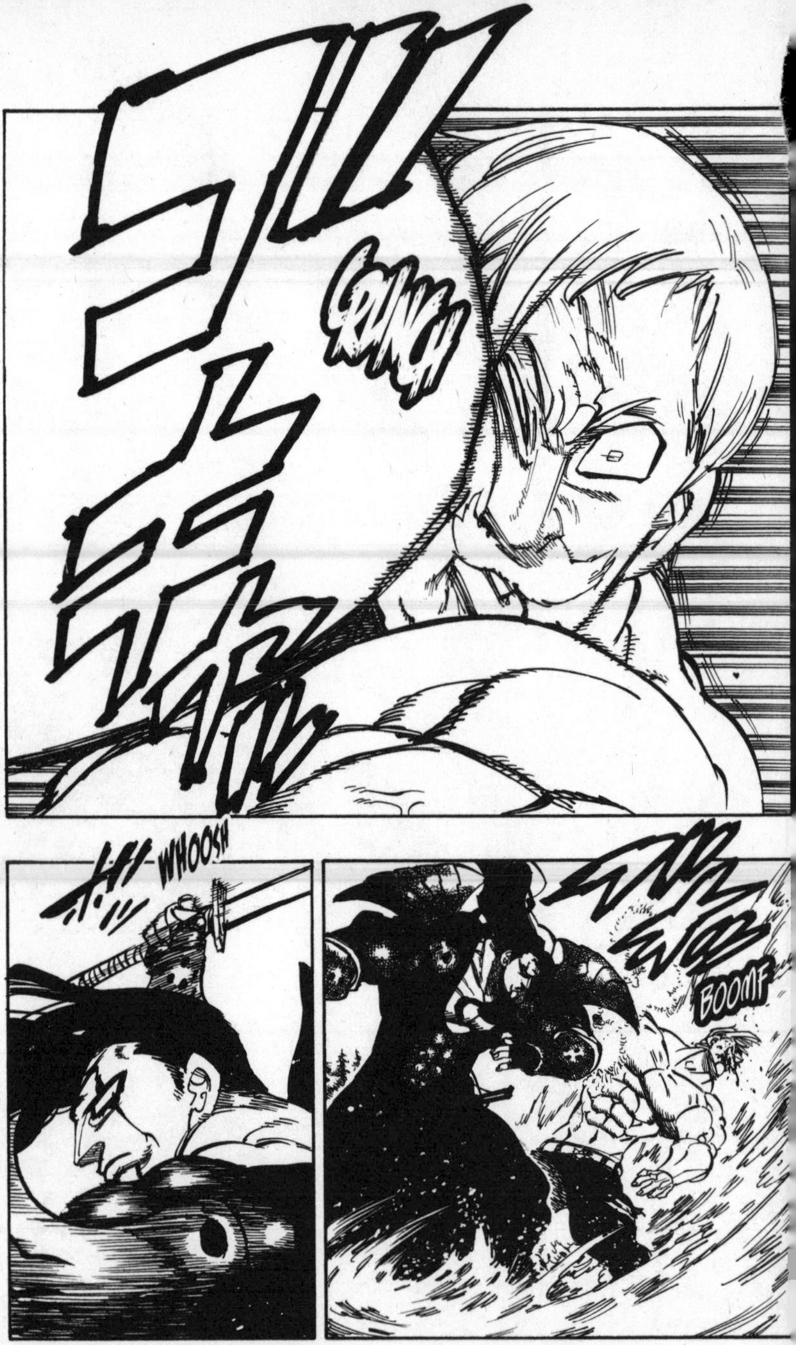
BOOMF
WHOOSH

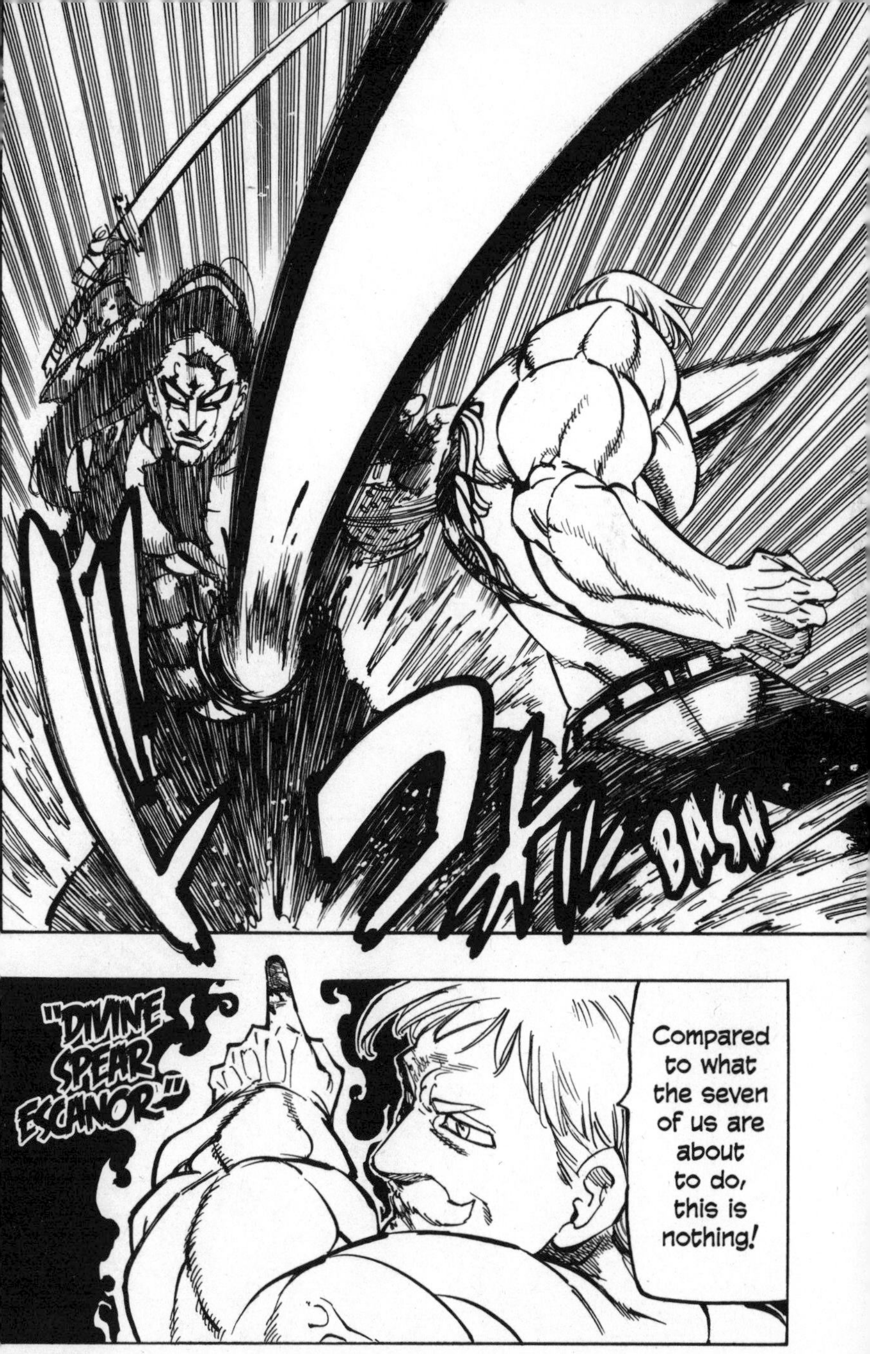
BASH
Compared to what the seven of us are about to do, this is nothing!
"DIVINE SPEAR ESCANOR!!"

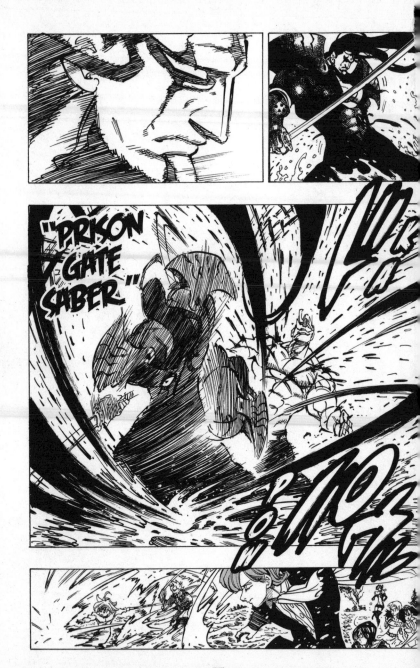

"PRISON GATE SABER"

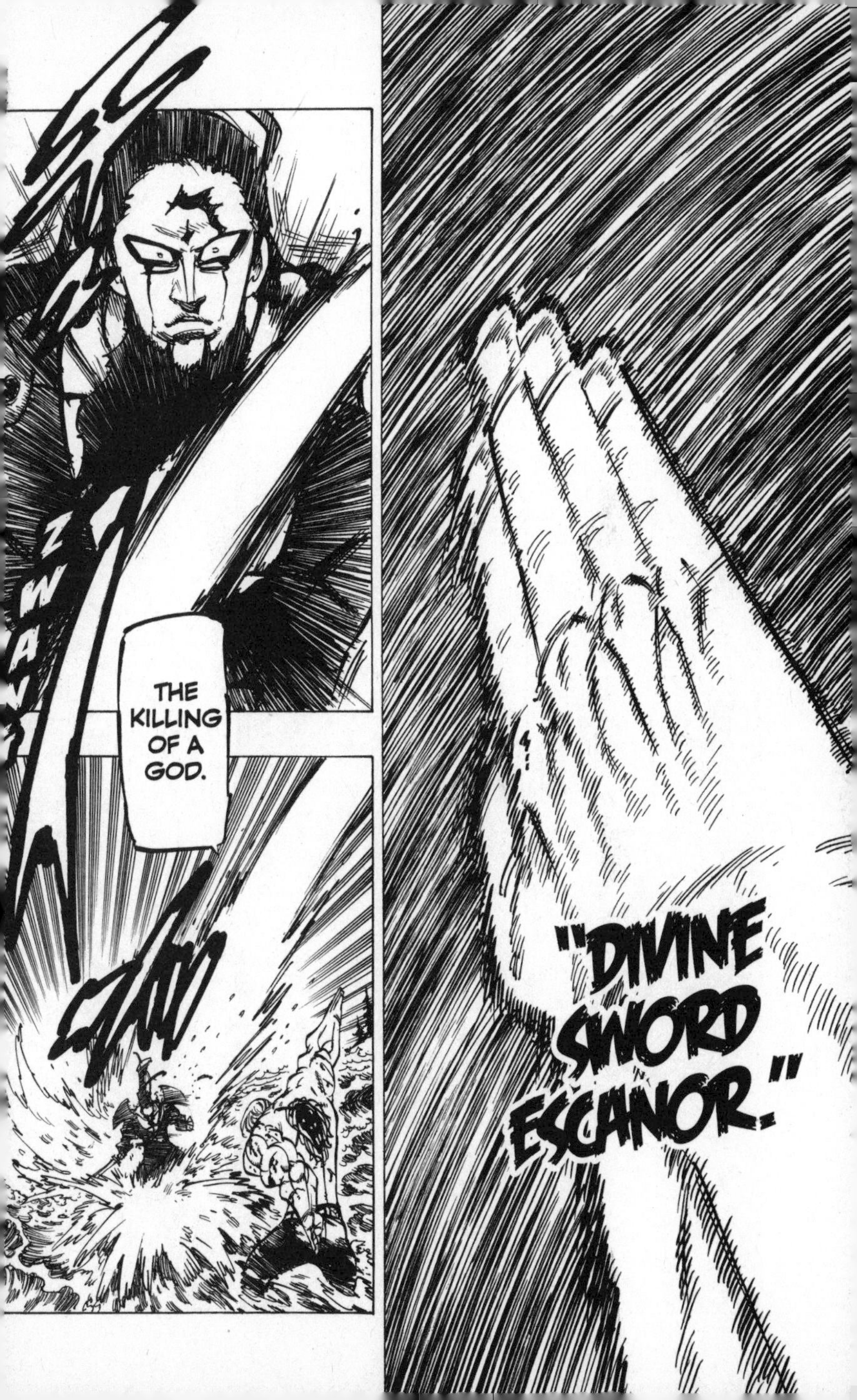
"DIVINE SWORD ESCANOR."
THE KILLING OF A GOD.

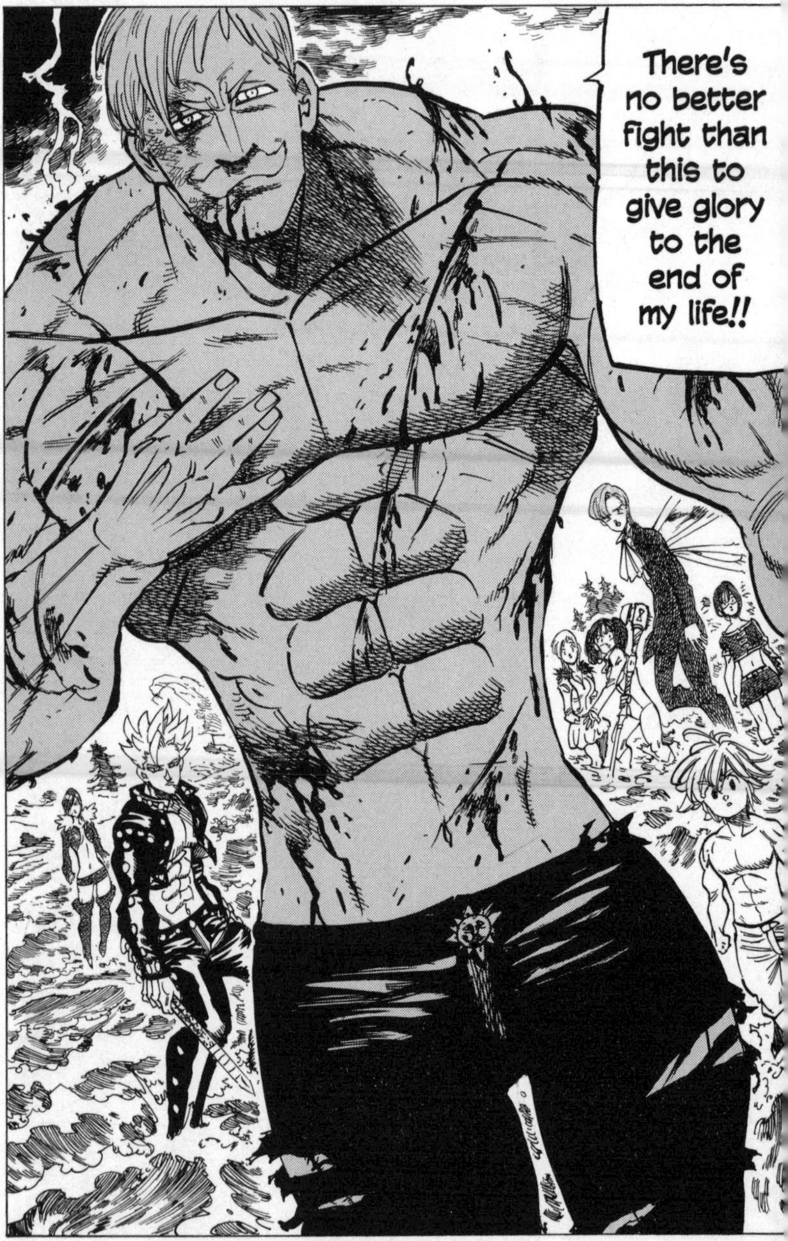
There's no better fight than this to give glory to the end of my life!!

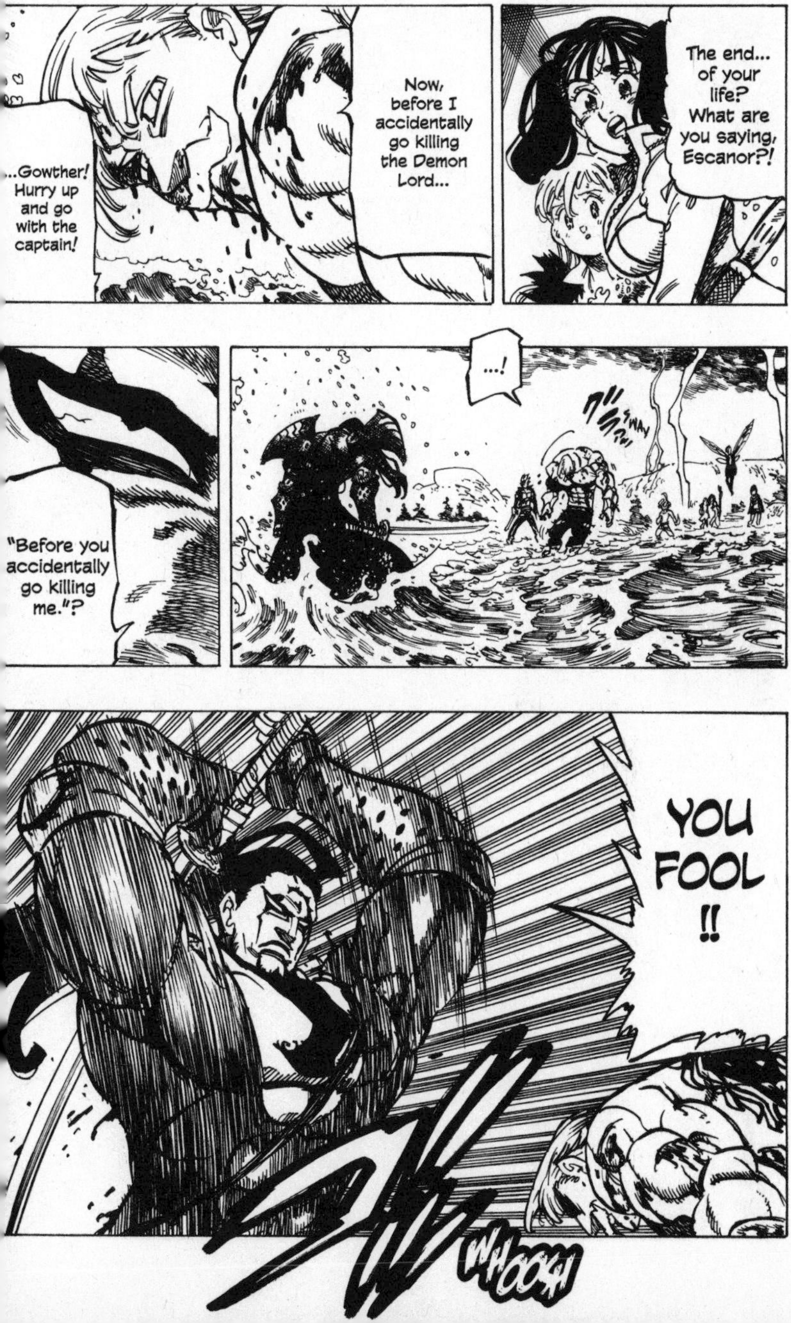
The end... of your life? What are you saying, Escanor?!
Now, before I accidentally go killing the Demon Lord...
...Gowther! Hurry up and go with the captain!
...!
SWAY
"Before you accidentally go killing me."?
YOU FOOL !!
WHOOSH

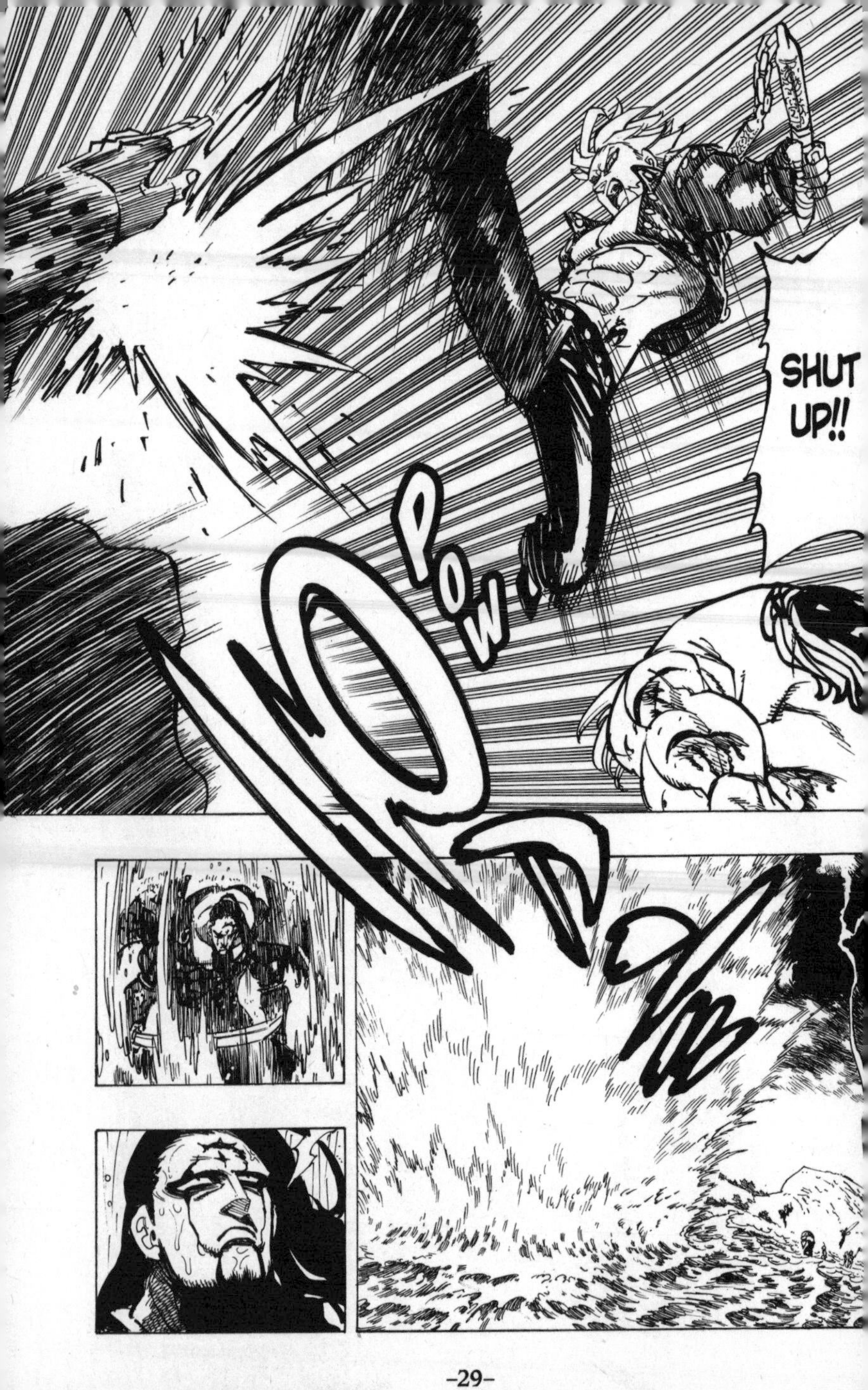
SHUT UP!!
POW
WHAM

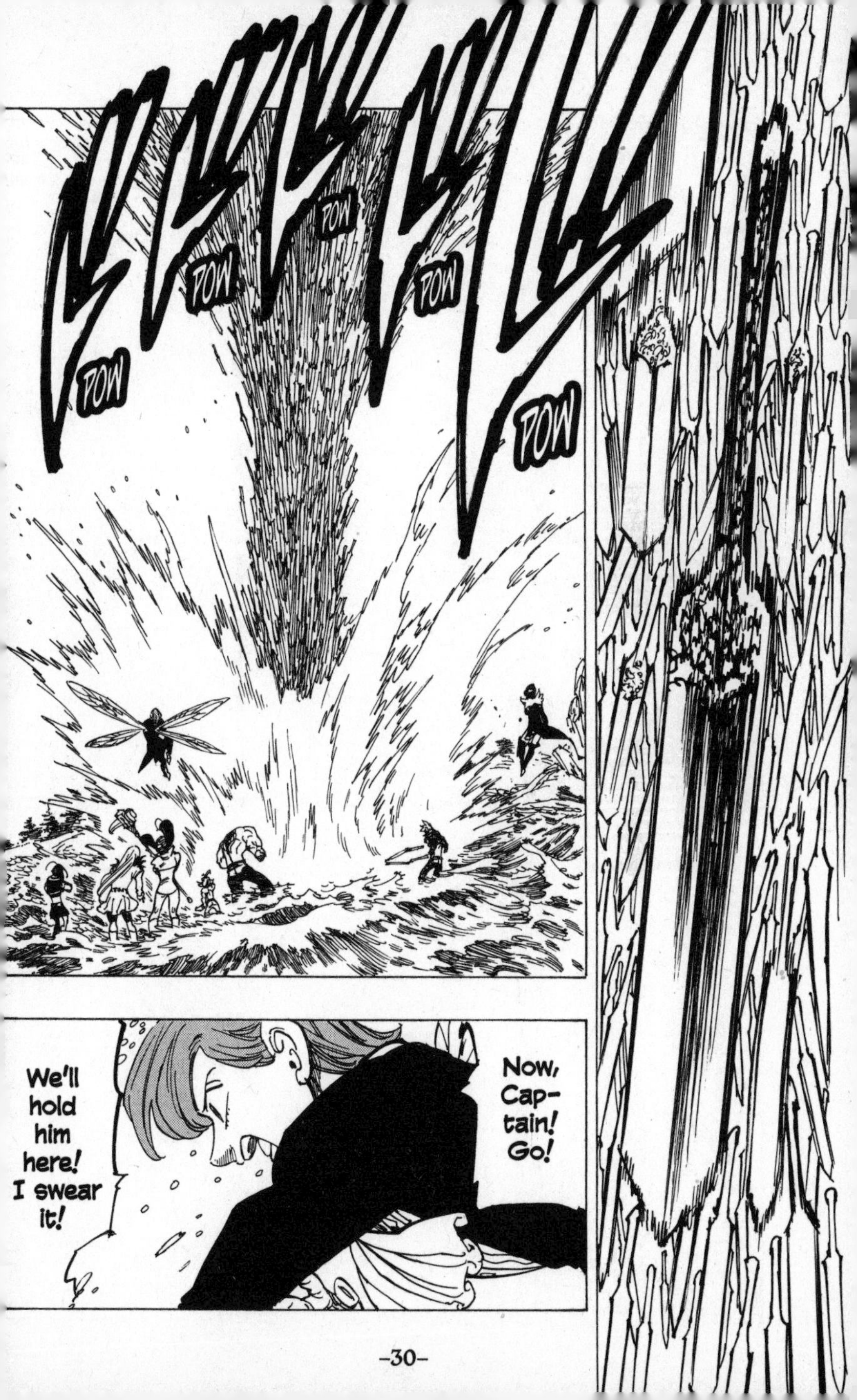
POW
POW
POW
POW
POW
Now, Captain! Go!
We'll hold him here! I swear it!

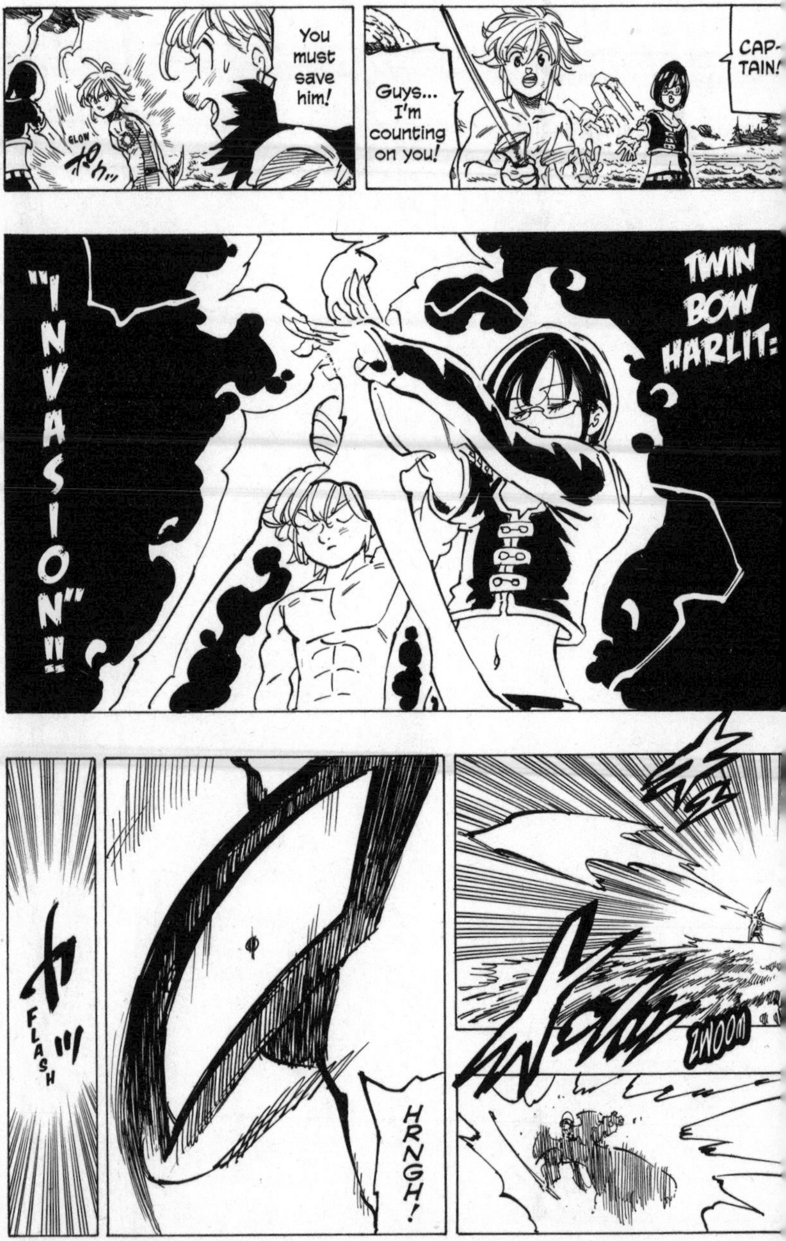
CAP-TAIN!
Guys... I'm counting on you!
You must save him!
GLOW
TWIN BOW HARLIT:
"INVASION"!!
ZWOOM
HRNGH!
FLASH

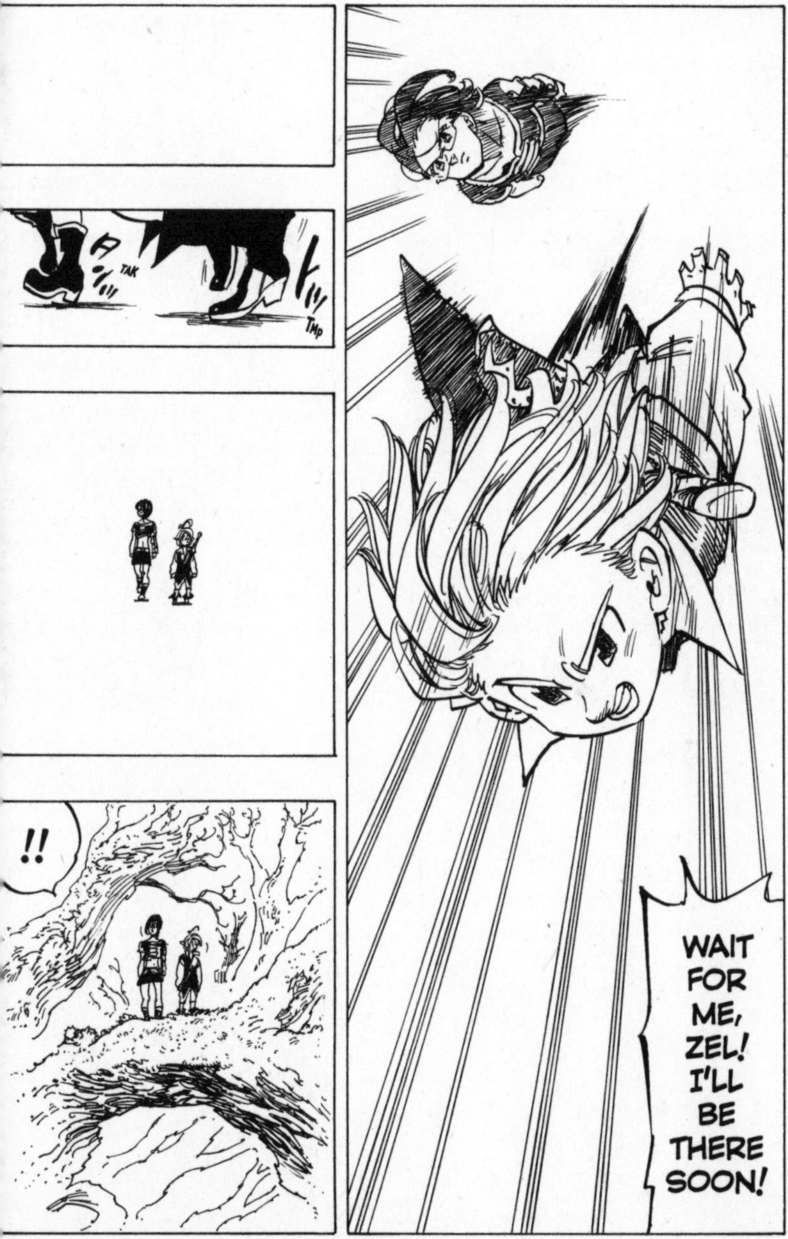
WAIT FOR ME, ZEL! I'LL BE THERE SOON!
TAK
TMP
!!

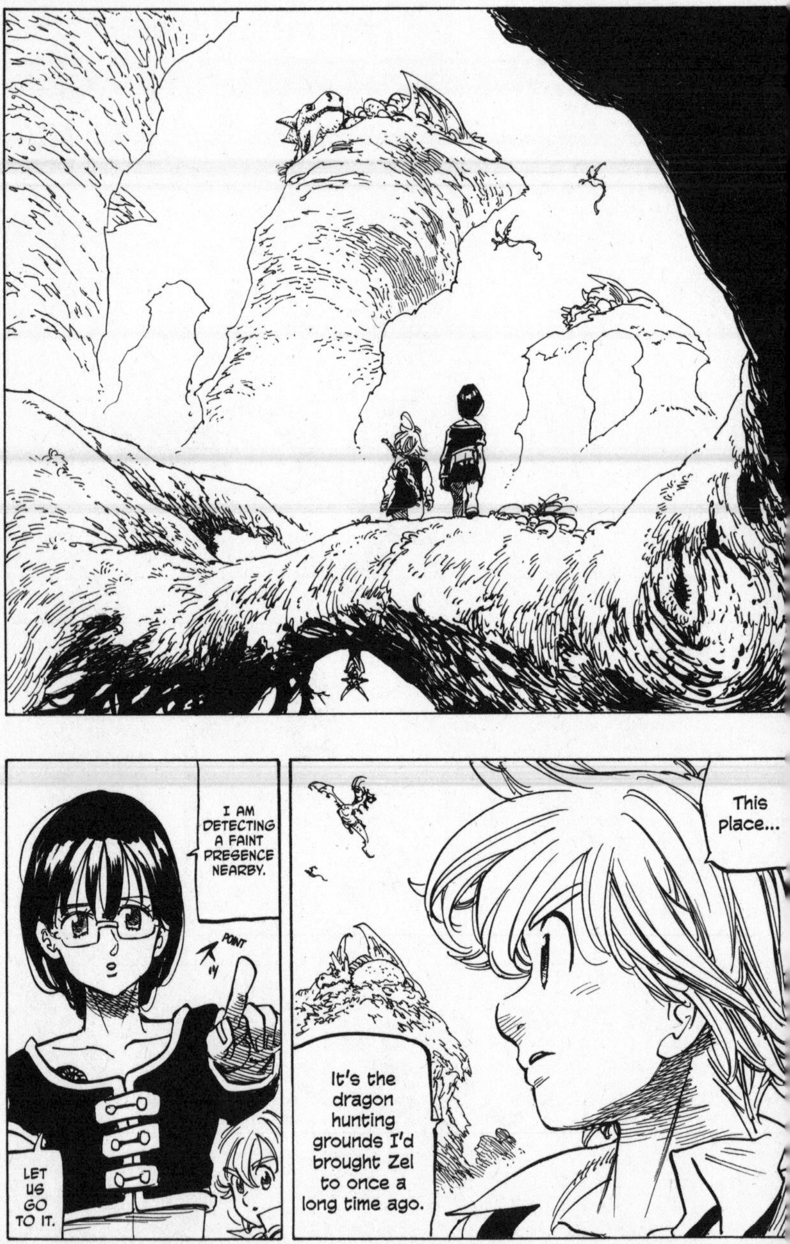
This place...
It's the dragon hunting grounds I'd brought Zel to once a long time ago.
I AM DETECTING A FAINT PRESENCE NEARBY.
POINT
LET US GO TO IT.

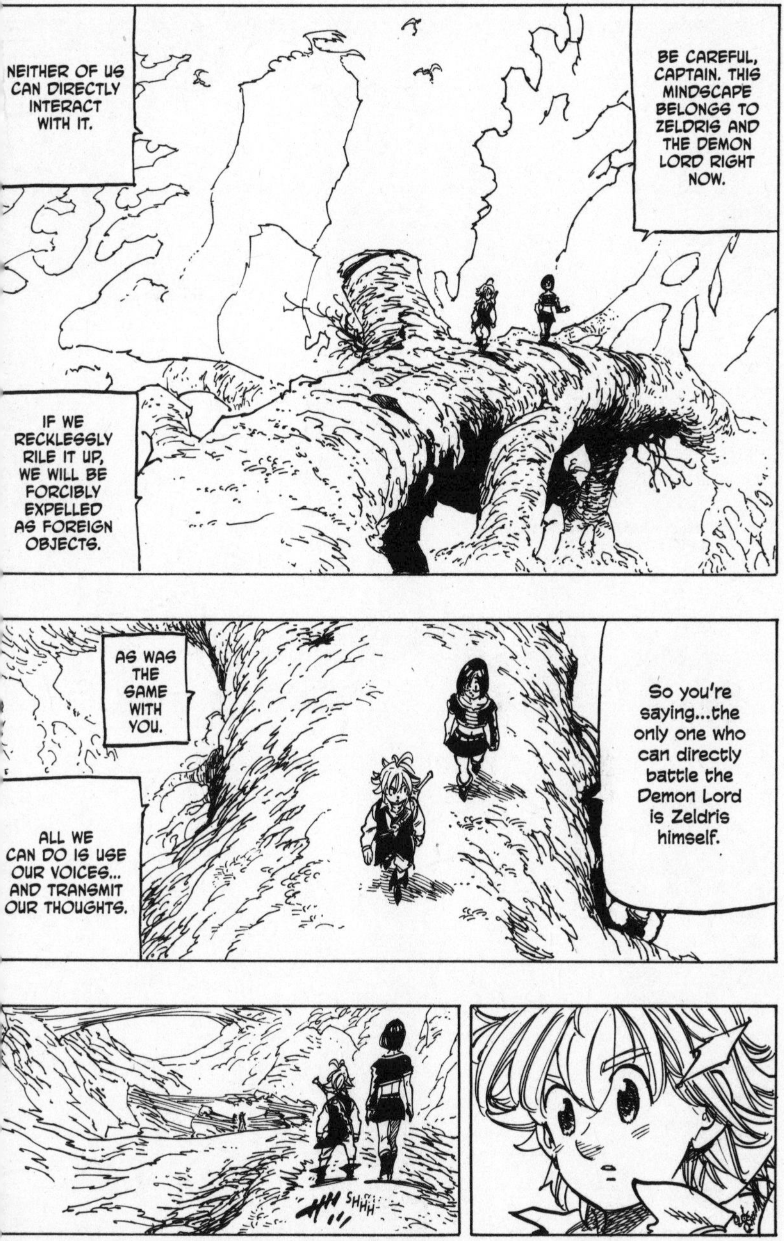
BE CAREFUL, CAPTAIN. THIS MINDSCAPE BELONGS TO ZELDRIS AND THE DEMON LORD RIGHT NOW.
NEITHER OF US CAN DIRECTLY INTERACT WITH IT.
IF WE RECKLESSLY RILE IT UP, WE WILL BE FORCIBLY EXPELLED AS FOREIGN OBJECTS.
So you're saying...the only one who can directly battle the Demon Lord is Zeldris himself.
AS WAS THE SAME WITH YOU.
ALL WE CAN DO IS USE OUR VOICES... AND TRANSMIT OUR THOUGHTS.
SHHH

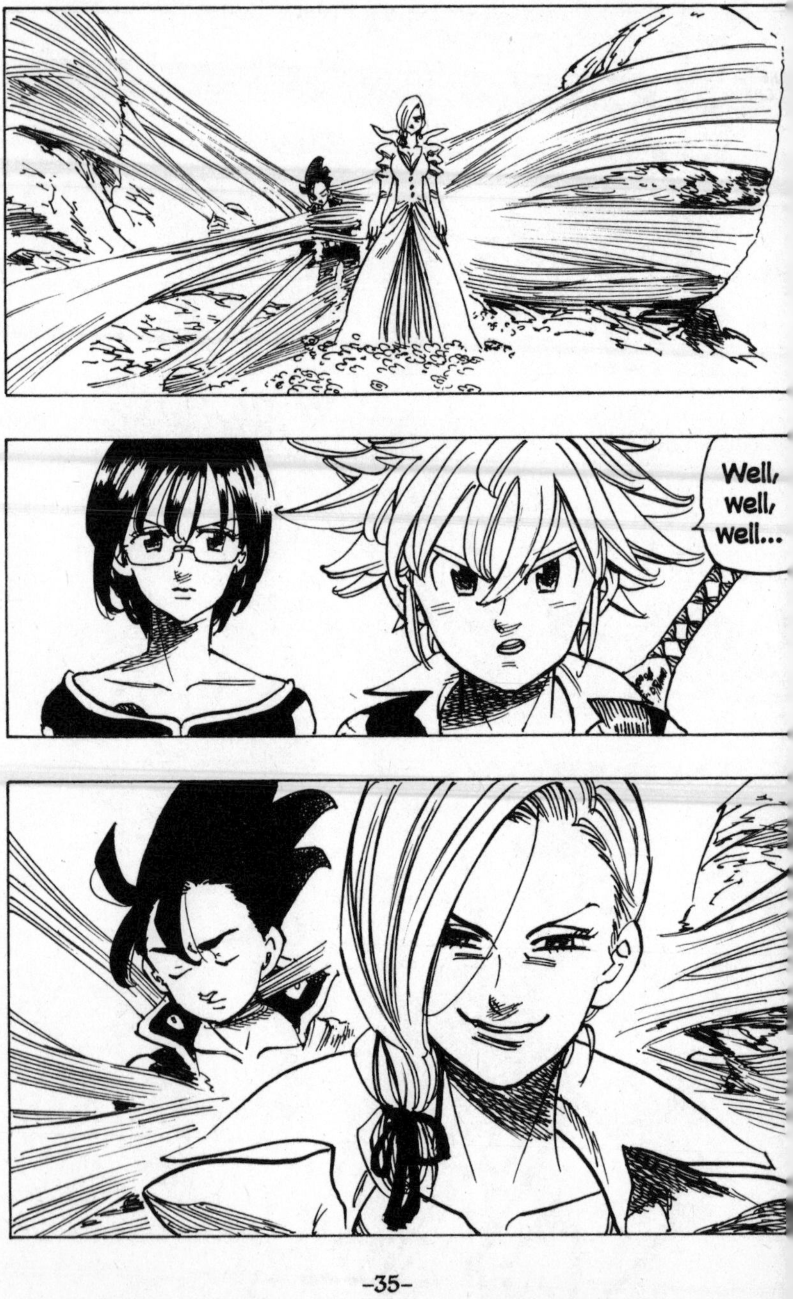
Well, well, well...

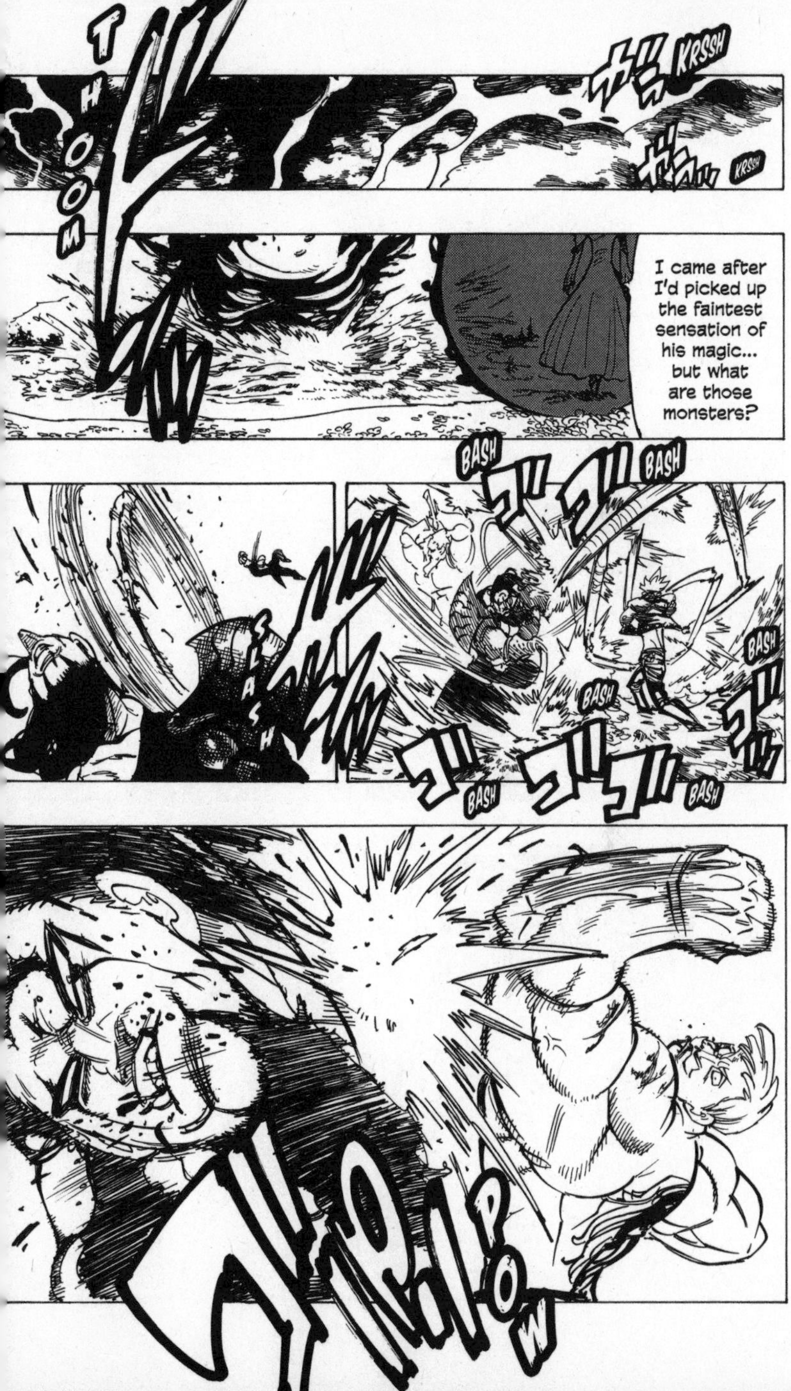
KRSSH
KRSSH
THOOM
I came after I'd picked up the faintest sensation of his magic... but what are those monsters?
BASH
BASH
BASH
BASH
BASH
BASH
SLASH
POW

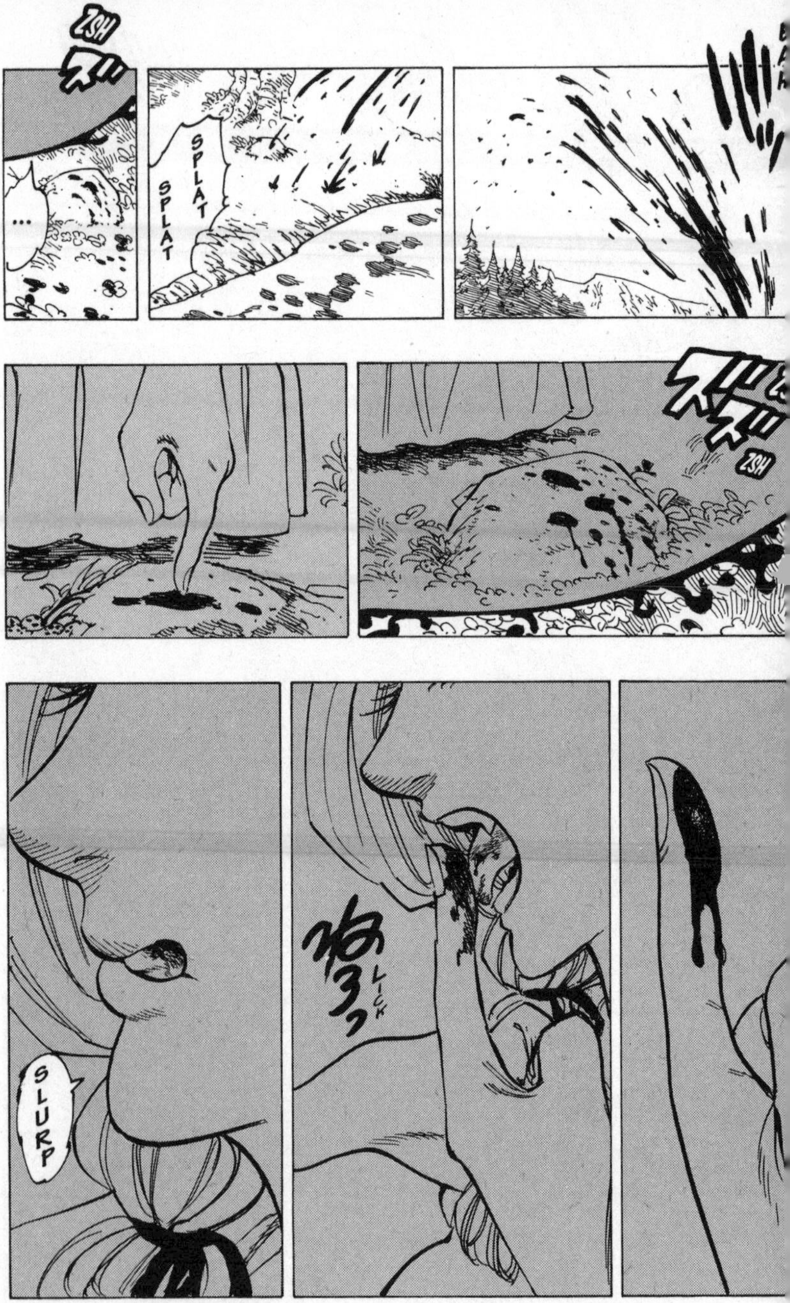
SPLAT
SPLAT
ZSH
...
ZSH
LICK
SLURP

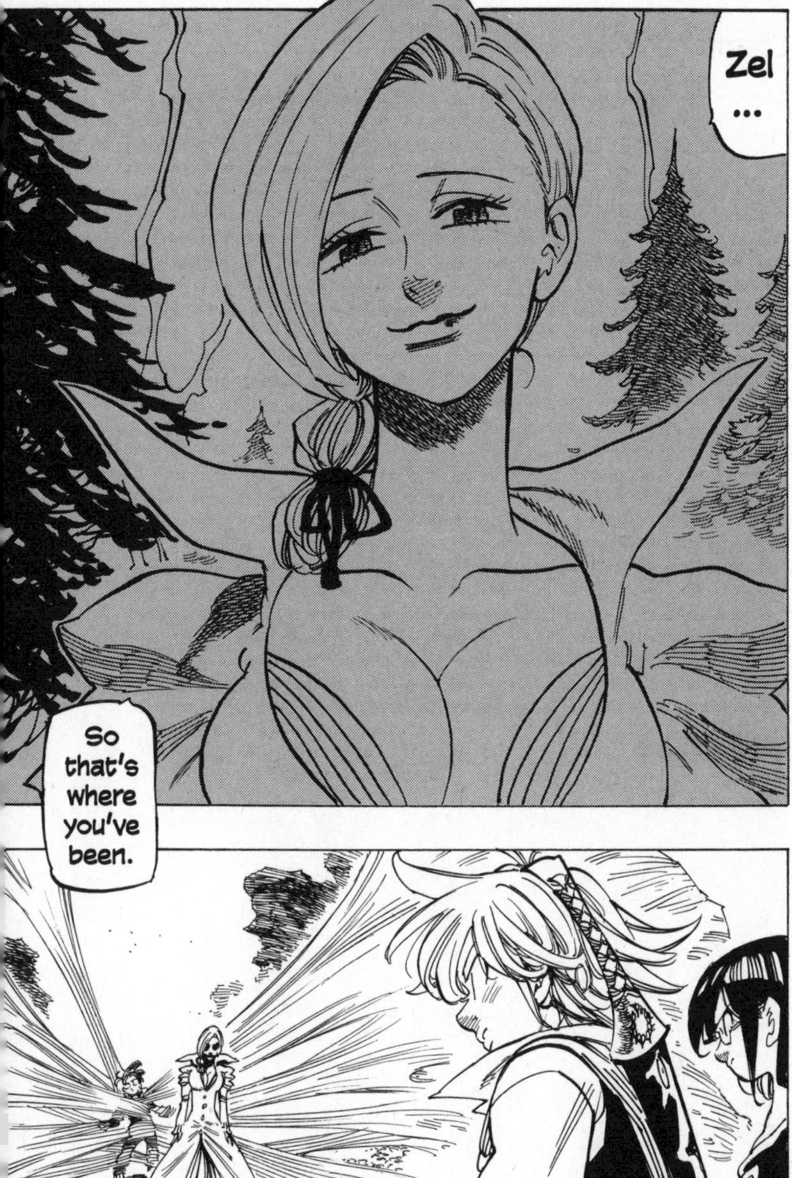
Zel...
So that's where you've been.

Chapter 323 - I'm Right Here

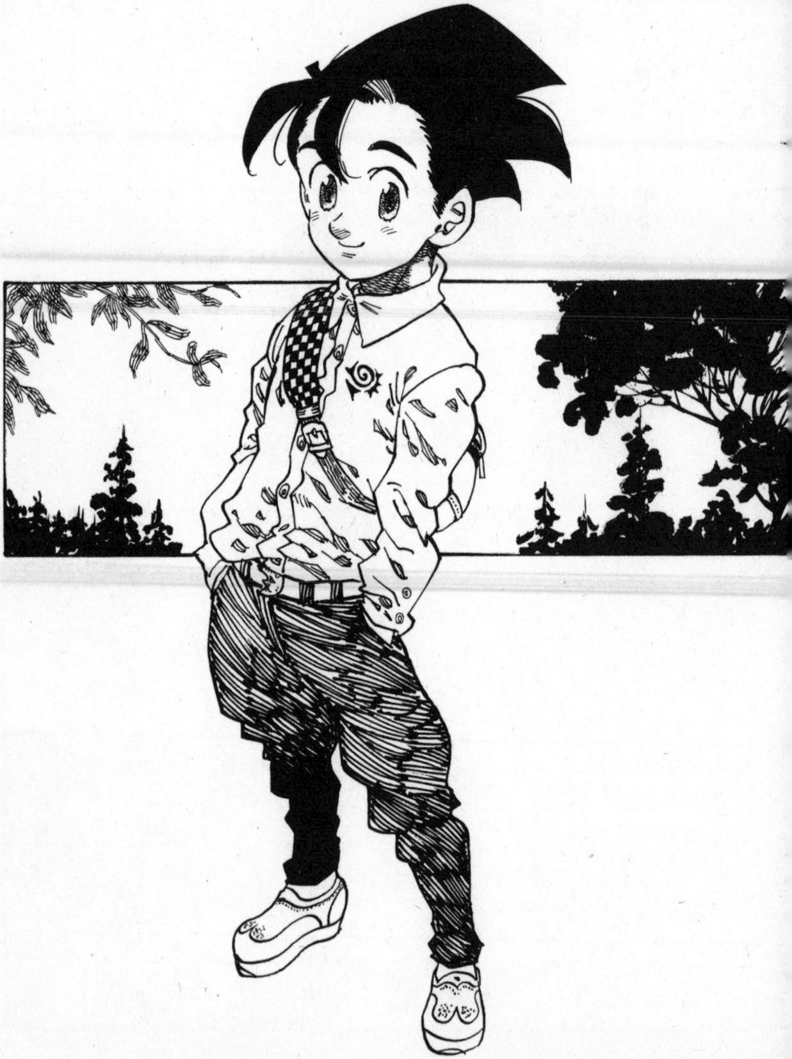

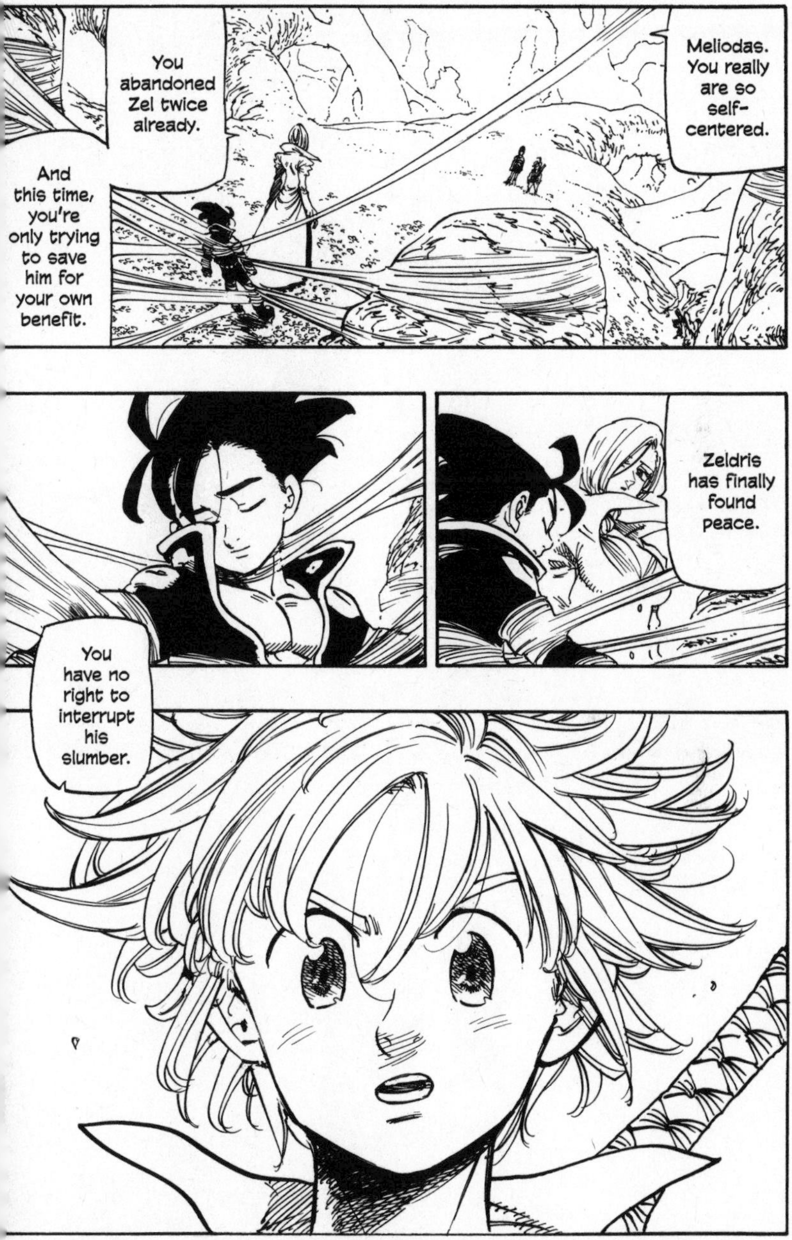
Meliodas. You really are so self-centered.
You abandoned Zel twice already.
And this time, you're only trying to save him for your own benefit.
Zeldris has finally found peace.
You have no right to interrupt his slumber.

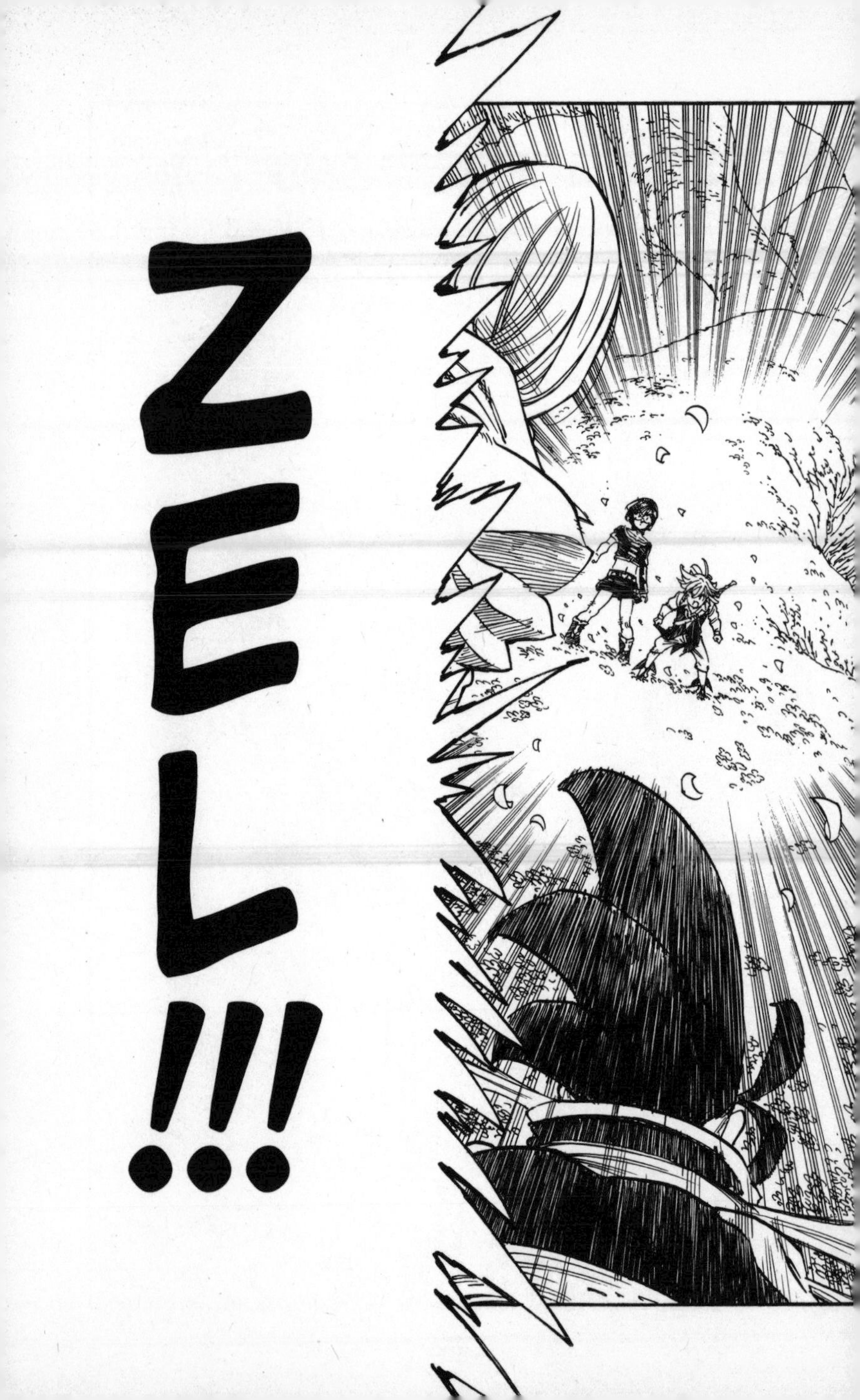
ZEL!!!

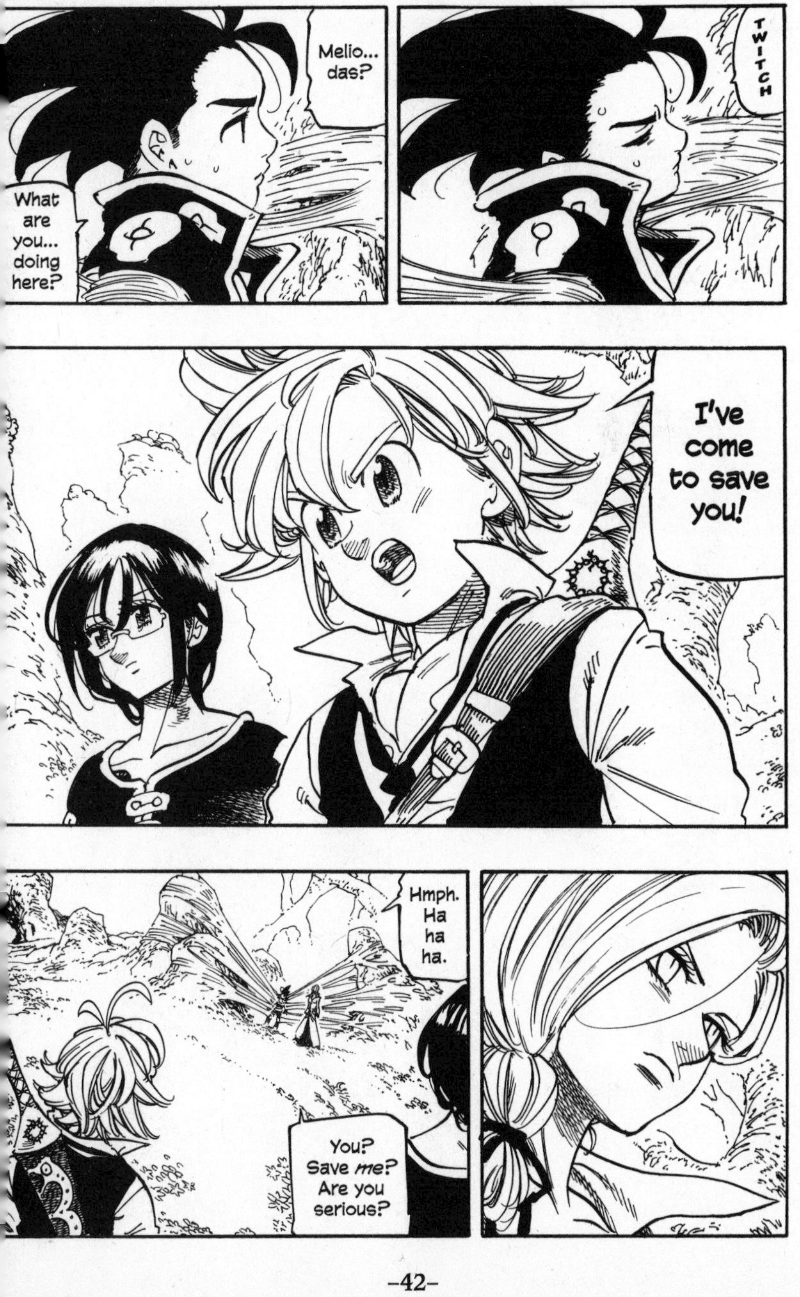
TWITCH
Melio... das?
What are you... doing here?
I've come to save you!
Hmph. Ha ha ha.
You? Save *me*? Are you serious?

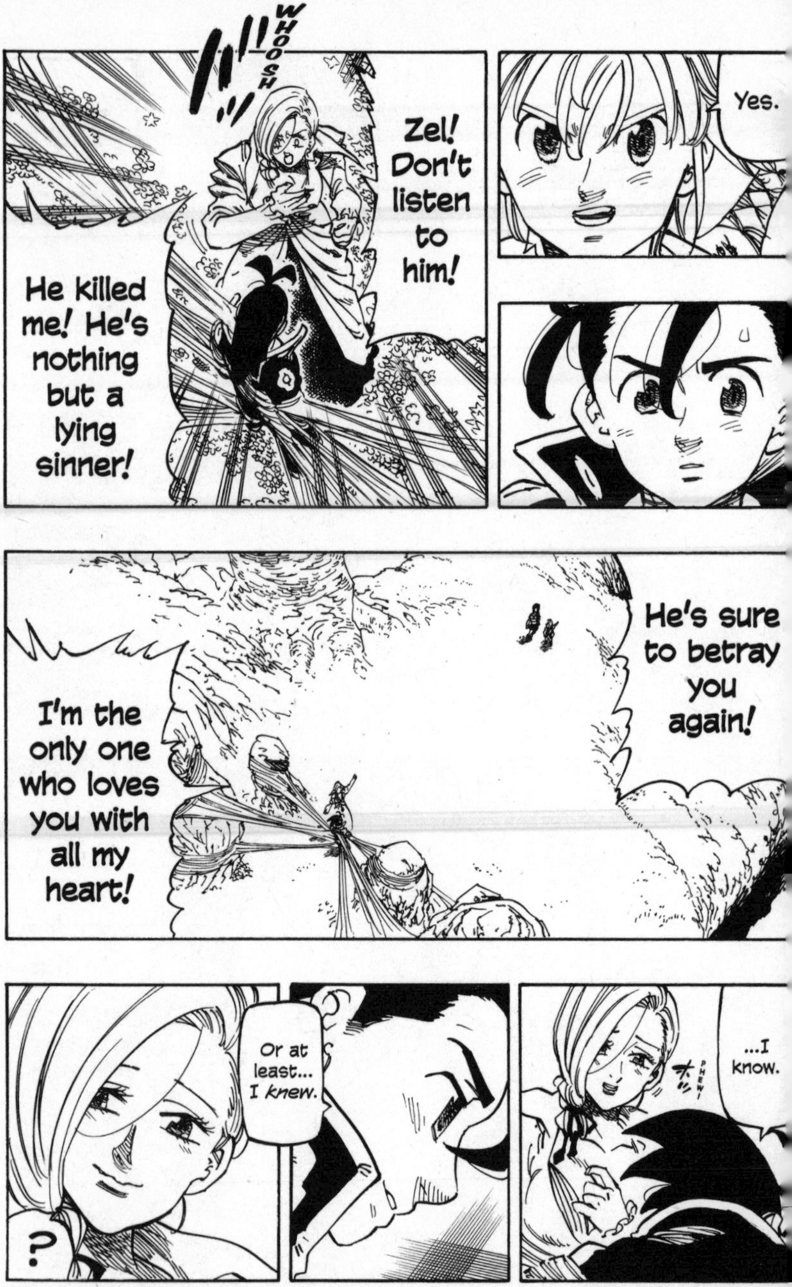
Yes.
WHOOSH
Zel! Don't listen to him!
He killed me! He's nothing but a lying sinner!
He's sure to betray you again!
I'm the only one who loves you with all my heart!
...I know.
PHEW
Or at least... I *knew*.
?

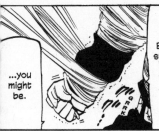

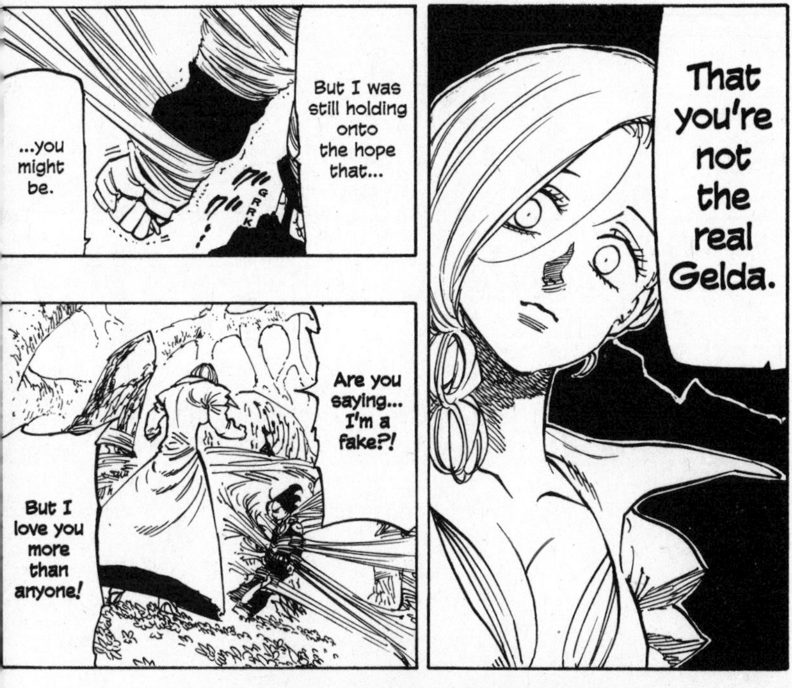

That you're not the real Gelda.
But I was still holding onto the hope that...
...you might be.
GRRK
Are you saying... I'm a fake?!
But I love you more than anyone!
That's how I know you're a fake.
The real Gelda would never say that to me!

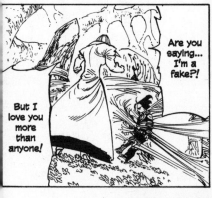

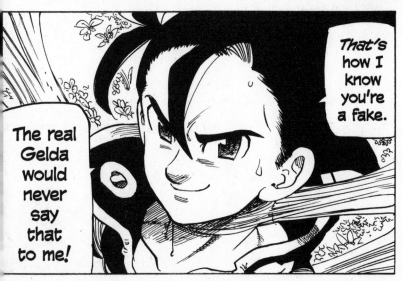

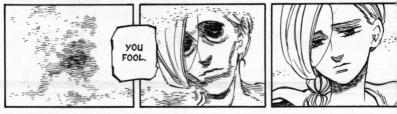

YOU FOOL,

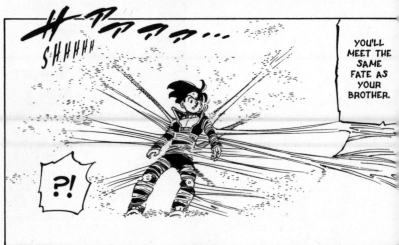

YOU'LL MEET THE SAME FATE AS YOUR BROTHER.

?!

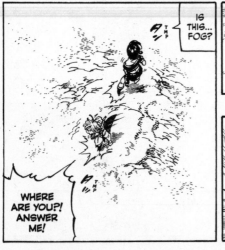

IS THIS... FOG?

WHERE ARE YOU?! ANSWER ME!

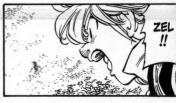

ZEL!!

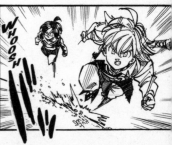

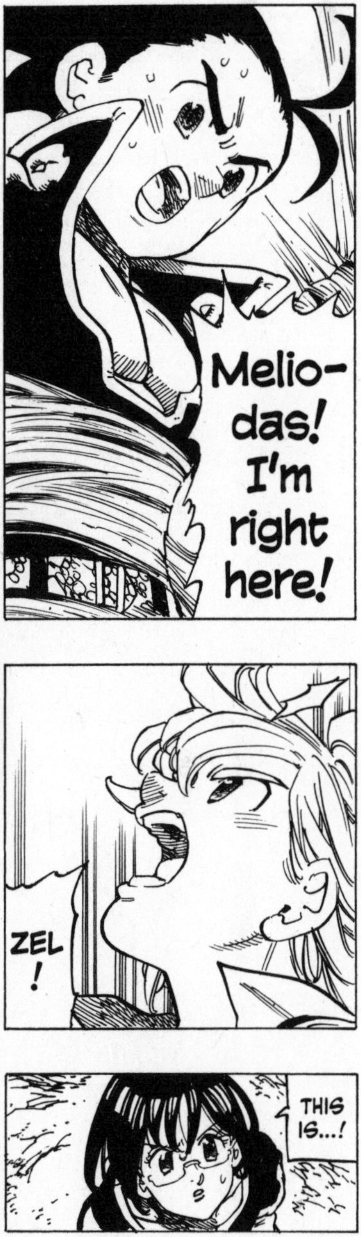
Melio-das! I'm right here!
ZEL!
THIS IS...!
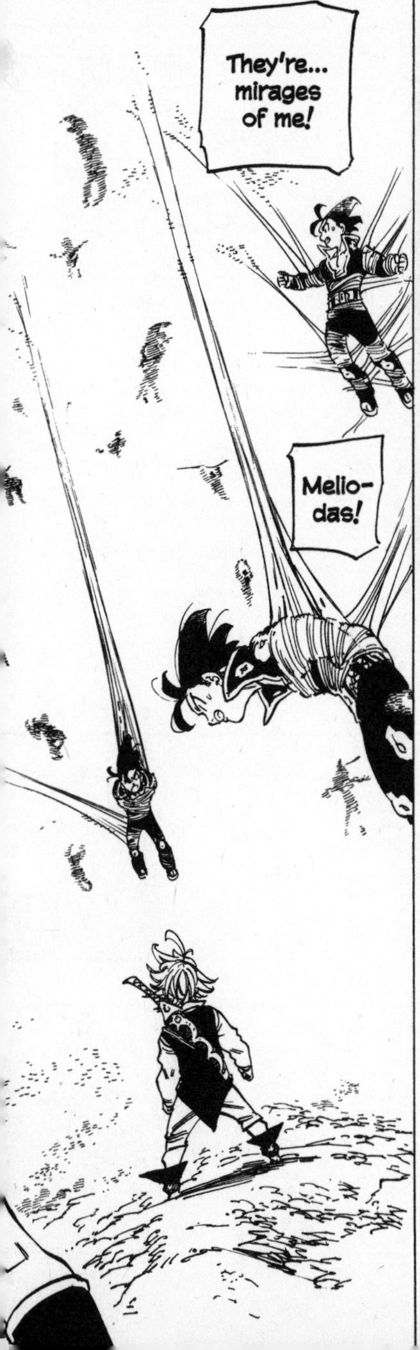
They're... mirages of me!
Melio-das!

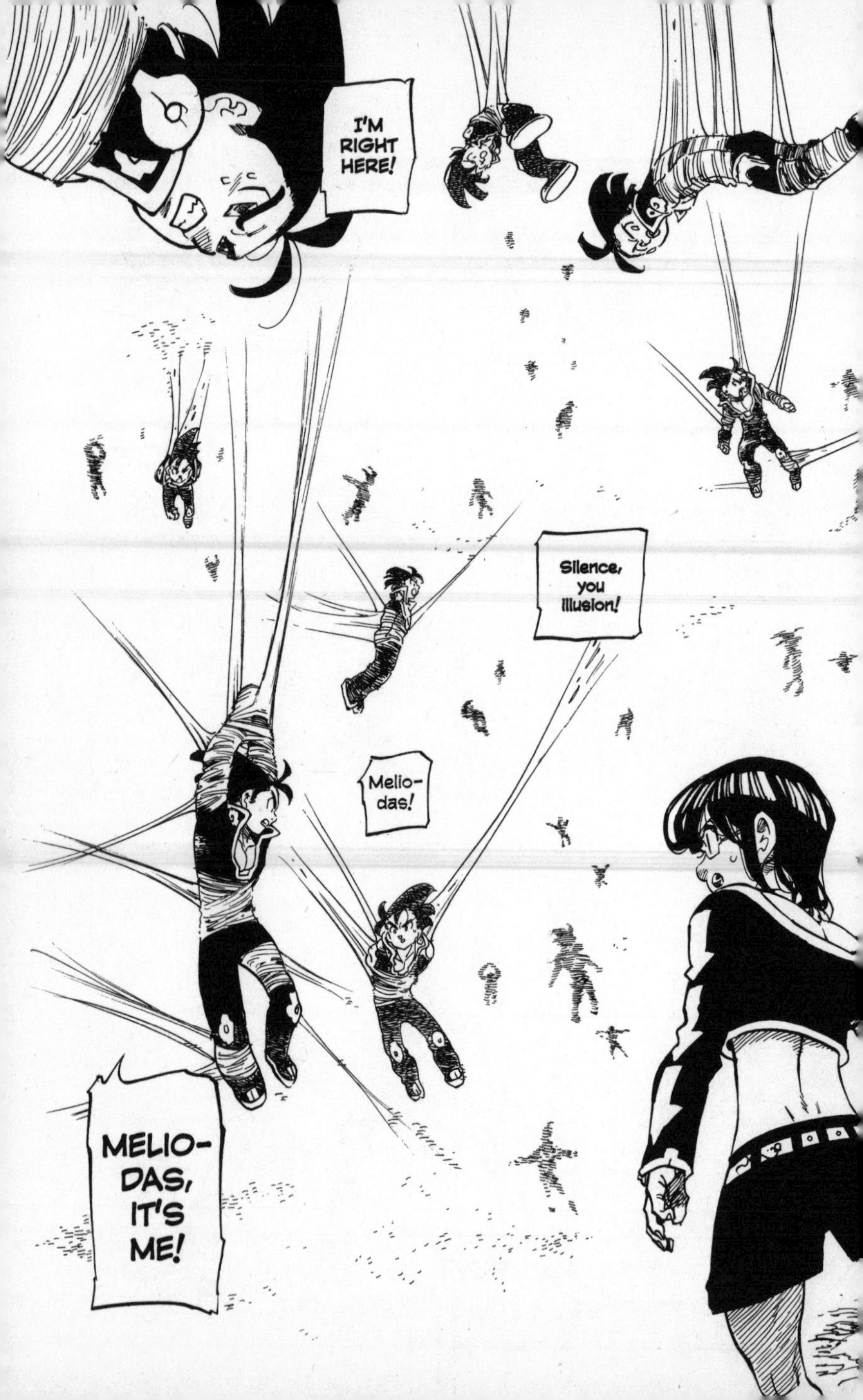
I'M RIGHT HERE!
Silence, you illusion!
Melio-das!
MELIO-DAS, IT'S ME!

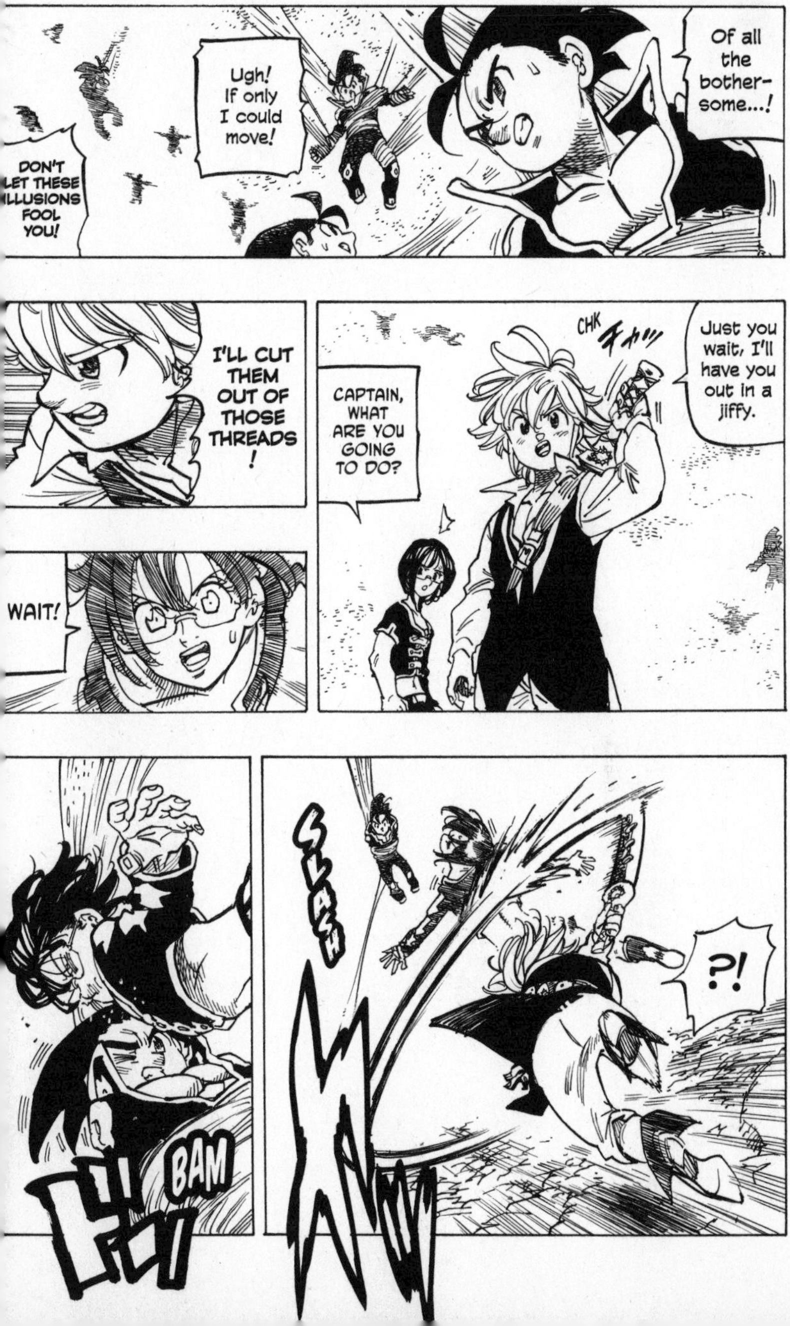

Of all the bother-some...!
Ugh! If only I could move!
DON'T LET THESE ILLUSIONS FOOL YOU!
Just you wait, I'll have you out in a jiffy.
CHK
CAPTAIN, WHAT ARE YOU GOING TO DO?
I'LL CUT THEM OUT OF THOSE THREADS!
WAIT!
?!
SLASH
BAM

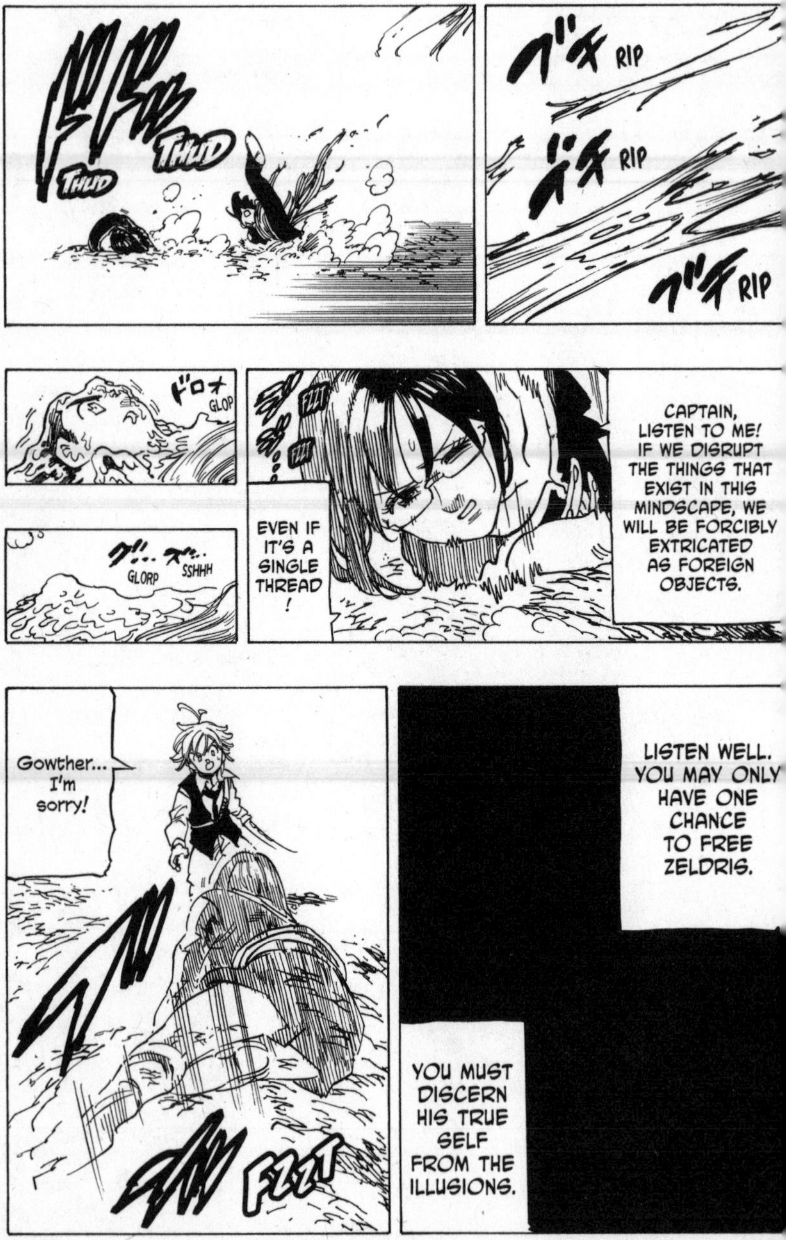
ブチ RIP
ブチ RIP
ブチ RIP
THUD
THUD
CAPTAIN, LISTEN TO ME! IF WE DISRUPT THE THINGS THAT EXIST IN THIS MINDSCAPE, WE WILL BE FORCIBLY EXTRICATED AS FOREIGN OBJECTS.
EVEN IF IT'S A SINGLE THREAD!
FZZT
FZZT
ドロォ GLOP
GLORP
SSHHH
LISTEN WELL. YOU MAY ONLY HAVE ONE CHANCE TO FREE ZELDRIS.
YOU MUST DISCERN HIS TRUE SELF FROM THE ILLUSIONS.
Gowther... I'm sorry!
FZZT

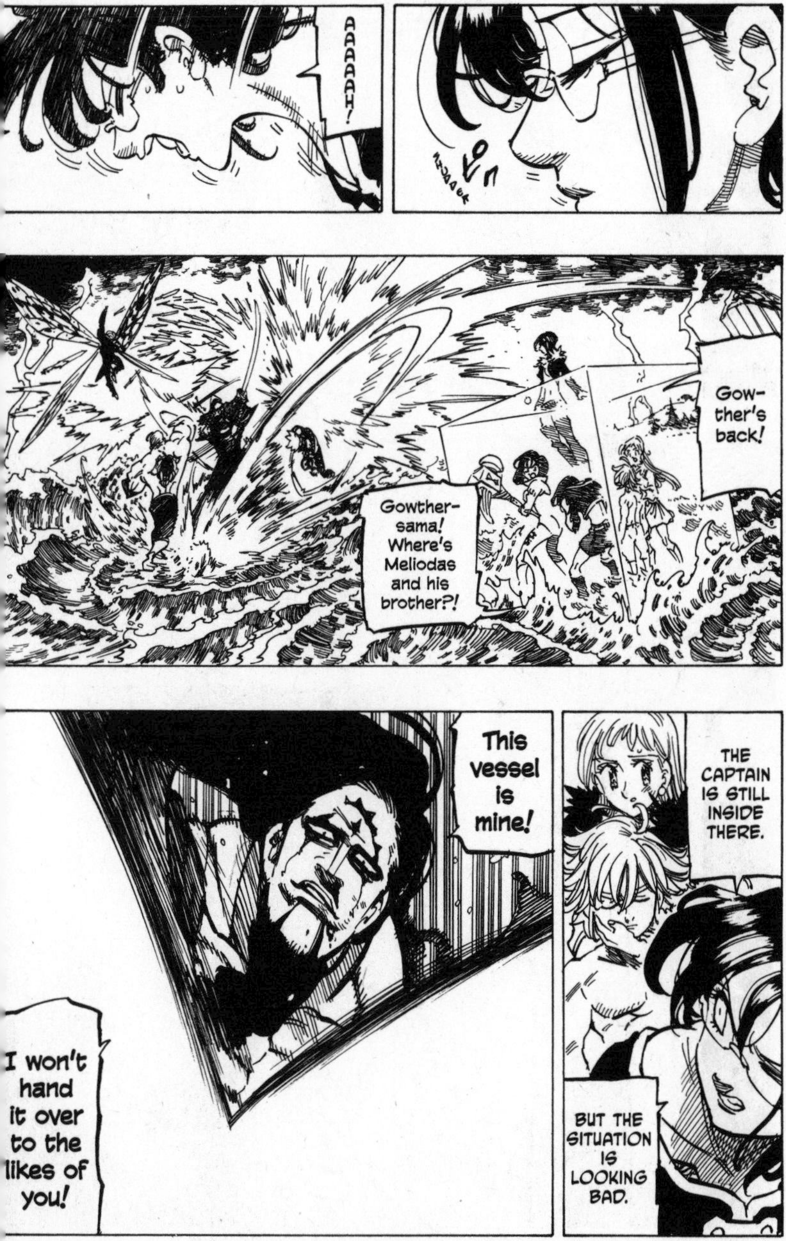
SHUDDER
AAAAAAH!
Gow-ther's back!
Gowther-sama! Where's Meliodas and his brother?!
THE CAPTAIN IS STILL INSIDE THERE.
BUT THE SITUATION IS LOOKING BAD.
This vessel is mine!
I won't hand it over to the likes of you!

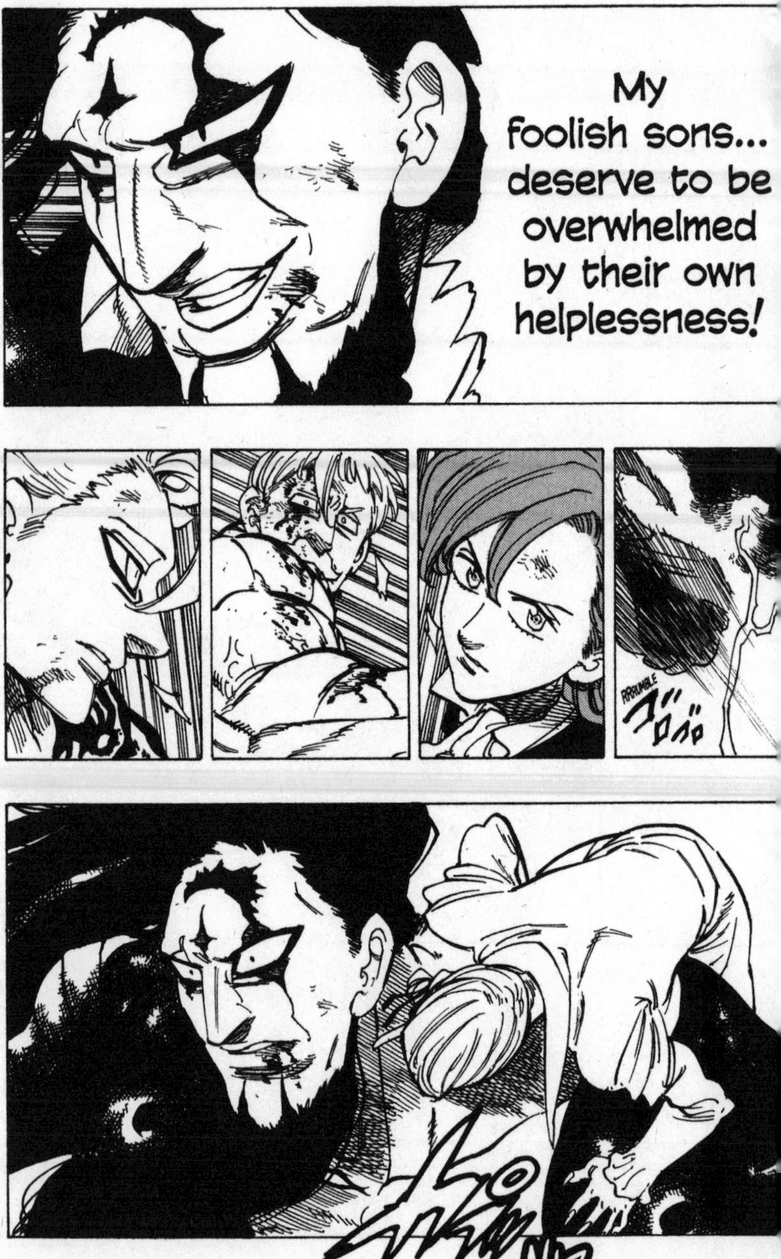
My foolish sons... deserve to be overwhelmed by their own helplessness!
RRRUMBLE
NIP

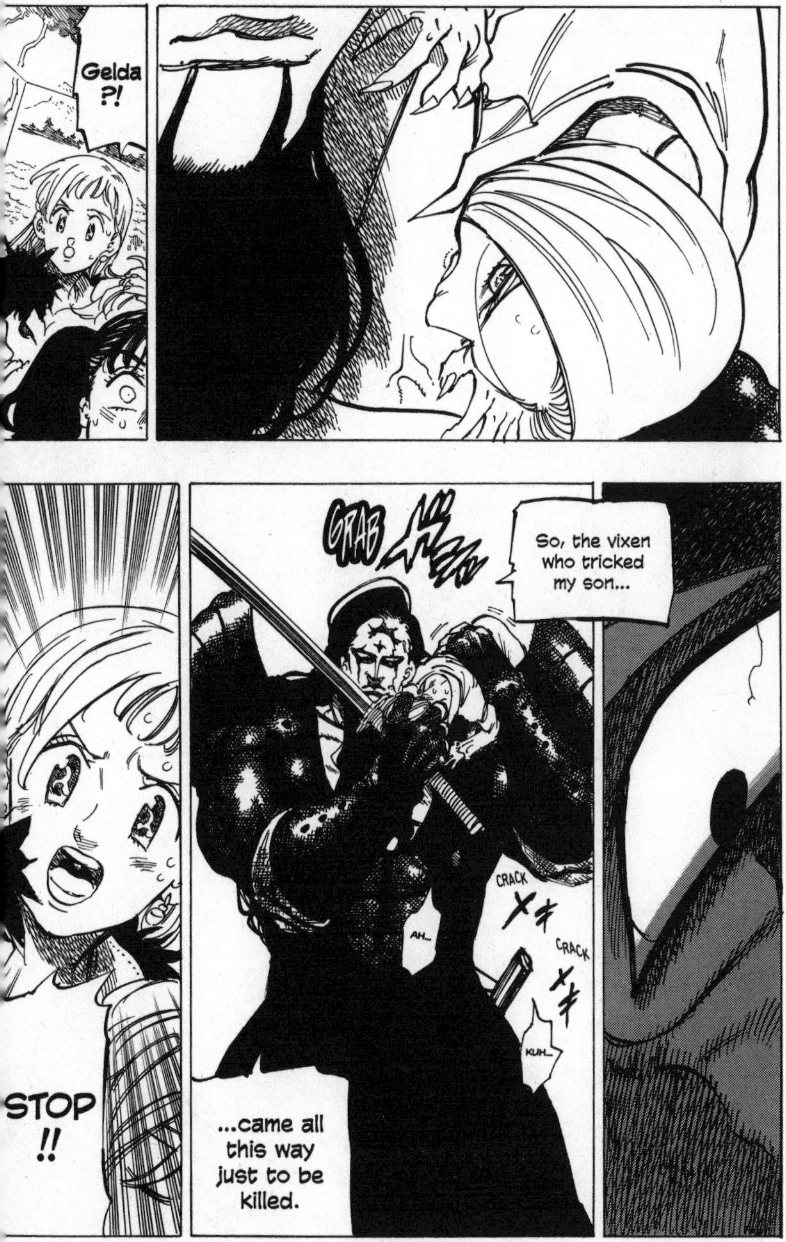
Gelda ?!
So, the vixen who tricked my son...
GRAB
CRACK
AH...
CRACK
KUH...
...came all this way just to be killed.
STOP !!

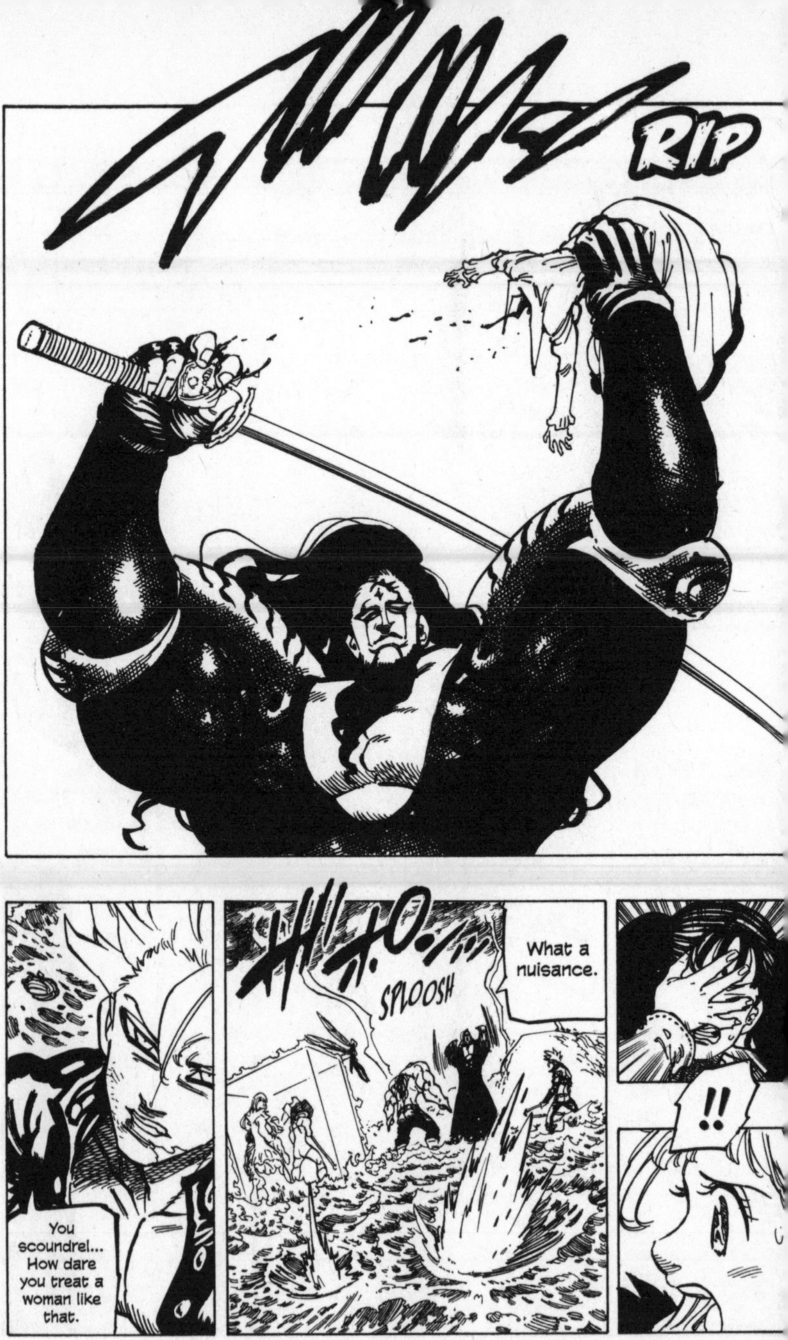
RIP
!!
What a nuisance.
SPLOOSH
You scoundrel... How dare you treat a woman like that.

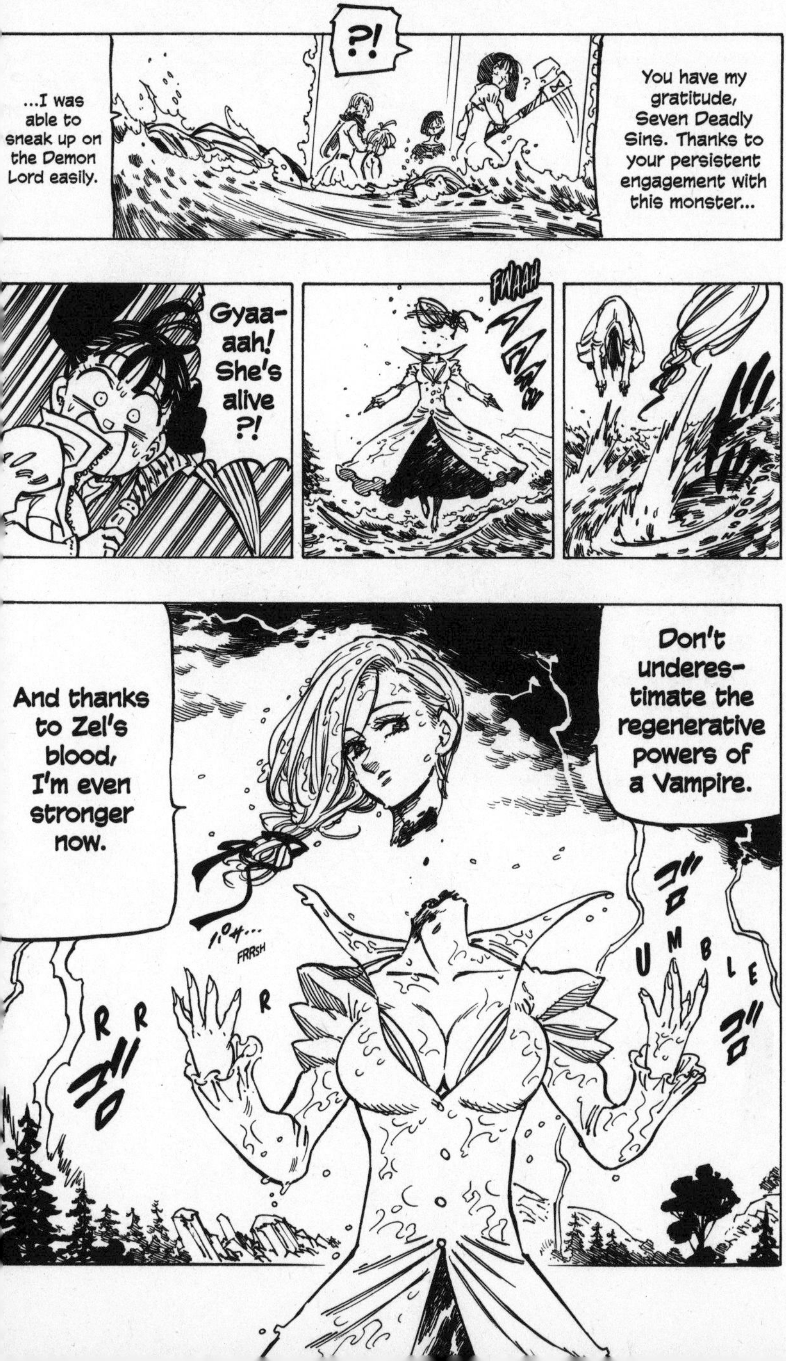
You have my gratitude, Seven Deadly Sins. Thanks to your persistent engagement with this monster...
?!
...I was able to sneak up on the Demon Lord easily.
SPLOOSH
FWAAH
Gyaa-aah! She's alive?!
Don't underes-timate the regenerative powers of a Vampire.
And thanks to Zel's blood, I'm even stronger now.
ゴロ
UMBLE
ゴロ
パサ...
FRRSH
RRR
ゴロ

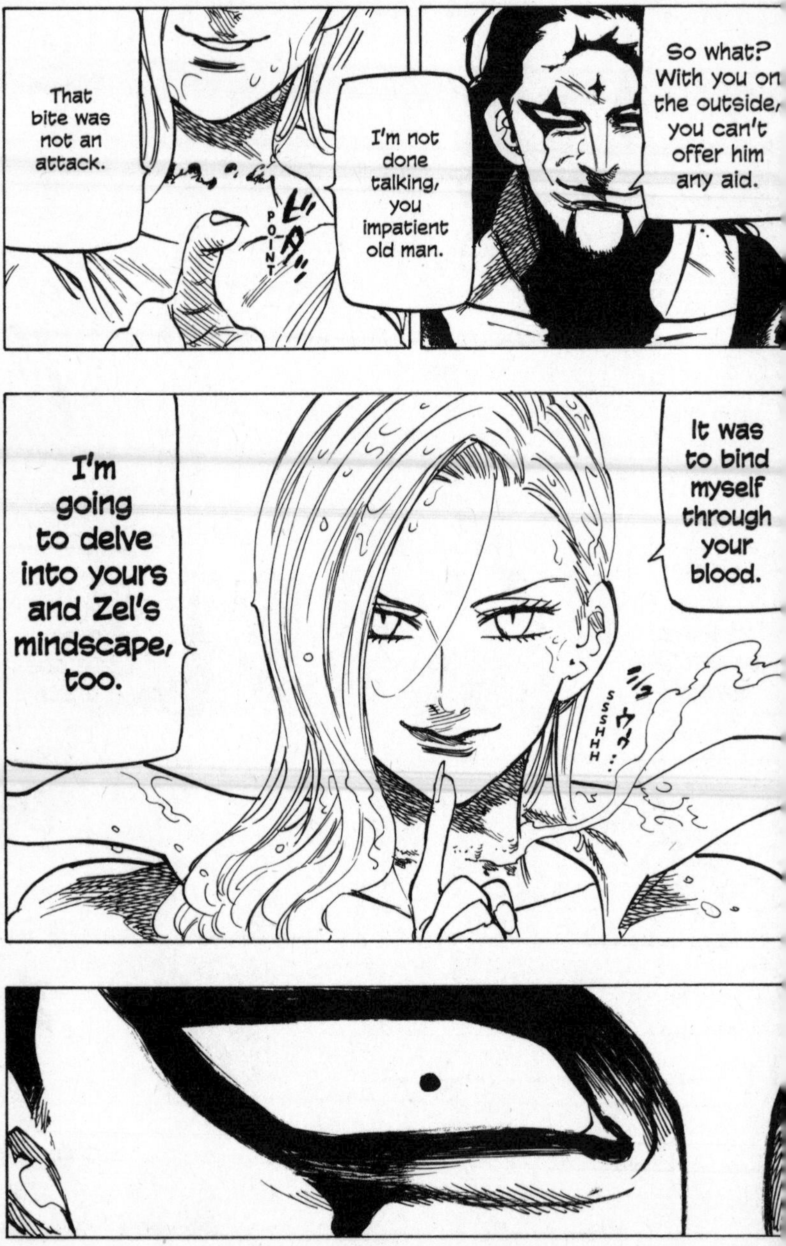
So what? With you on the outside, you can't offer him any aid.
I'm not done talking, you impatient old man.
That bite was not an attack.
POINT
It was to bind myself through your blood.
I'm going to delve into yours and Zel's mindscape, too.
SSSHHH

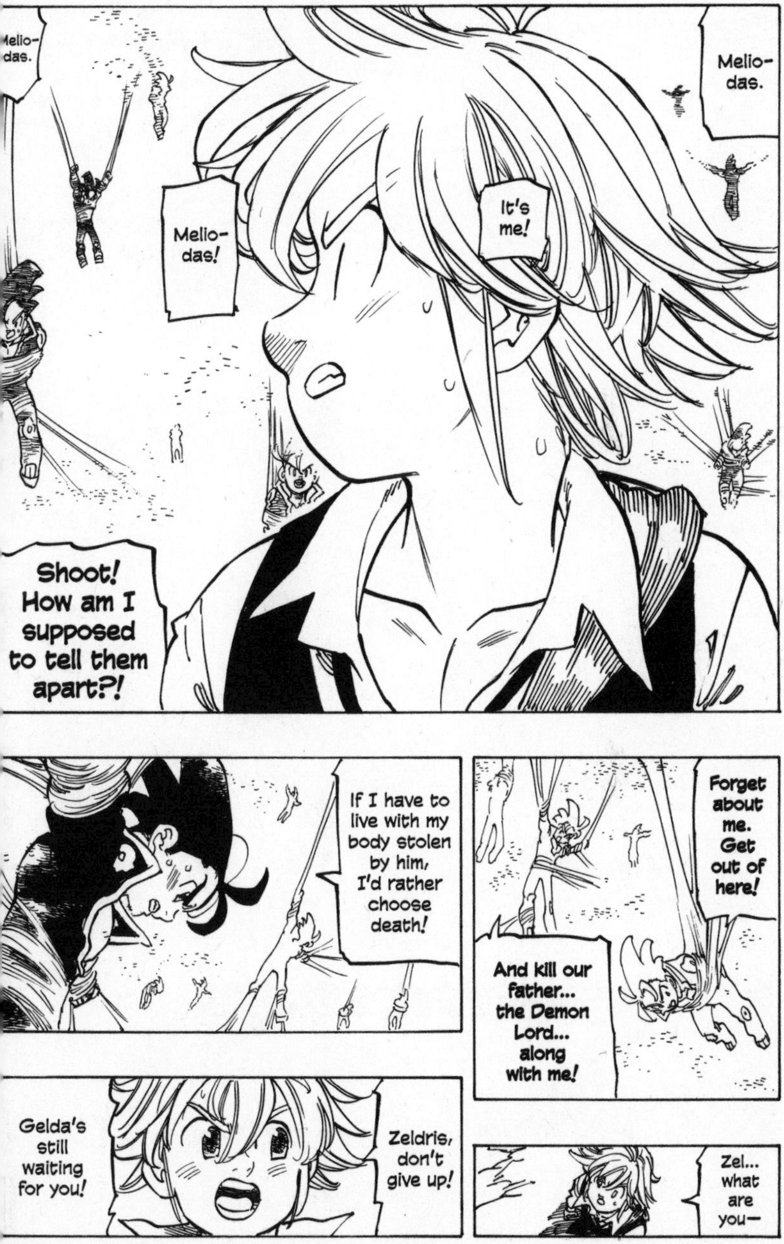
Melio-das.
It's me!
Melio-das!
Melio-das.
Shoot! How am I supposed to tell them apart?!
Forget about me. Get out of here!
And kill our father... the Demon Lord... along with me!
If I have to live with my body stolen by him, I'd rather choose death!
Zel... what are you—
Zeldris, don't give up!
Gelda's still waiting for you!

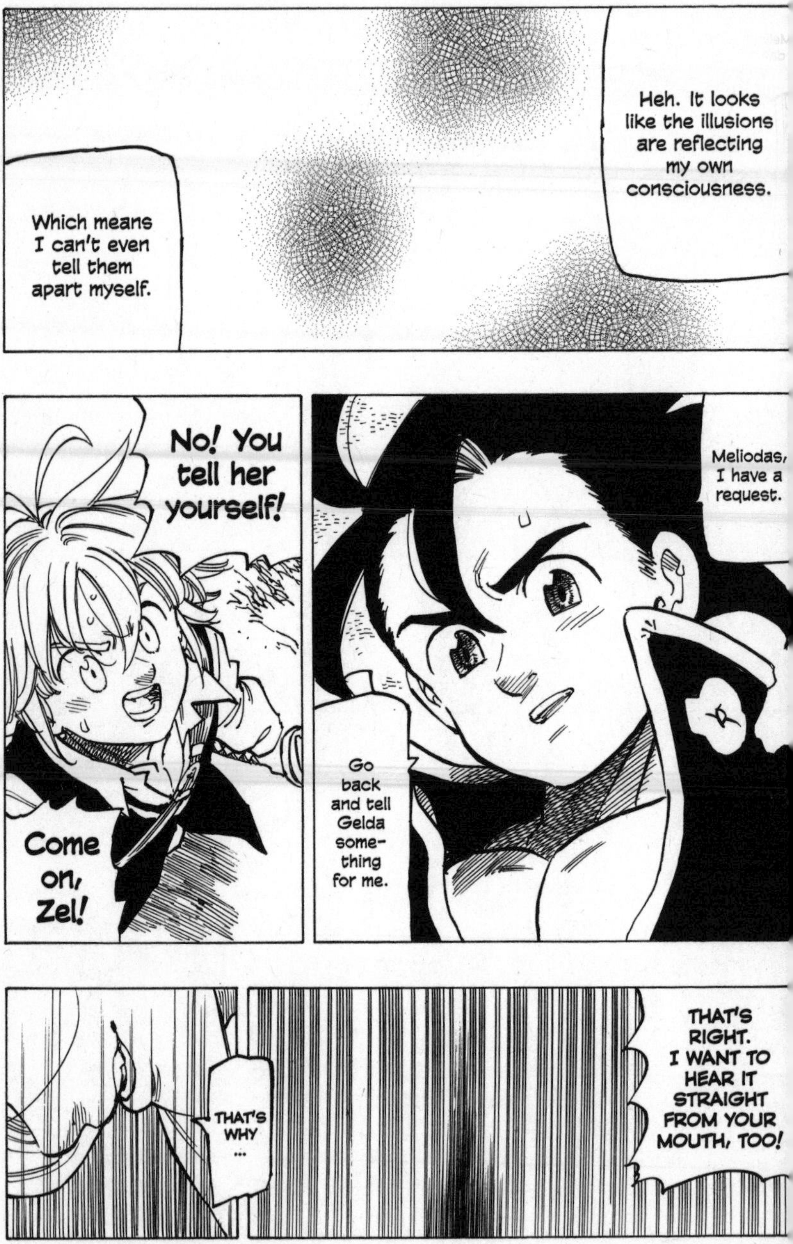
Heh. It looks like the illusions are reflecting my own consciousness.
Which means I can't even tell them apart myself.
Meliodas, I have a request.
Go back and tell Gelda something for me.
No! You tell her yourself!
Come on, Zel!
THAT'S RIGHT. I WANT TO HEAR IT STRAIGHT FROM YOUR MOUTH, TOO!
THAT'S WHY ...

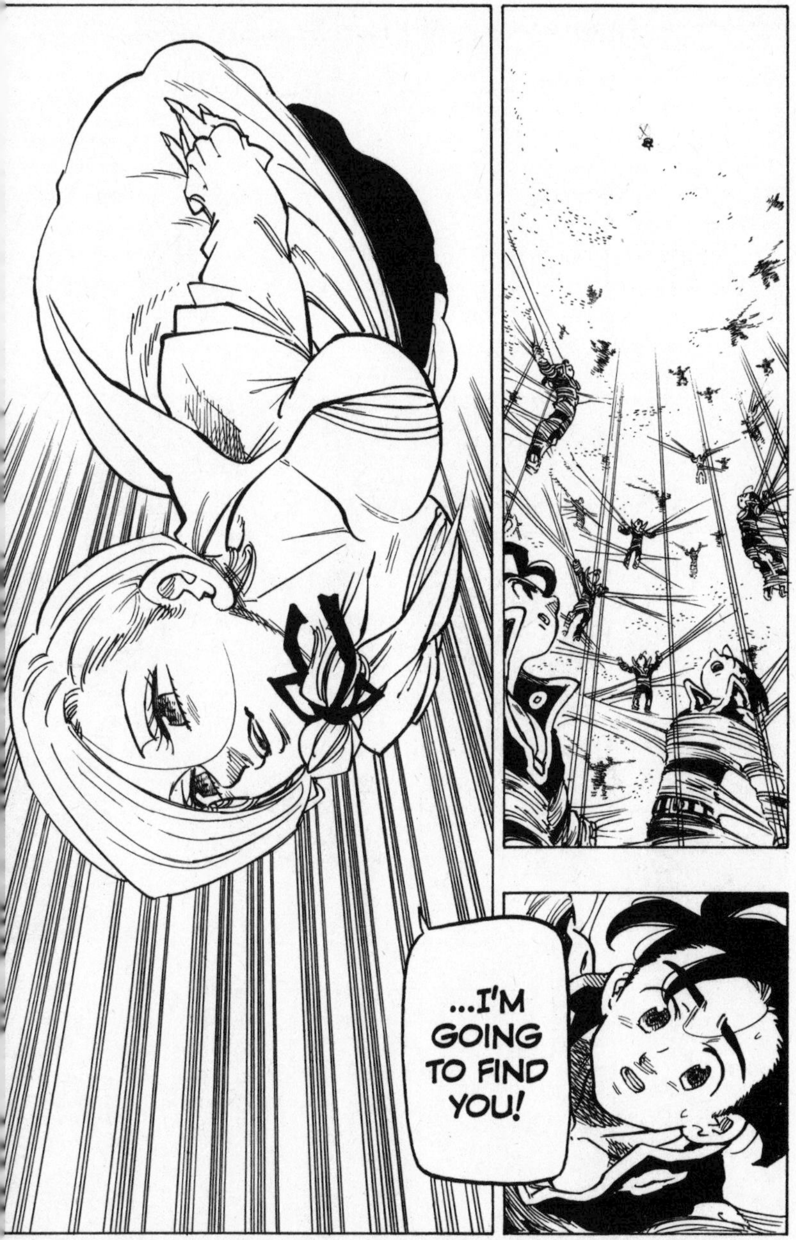
...I'M GOING TO FIND YOU!

Chapter 324 - A Promise Between Brothers

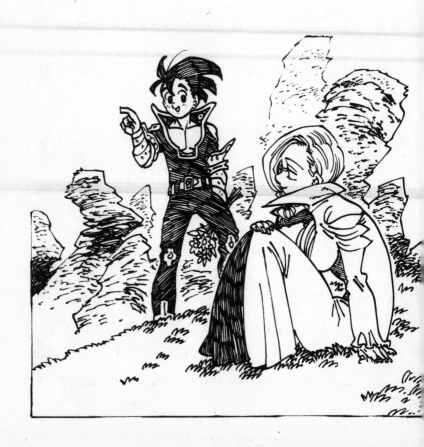

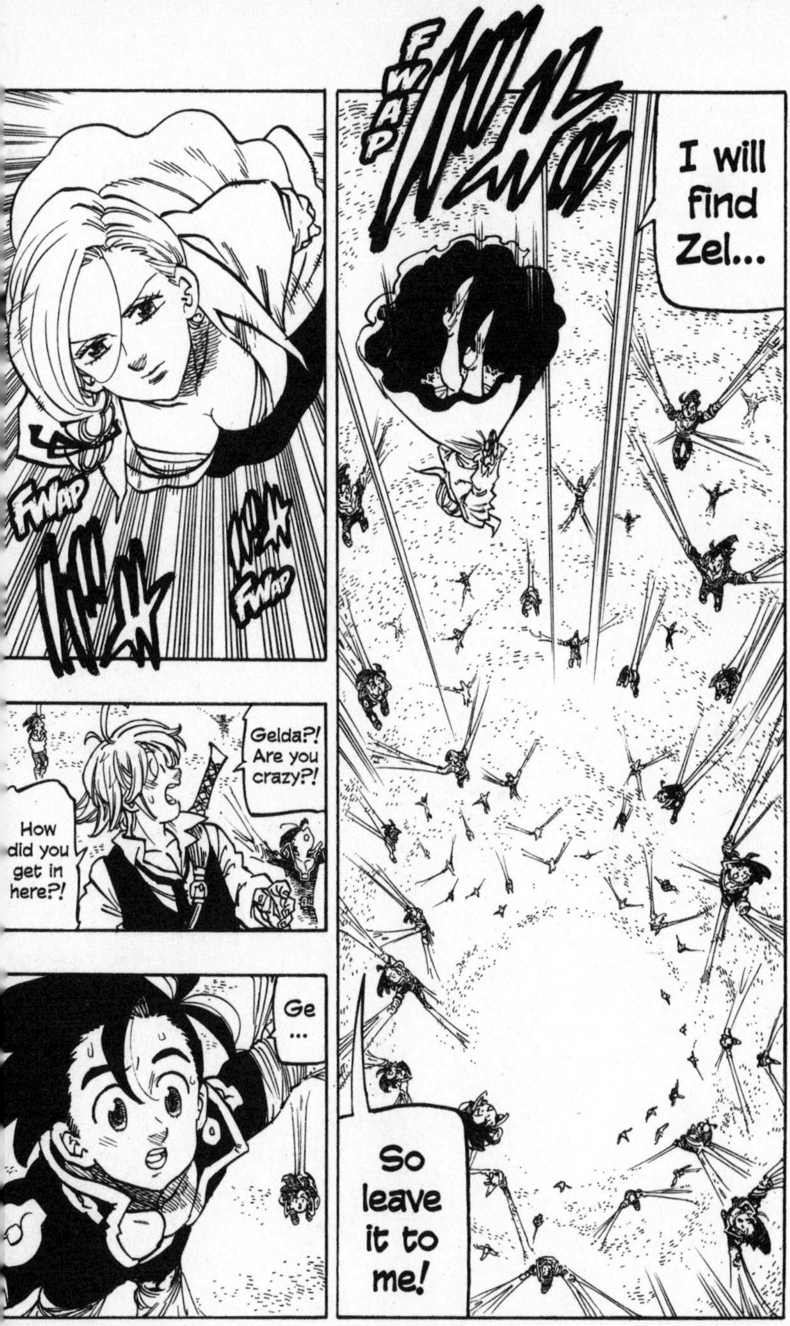
FWAP
I will find Zel...
So leave it to me!
FWAP
FWAP
Gelda?! Are you crazy?!
How did you get in here?!
Ge ...

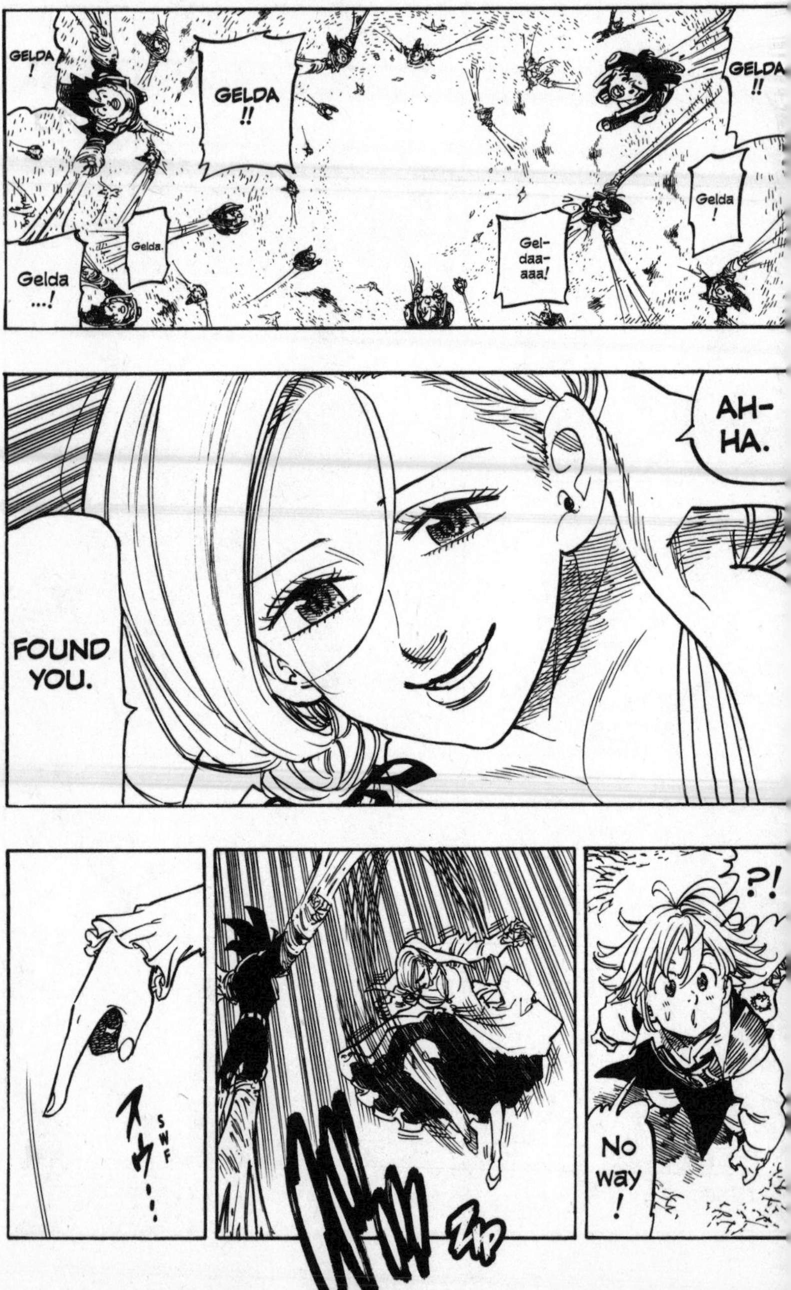
GELDA !!
Gelda !
Gel-daaa-aaa!
GELDA !!
GELDA !
Gelda.
Gelda ...!
AH-HA.
FOUND YOU.
?!
No way !
ZIP
SWF

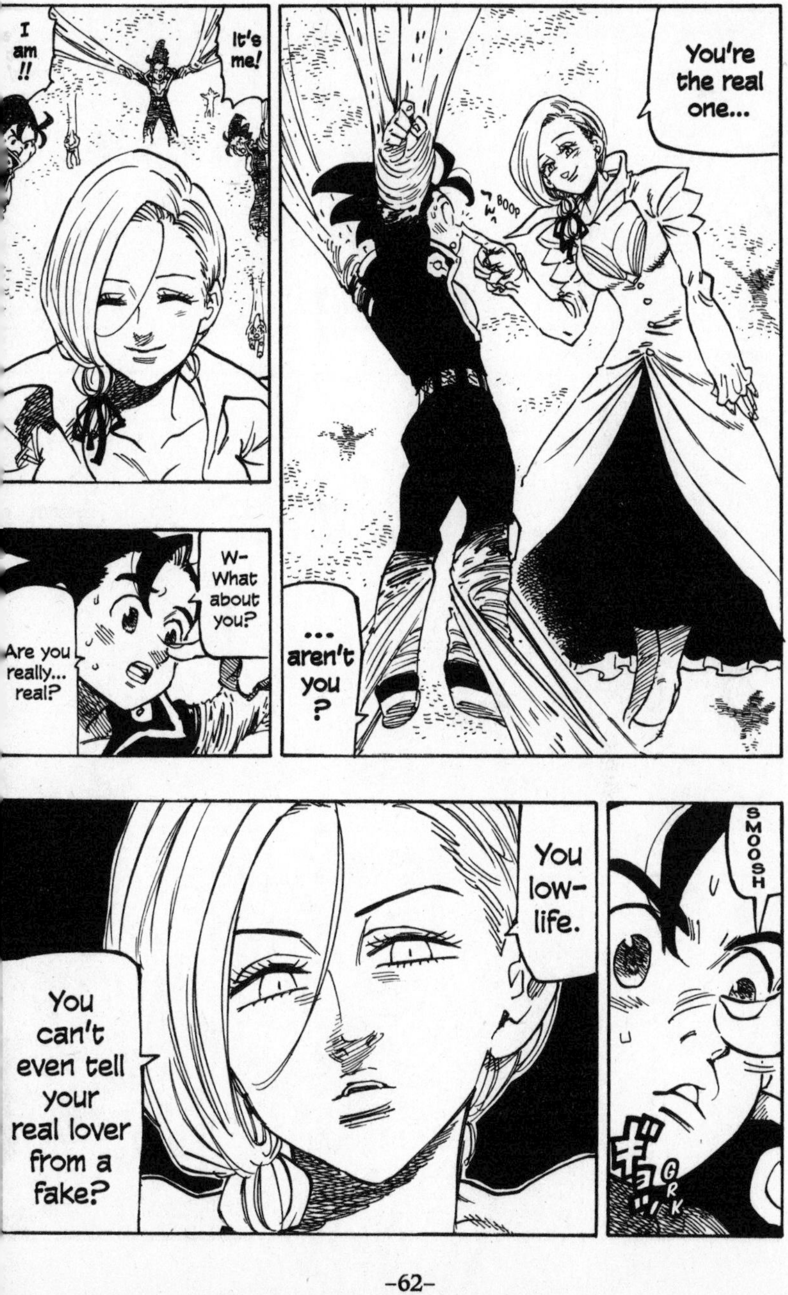
You're the real one...
BOOP
...aren't you?
It's me!
I am!!
W- What about you?
Are you really... real?
SMOOSH
GRK
You low-life.
You can't even tell your real lover from a fake?

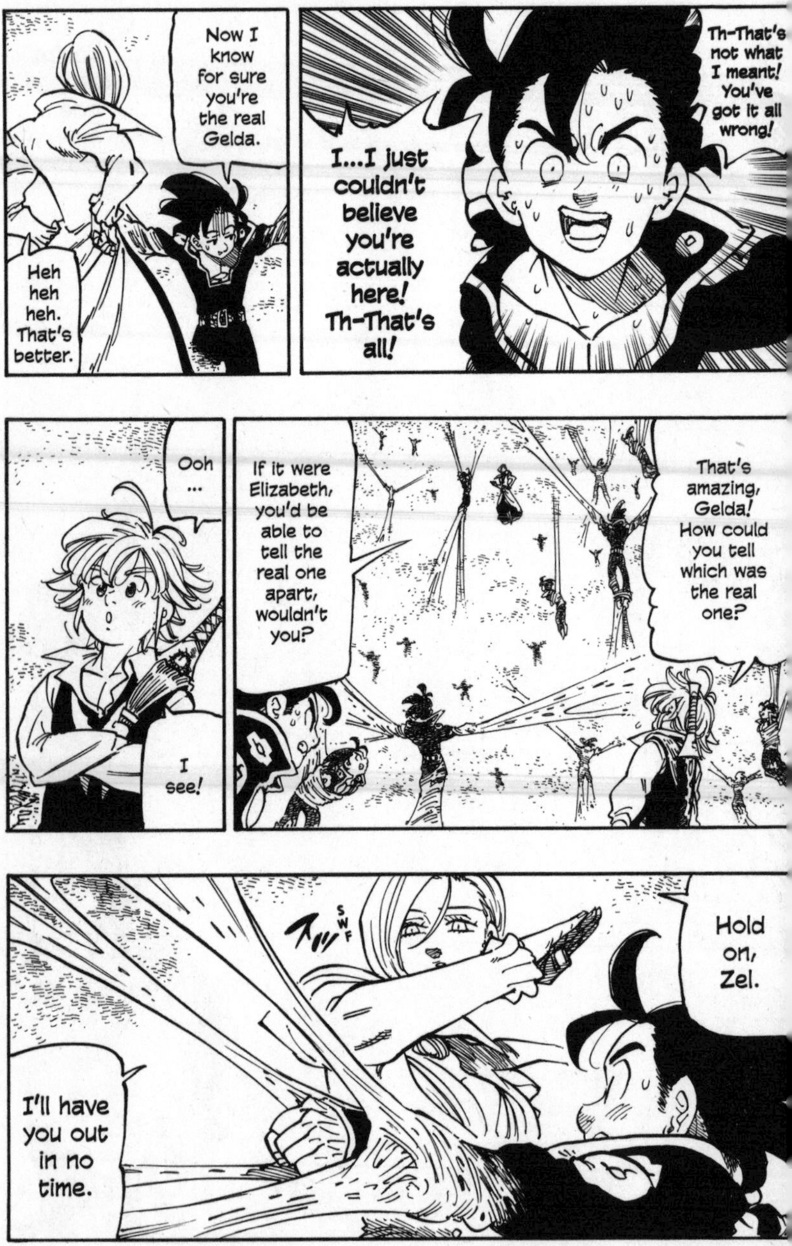
Th-That's not what I meant! You've got it all wrong!
I...I just couldn't believe you're actually here! Th-That's all!
Now I know for sure you're the real Gelda.
Heh heh heh. That's better.
That's amazing, Gelda! How could you tell which was the real one?
If it were Elizabeth, you'd be able to tell the real one apart, wouldn't you?
Ooh ...
I see!
Hold on, Zel.
SWF
I'll have you out in no time.

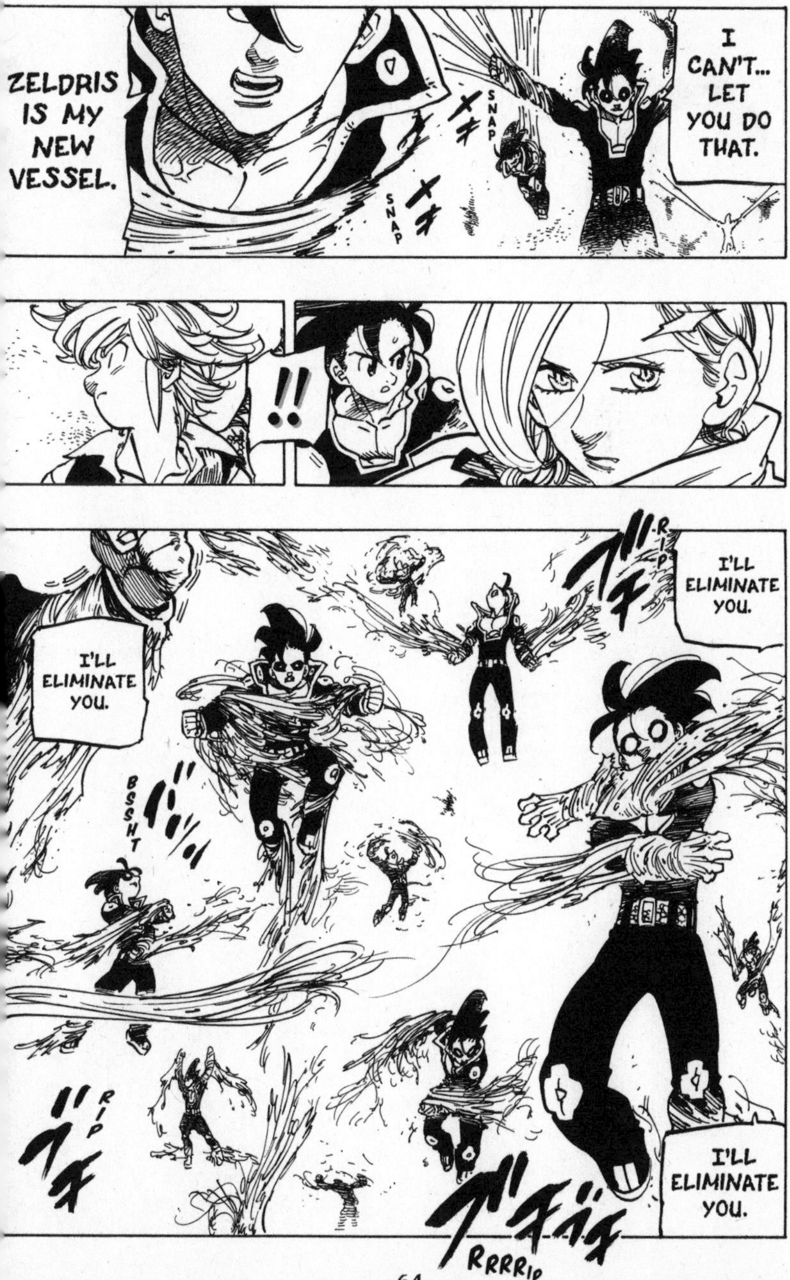

I CAN'T... LET YOU DO THAT.
SNAP
SNAP
ZELDRIS IS MY NEW VESSEL.
!!
RIP
I'LL ELIMINATE YOU.
I'LL ELIMINATE YOU.
BSSHT
I'LL ELIMINATE YOU.
RRRRIP
RIP

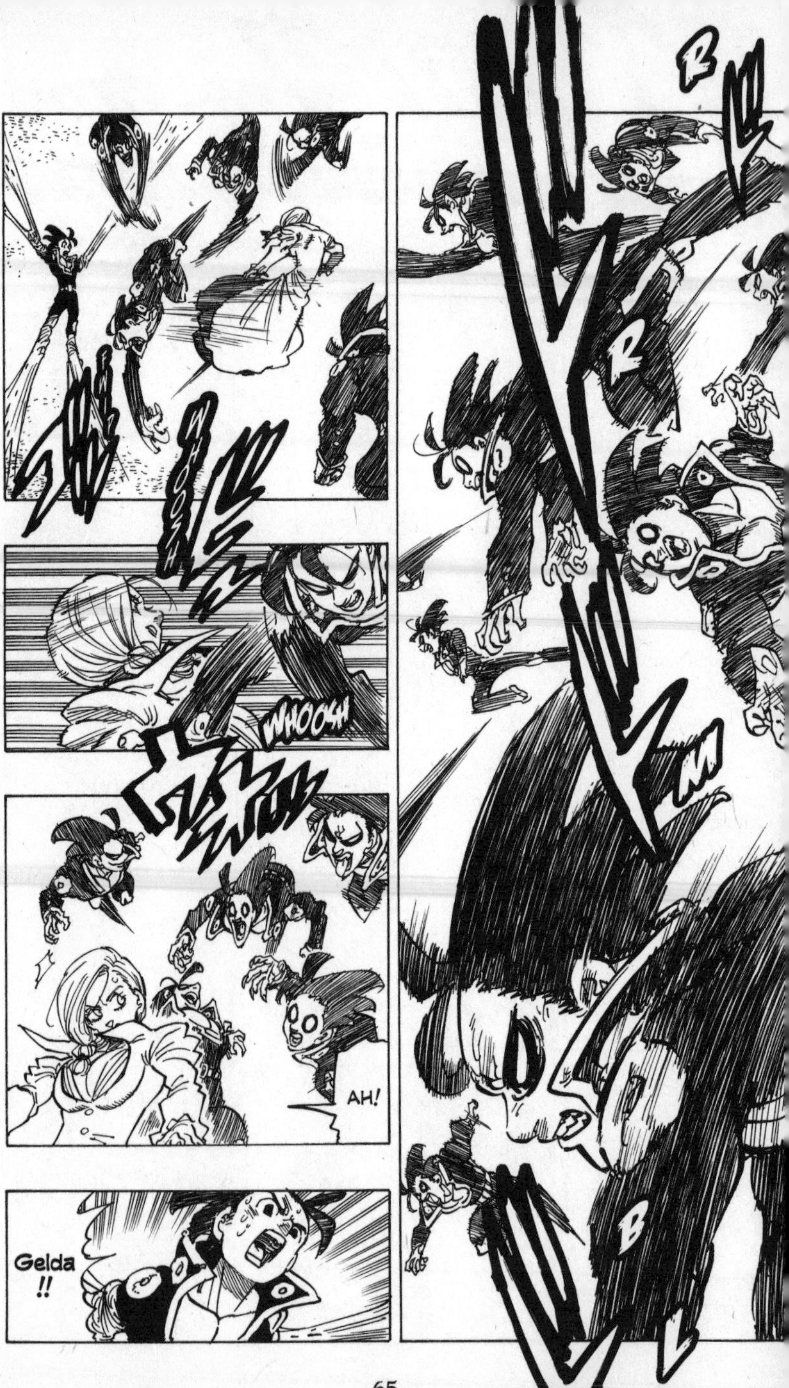
WHOOSH
WHOOSH
AH!
Gelda !!

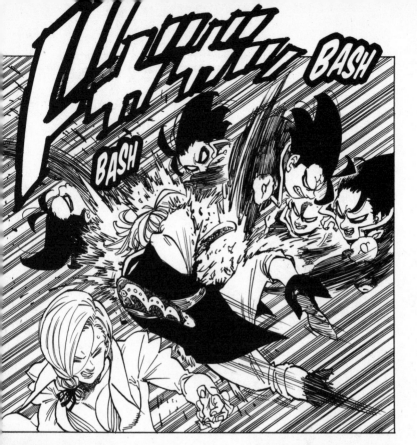

BASH

BASH

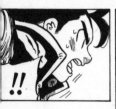

!!

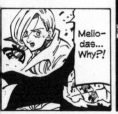

Melio-
das...
Why?!

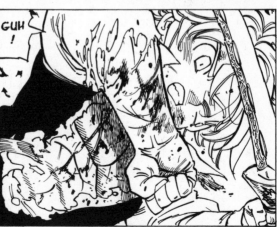

GUH
!

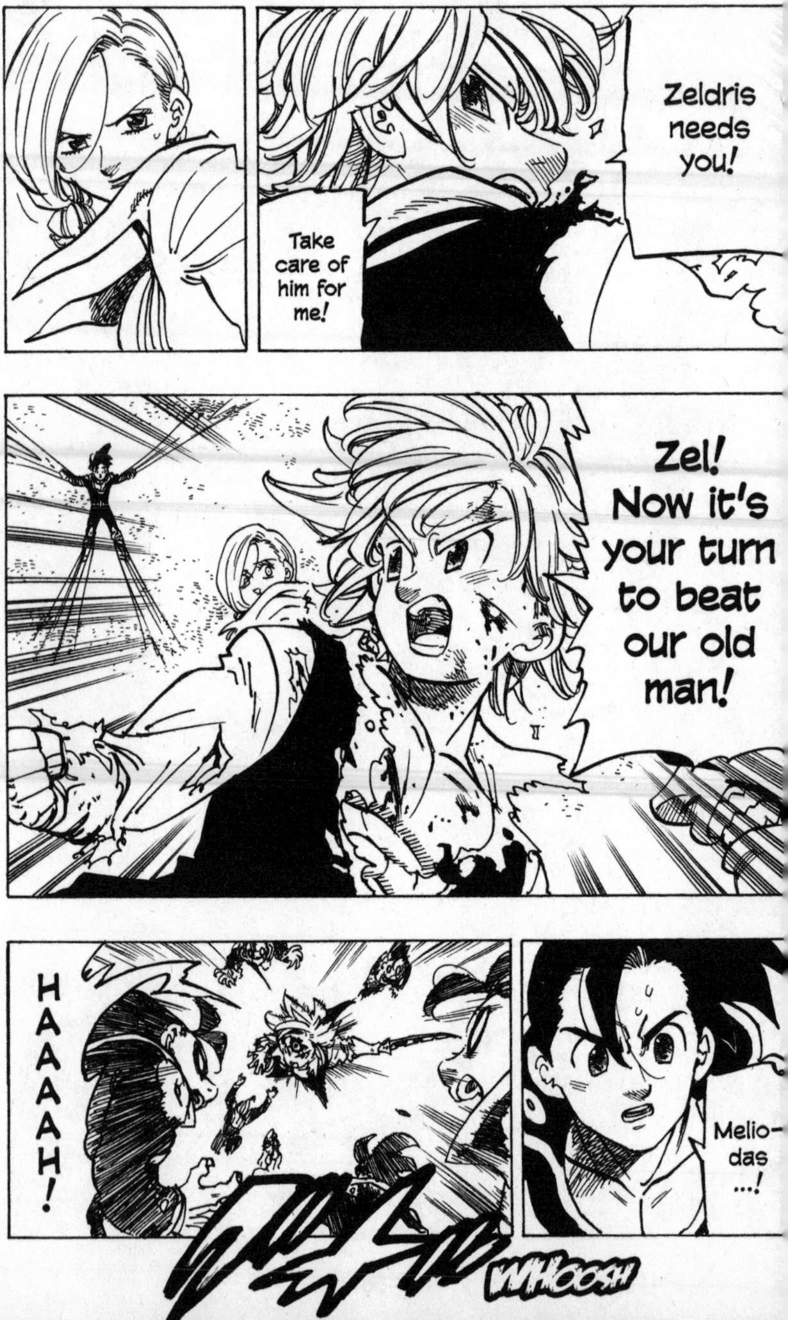
Zeldris needs you!
Take care of him for me!
Zel! Now it's your turn to beat our old man!
Melio-das ...!
HAAAAAH!
WHOOSH

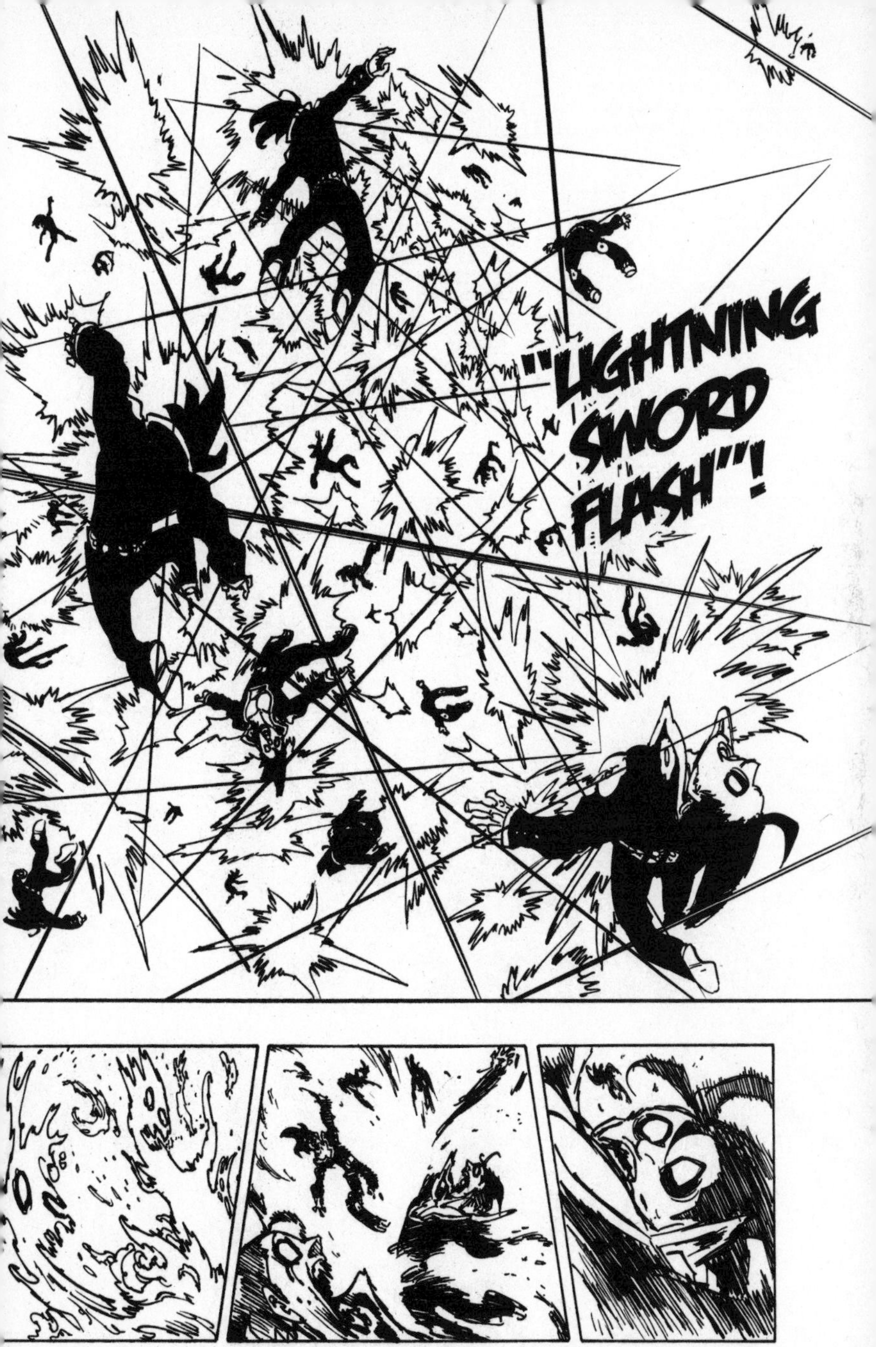
"LIGHTNING SWORD FLASH"!

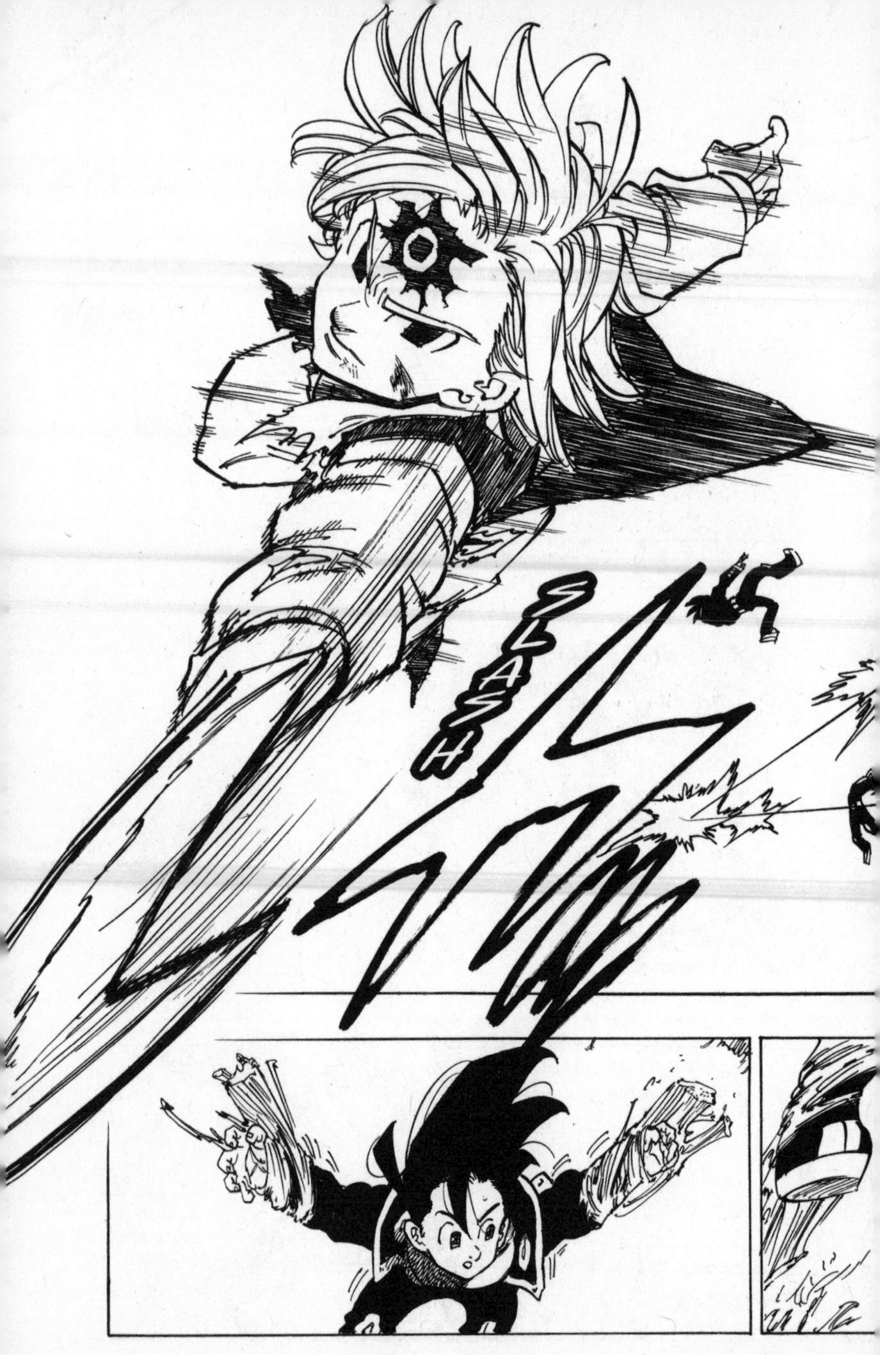
SLASH

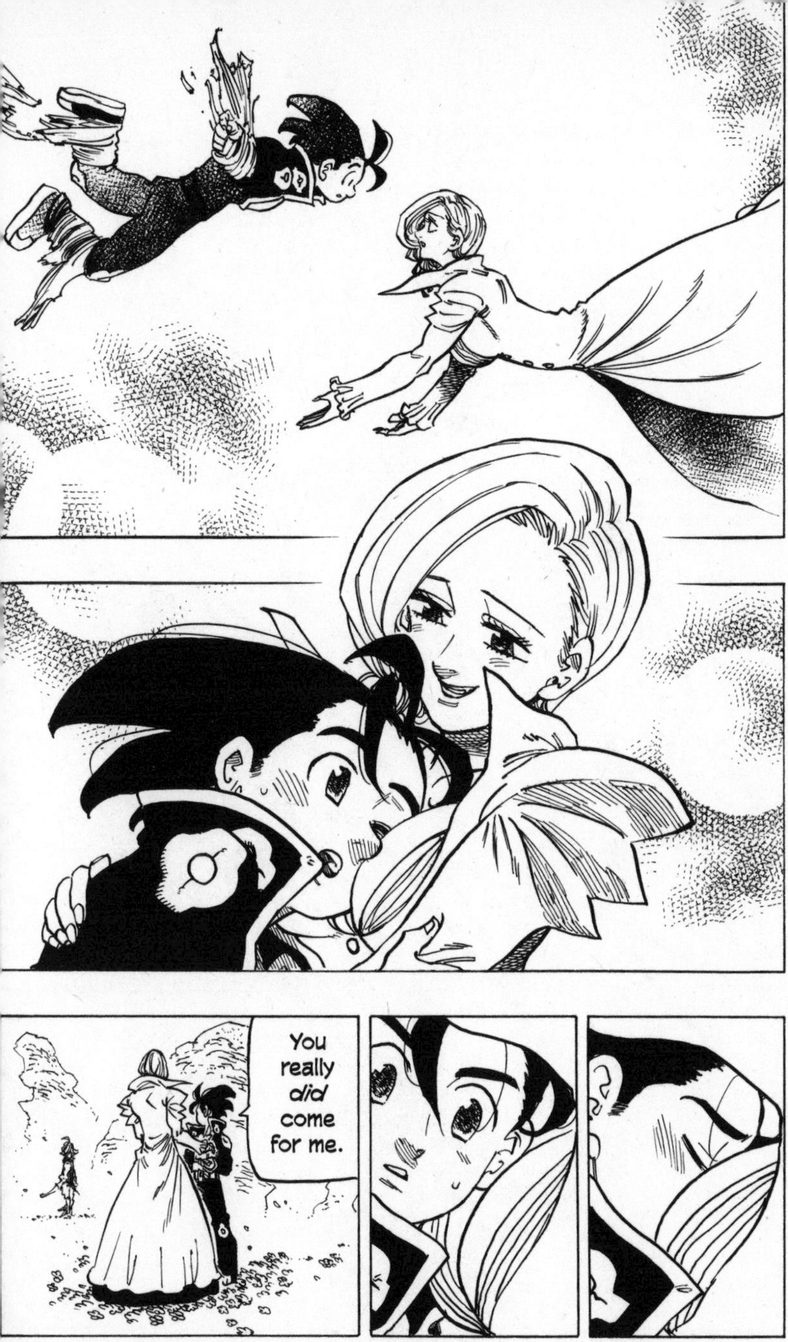
You really *did* come for me.

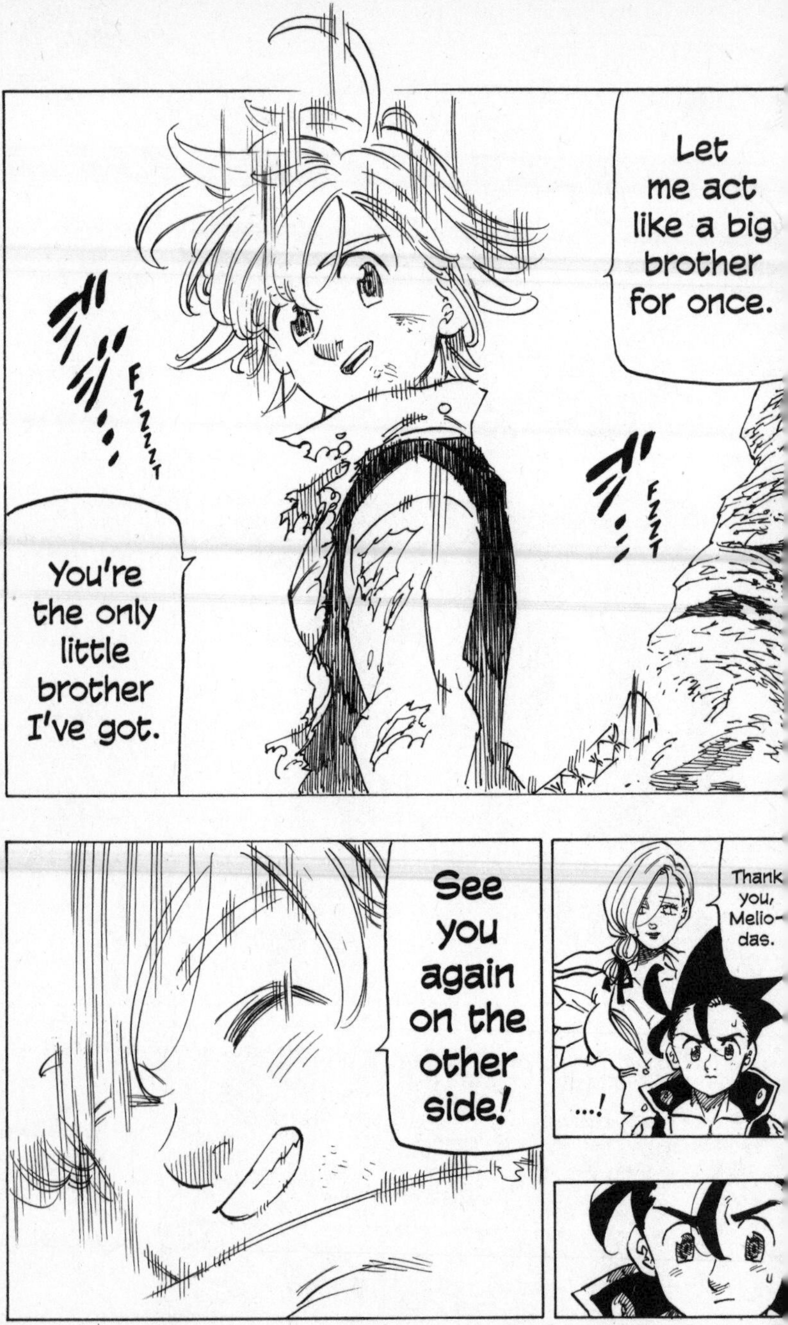
Let me act like a big brother for once.
FZZZT
FZZZZZT
You're the only little brother I've got.
Thank you, Melio-das.
...!
See you again on the other side!

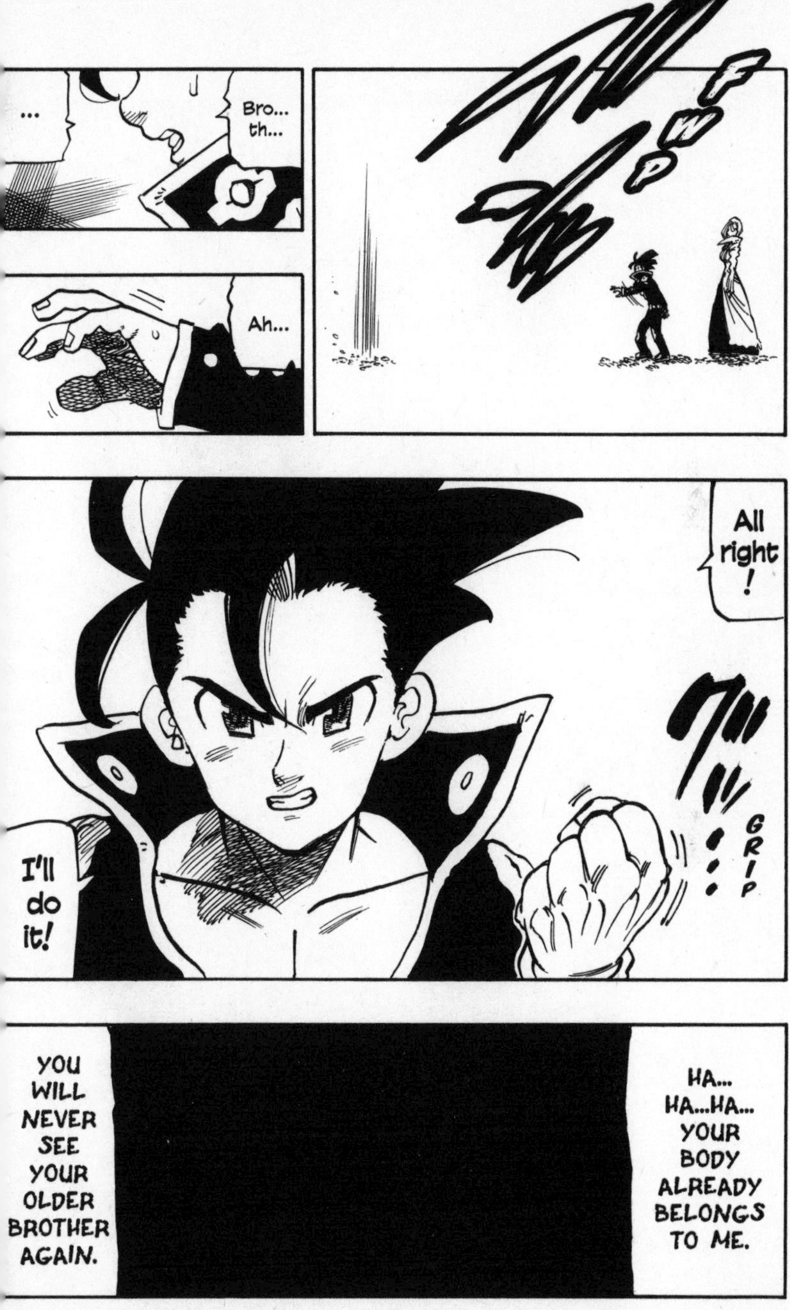
FWP
Bro... th...
...
Ah...
All right!
GRIP
I'll do it!
HA... HA...HA... YOUR BODY ALREADY BELONGS TO ME.
YOU WILL NEVER SEE YOUR OLDER BROTHER AGAIN.

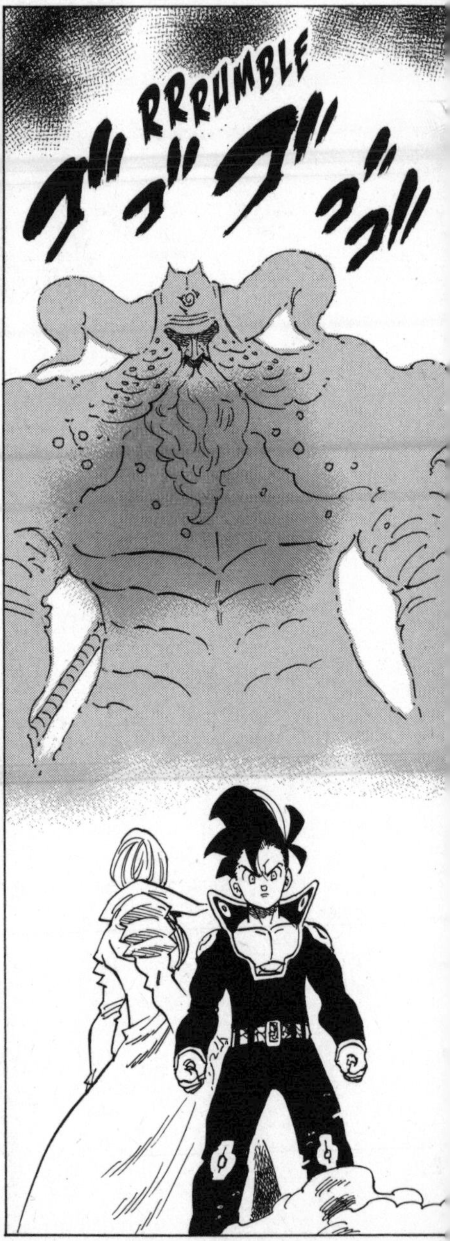
RRRUMBLE
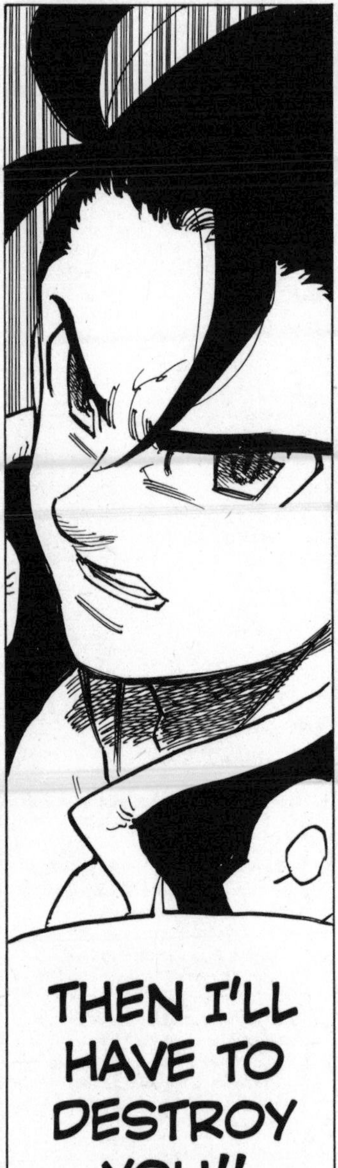
THEN I'LL HAVE TO DESTROY YOU!!

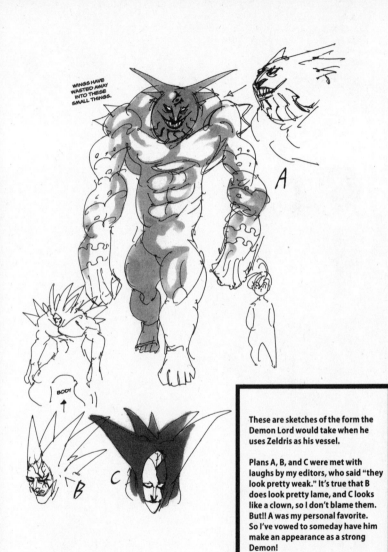

WINGS HAVE
WASTED AWAY
INTO THESE
SMALL THINGS.

A

BODY

B

C

These are sketches of the form the Demon Lord would take when he uses Zeldris as his vessel.

Plans A, B, and C were met with laughs by my editors, who said "they look pretty weak." It's true that B does look pretty lame, and C looks like a clown, so I don't blame them. But!! A was my personal favorite. So I've vowed to someday have him make an appearance as a strong Demon!

THE SEVEN DEADLY SINS

Chapter 325 - The Challengers

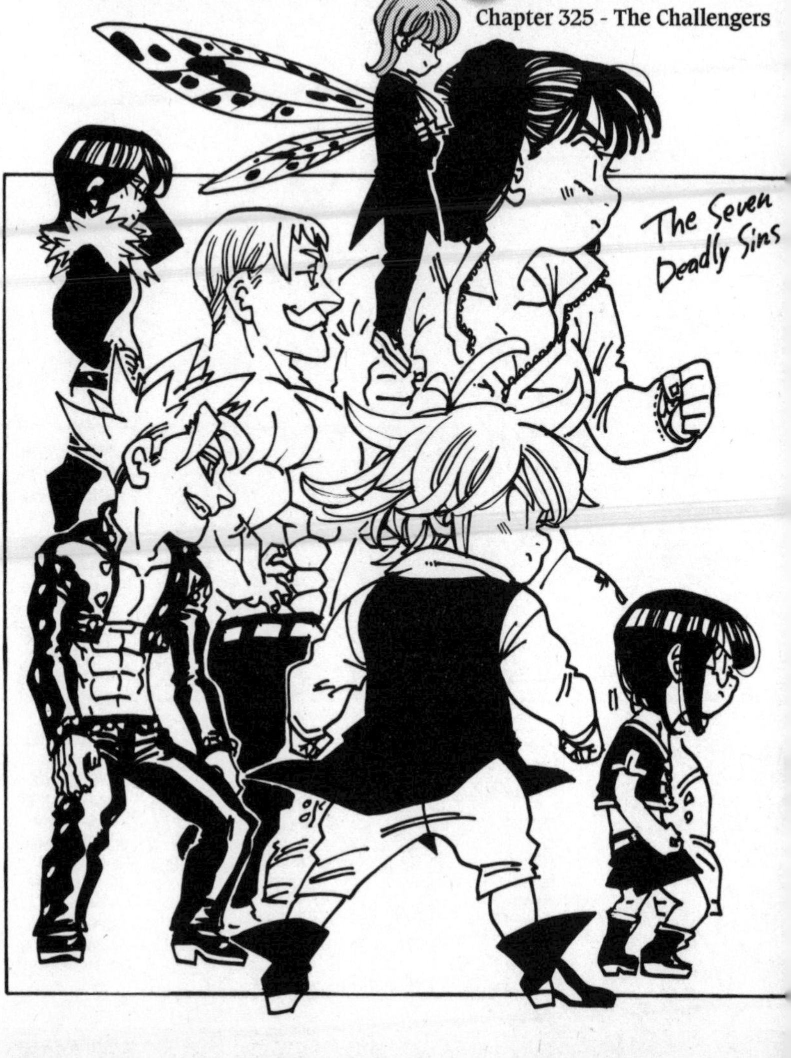
The Seven Deadly Sins

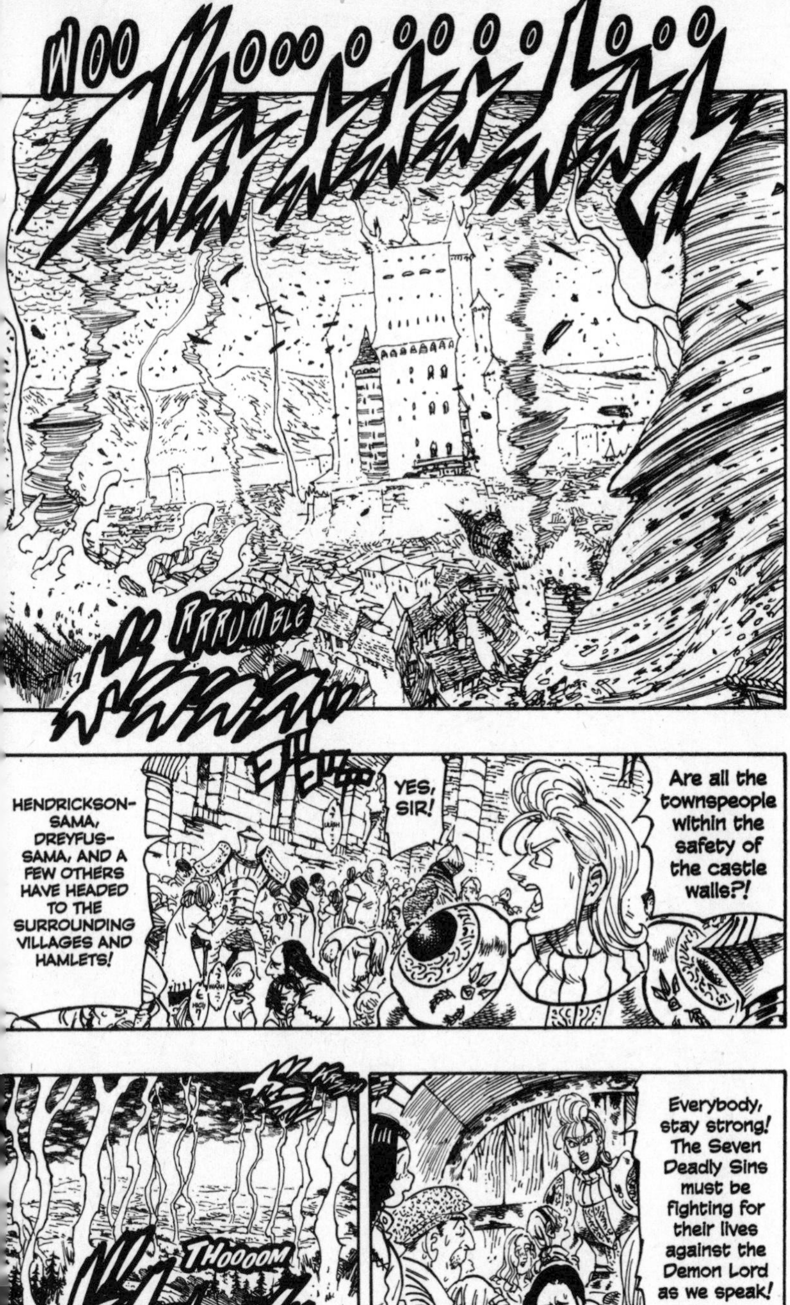
WOOOOOOOOOOOOO
RRRUMBLE
Are all the townspeople within the safety of the castle walls?!
YES, SIR!
HENDRICKSON-SAMA, DREYFUS-SAMA, AND A FEW OTHERS HAVE HEADED TO THE SURROUNDING VILLAGES AND HAMLETS!
Everybody, stay strong! The Seven Deadly Sins must be fighting for their lives against the Demon Lord as we speak!
THOOOOM

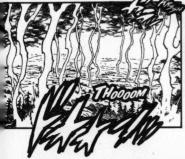

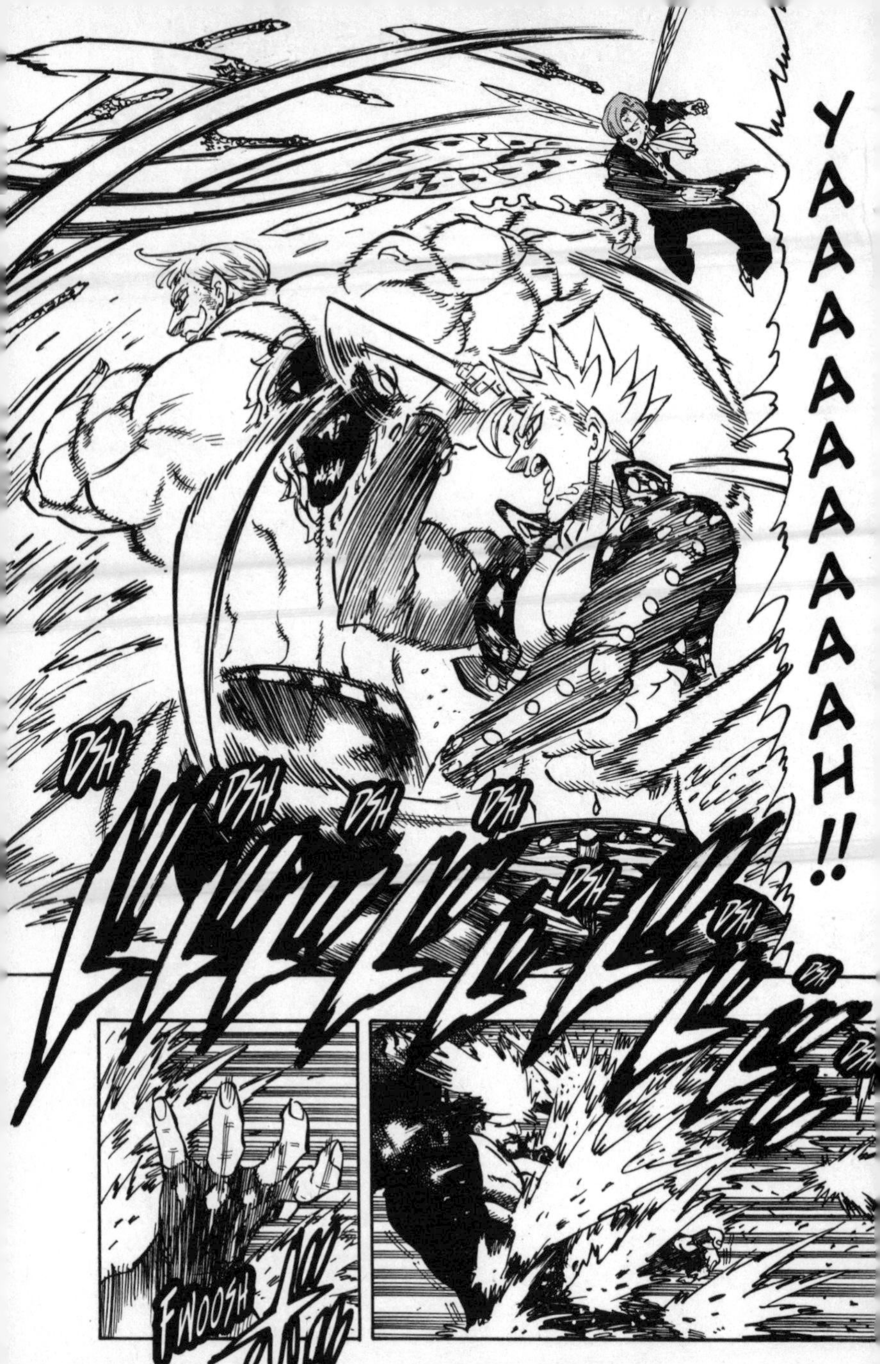
YAAAAAAAAAAH!!
DSH
DSH
DSH
DSH
DSH
DSH
FWOOSH

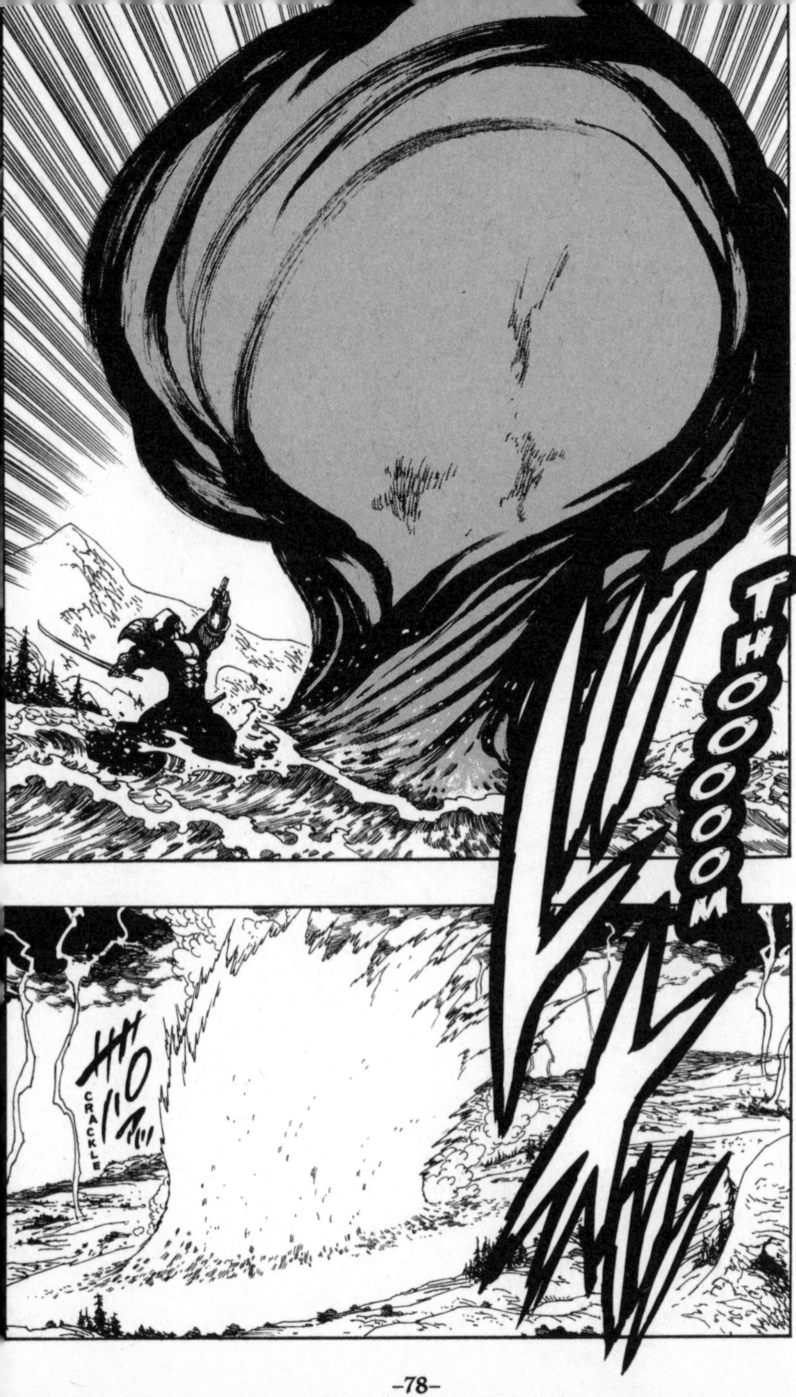
THOOOOOM
CRACKLE

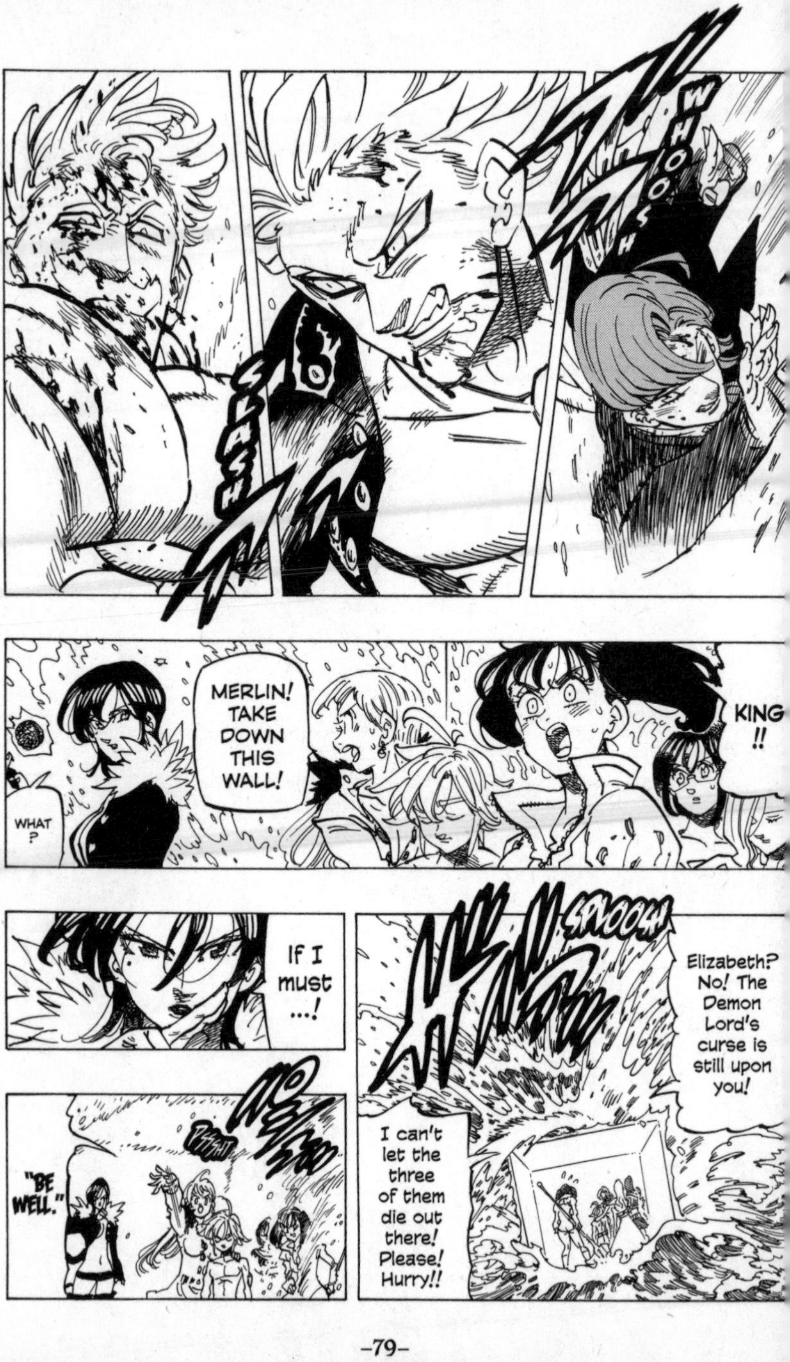
WHOOSH
SLASH
KING !!
MERLIN! TAKE DOWN THIS WALL!
WHAT ?
SPLOOSH
Elizabeth? No! The Demon Lord's curse is still upon you!
I can't let the three of them die out there! Please! Hurry!!
If I must ...!
"BE WELL."

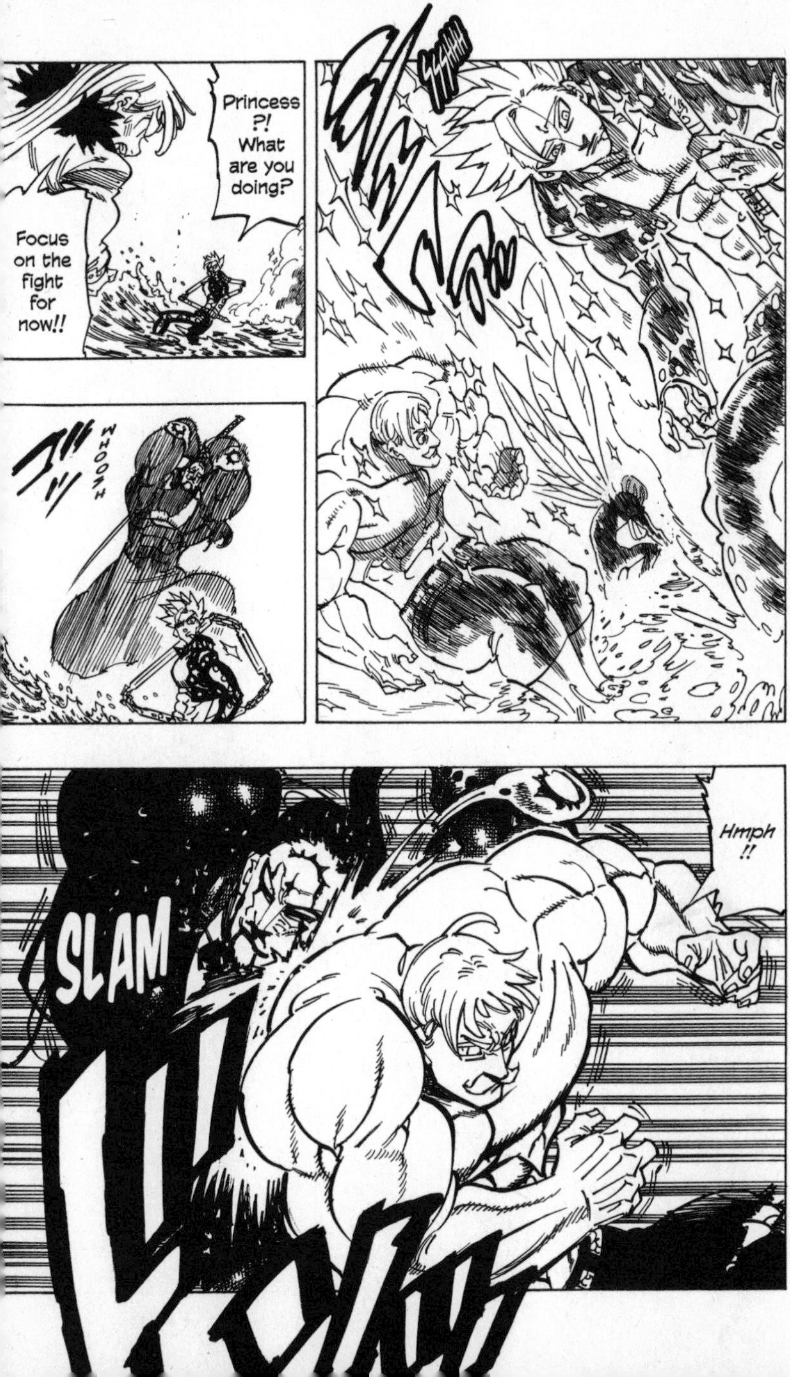
Princess?! What are you doing?
Focus on the fight for now!!
WHOOSH
Hmph!!
SLAM

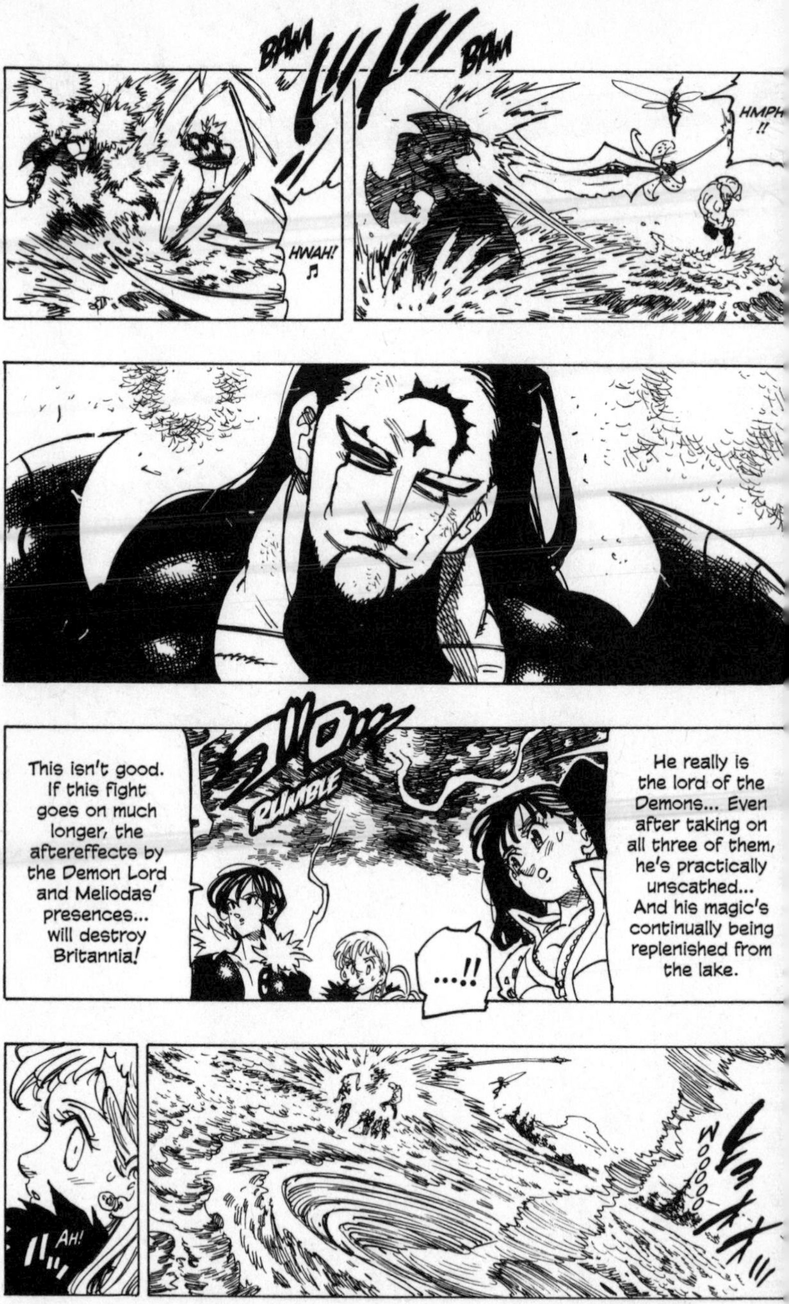
BAM
HMPH!!
BAM
HWAH! ♫
RUMBLE
He really is the lord of the Demons... Even after taking on all three of them, he's practically unscathed... And his magic's continually being replenished from the lake.
...!!
This isn't good. If this fight goes on much longer, the aftereffects by the Demon Lord and Meliodas' presences... will destroy Britannia!
WOOOOO
AH!

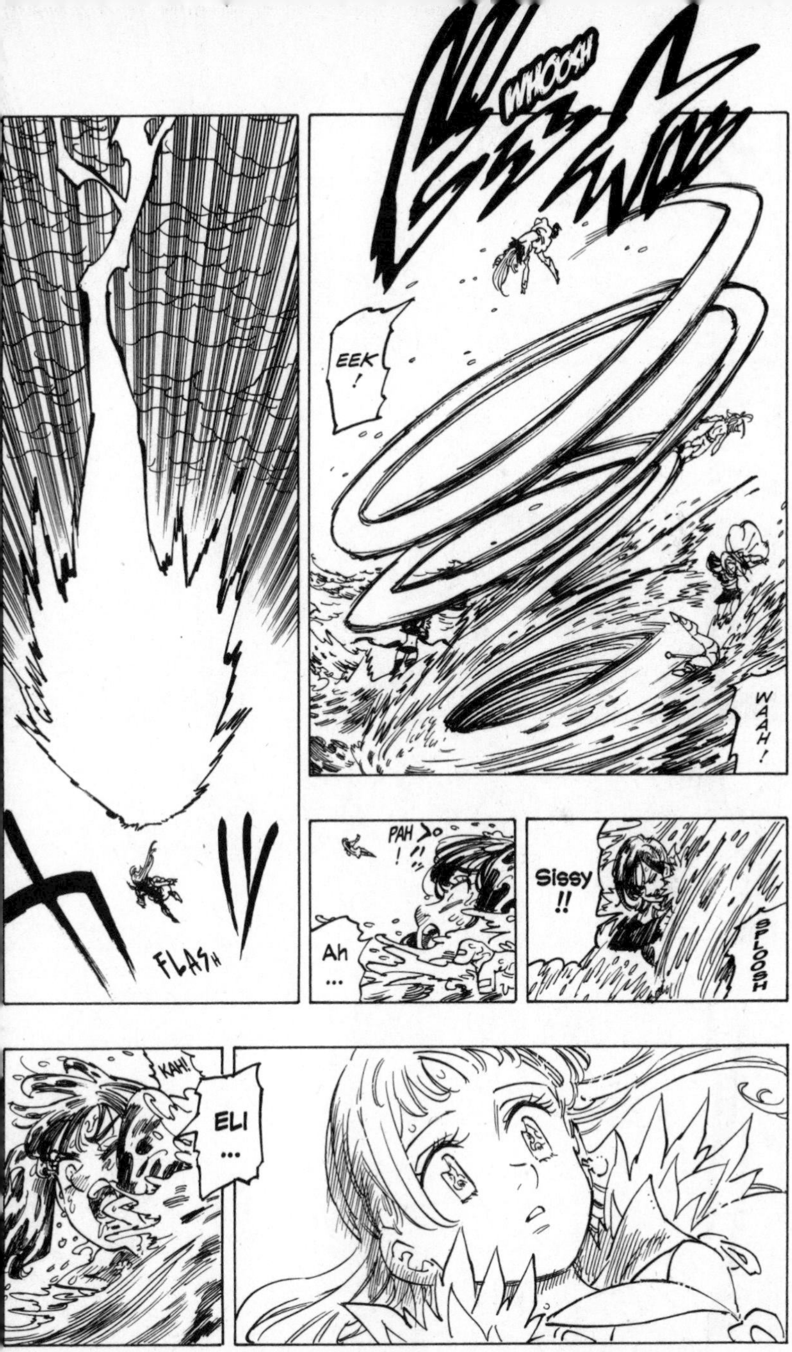
WHOOSH
EEK!
WAAH!
Sissy!!
SPLOOSH
PAH
Ah...
FLASH
KAH!
ELI...

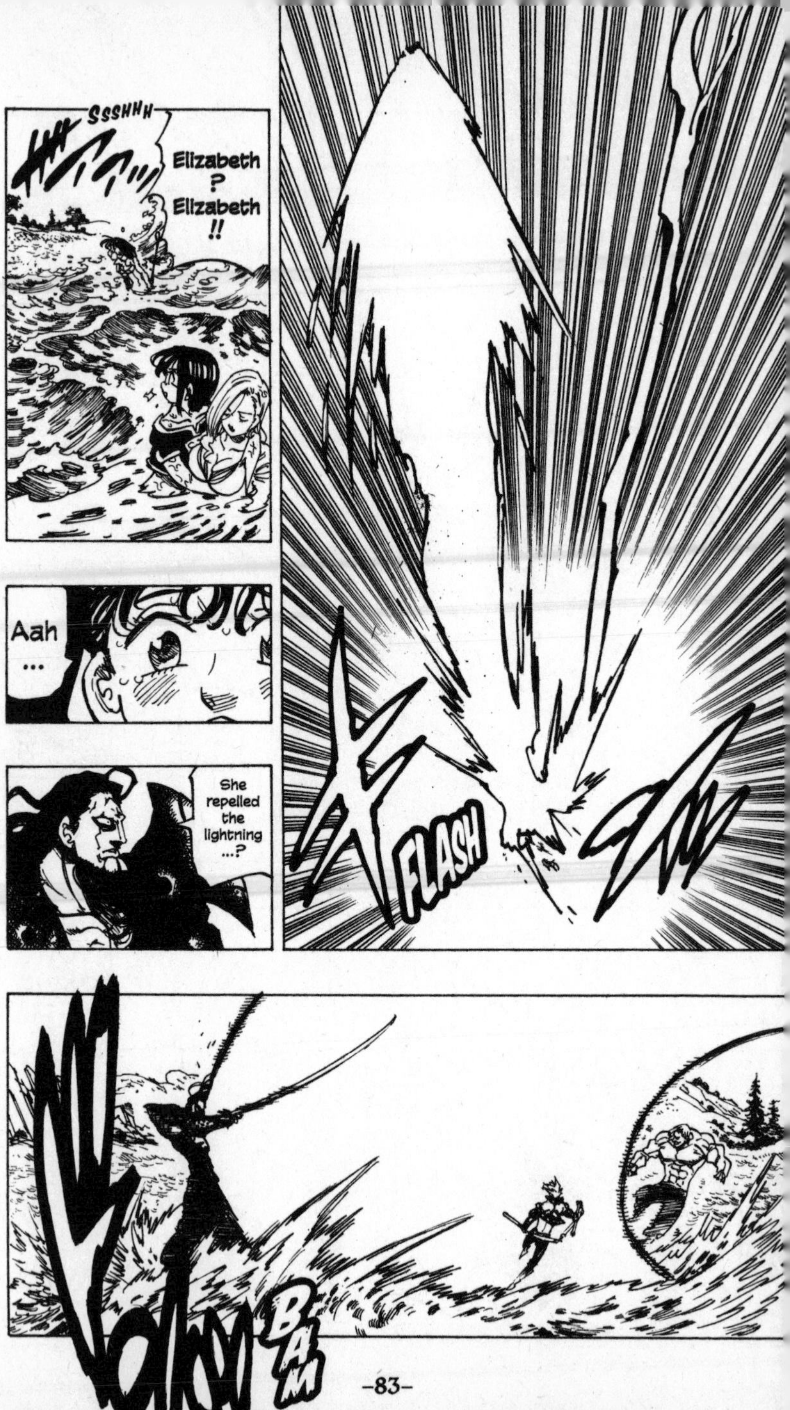
FLASH
SSSHHH
Elizabeth? Elizabeth!!
Aah...
She repelled the lightning...?
BAM

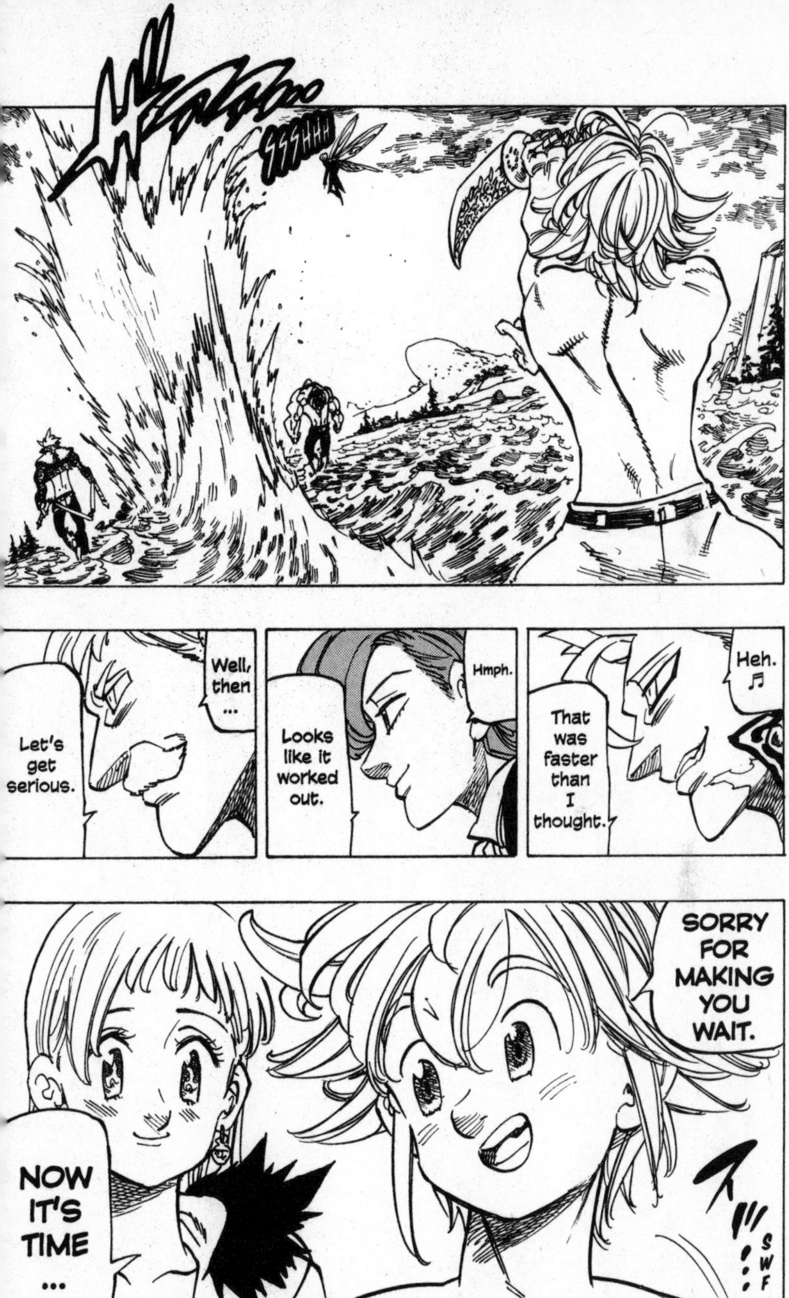
SSSHHH
Heh. ♫
That was faster than I thought.
Hmph.
Looks like it worked out.
Well, then ...
Let's get serious.
SORRY FOR MAKING YOU WAIT.
SWF
NOW IT'S TIME ...

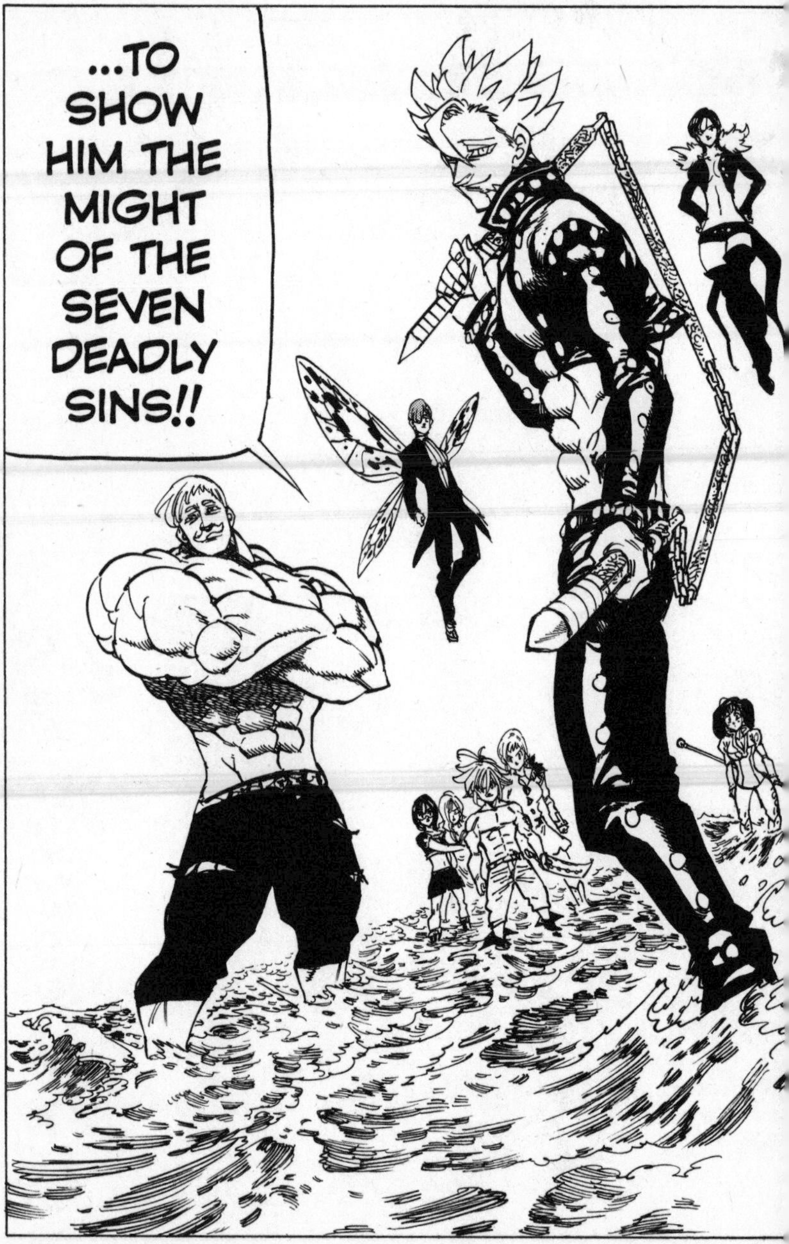
...TO SHOW HIM THE MIGHT OF THE SEVEN DEADLY SINS!!

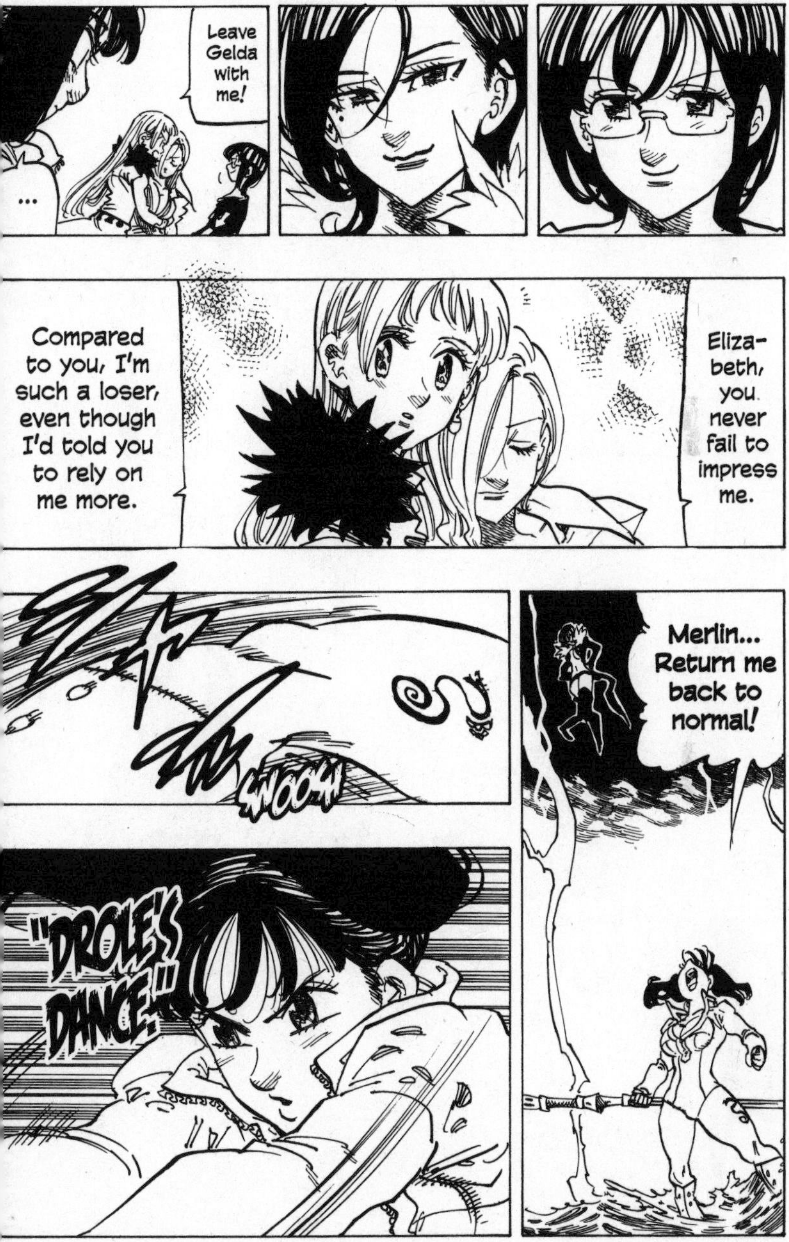
Leave Gelda with me!
...
Eliza-beth, you never fail to impress me.
Compared to you, I'm such a loser, even though I'd told you to rely on me more.
Merlin... Return me back to normal!
SWOOSH
"DROLE'S DANCE!!"

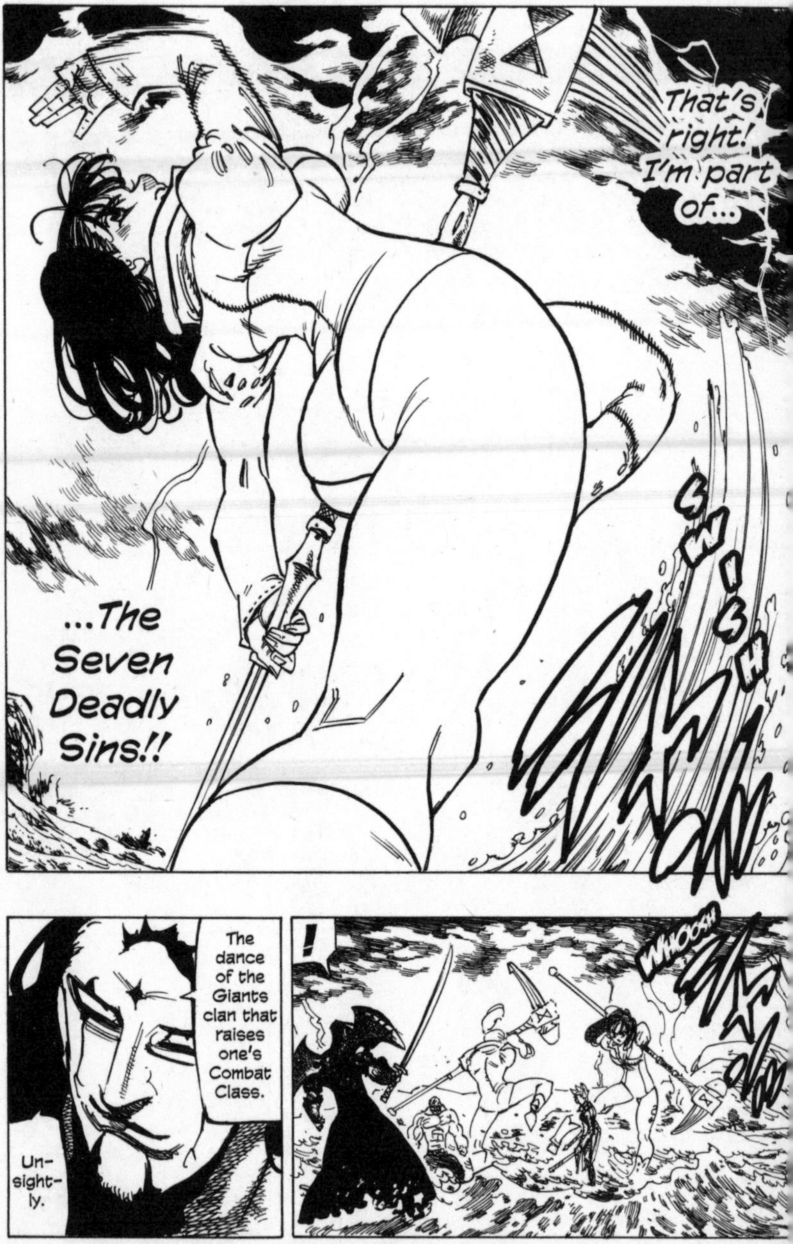
That's right! I'm part of...
SWISH
...The Seven Deadly Sins!!
WHOOSH
!
The dance of the Giants clan that raises one's Combat Class.
Un-sight-ly.

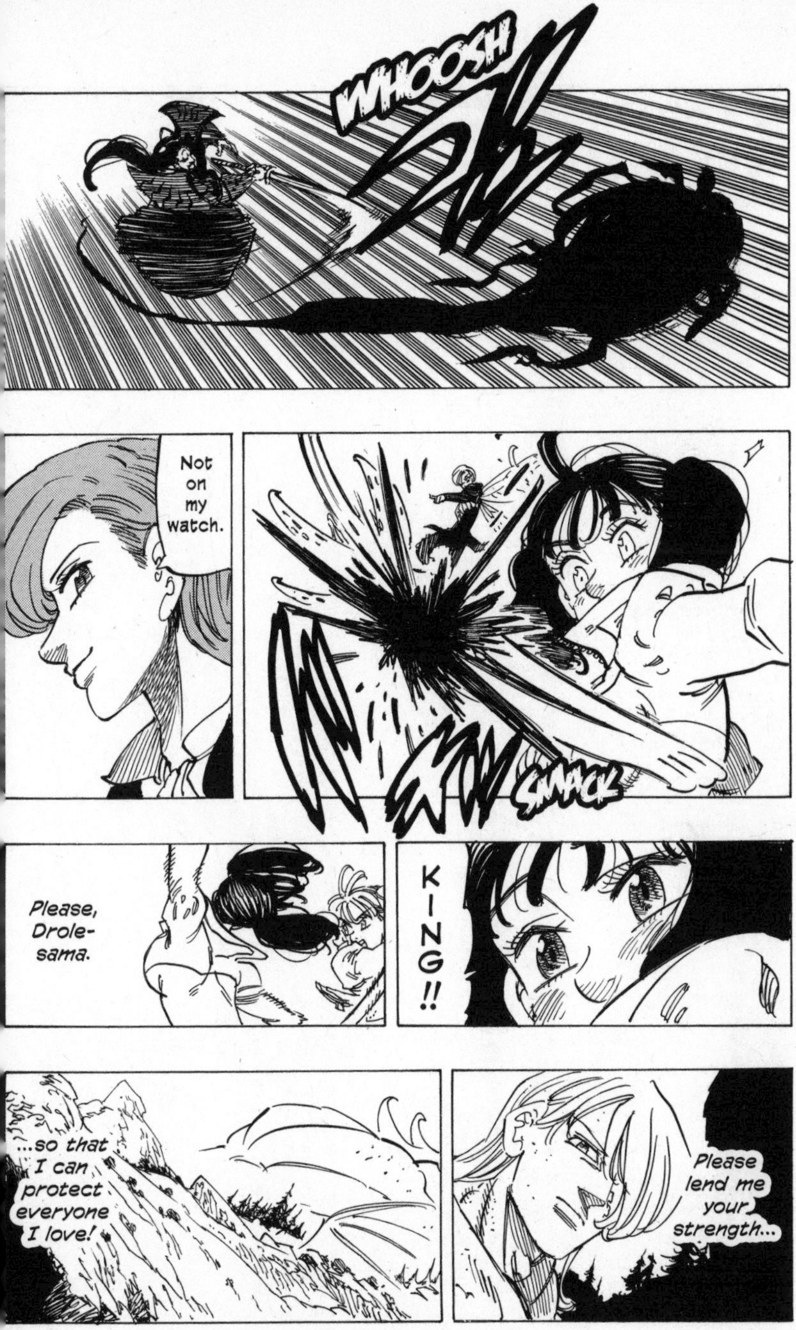
WHOOSH
SMACK
Not on my watch.
KING!!
Please, Drole-sama.
Please lend me your strength...
...so that I can protect everyone I love!

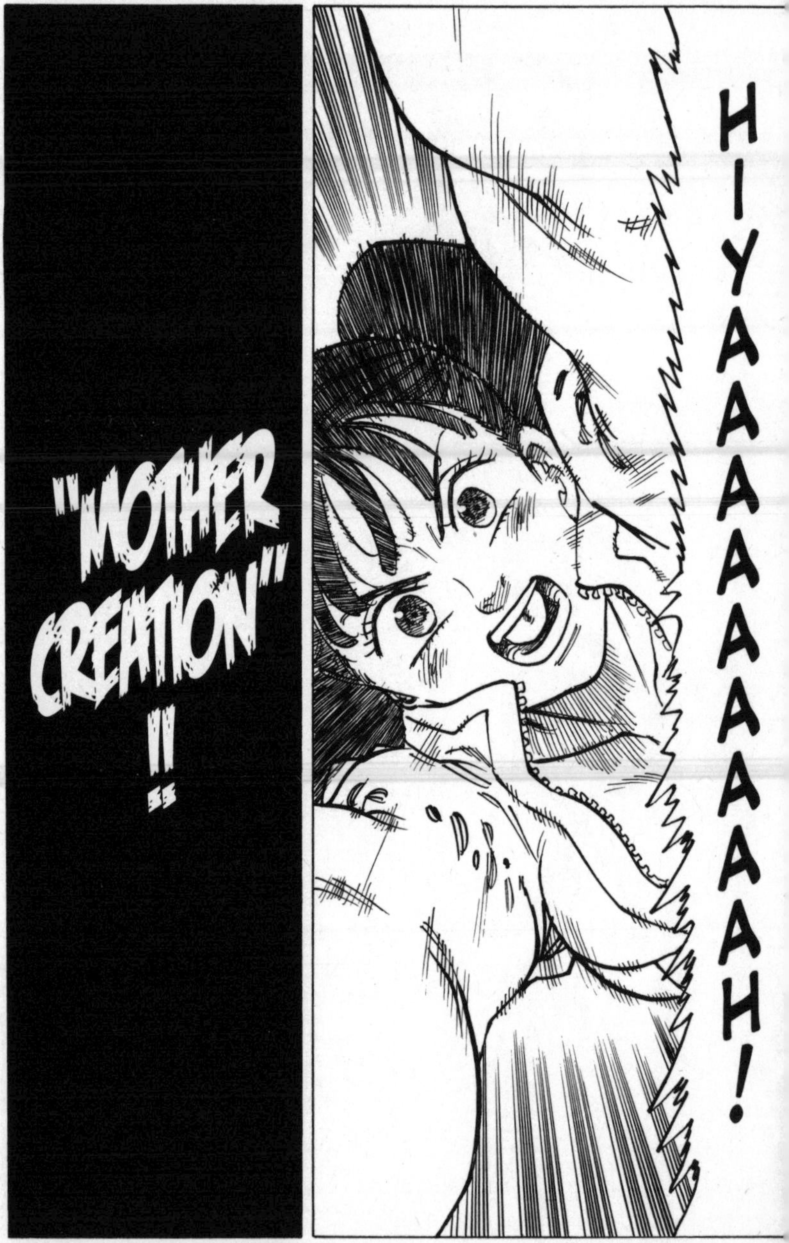
HIYAAAAAAAAAH!
"MOTHER CREATION"!!

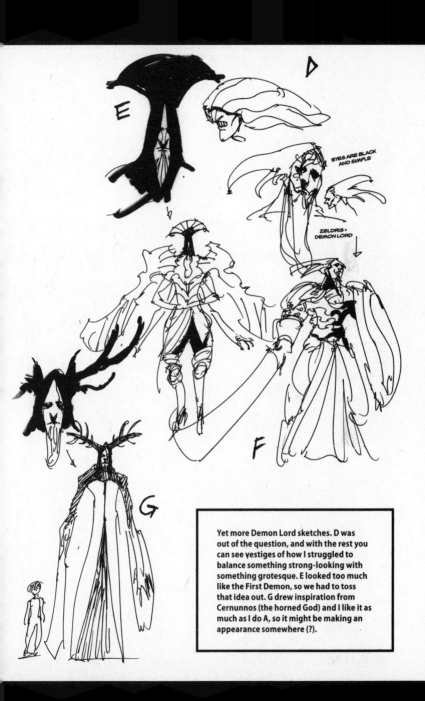

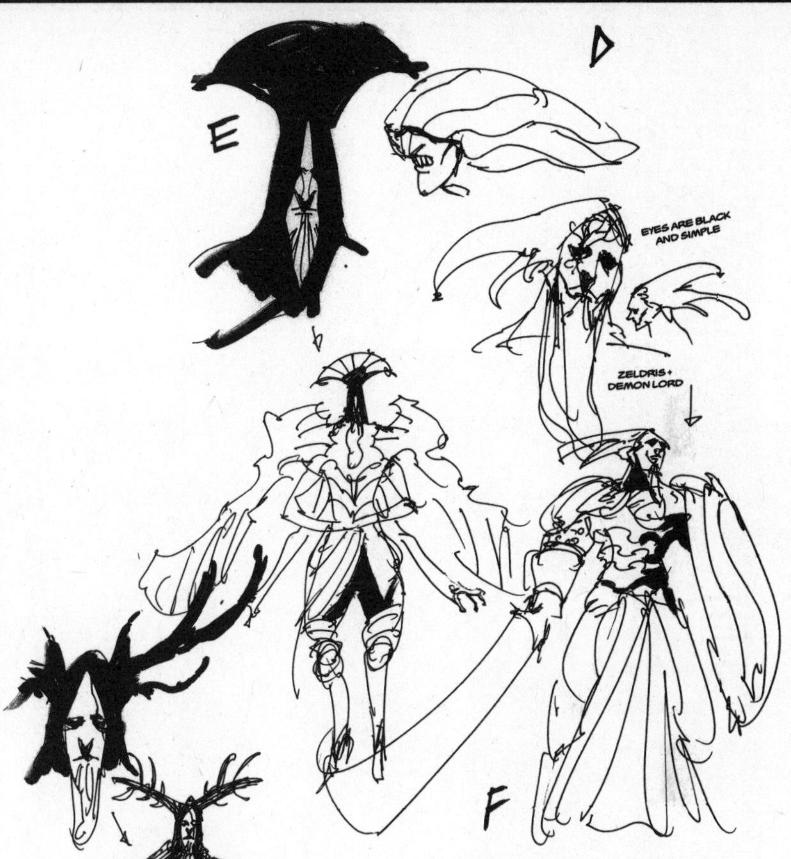
D
E
EYES ARE BLACK AND SIMPLE
ZELDRIS + DEMON LORD
F

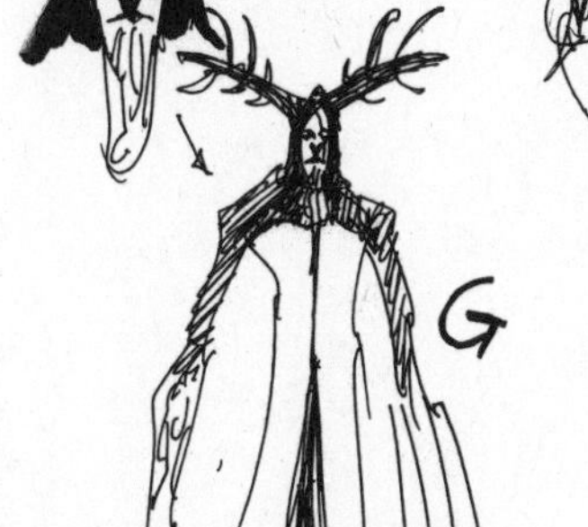
G

Yet more Demon Lord sketches. D was out of the question, and with the rest you can see vestiges of how I struggled to balance something strong-looking with something grotesque. E looked too much like the First Demon, so we had to toss that idea out. G drew inspiration from Cernunnos (the horned God) and I like it as much as I do A, so it might be making an appearance somewhere (?).

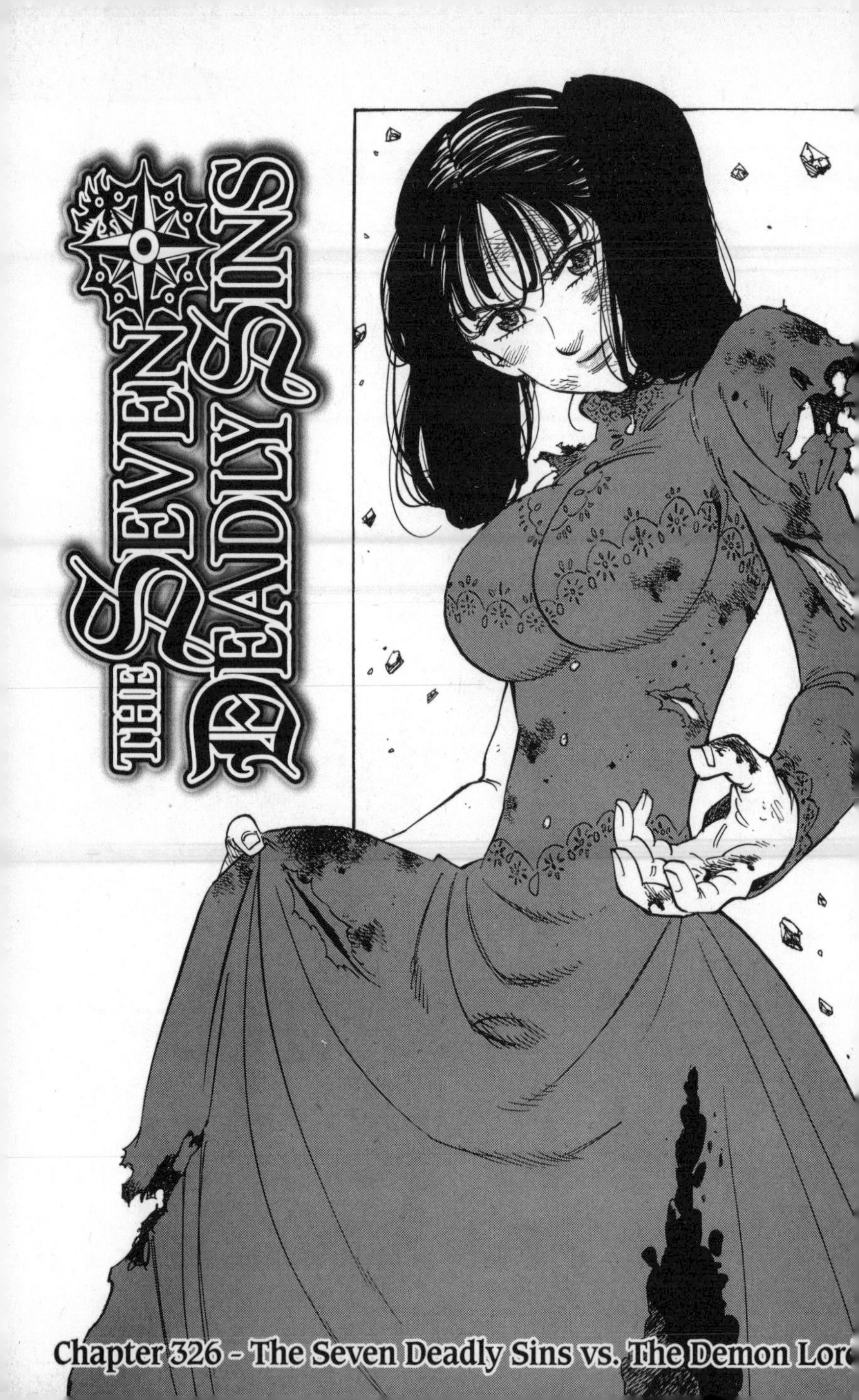
THE SEVEN DEADLY SINS
Chapter 326 - The Seven Deadly Sins vs. The Demon Lord

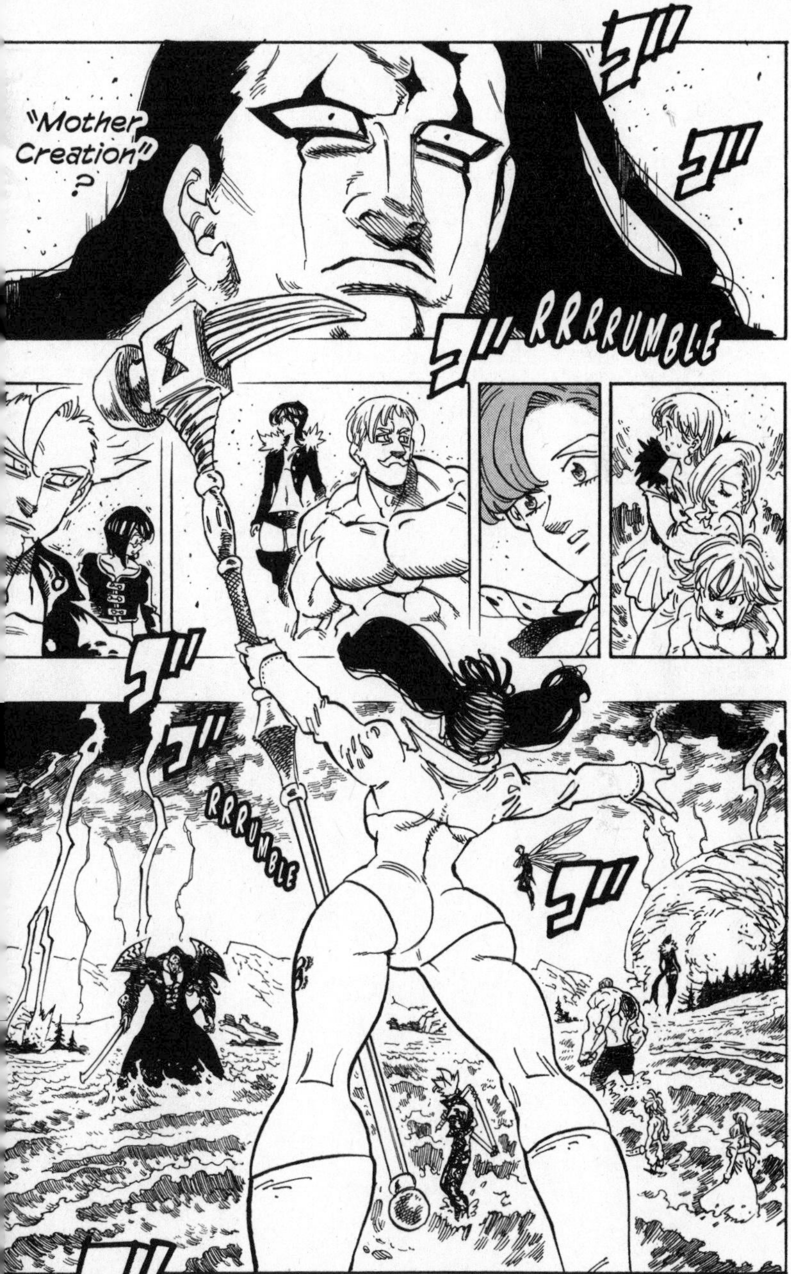
"Mother Creation"?
RRRRUMBLE
RRRUMBLE

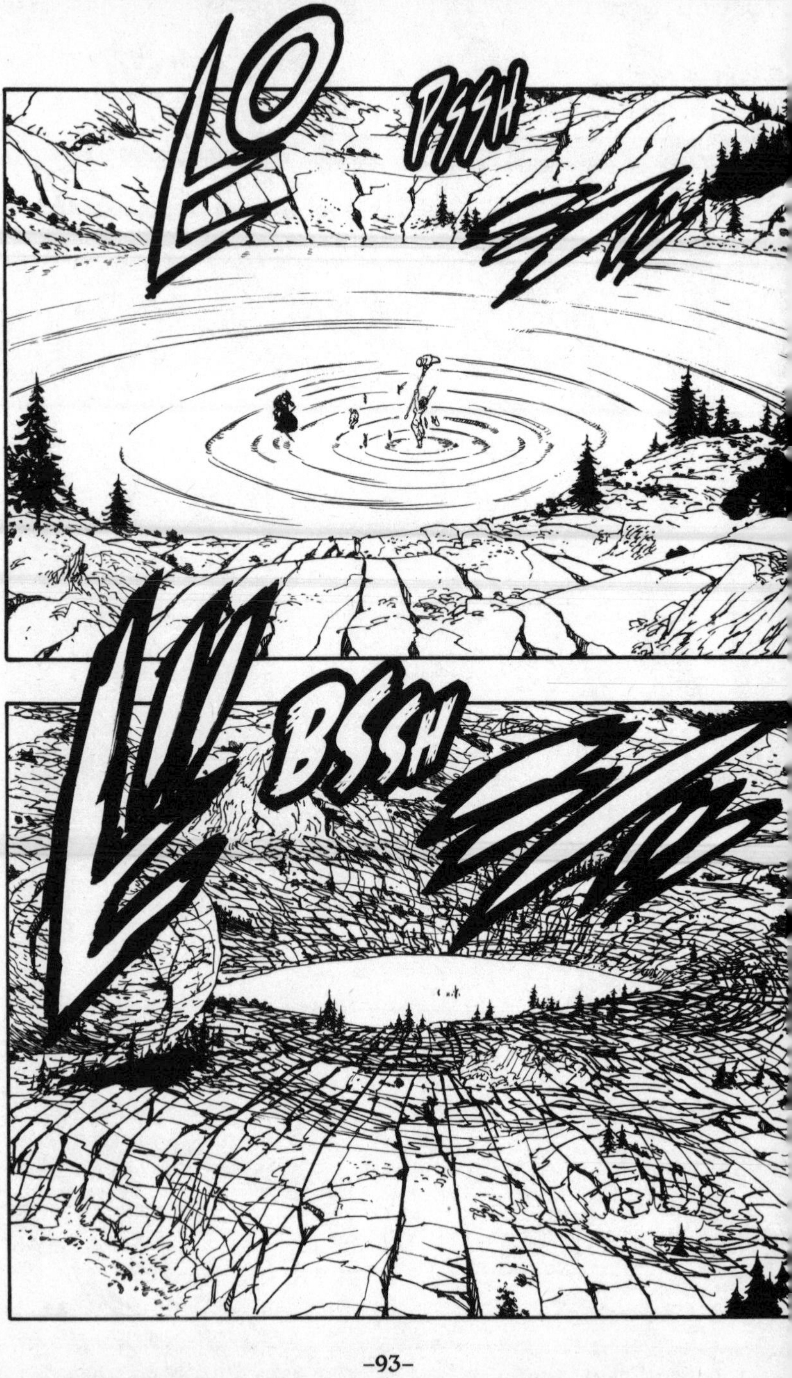
PSSH
BSSH

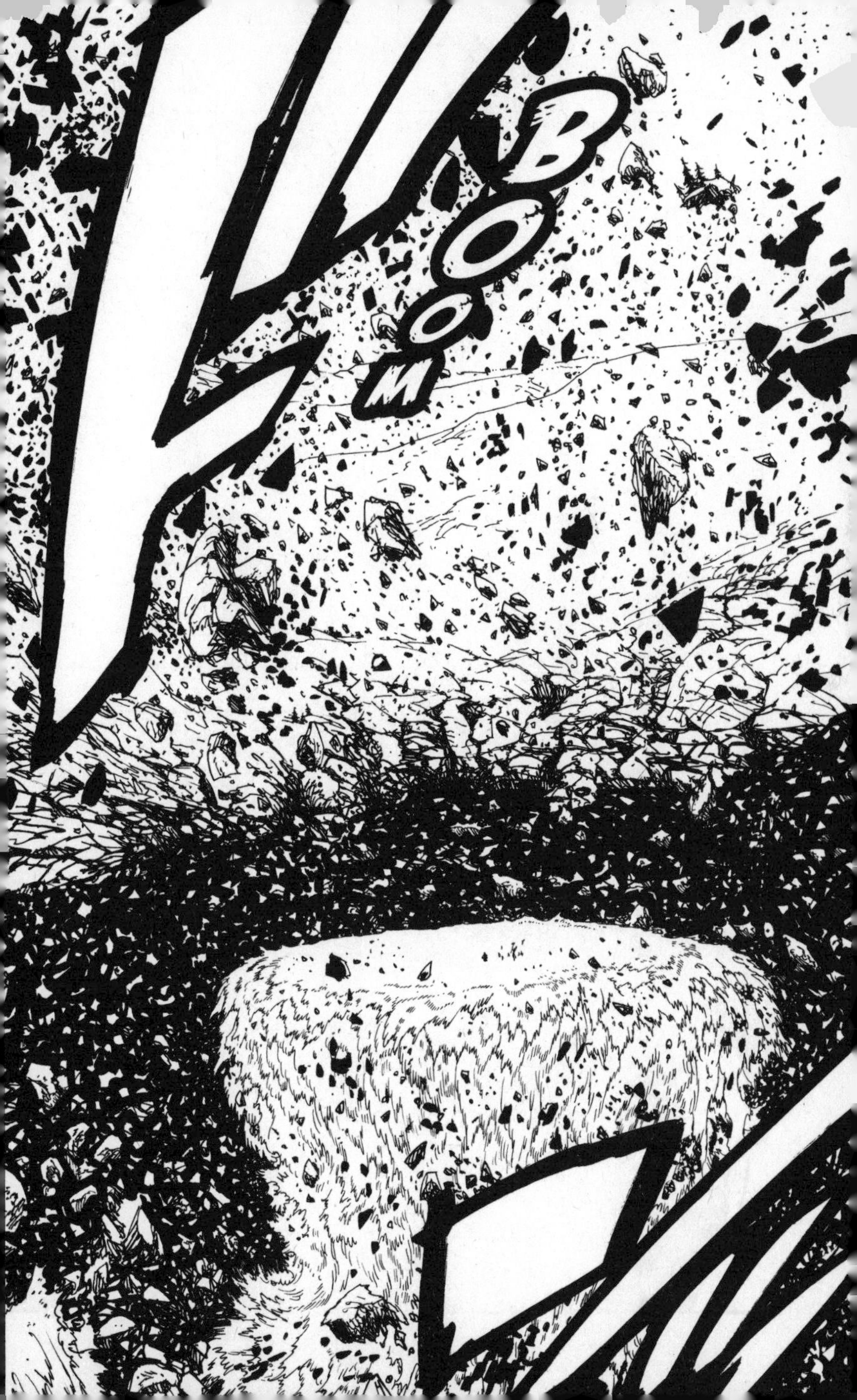
BOOM

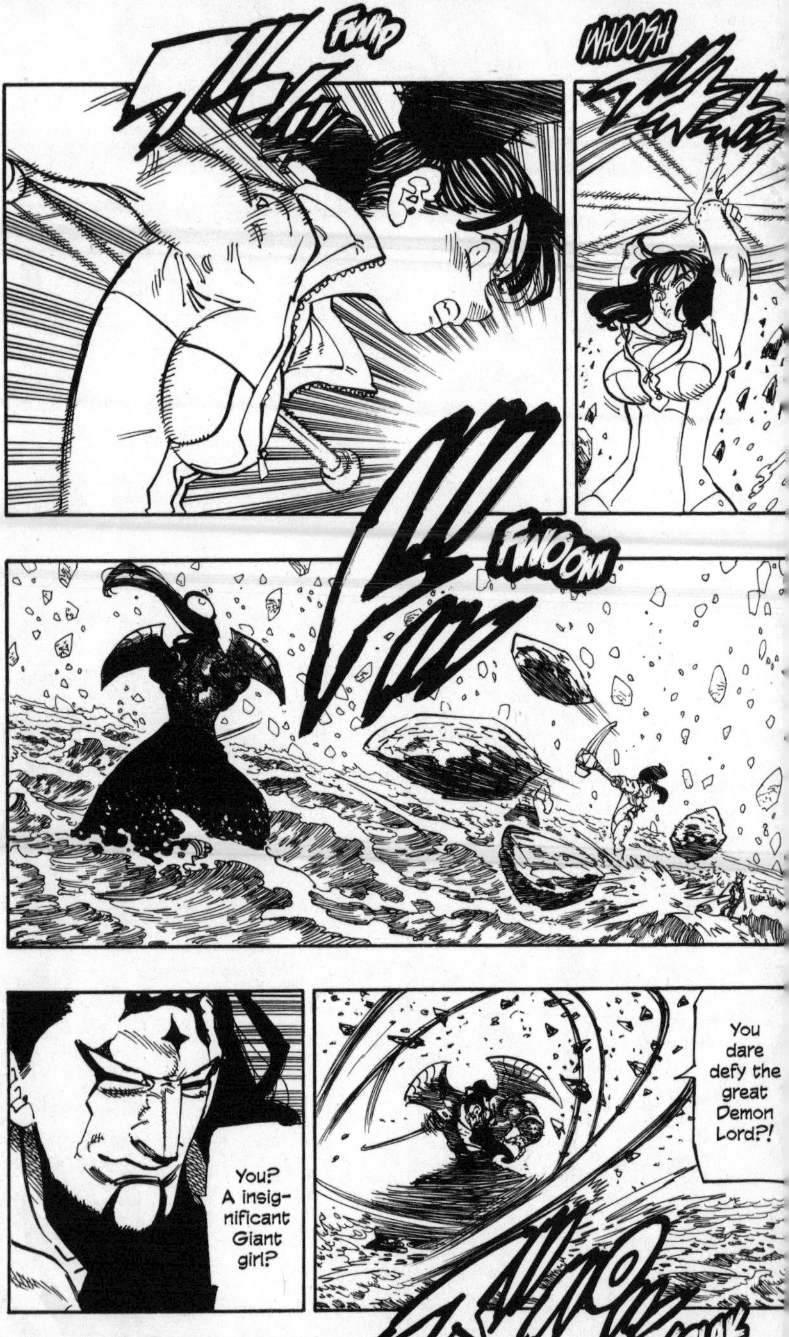
WHOOSH
FWIP
FWOOM
You dare defy the great Demon Lord?!
SPLAK
You? A insig-nificant Giant girl?

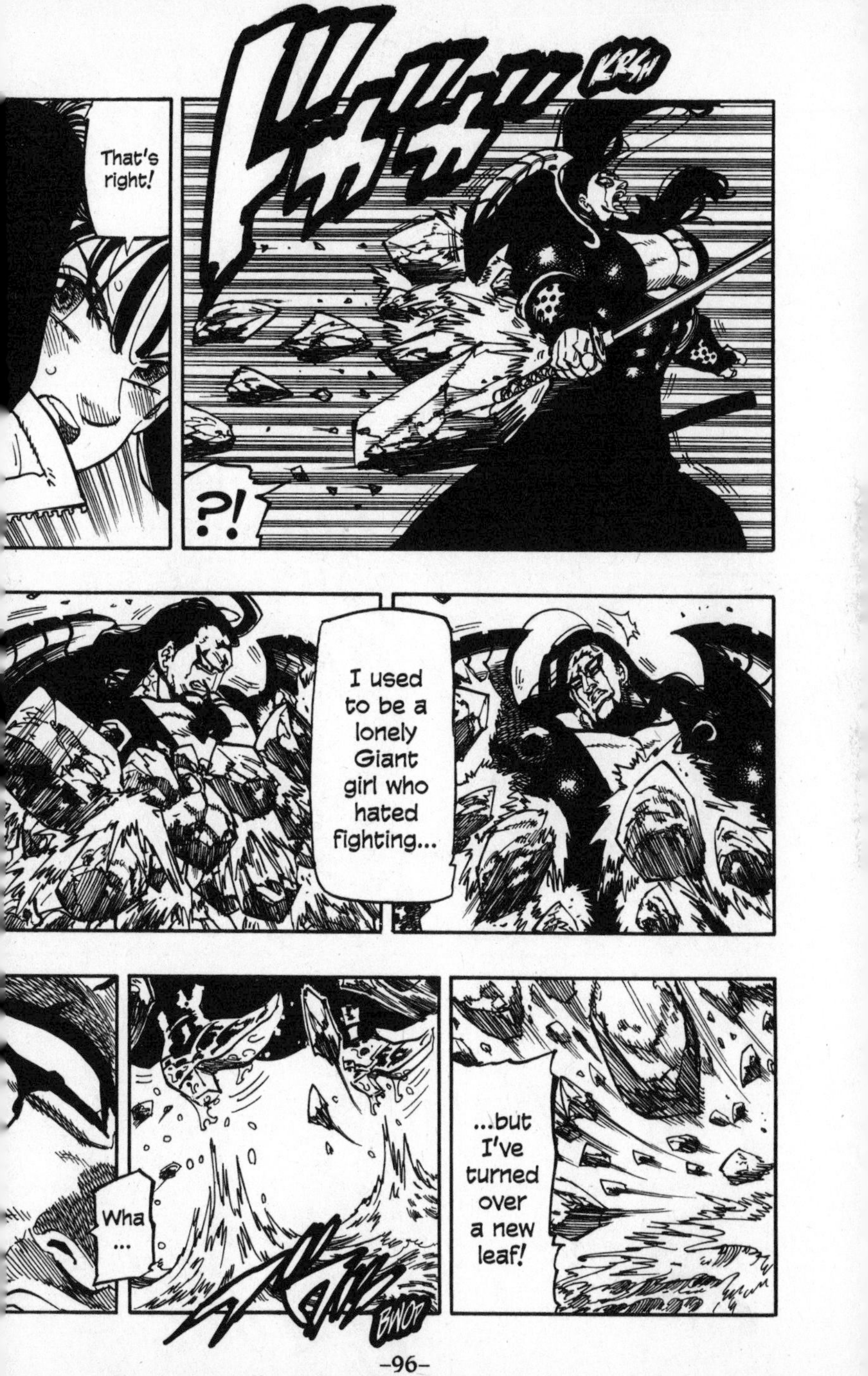
KRSH
?!
That's right!
I used to be a lonely Giant girl who hated fighting...
...but I've turned over a new leaf!
BWOP
Wha ...

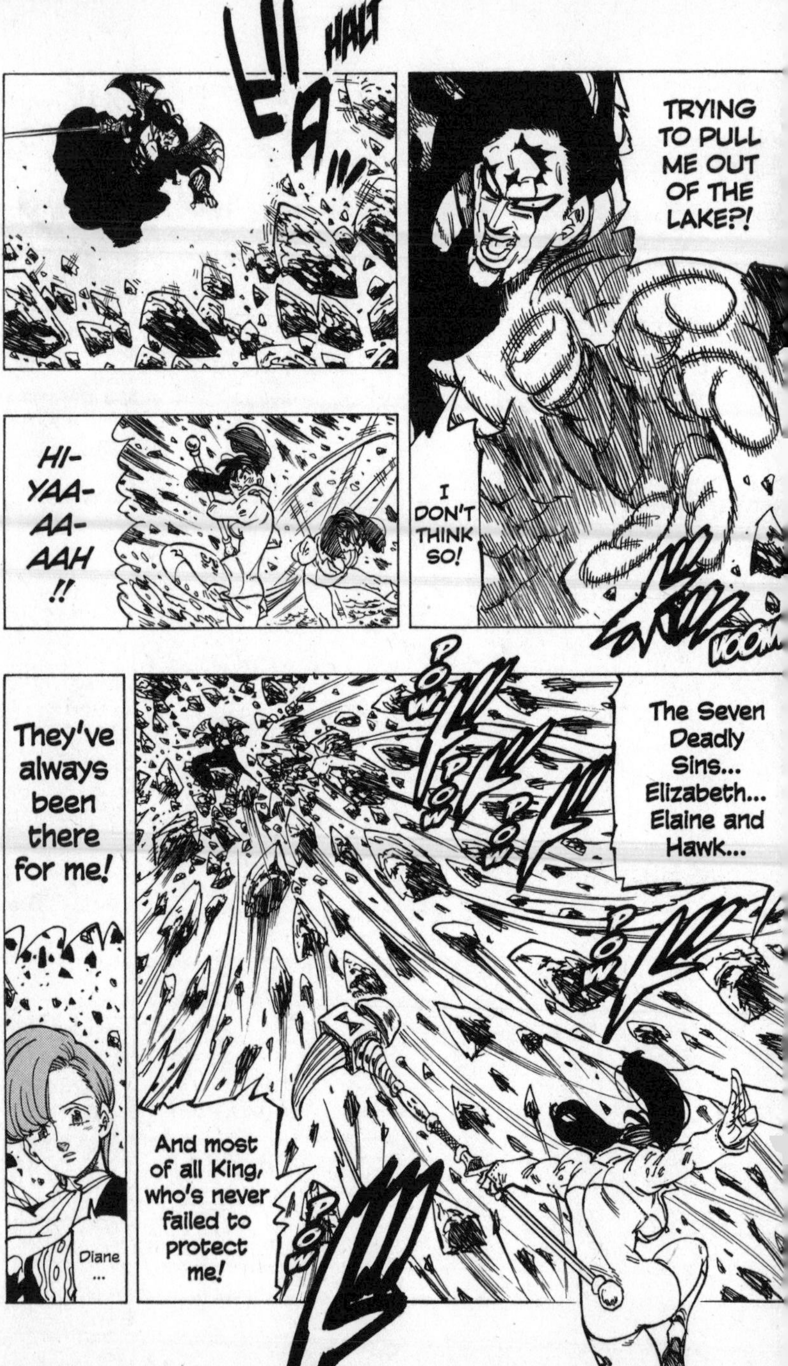
TRYING TO PULL ME OUT OF THE LAKE?!
I DON'T THINK SO!
VOOM
HALT
HI-YAAA-AA-AAH!!
The Seven Deadly Sins... Elizabeth... Elaine and Hawk...
POW
POW
POW
POW
And most of all King, who's never failed to protect me!
POW
They've always been there for me!
Diane ...

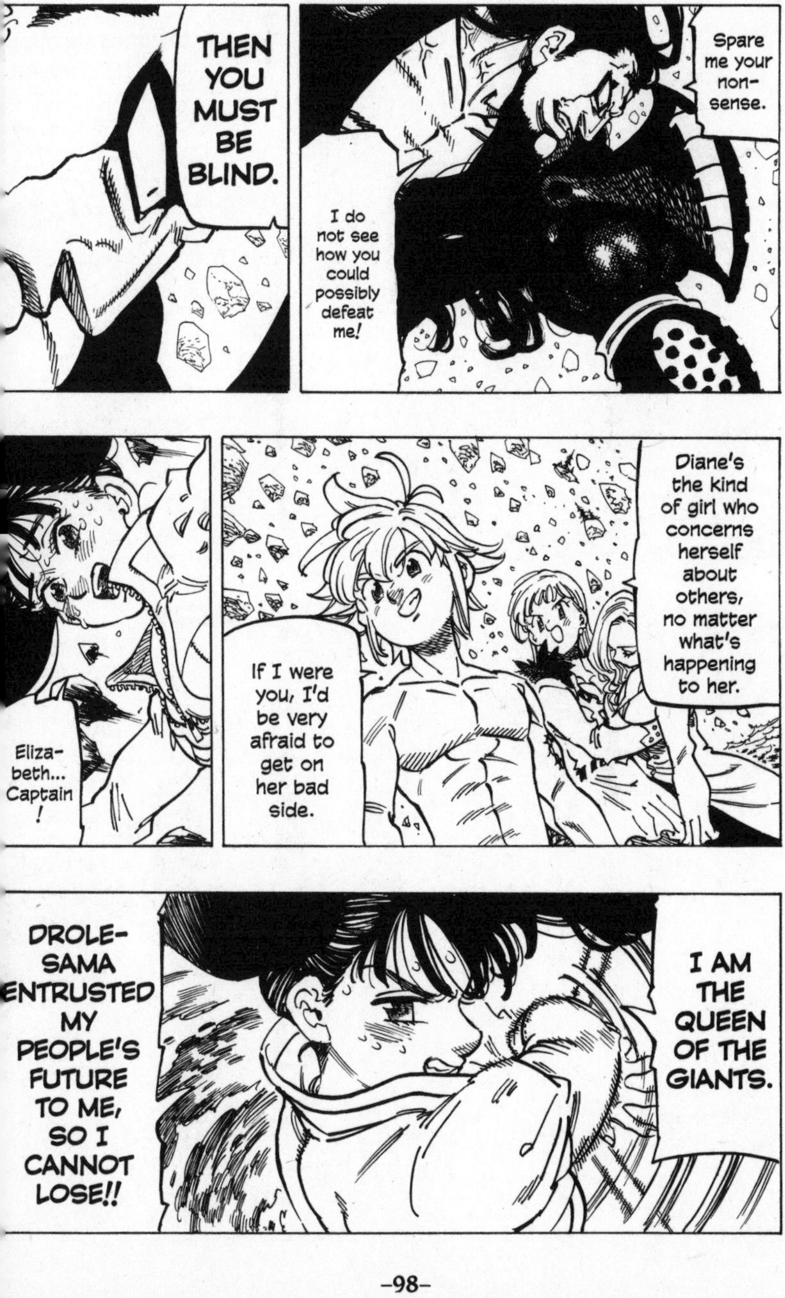
Spare me your non-sense.
I do not see how you could possibly defeat me!
THEN YOU MUST BE BLIND.
Diane's the kind of girl who concerns herself about others, no matter what's happening to her.
If I were you, I'd be very afraid to get on her bad side.
Eliza-beth... Captain!
I AM THE QUEEN OF THE GIANTS.
DROLE-SAMA ENTRUSTED MY PEOPLE'S FUTURE TO ME, SO I CANNOT LOSE!!

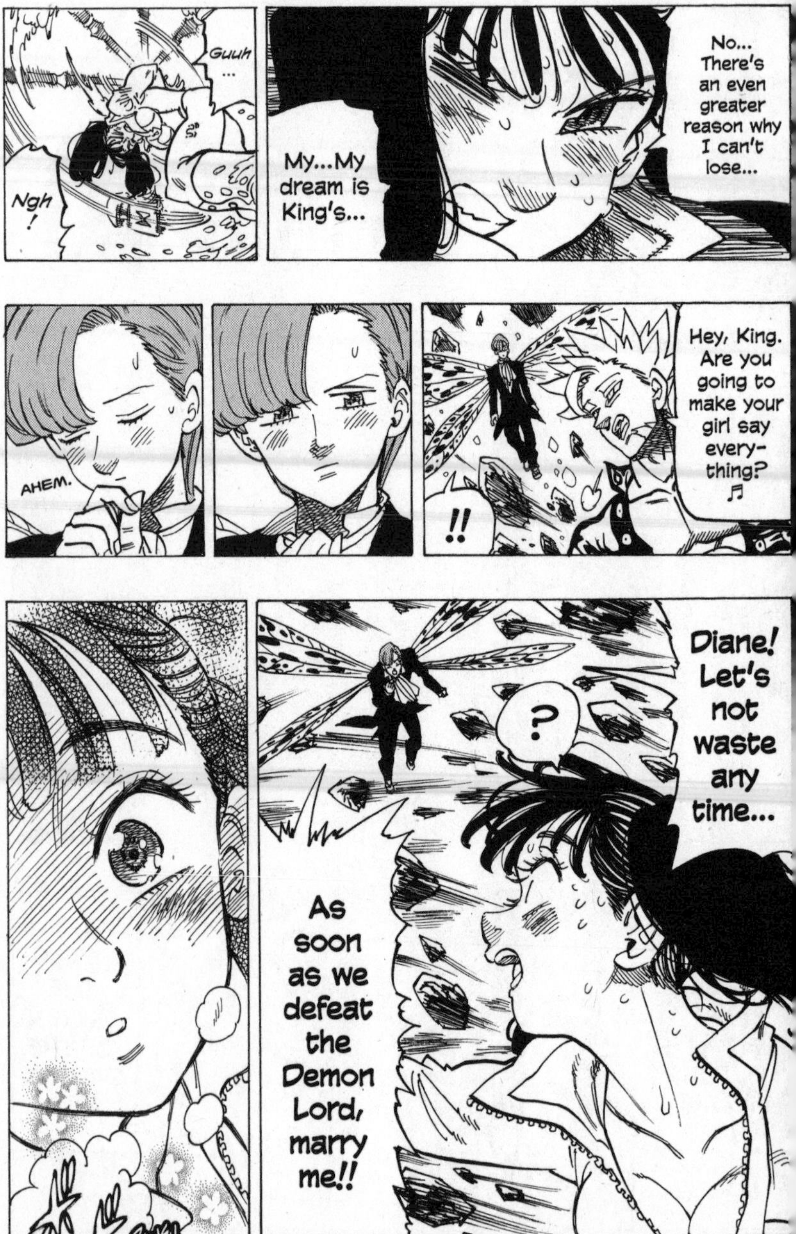
No... There's an even greater reason why I can't lose...
My...My dream is King's...
Guuh ...
Ngh !
Hey, King. Are you going to make your girl say every-thing? ♫
!!
AHEM.
Diane! Let's not waste any time...
?
As soon as we defeat the Demon Lord, marry me!!
BLUSH

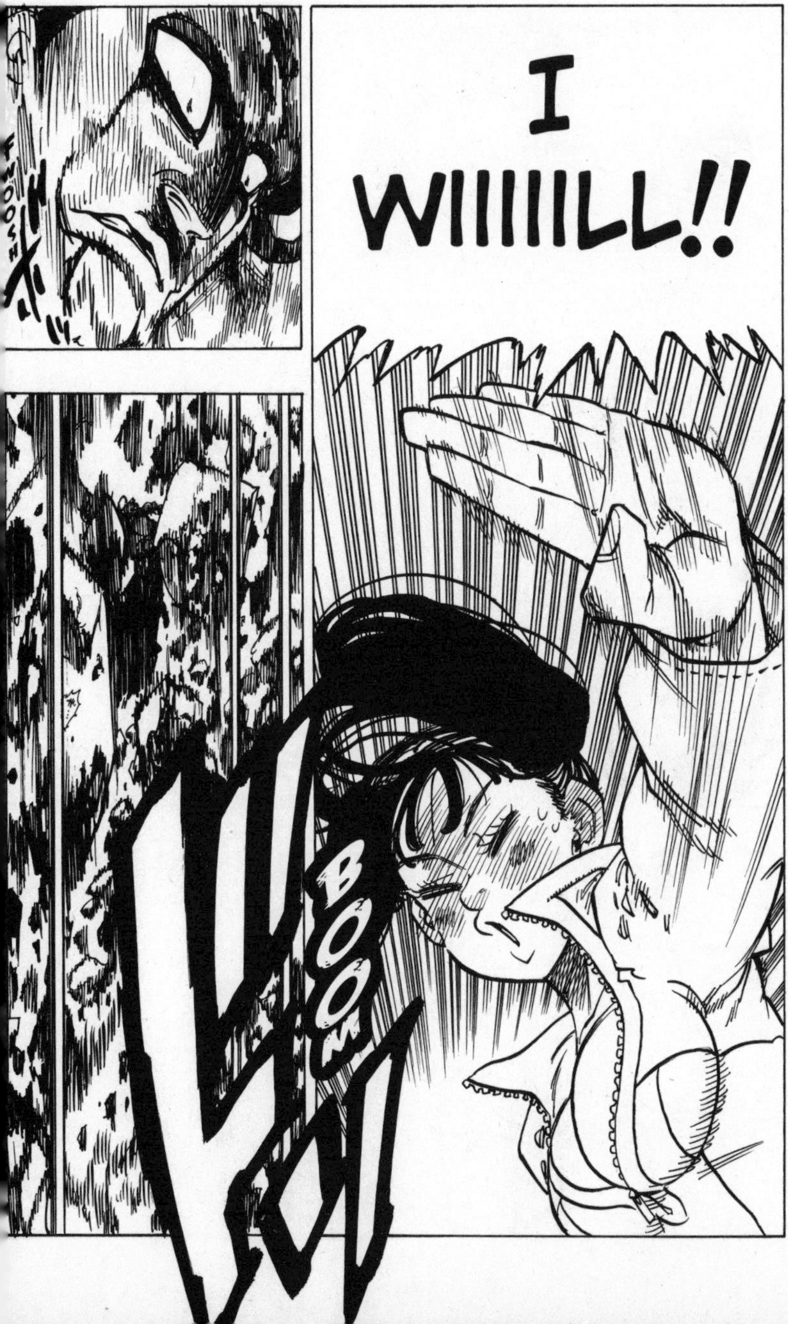
I WIIIIILL!!
BOOOM
FWOOSH

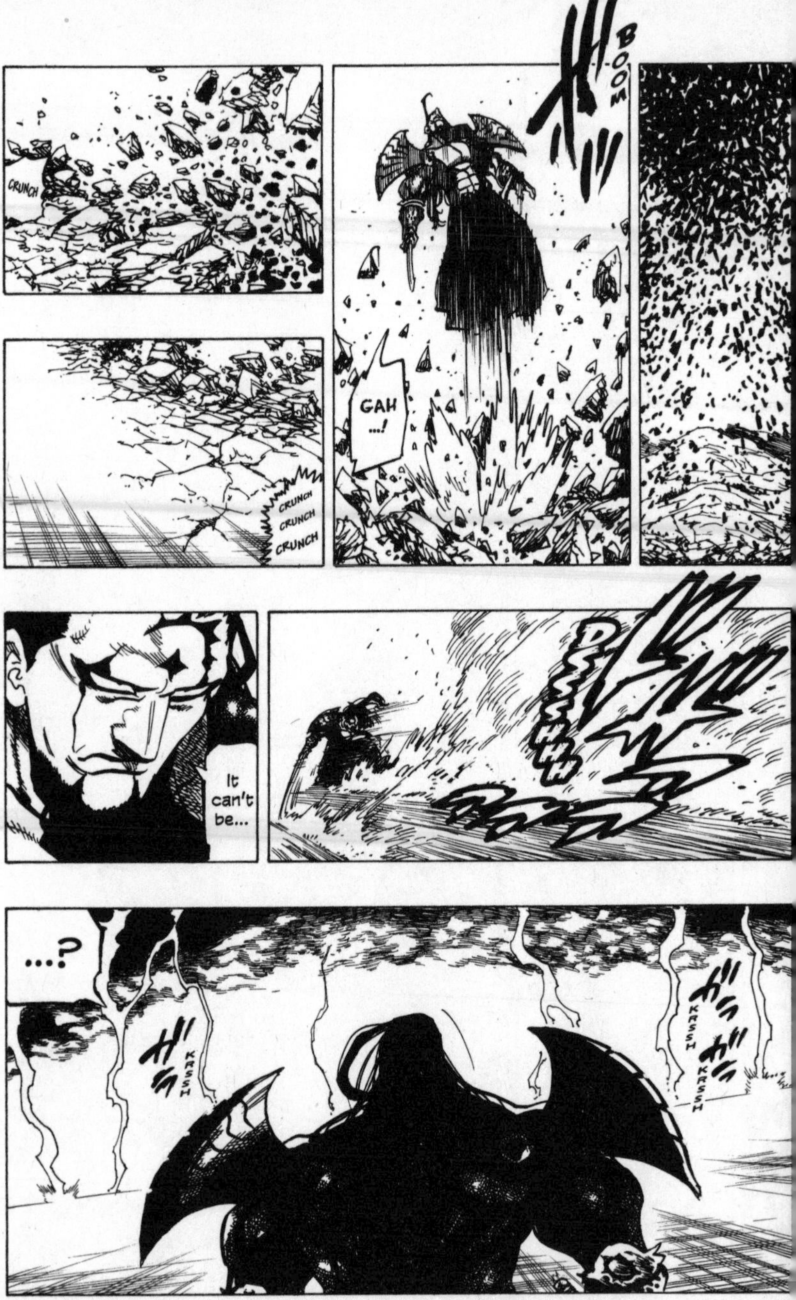
BOOM
GAH ...!
CRUNCH
CRUNCH CRUNCH CRUNCH
DSSSSHHH
It can't be...
...?
KRSSH
KRSSH
KRSSH

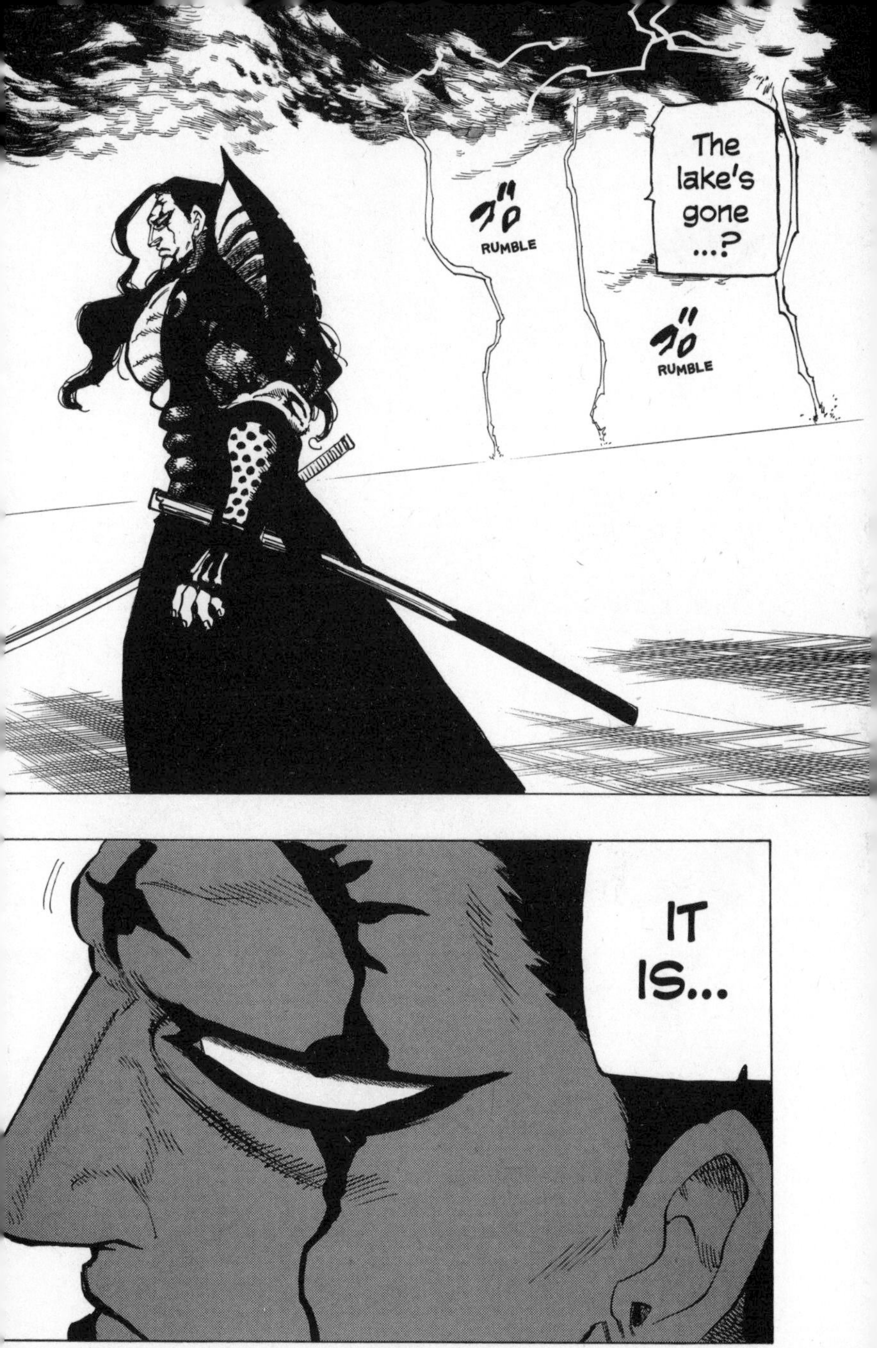
The lake's gone ...?
ゴロ RUMBLE
ゴロ RUMBLE
IT IS...

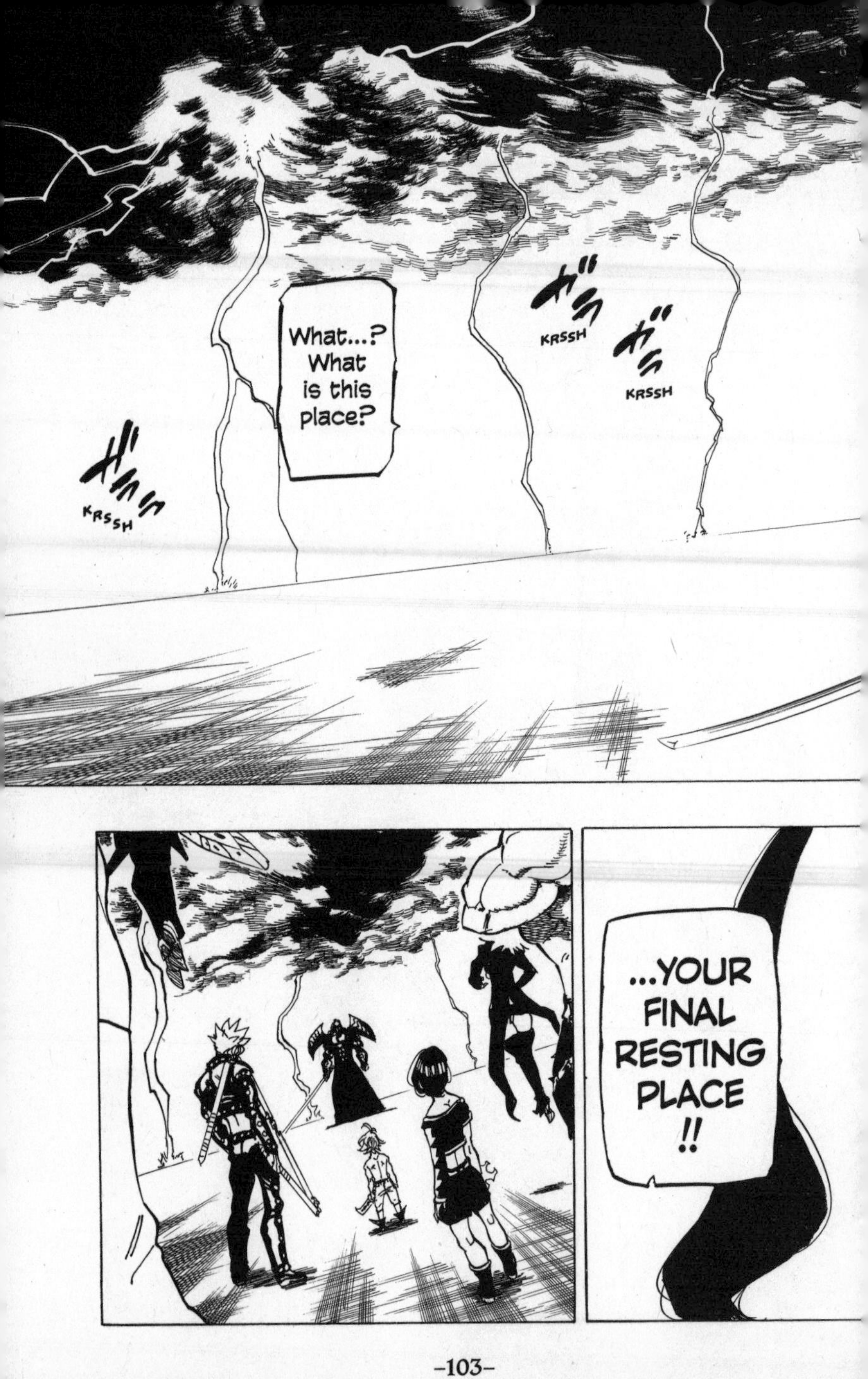
KRSSH
KRSSH
What...? What is this place?
KRSSH
...YOUR FINAL RESTING PLACE!!

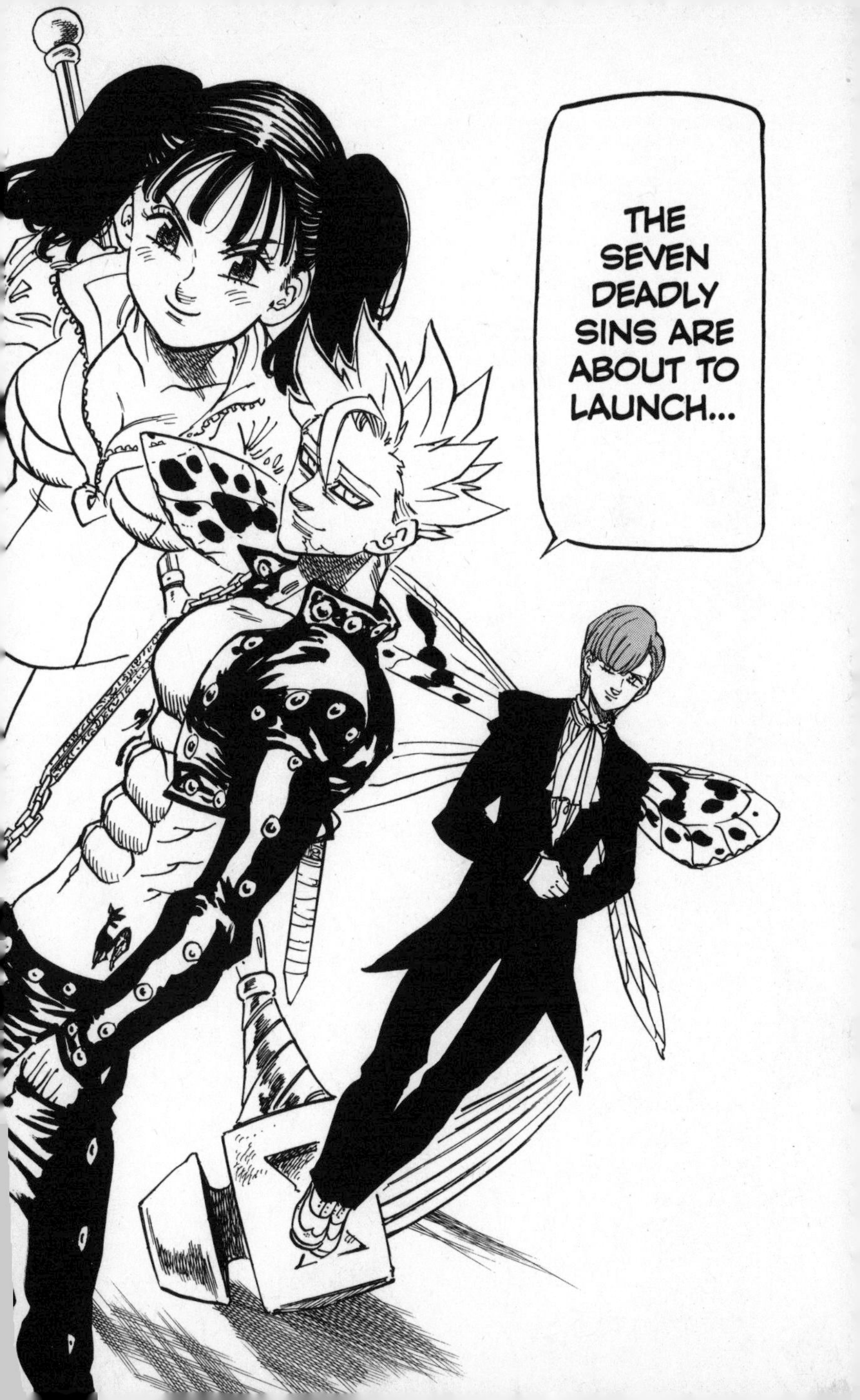
THE SEVEN DEADLY SINS ARE ABOUT TO LAUNCH...

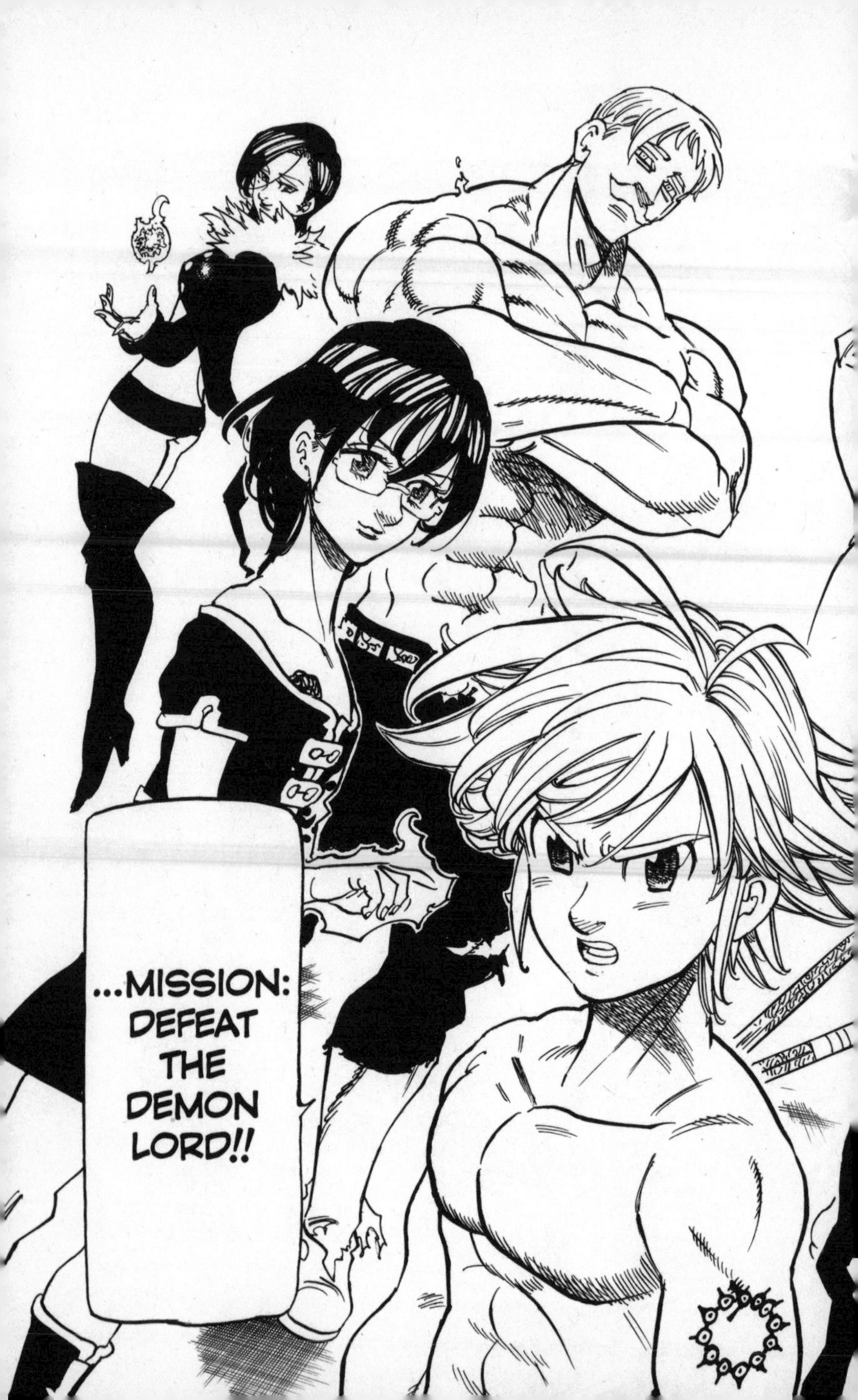
...MISSION: DEFEAT THE DEMON LORD!!

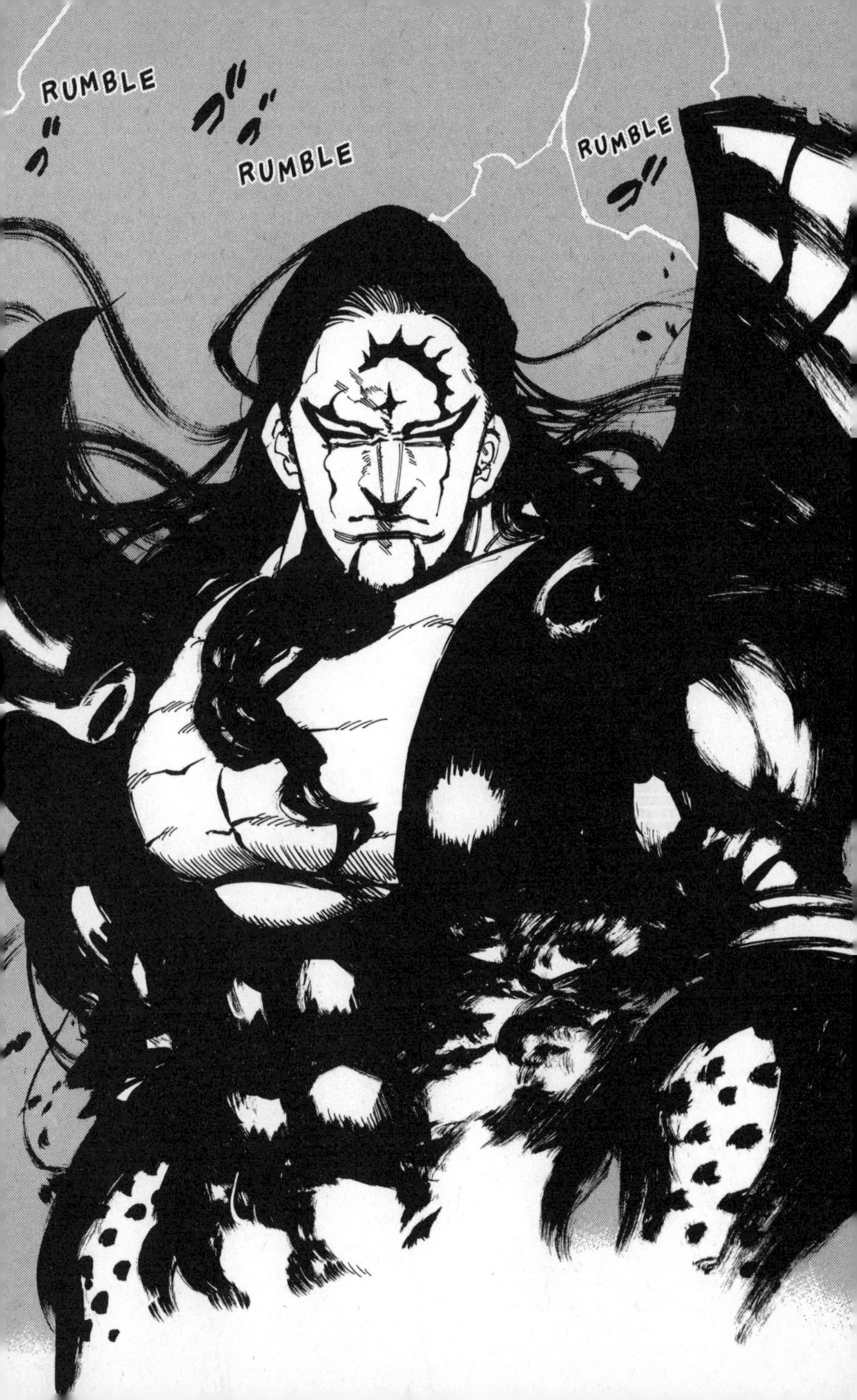
RUMBLE
ゴ
ゴゴ
RUMBLE
RUMBLE
ゴ

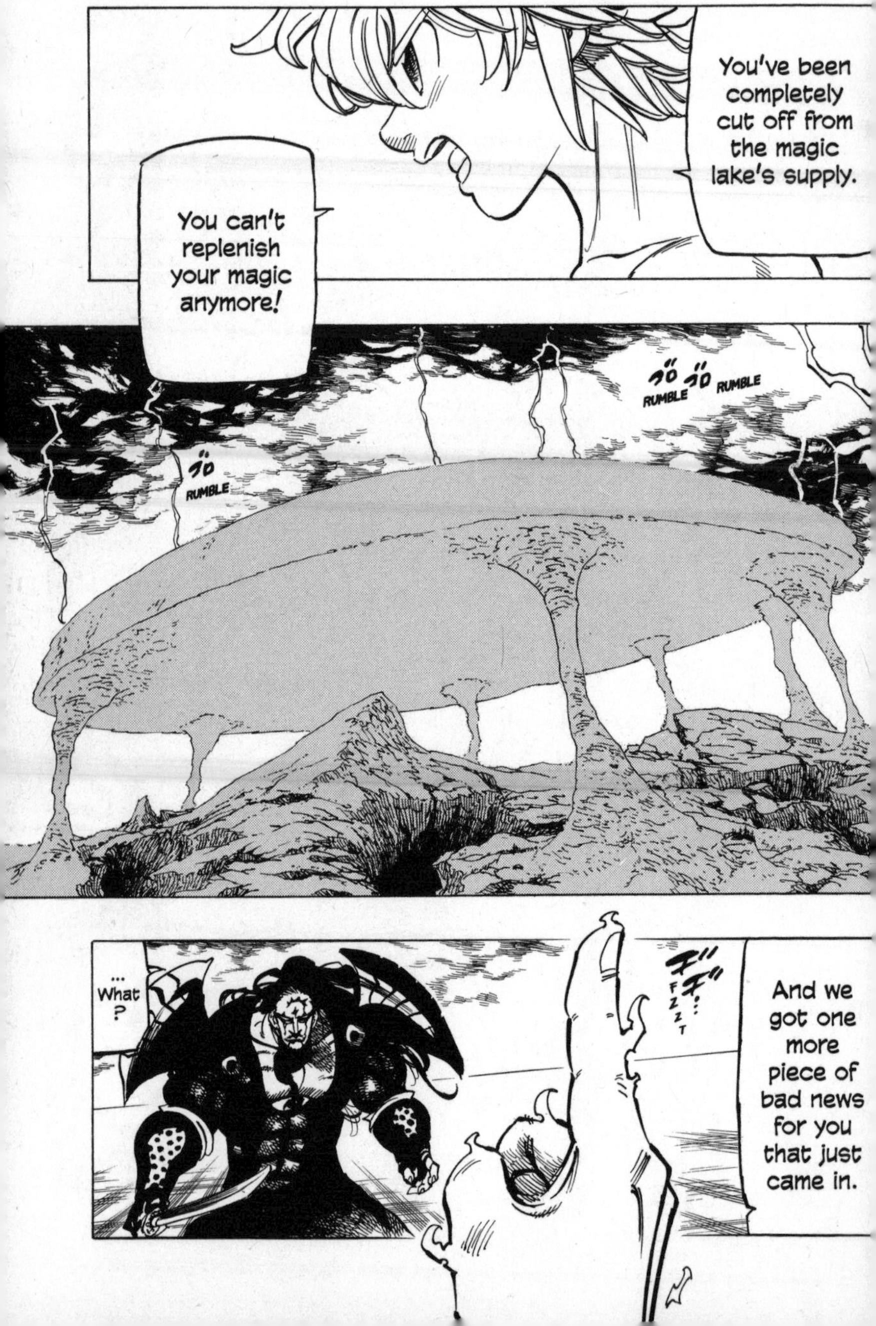
You've been completely cut off from the magic lake's supply.
You can't replenish your magic anymore!
ゴロ ゴロ RUMBLE RUMBLE
ゴロ RUMBLE
And we got one more piece of bad news for you that just came in.
ヂヂ… FZZT
... What?

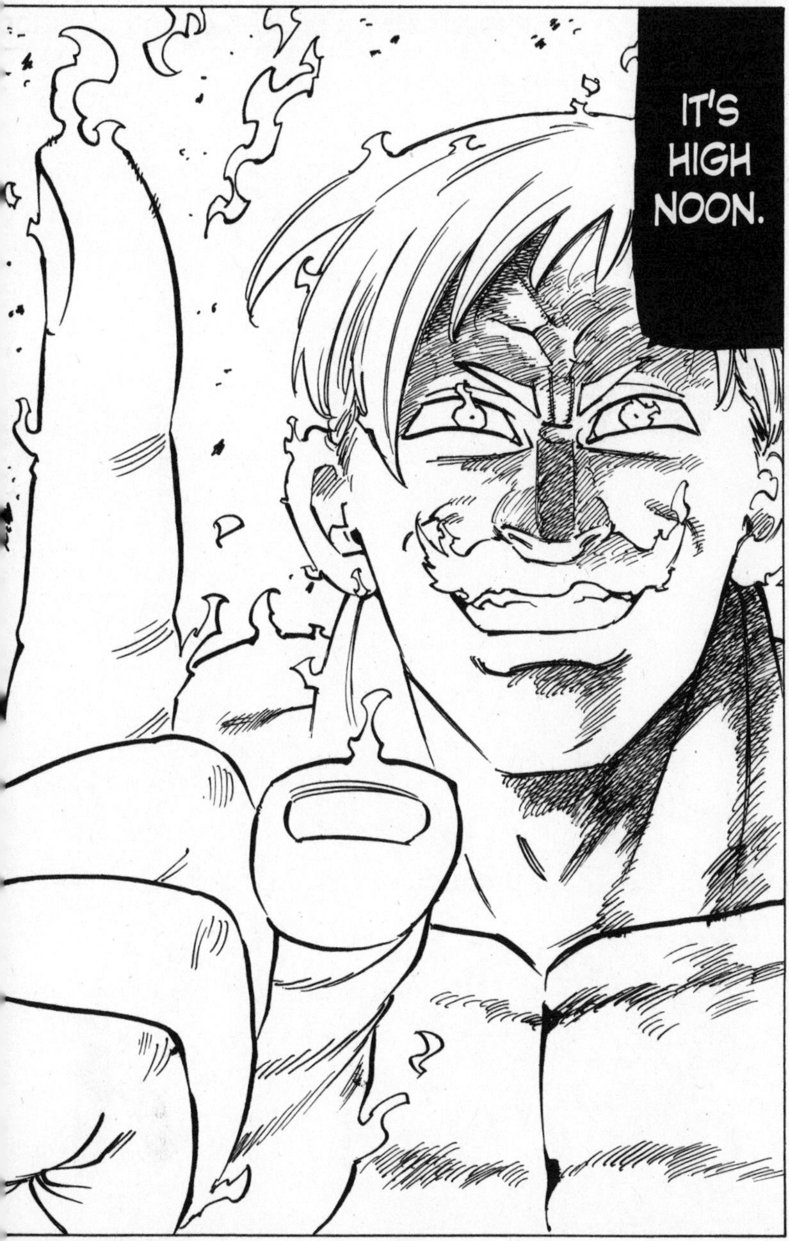
IT'S HIGH NOON.

Chapter 327 - The Man Called Escanor

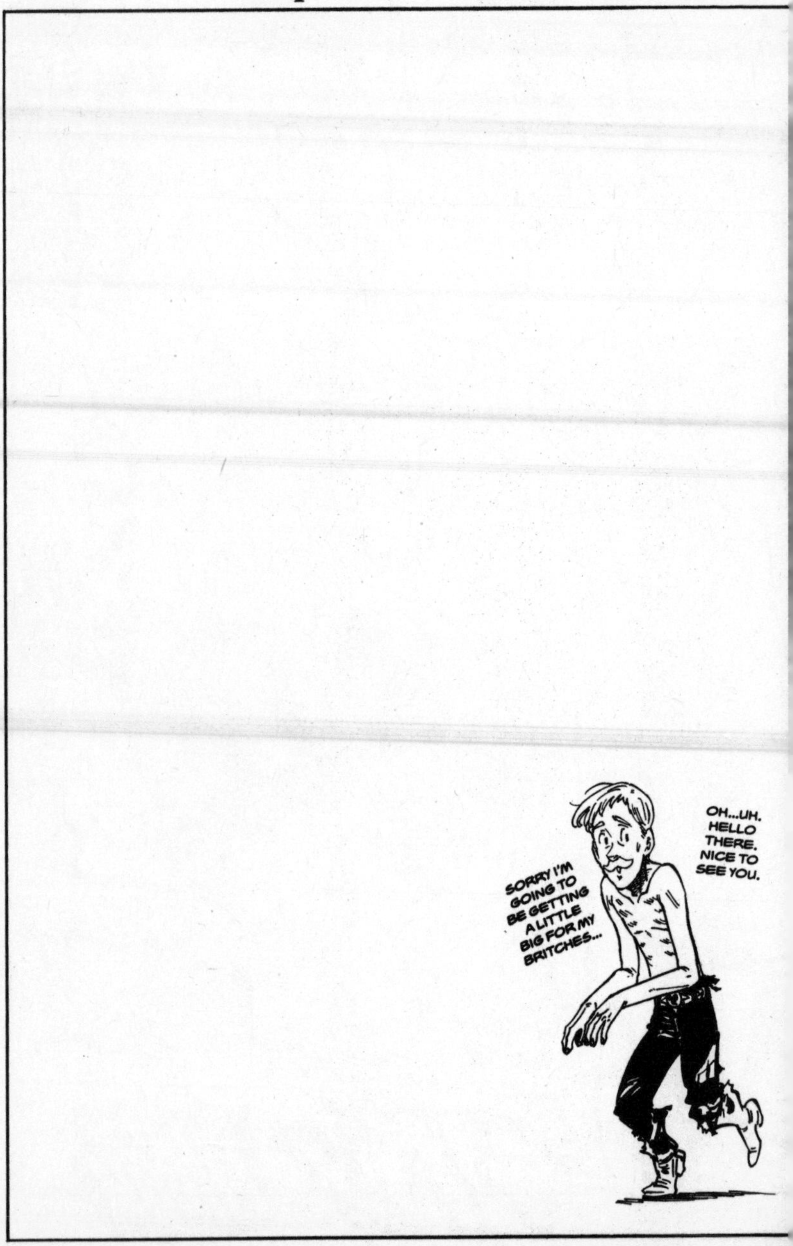
OH...UH. HELLO THERE. NICE TO SEE YOU.
SORRY I'M GOING TO BE GETTING A LITTLE BIG FOR MY BRITCHES...

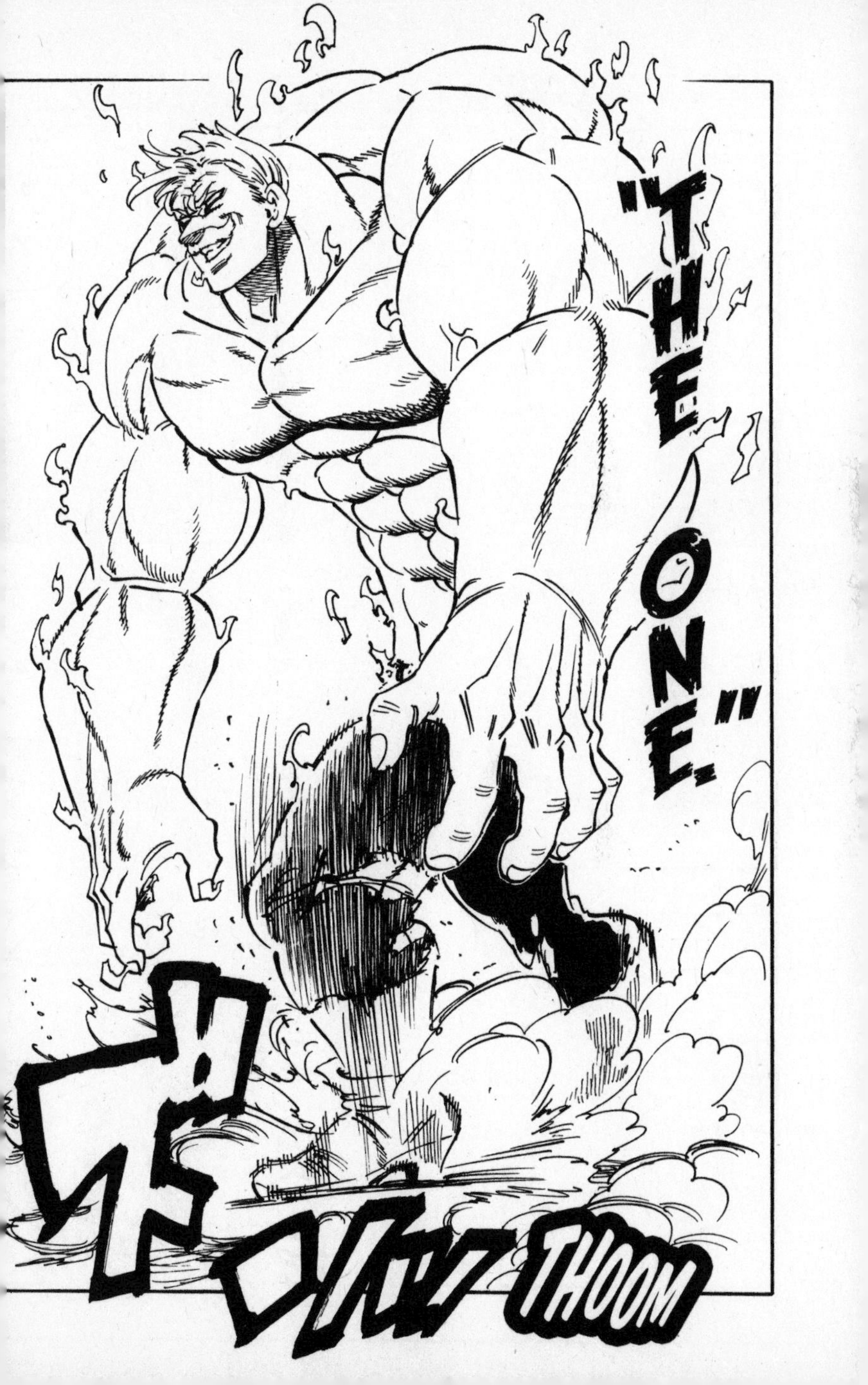
"THE ONE."
THOOM

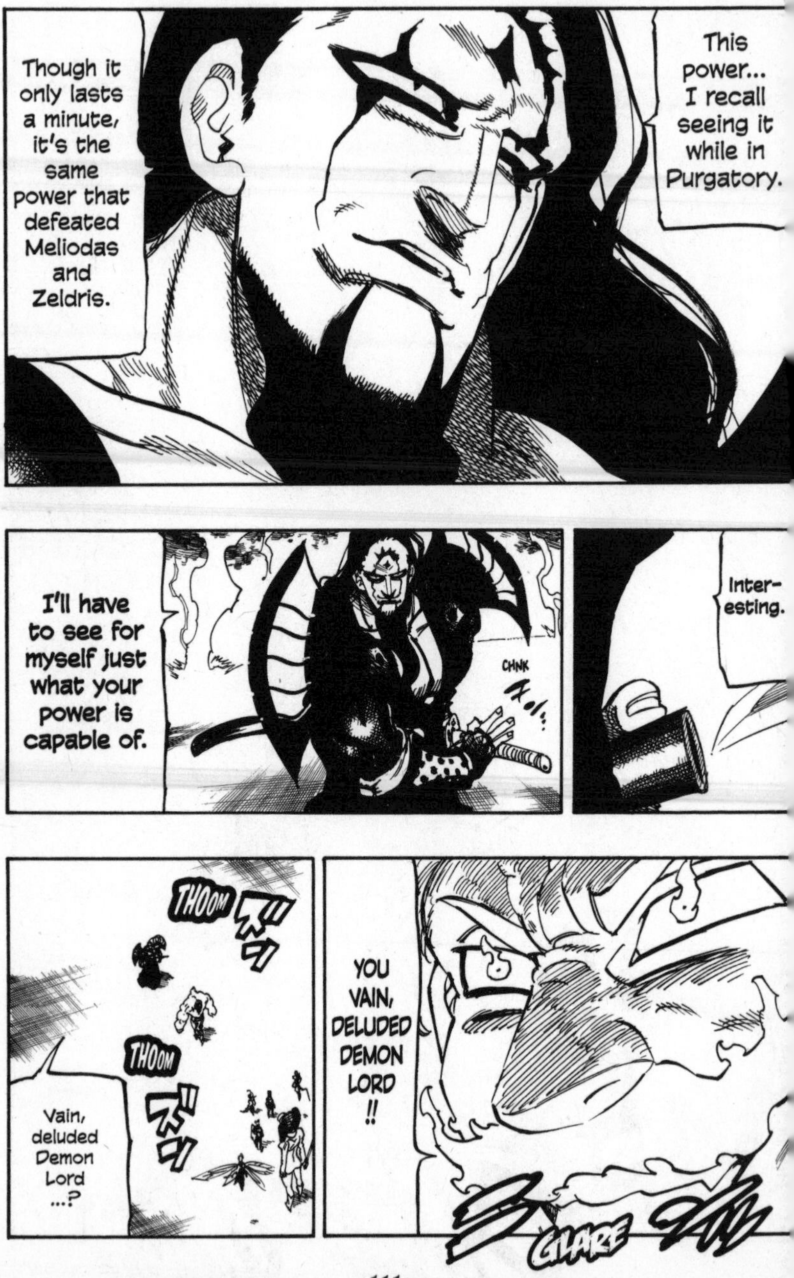
This power... I recall seeing it while in Purgatory.
Though it only lasts a minute, it's the same power that defeated Meliodas and Zeldris.
Inter-esting.
CHNK
I'll have to see for myself just what your power is capable of.
YOU VAIN, DELUDED DEMON LORD !!
GLARE
THOOM
THOOM
Vain, deluded Demon Lord ...?

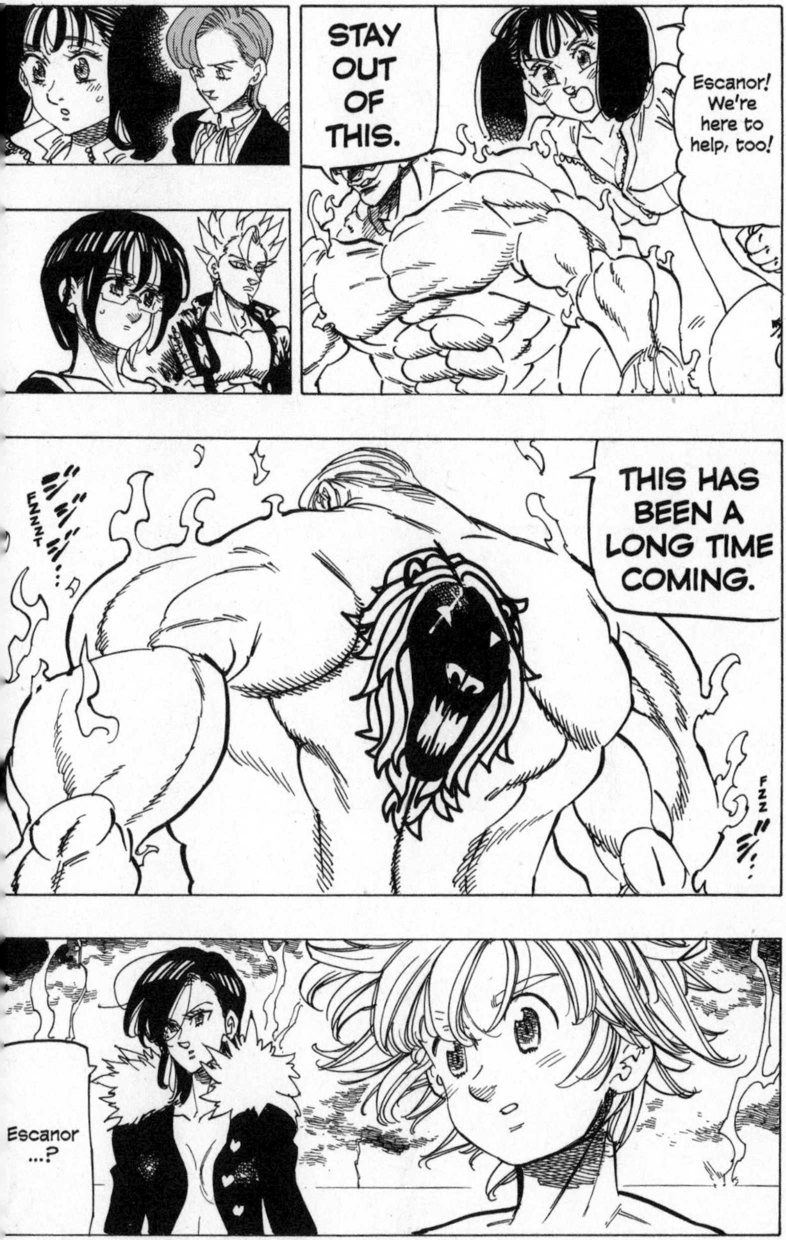
Escanor! We're here to help, too!
STAY OUT OF THIS.
THIS HAS BEEN A LONG TIME COMING.
FZZZT
FZZ
Escanor ...?

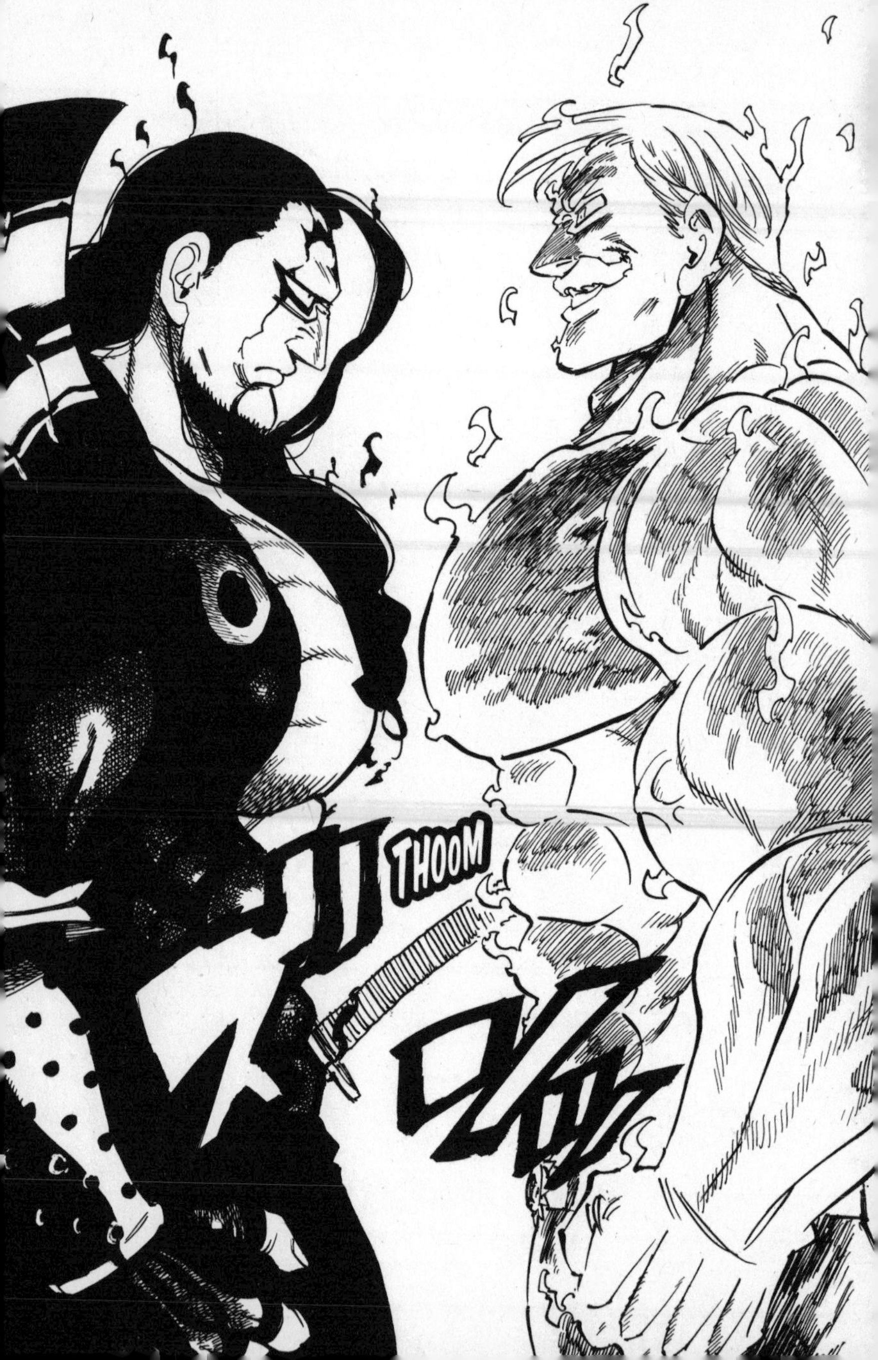
THOOM

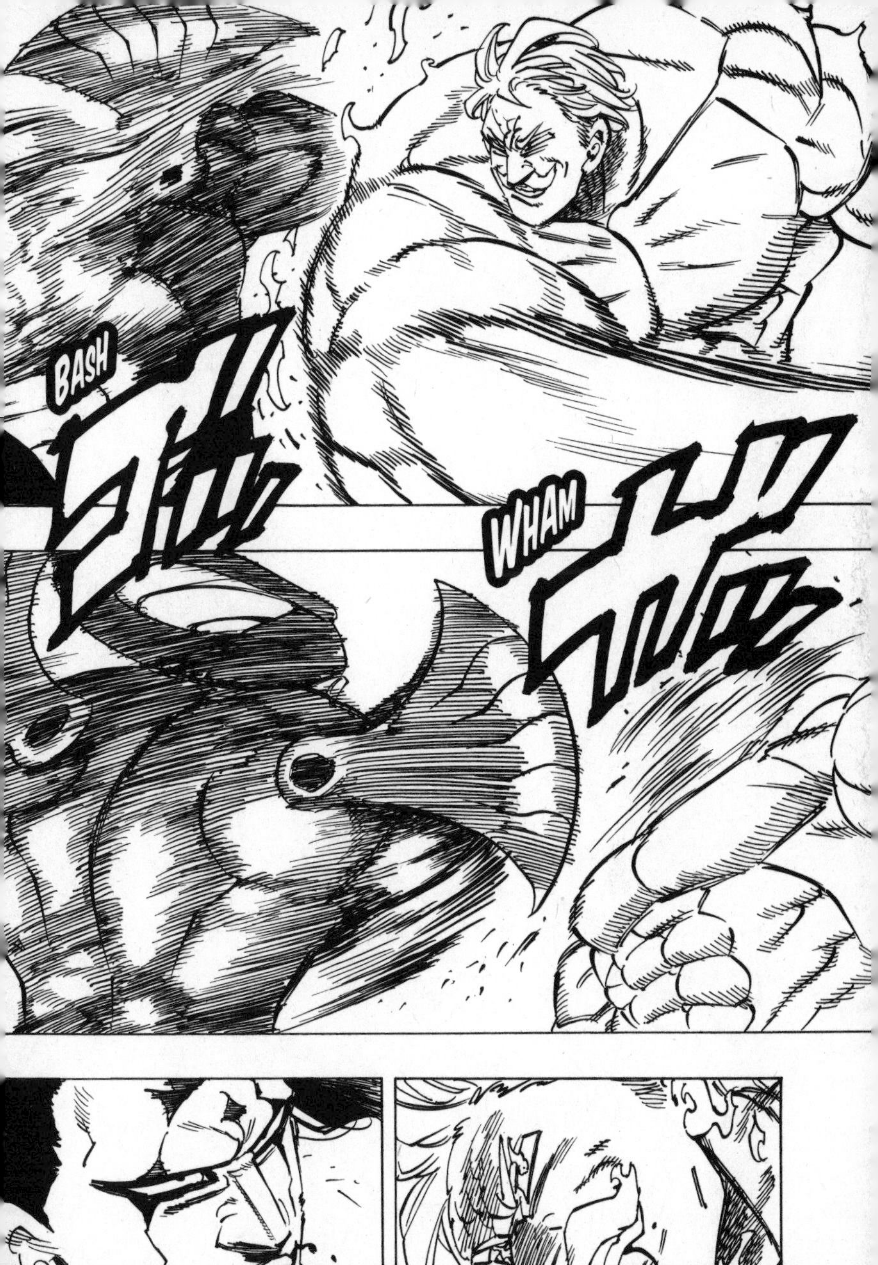
BASH
WHAM

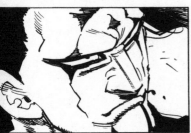

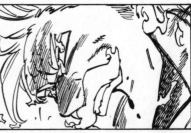

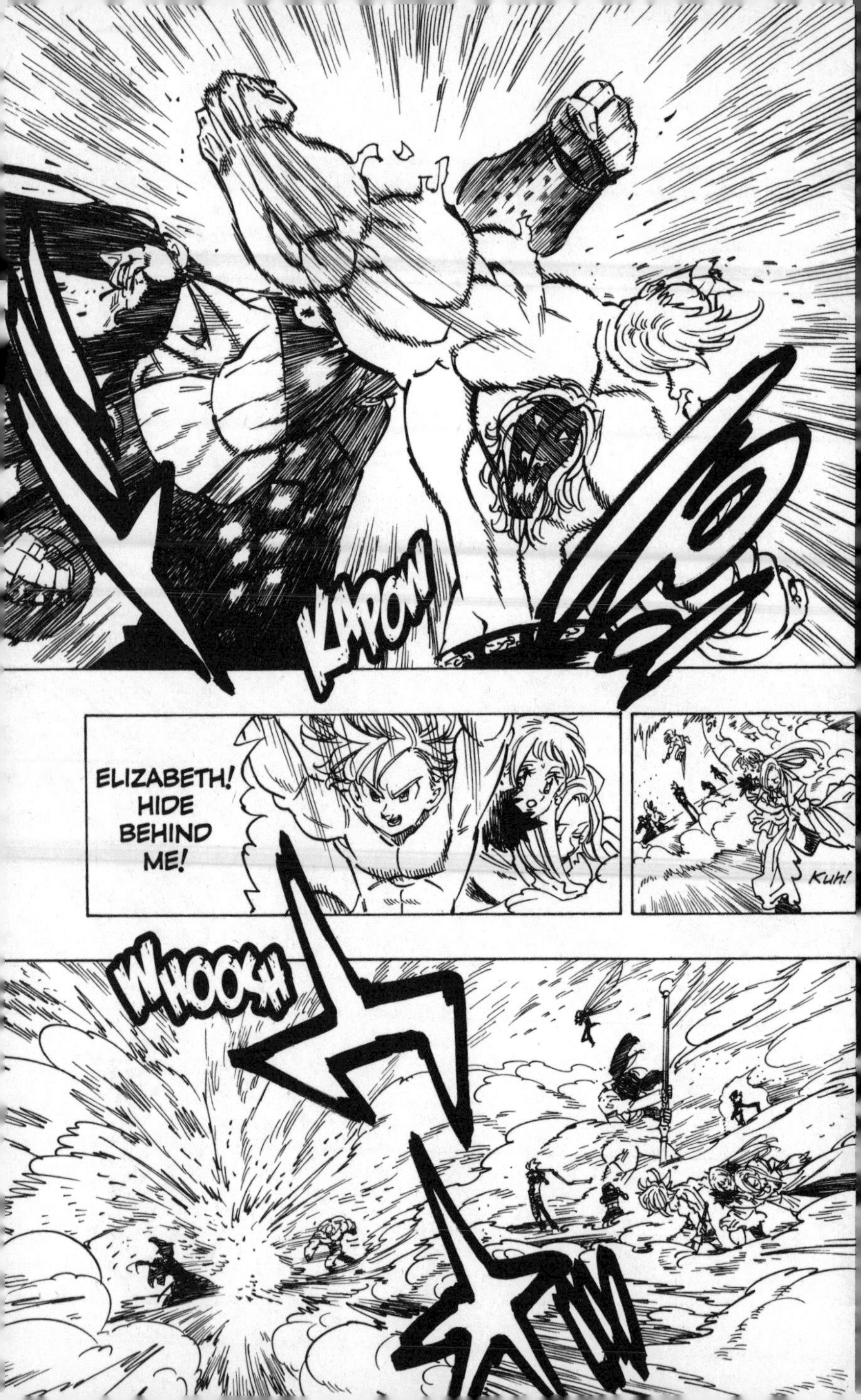
KAPOW
Kuh!
ELIZABETH! HIDE BEHIND ME!
WHOOSH

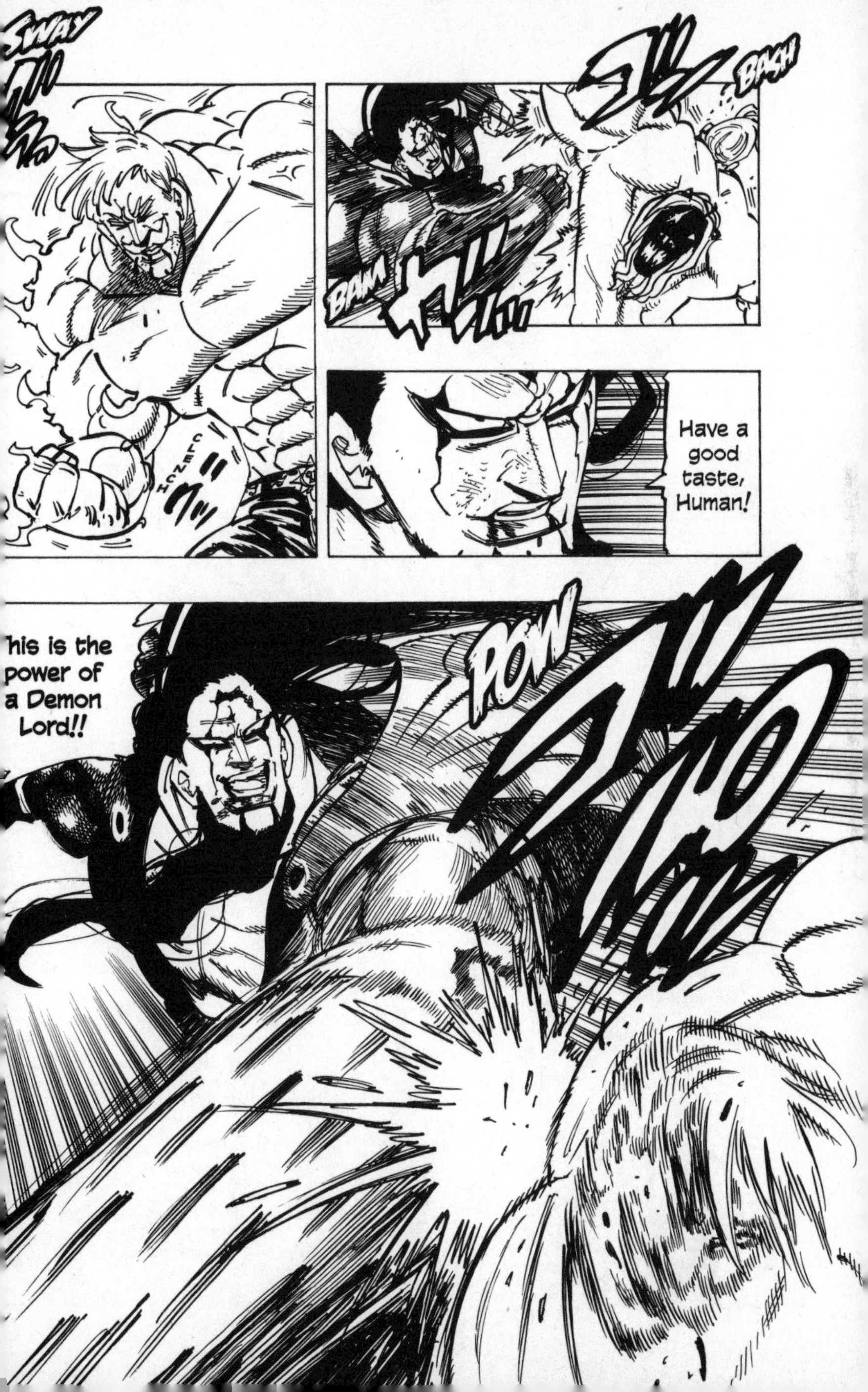

BASH
BAM
Have a good taste, Human!
SWAY
CLENCH
POW
his is the power of a Demon Lord!!

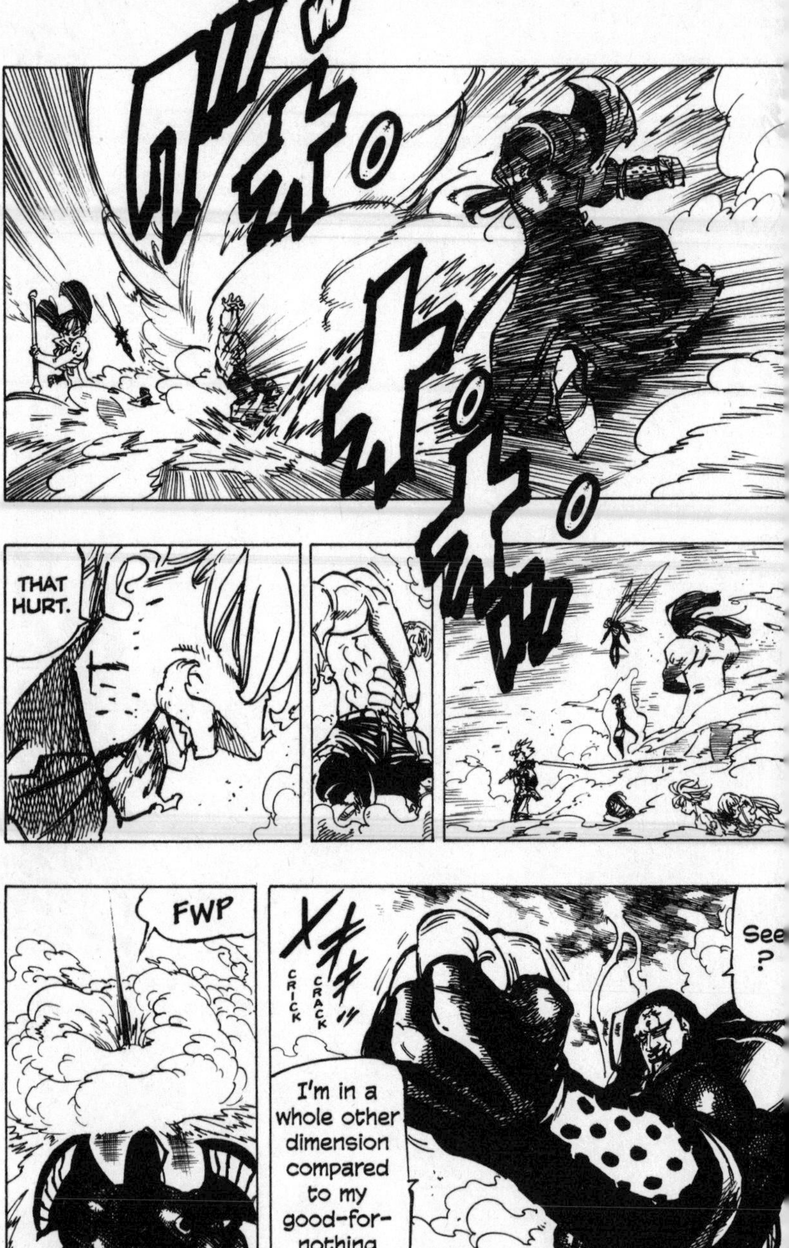
THAT HURT.
See?
CRICK CRACK
I'm in a whole other dimension compared to my good-for-nothing sons.
FWP
!

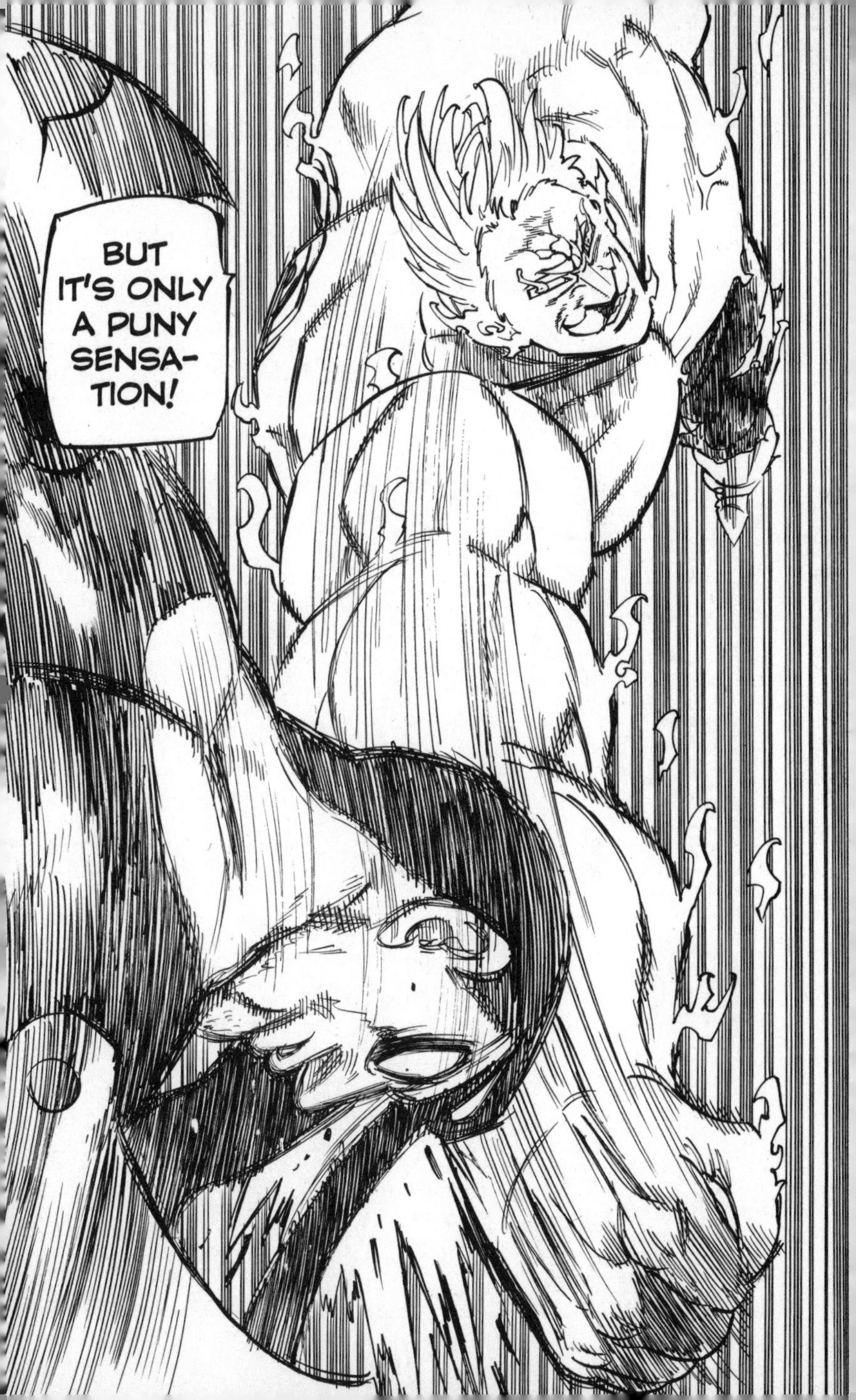
BUT IT'S ONLY A PUNY SENSA-TION!

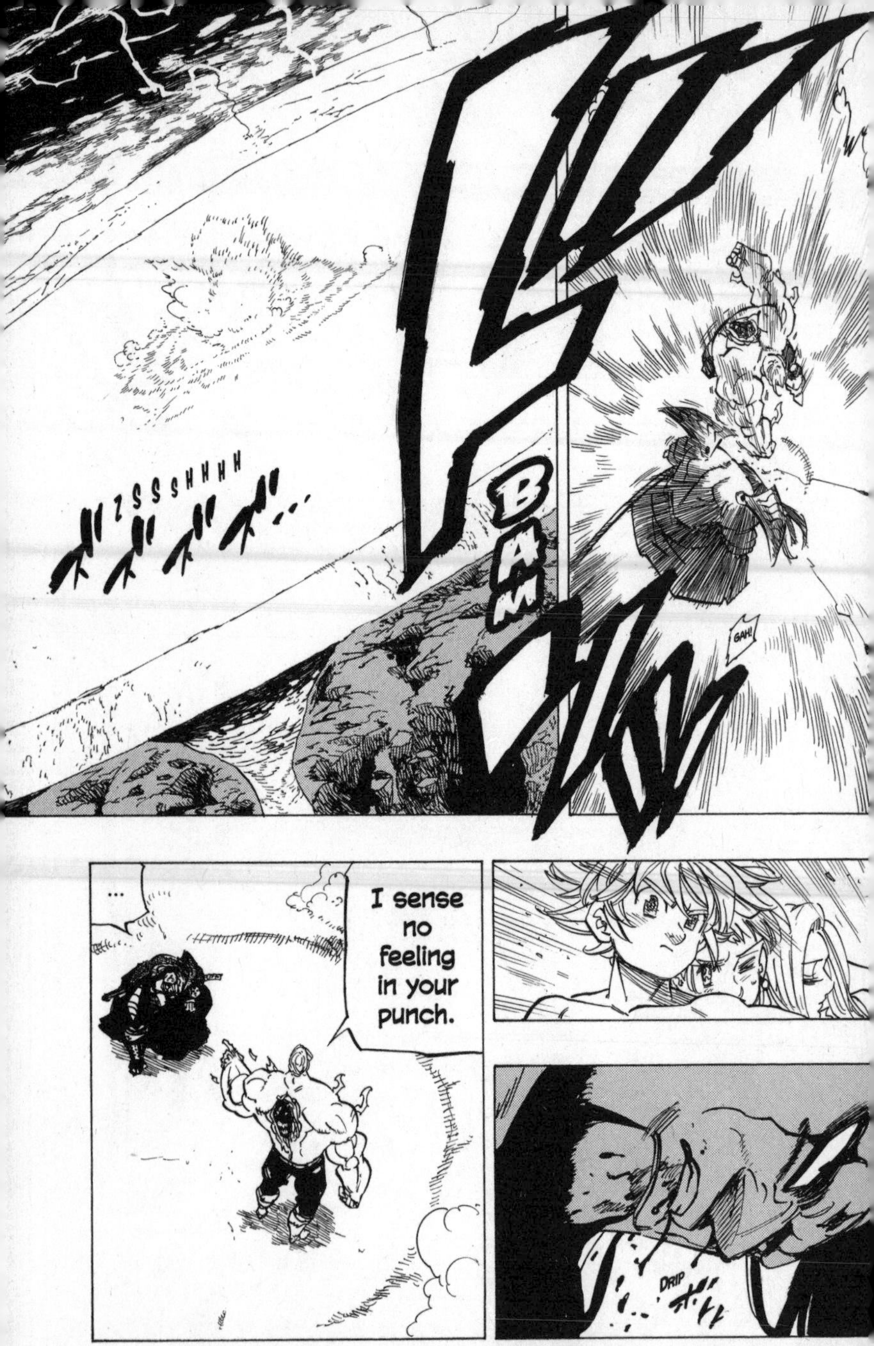
BAM
GAH!
ZZSSHHHH
ズズズ…
DRIP
I sense no feeling in your punch.
...

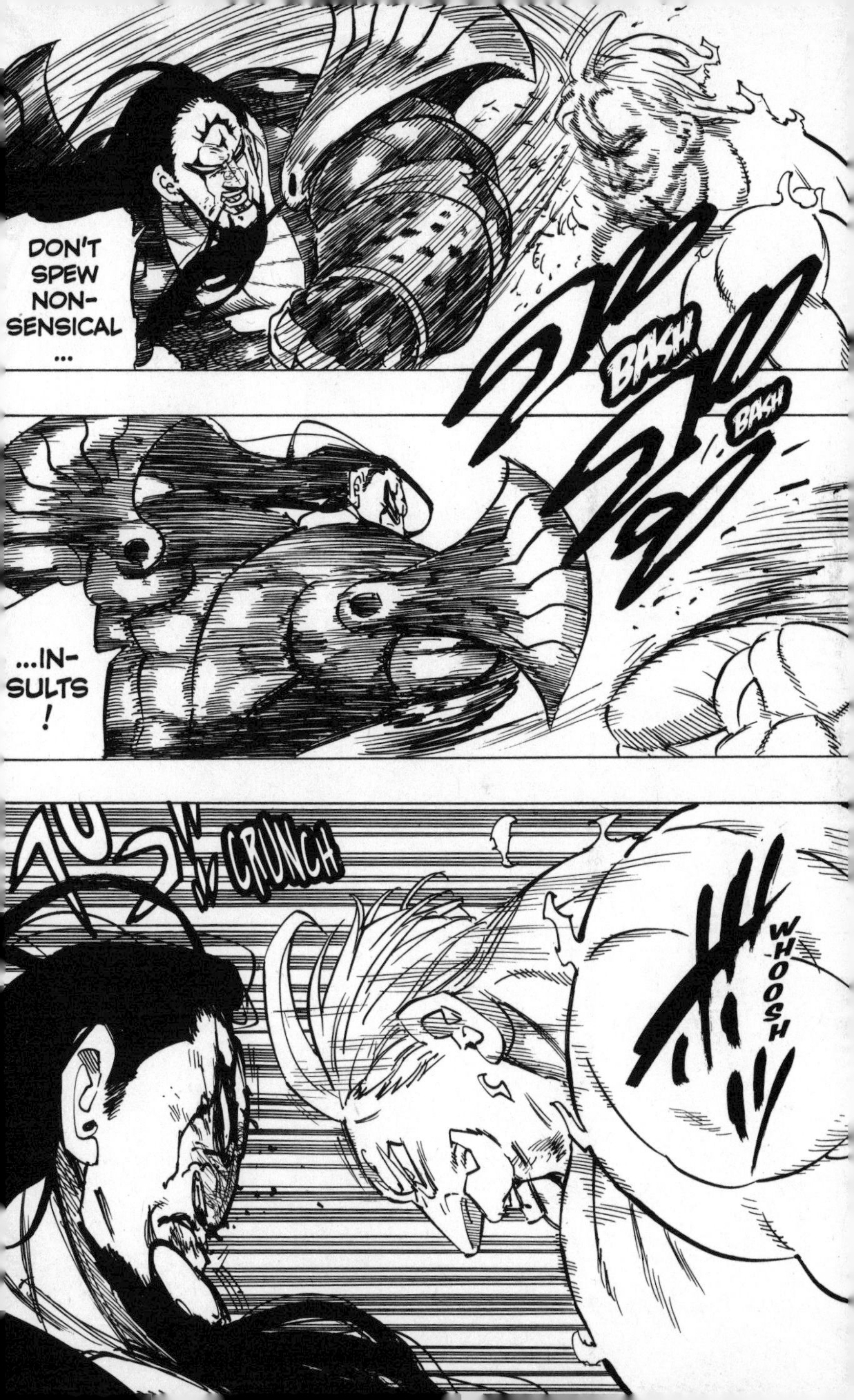
BASH
DON'T SPEW NON-SENSICAL ...
BASH
...IN-SULTS!
WHOOSH
CRUNCH

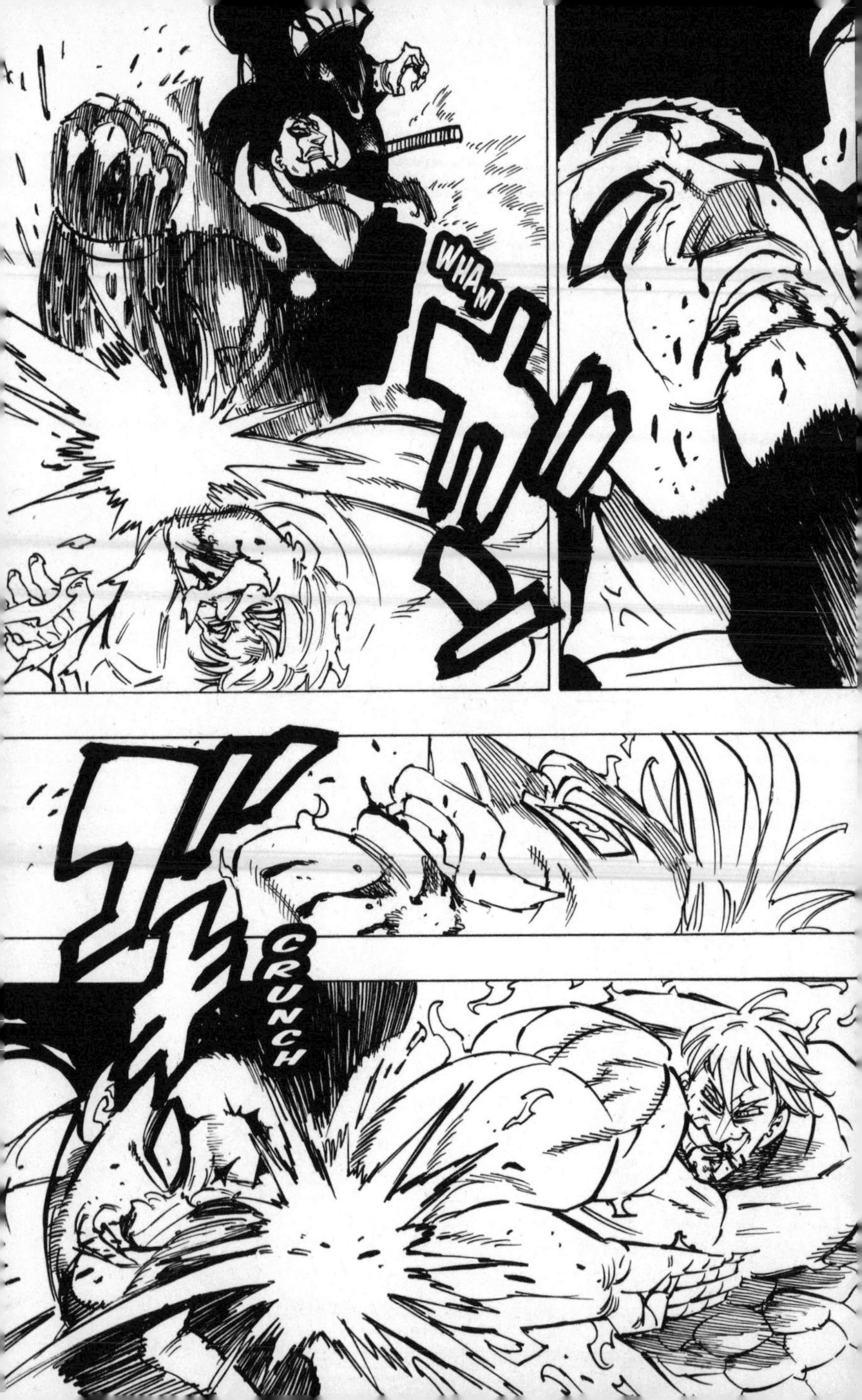
WHAM
CRUNCH

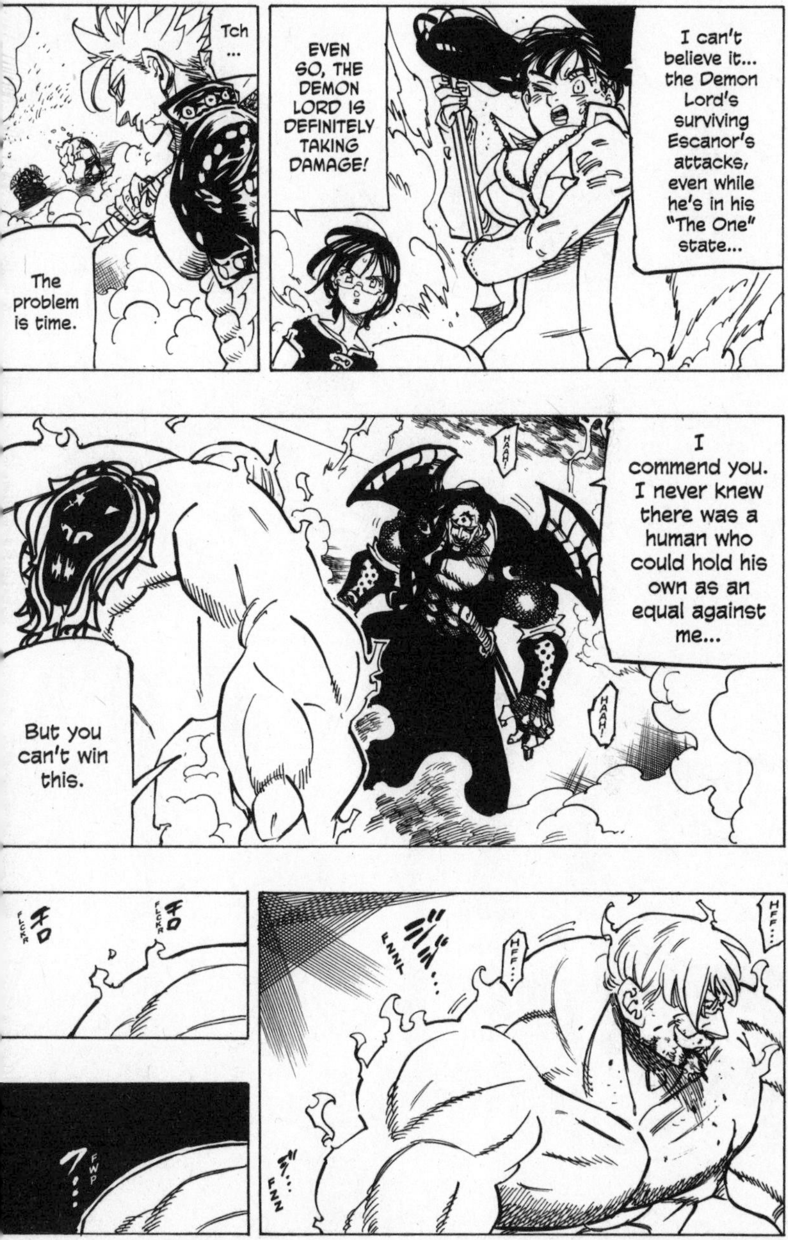
I can't believe it... the Demon Lord's surviving Escanor's attacks, even while he's in his "The One" state...
EVEN SO, THE DEMON LORD IS DEFINITELY TAKING DAMAGE!
Tch ...
The problem is time.
I commend you. I never knew there was a human who could hold his own as an equal against me...
HAAH!
HAAH!
But you can't win this.
HFF...
HFF...
FZZT
FZZ
FLCKR
FLCKR
FWP

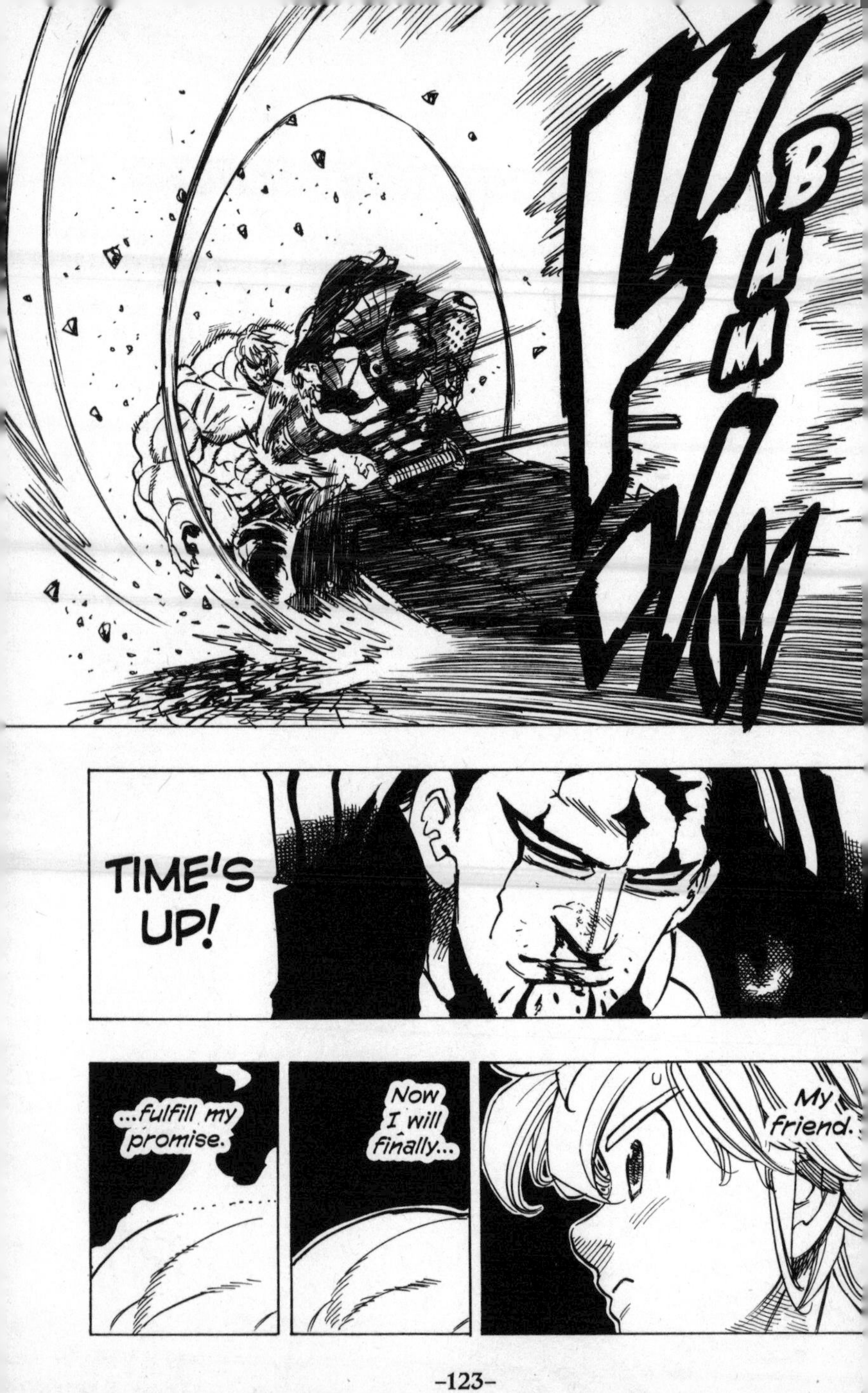
BAM
TIME'S UP!
My friend.
Now I will finally...
...fulfill my promise.

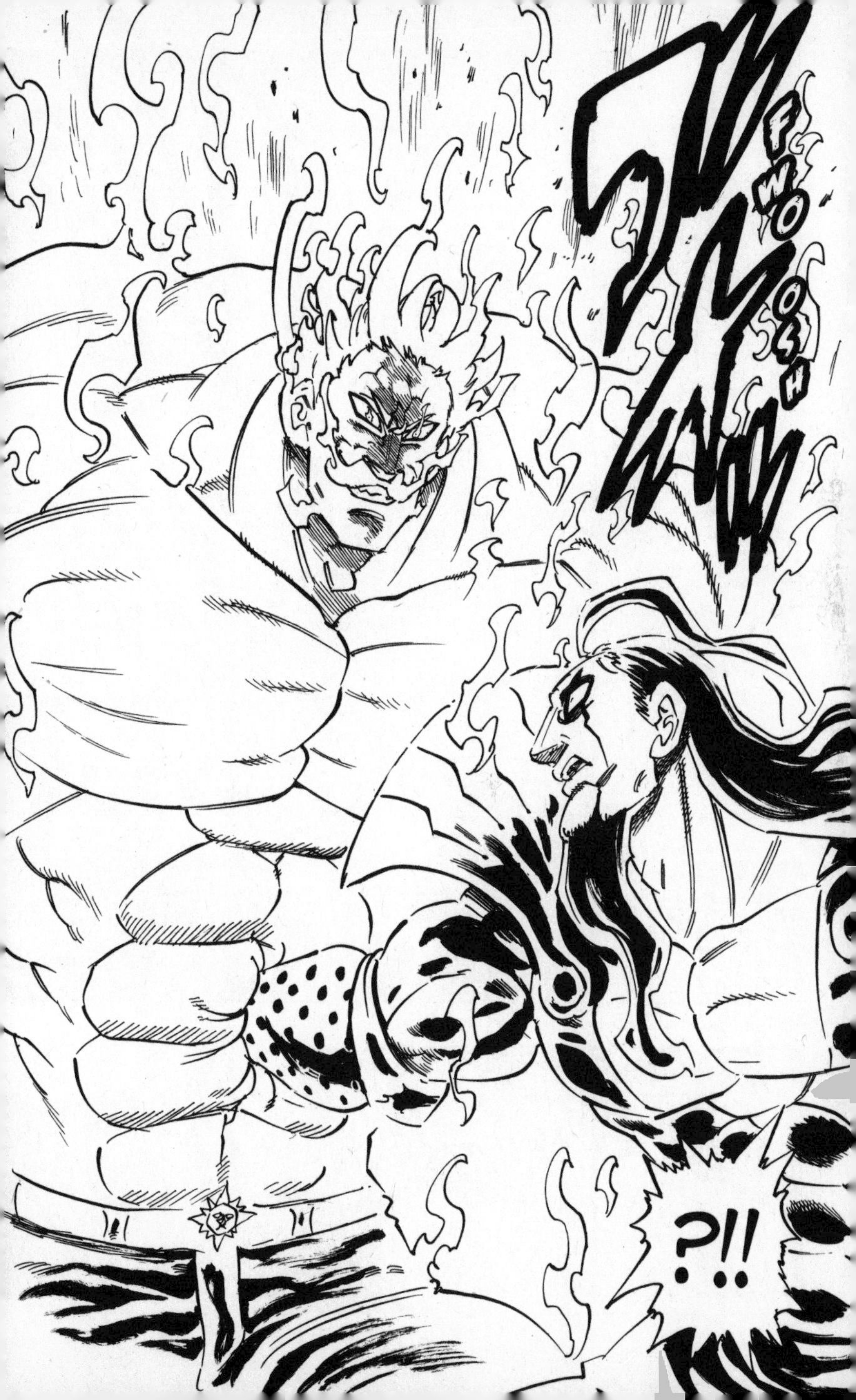
FWOOSH
?!!

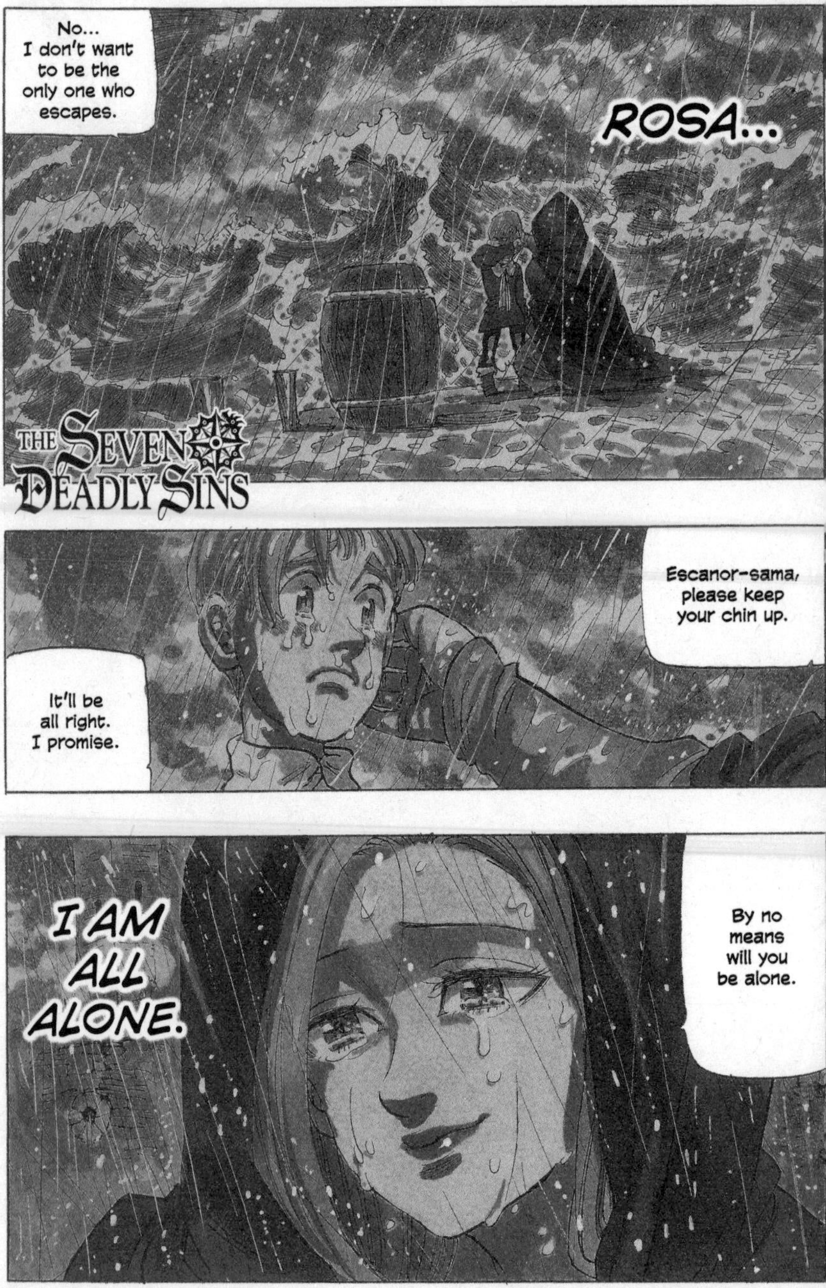
ROSA...
No... I don't want to be the only one who escapes.
THE SEVEN DEADLY SINS
Escanor-sama, please keep your chin up.
It'll be all right. I promise.
By no means will you be alone.
I AM ALL ALONE.

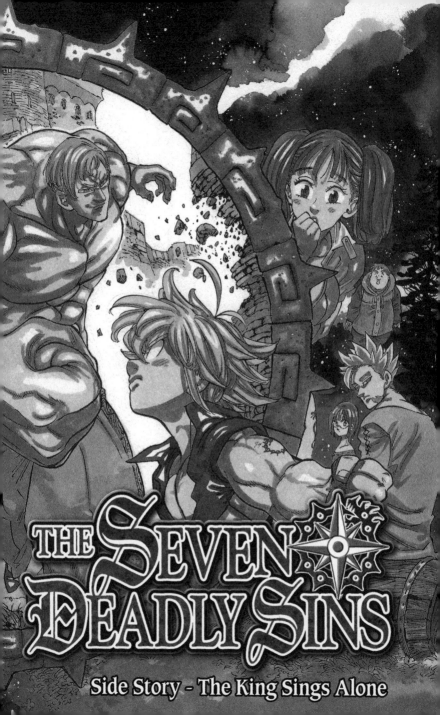

THE SEVEN DEADLY SINS

Side Story - The King Sings Alone

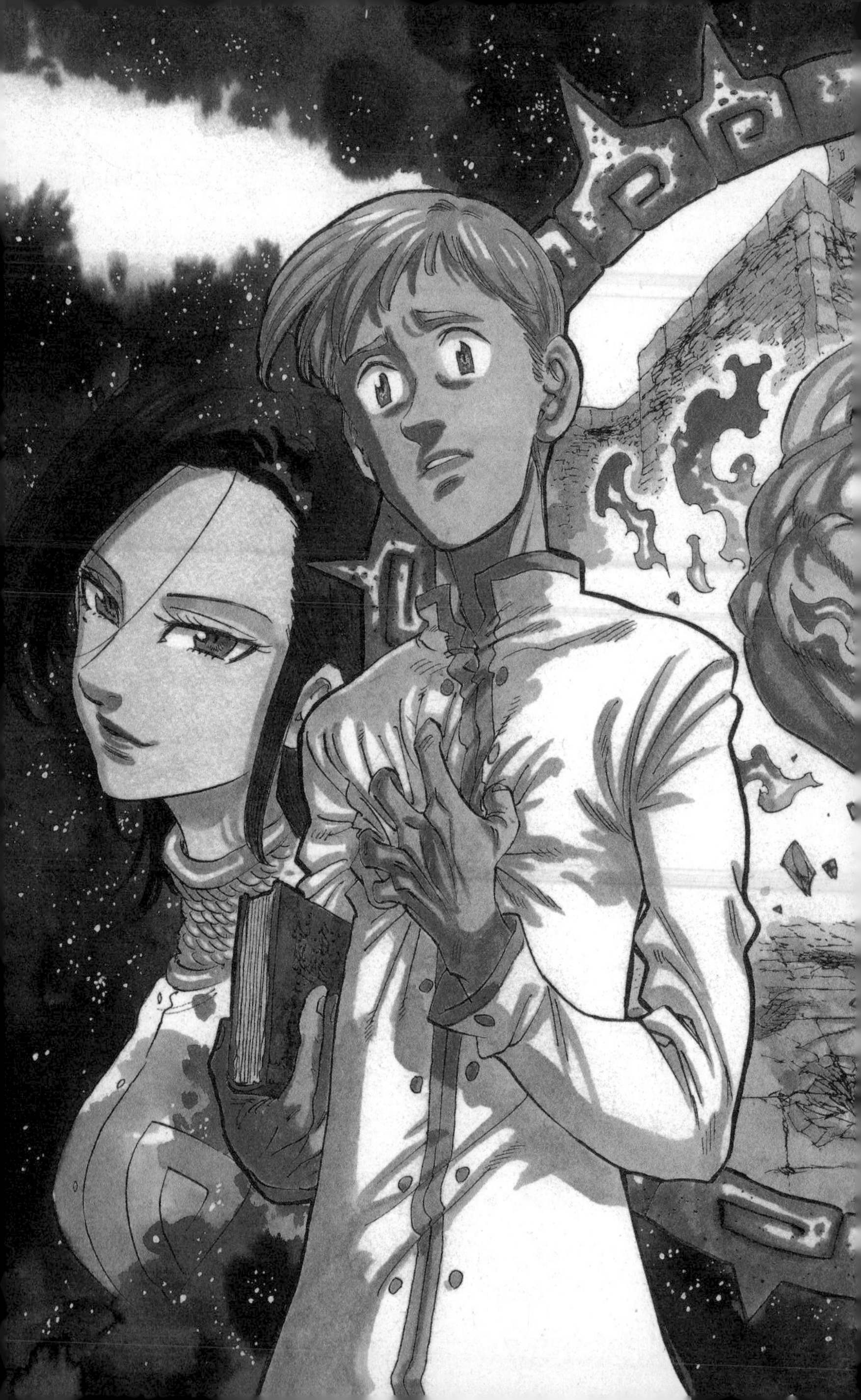

This was the final sketch proposed for the Demon Lord. I designed it to be less ugly and put more emphasis on the fact that Zeldris has been taken over. I wanted to see what a fully grown Zeldris would look like (who knows how long that would take...) at the prime of his life... And at the same time it'd probably look like how the Demon Lord in his youth. Unlike Meliodas, who psychologically resisted him the whole time, he's been very eroded away at, so his form is more fully seeped in a Demon Lord appearance.

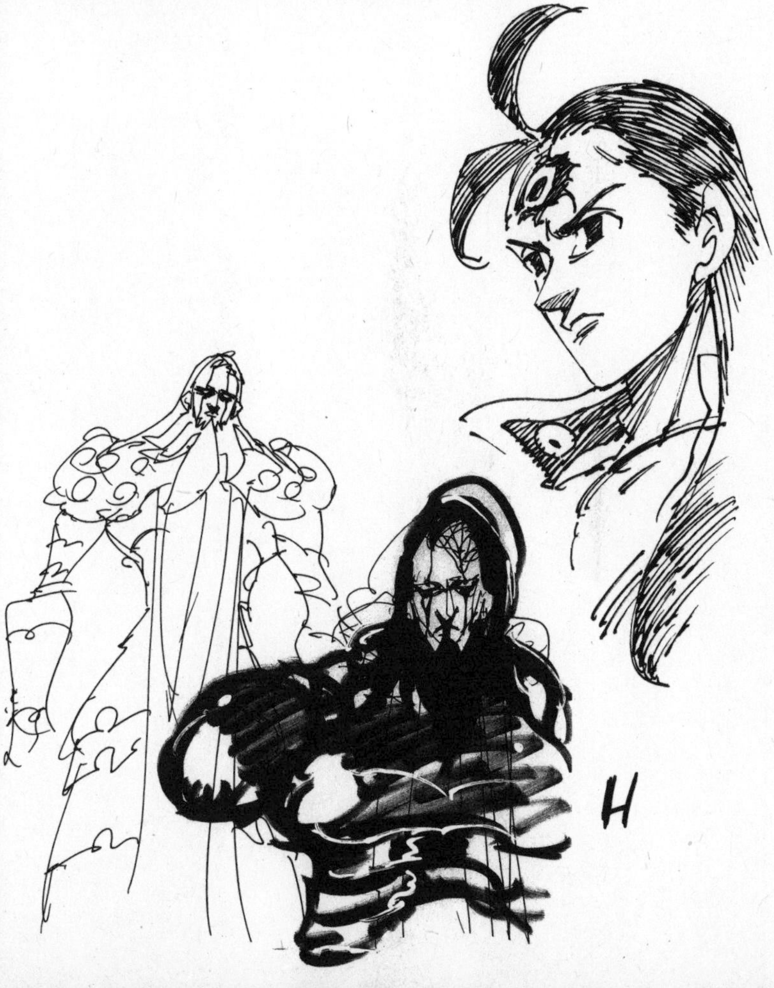
H

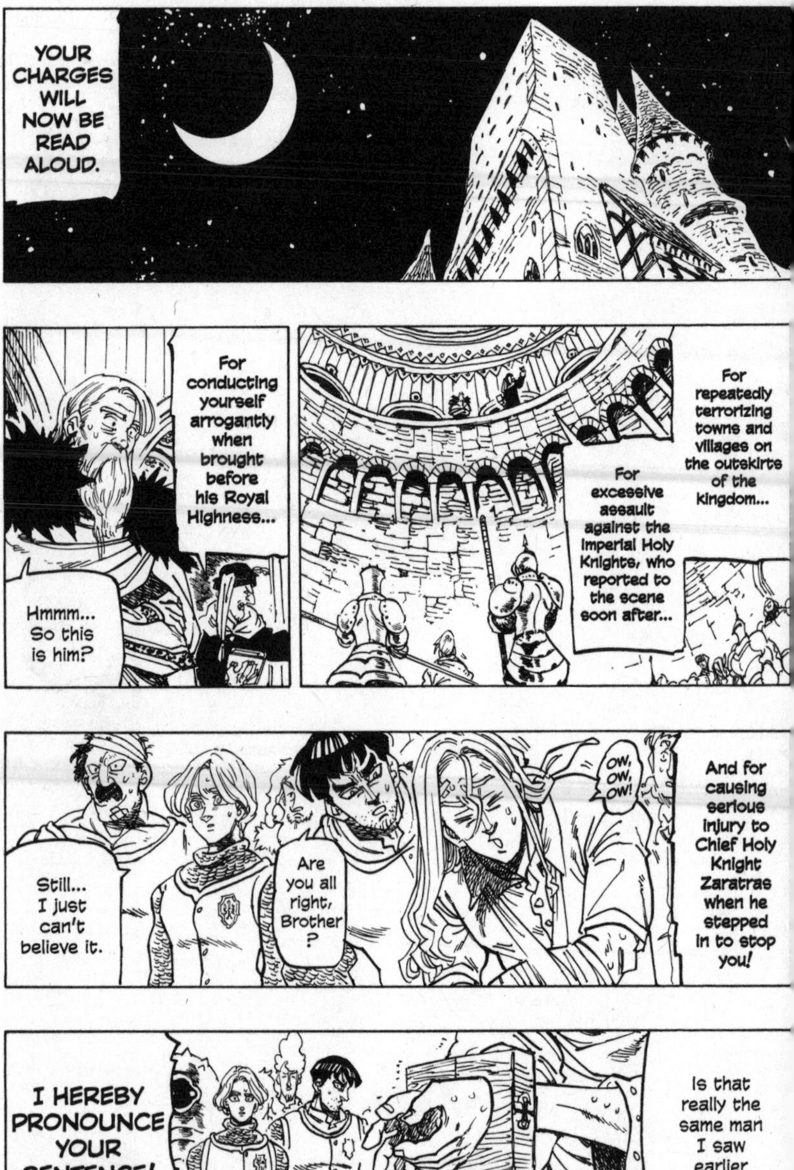
YOUR CHARGES WILL NOW BE READ ALOUD.
For repeatedly terrorizing towns and villages on the outskirts of the kingdom...
For excessive assault against the Imperial Holy Knights, who reported to the scene soon after...
For conducting yourself arrogantly when brought before his Royal Highness...
Hmmm... So this is him?
And for causing serious injury to Chief Holy Knight Zaratras when he stepped in to stop you!
OW, OW, OW!
Are you all right, Brother?
Still... I just can't believe it.
Is that really the same man I saw earlier today?
I HEREBY PRONOUNCE YOUR SENTENCE!

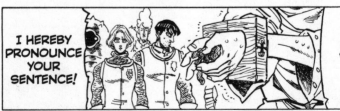

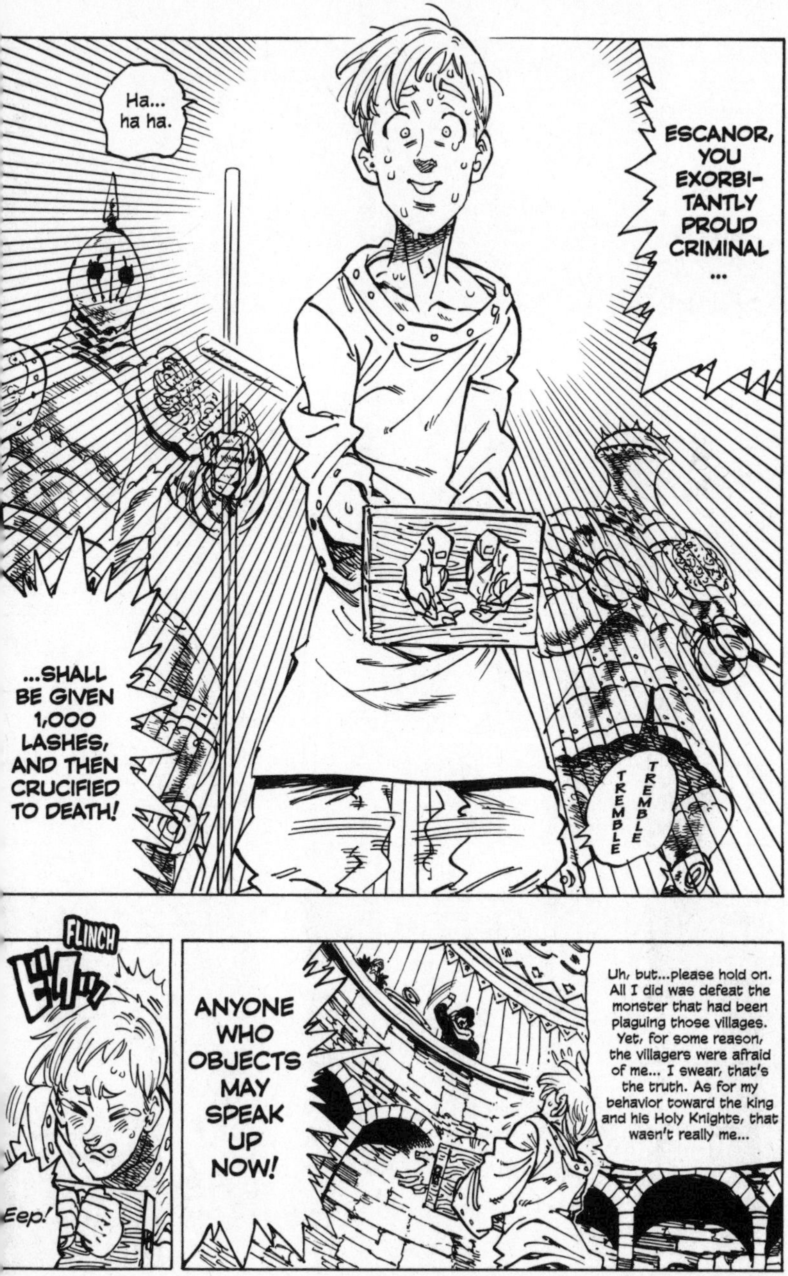
ESCANOR, YOU EXORBITANTLY PROUD CRIMINAL...
Ha... ha ha.
TREMBLE
TREMBLE
...SHALL BE GIVEN 1,000 LASHES, AND THEN CRUCIFIED TO DEATH!
Uh, but...please hold on. All I did was defeat the monster that had been plaguing those villages. Yet, for some reason, the villagers were afraid of me... I swear, that's the truth. As for my behavior toward the king and his Holy Knights, that wasn't really me...
ANYONE WHO OBJECTS MAY SPEAK UP NOW!
FLINCH
Eep!

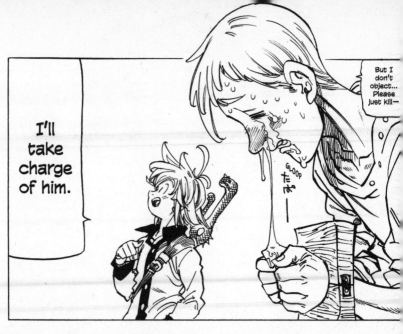

But I don't object... Please just kill—
GLOOP
I'll take charge of him.
Huh?
SNORT!
Ah...
Y- You're—
HEH HEH HEH.

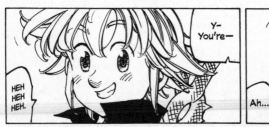

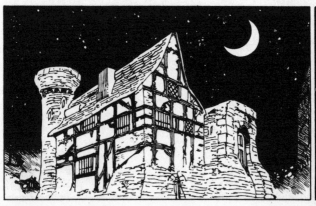

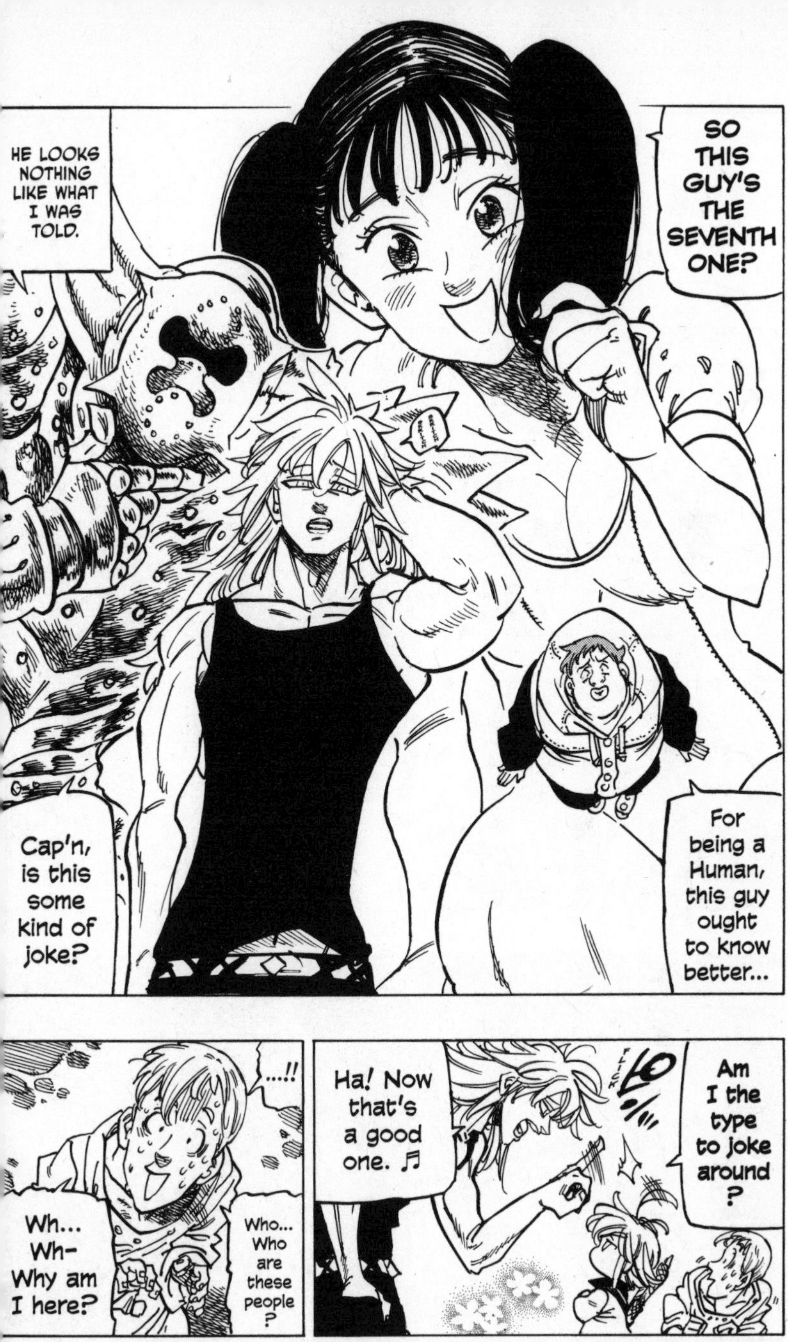
SO THIS GUY'S THE SEVENTH ONE?
HE LOOKS NOTHING LIKE WHAT I WAS TOLD.
For being a Human, this guy ought to know better...
Cap'n, is this some kind of joke?
Am I the type to joke around?
FLICK
Ha! Now that's a good one. ♫
...!!
Who... Who are these people?
Wh... Wh- Why am I here?

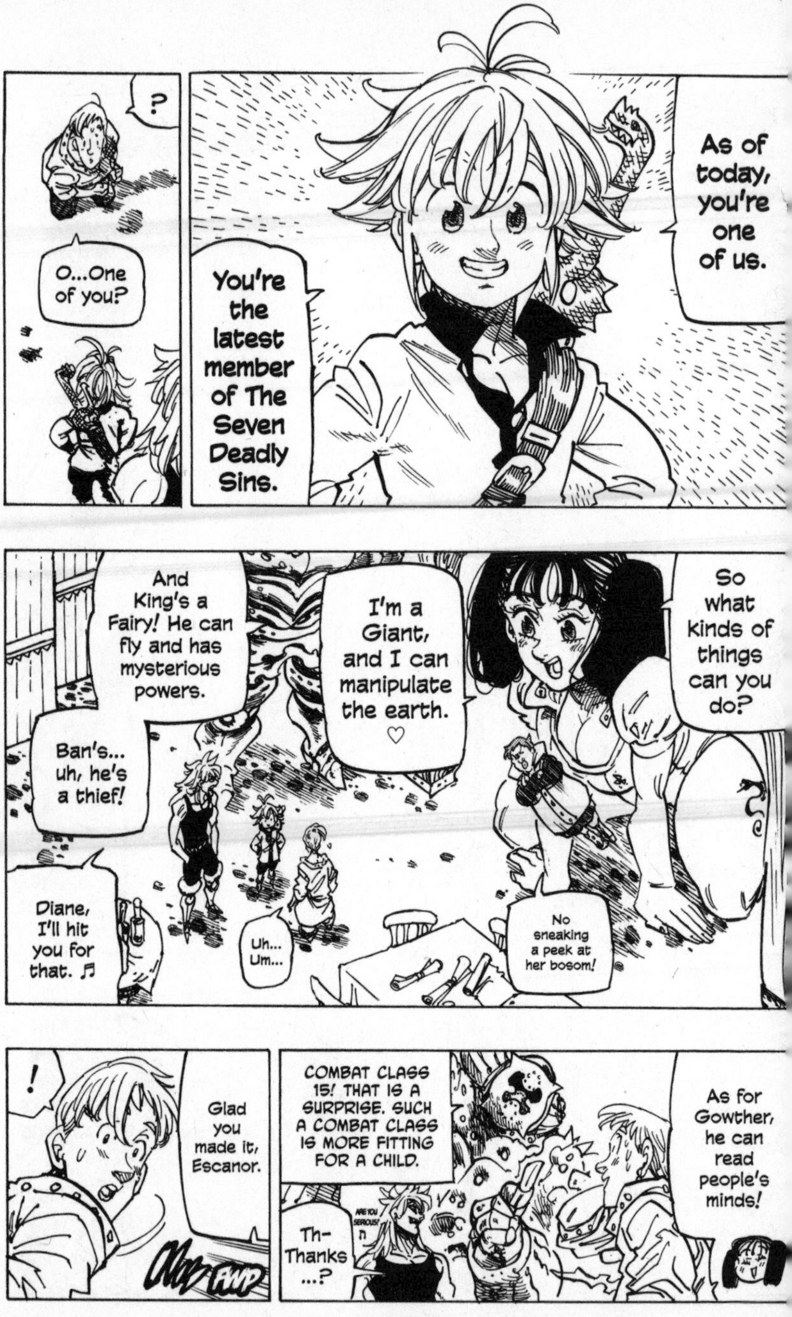

As of today, you're one of us.
You're the latest member of The Seven Deadly Sins.
?
O...One of you?
So what kinds of things can you do?
No sneaking a peek at her bosom!
I'm a Giant, and I can manipulate the earth. ♡
And King's a Fairy! He can fly and has mysterious powers.
Uh... Um...
Ban's... uh, he's a thief!
Diane, I'll hit you for that. ♫
As for Gowther, he can read people's minds!
COMBAT CLASS 15! THAT IS A SURPRISE. SUCH A COMBAT CLASS IS MORE FITTING FOR A CHILD.
ARE YOU SERIOUS!?
Th- Thanks ...?
!
Glad you made it, Escanor.
FWP

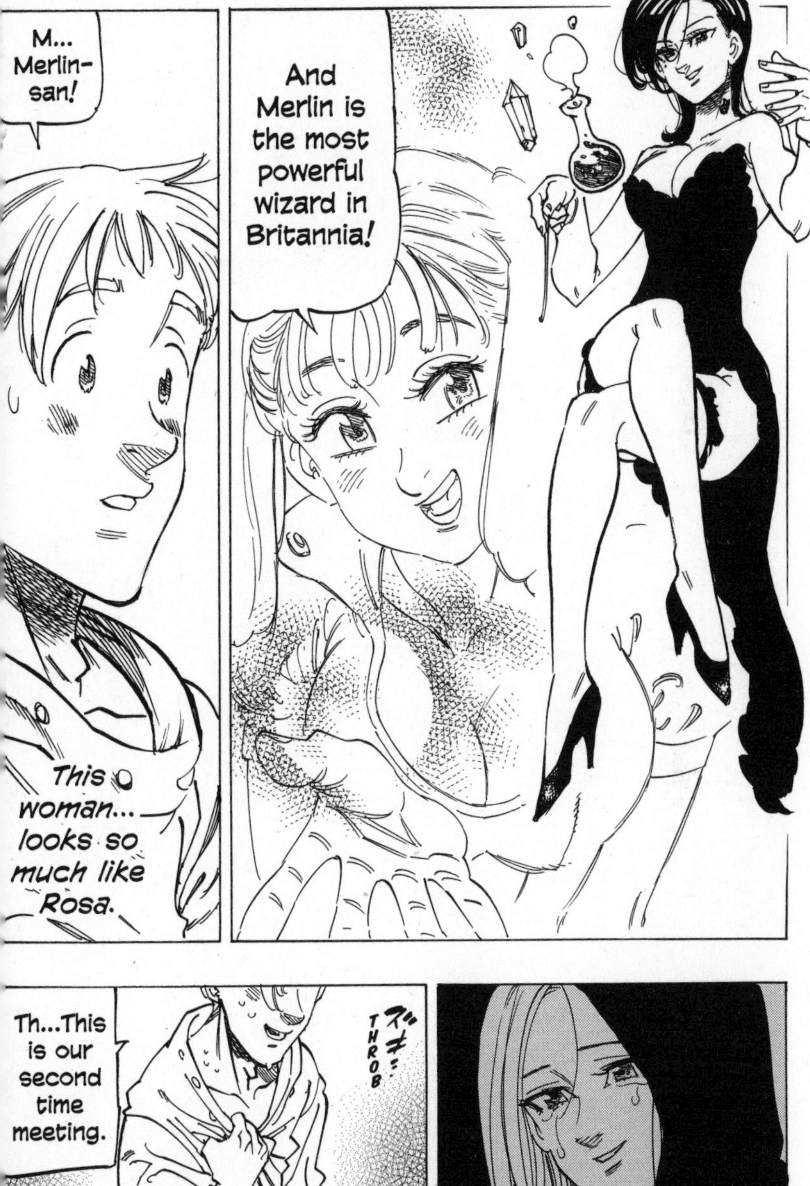
And Merlin is the most powerful wizard in Britannia!
M... Merlin-san!
This woman... looks so much like Rosa.
THROB
Th...This is our second time meeting.

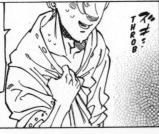

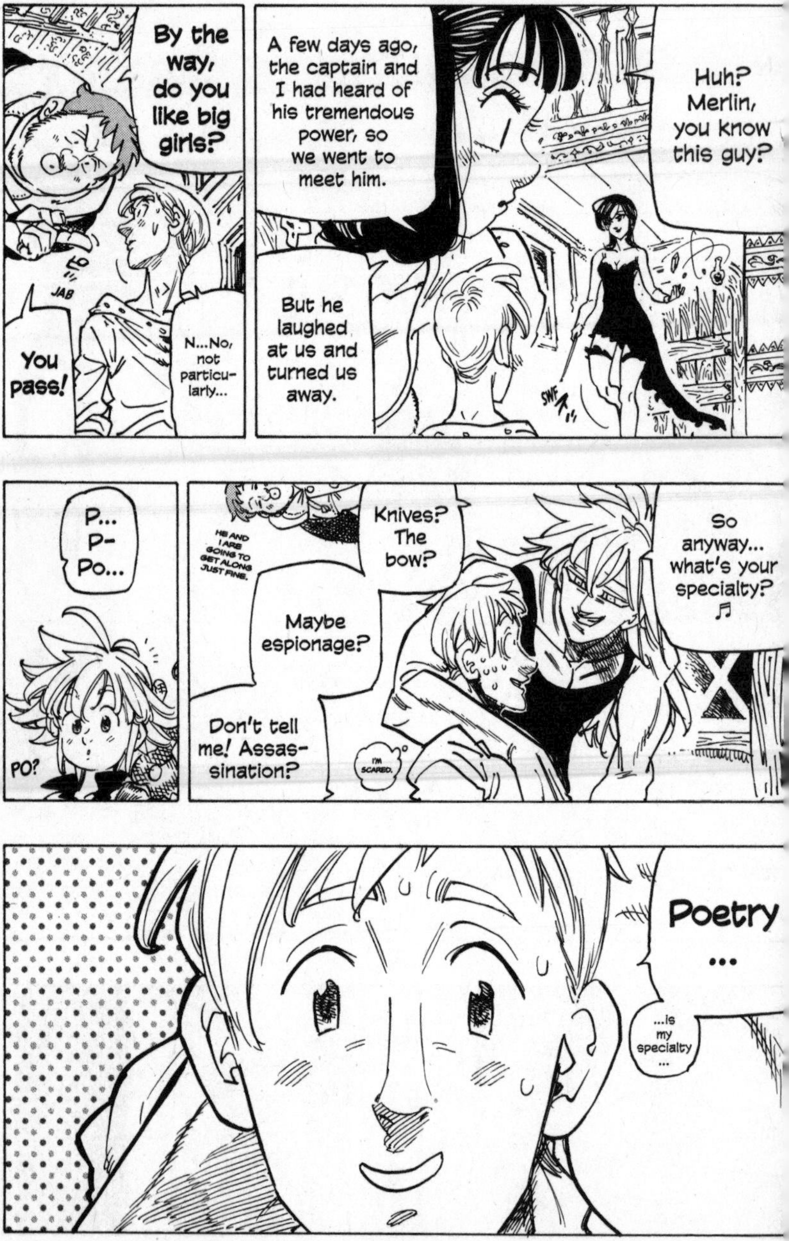
Huh? Merlin, you know this guy?
SWF
A few days ago, the captain and I had heard of his tremendous power, so we went to meet him.
But he laughed at us and turned us away.
By the way, do you like big girls?
JAB
N...No, not particu-larly...
You pass!
So anyway... what's your specialty? ♬
Knives? The bow?
HE AND I ARE GOING TO GET ALONG JUST FINE.
Maybe espionage?
Don't tell me! Assas-sination?
I'M SCARED.
P... P- Po...
PO?
Poetry ...
...is my specialty ...

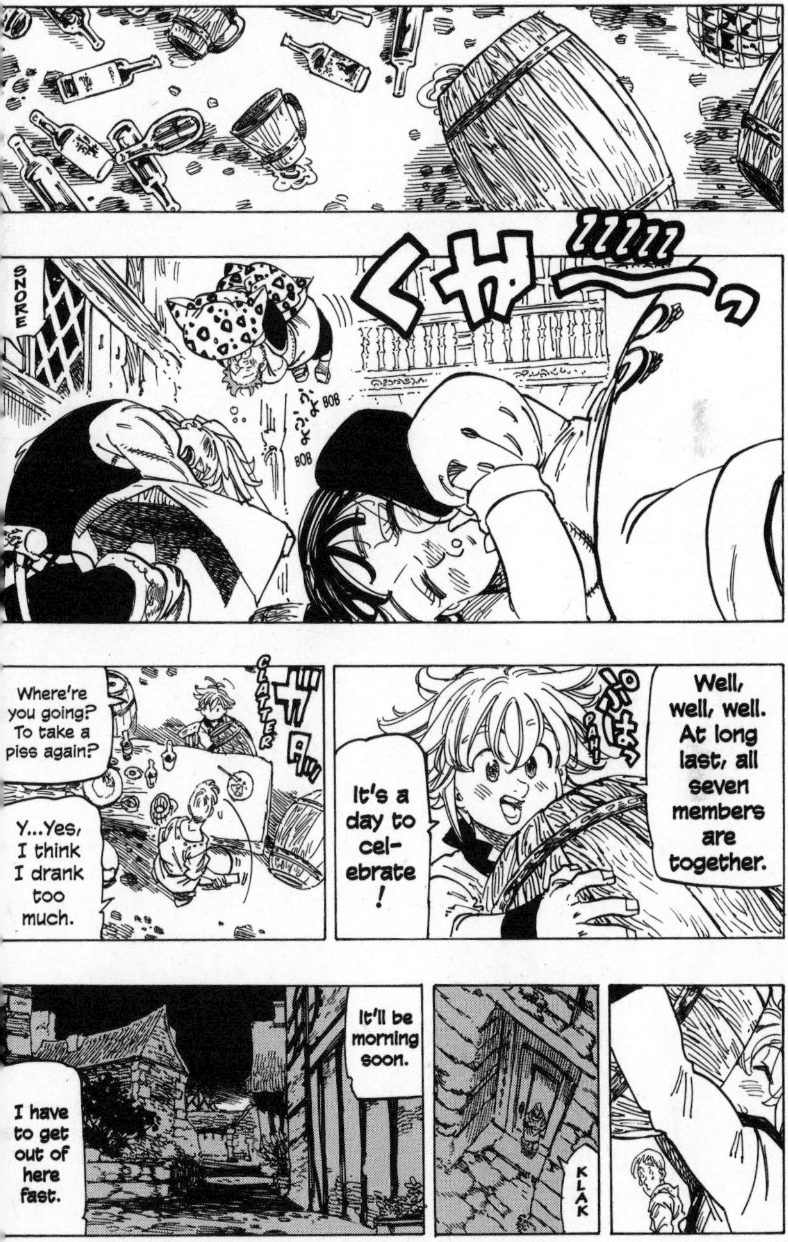
ZZZZZ
くかーーっ
SNORE
BOB
BOB
Well, well, well. At long last, all seven members are together.
PAH
It's a day to cel-ebrate!
CLATTER
Where're you going? To take a piss again?
Y...Yes, I think I drank too much.
KLAK
It'll be morning soon.
I have to get out of here fast.

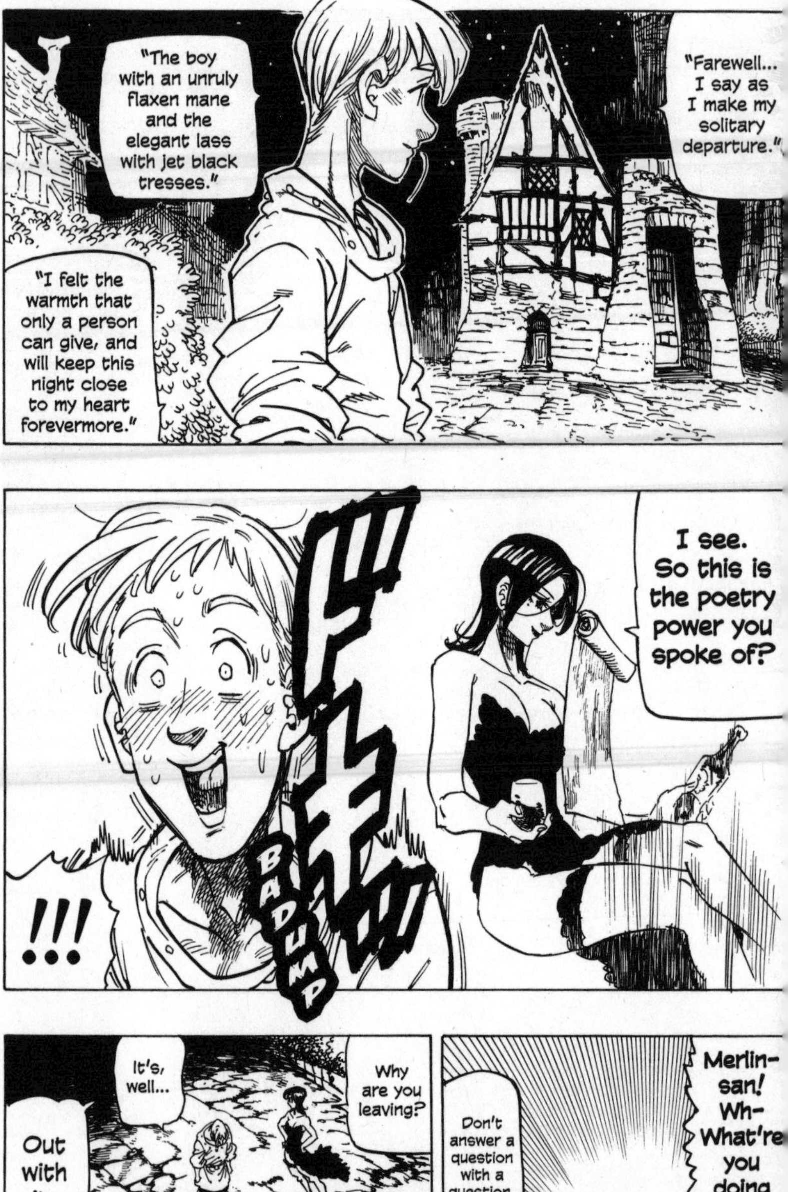
"Farewell... I say as I make my solitary departure."
"The boy with an unruly flaxen mane and the elegant lass with jet black tresses."
"I felt the warmth that only a person can give, and will keep this night close to my heart forevermore."
I see. So this is the poetry power you spoke of?
BADUMP
!!!
Merlin-san! Wh- What're you doing here?!
Don't answer a question with a question.
Why are you leaving?
It's, well...
Out with it.

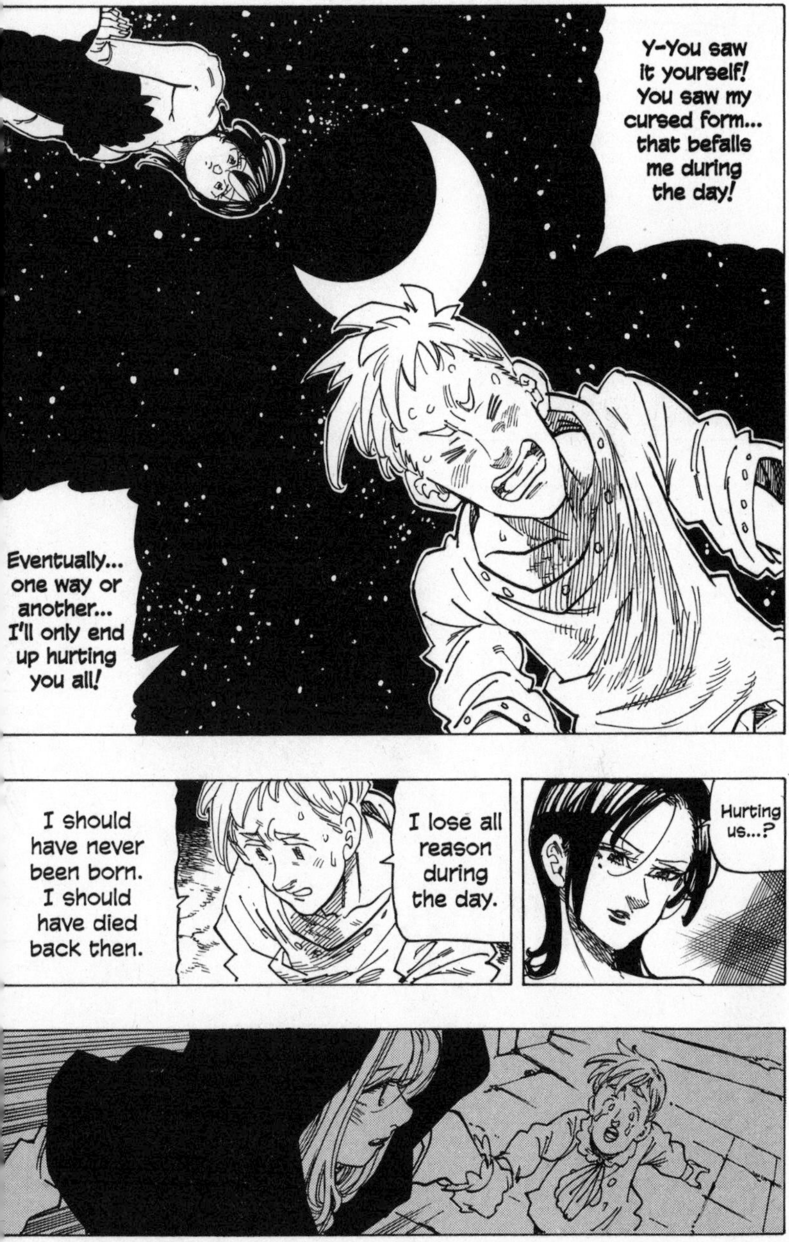
Y-You saw it yourself! You saw my cursed form... that befalls me during the day!
Eventually... one way or another... I'll only end up hurting you all!
Hurting us...?
I lose all reason during the day.
I should have never been born. I should have died back then.

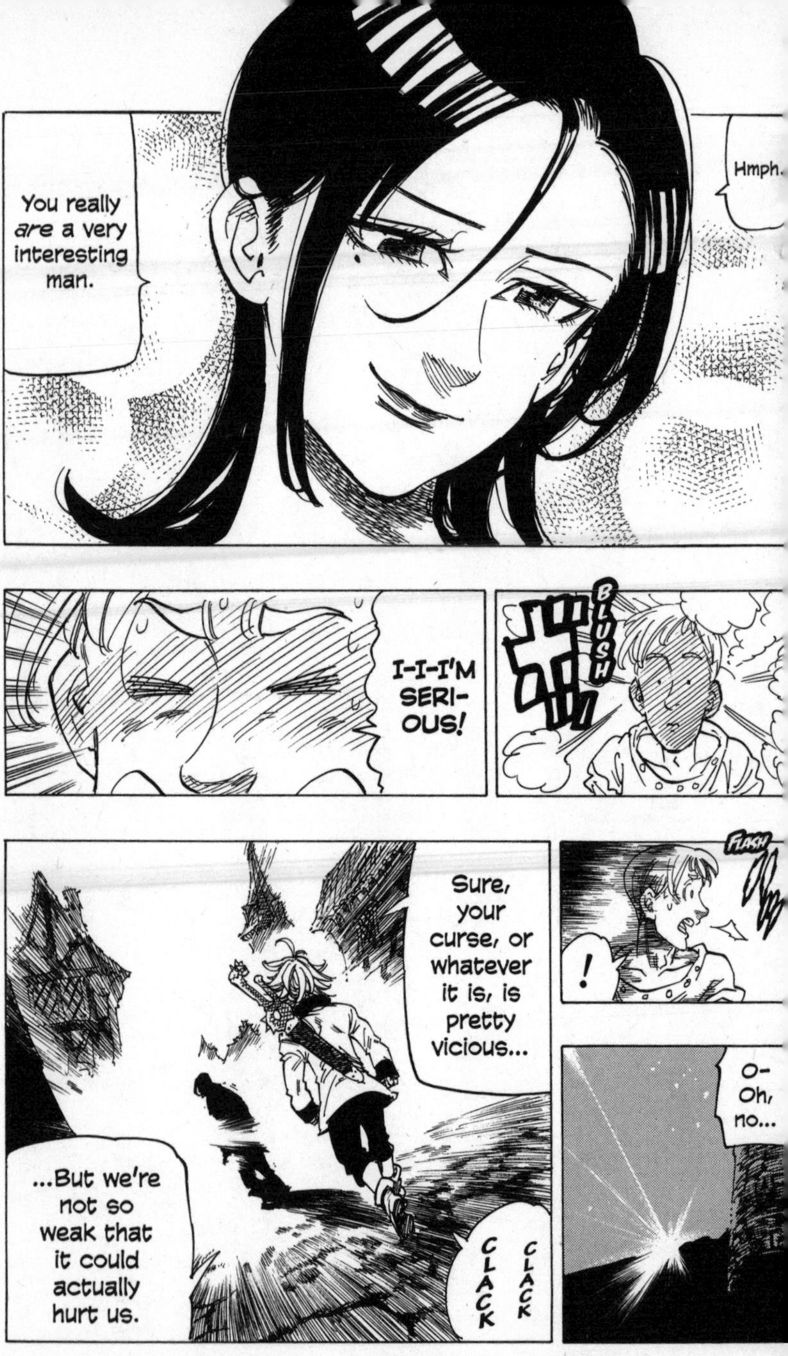
Hmph.
You really *are* a very interesting man.
BLUSH
I-I-I'M SERIOUS!
FLASH
!
O- Oh, no...
Sure, your curse, or whatever it is, is pretty vicious...
...But we're not so weak that it could actually hurt us.
CLACK CLACK

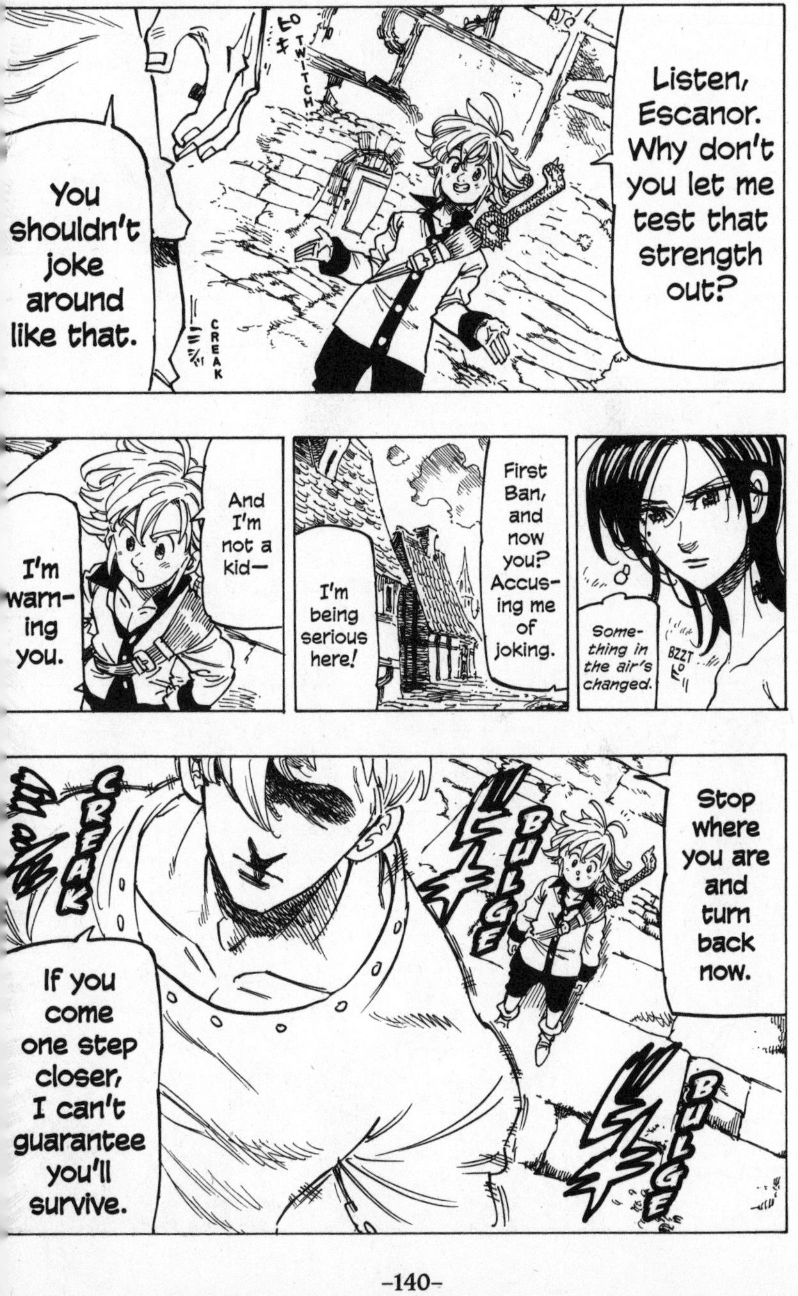
Listen, Escanor. Why don't you let me test that strength out?
TWITCH
You shouldn't joke around like that.
CREAK
Something in the air's changed.
BZZT
First Ban, and now you? Accusing me of joking.
I'm being serious here!
And I'm not a kid—
I'm warning you.
Stop where you are and turn back now.
BULGE
BULGE
CREAK
If you come one step closer, I can't guarantee you'll survive.

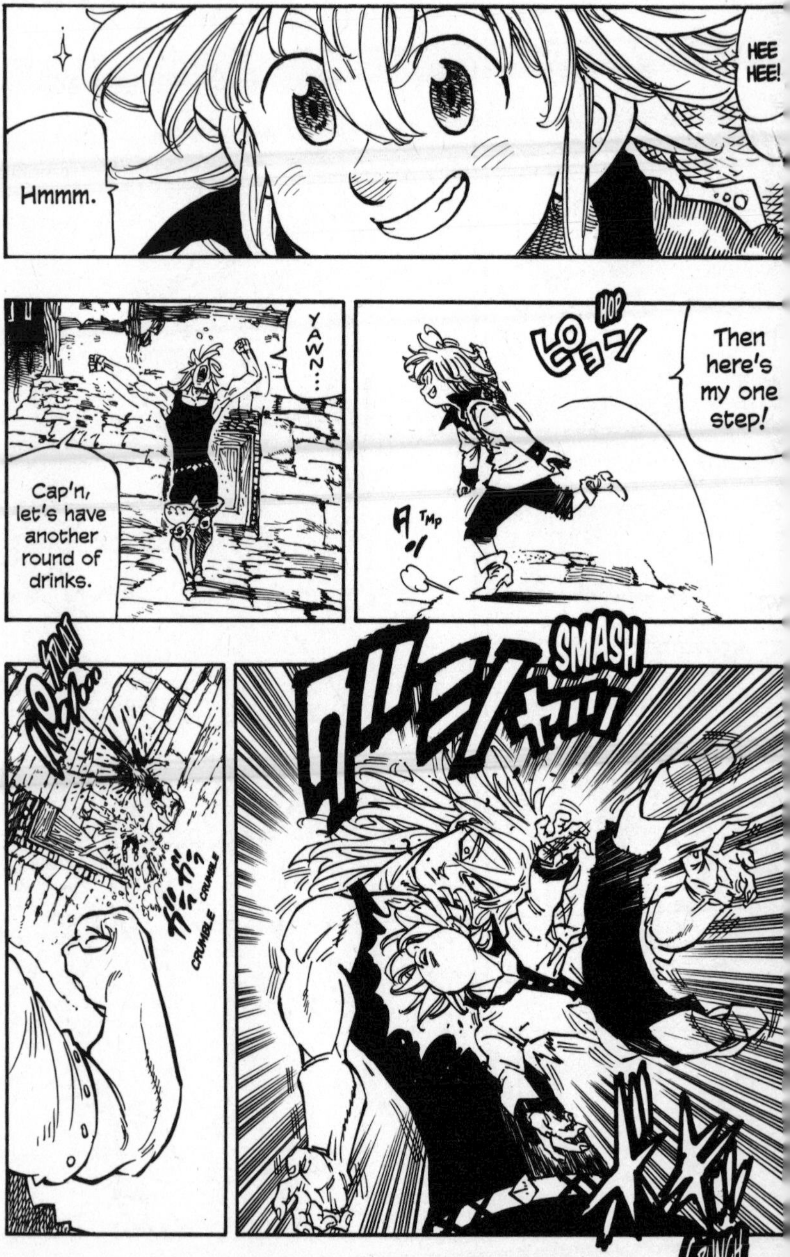
HEE HEE!
Hmmm.
HOP
Then here's my one step!
TMP
YAWN...
Cap'n, let's have another round of drinks.
SMASH
CRUNCH
SPLAT
CRUMBLE
CRUMBLE

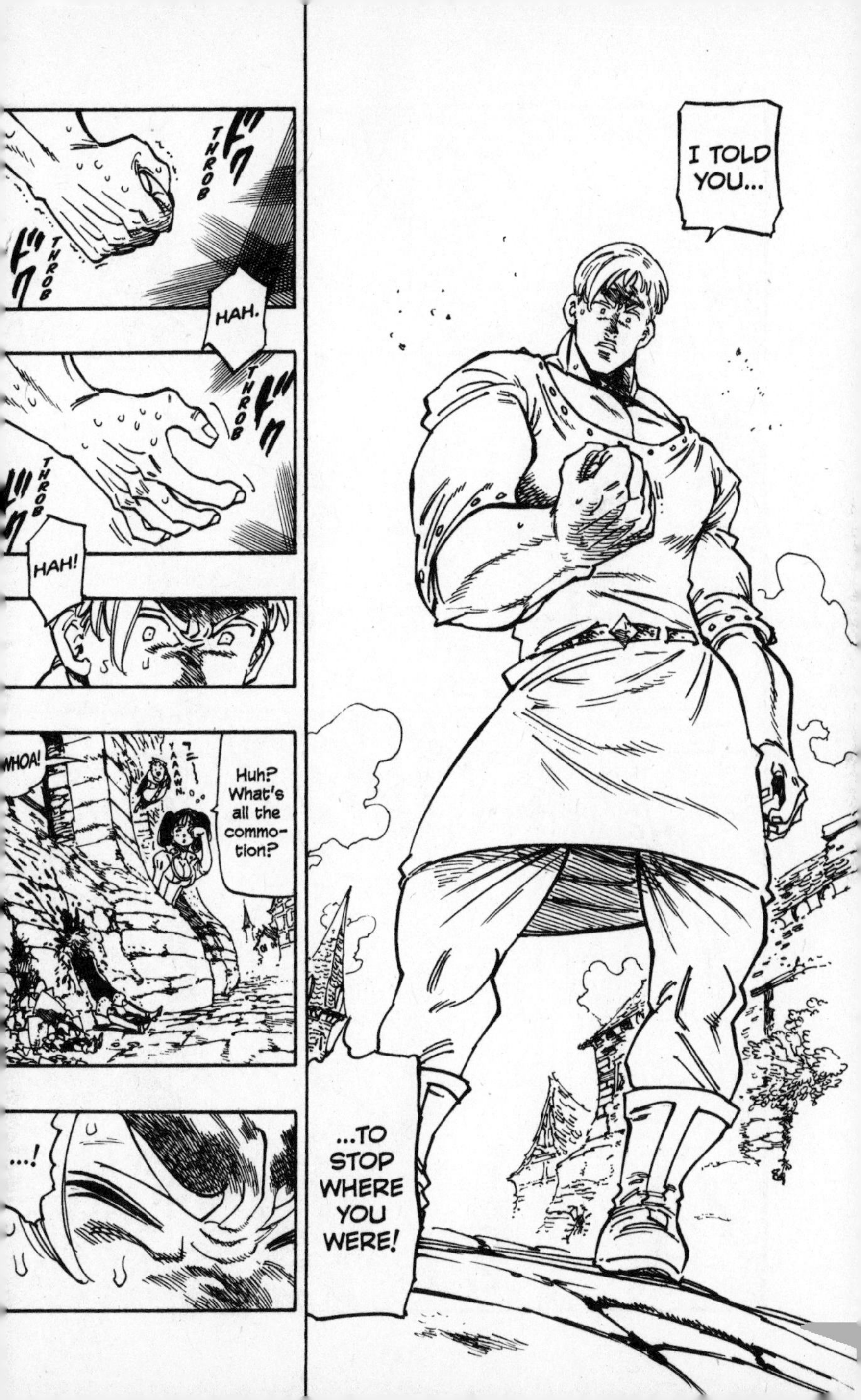
I TOLD YOU...
...TO STOP WHERE YOU WERE!
THROB
THROB
HAH.
THROB
THROB
HAH!
YAAAWN.
Huh? What's all the commotion?
WHOA!
...!

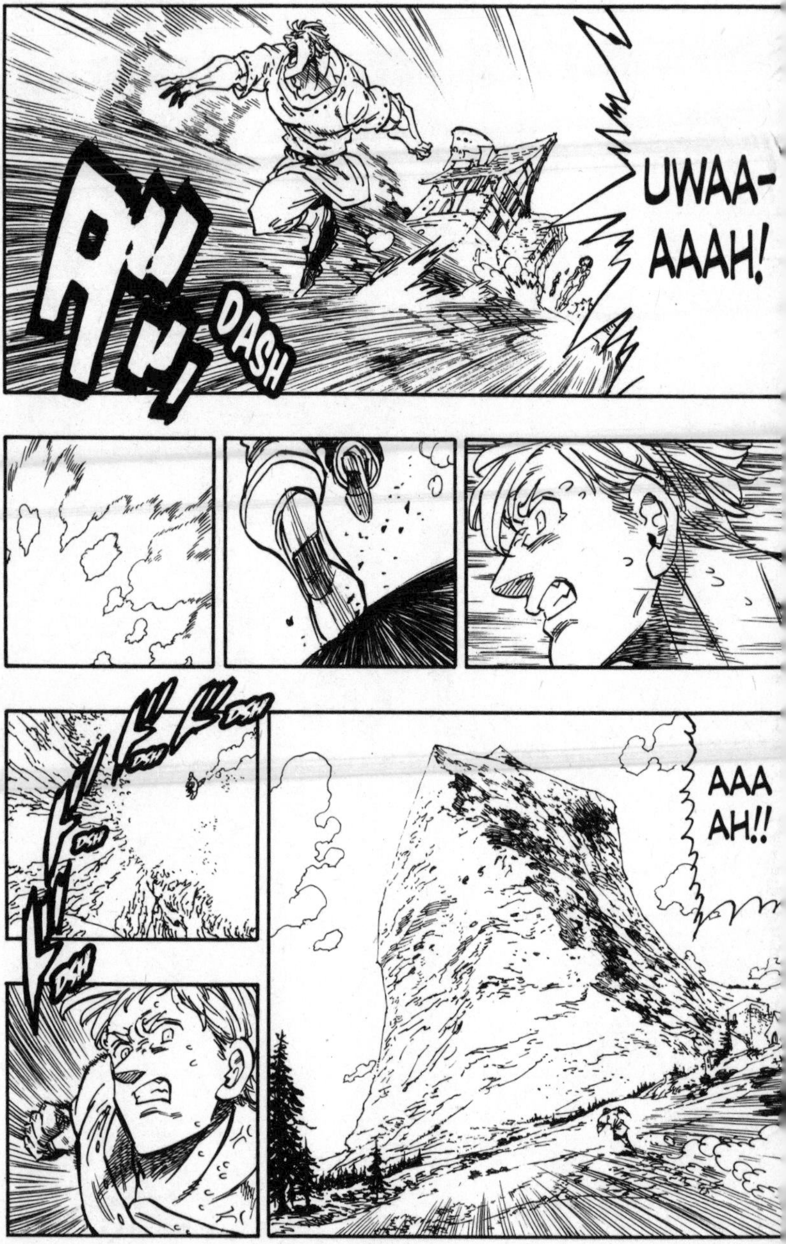
UWAA-AAAH!
DASH
AAA AH!!
DSH
DSH
DSH
DSH

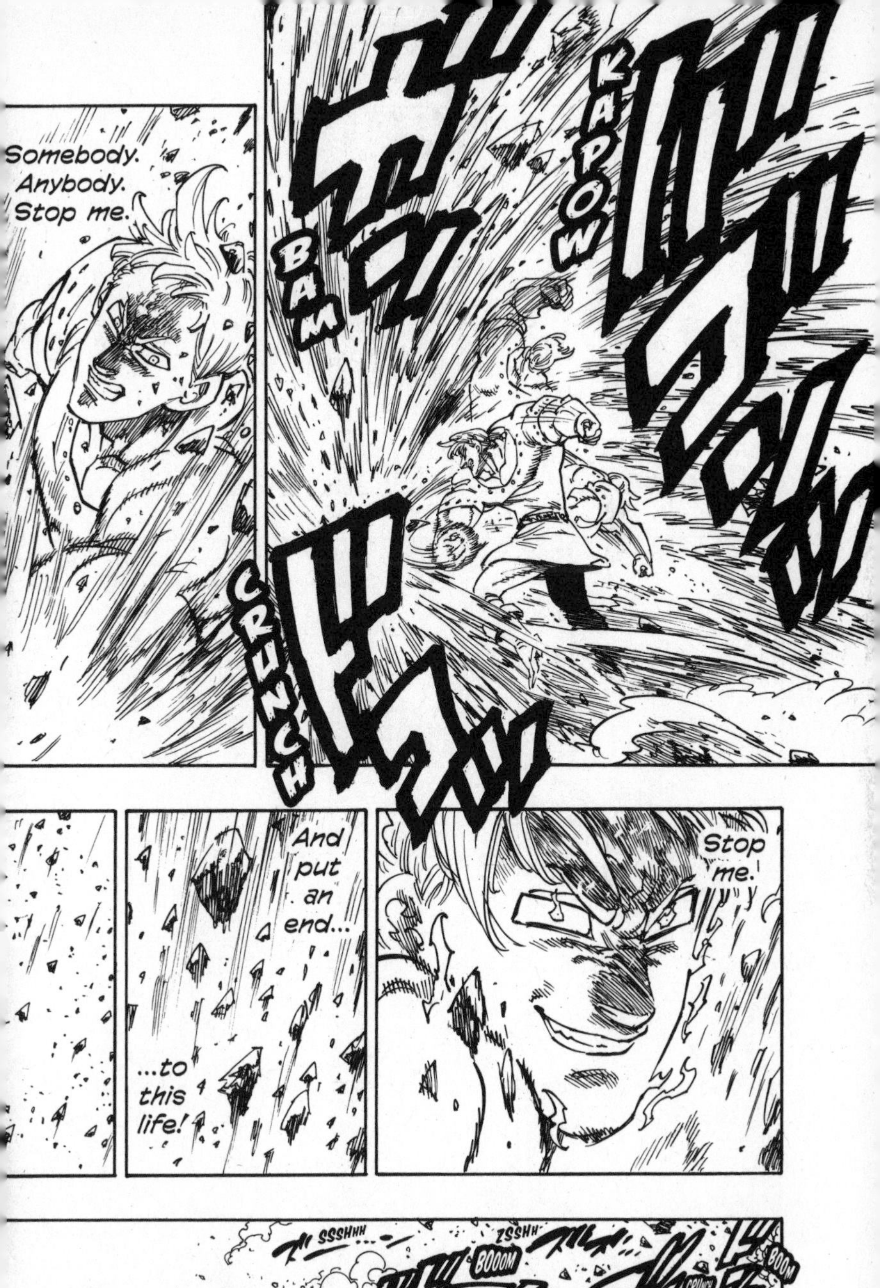
KAPOW
BAM
CRUNCH
Somebody. Anybody. Stop me.
Stop me.
And put an end...
...to this life!
BOOM
ZSSHH
SSSHHH
BOOOM
CRUNCH
SHAM
CRUMBLE
CRUMBLE

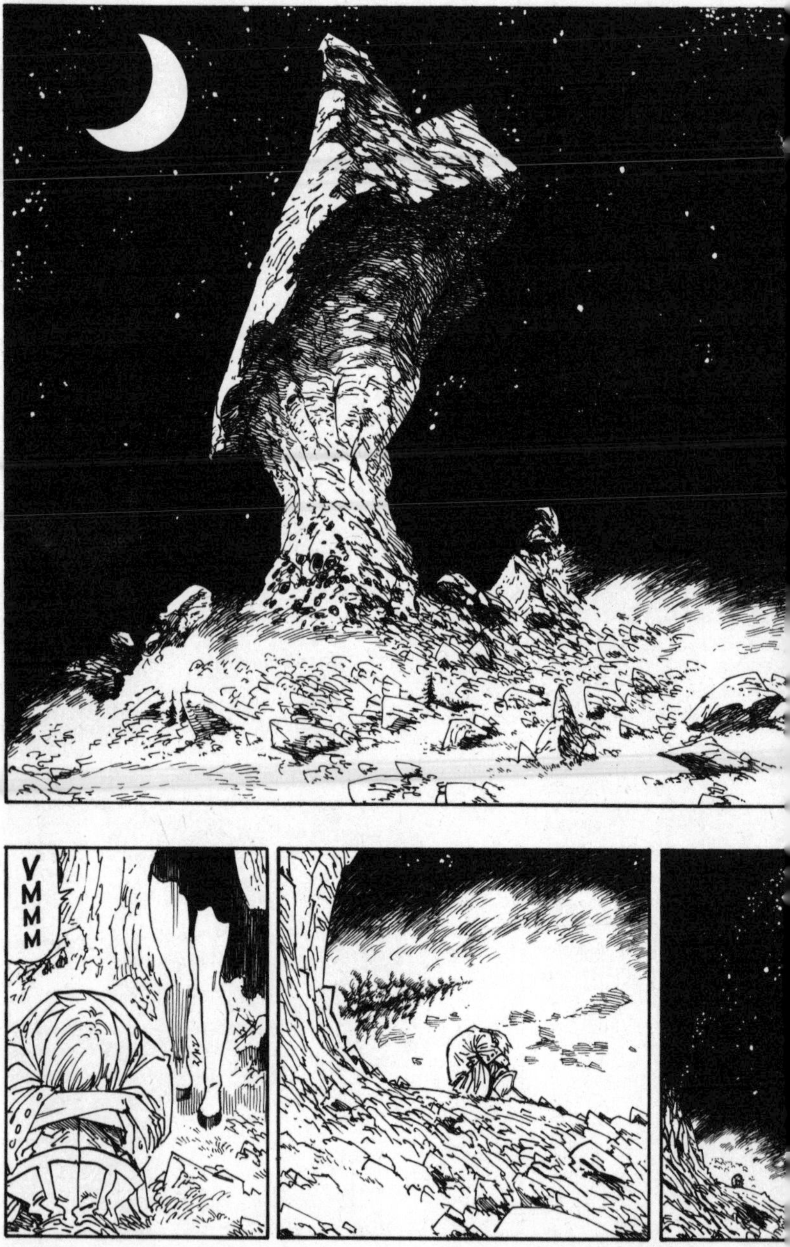
VMMM

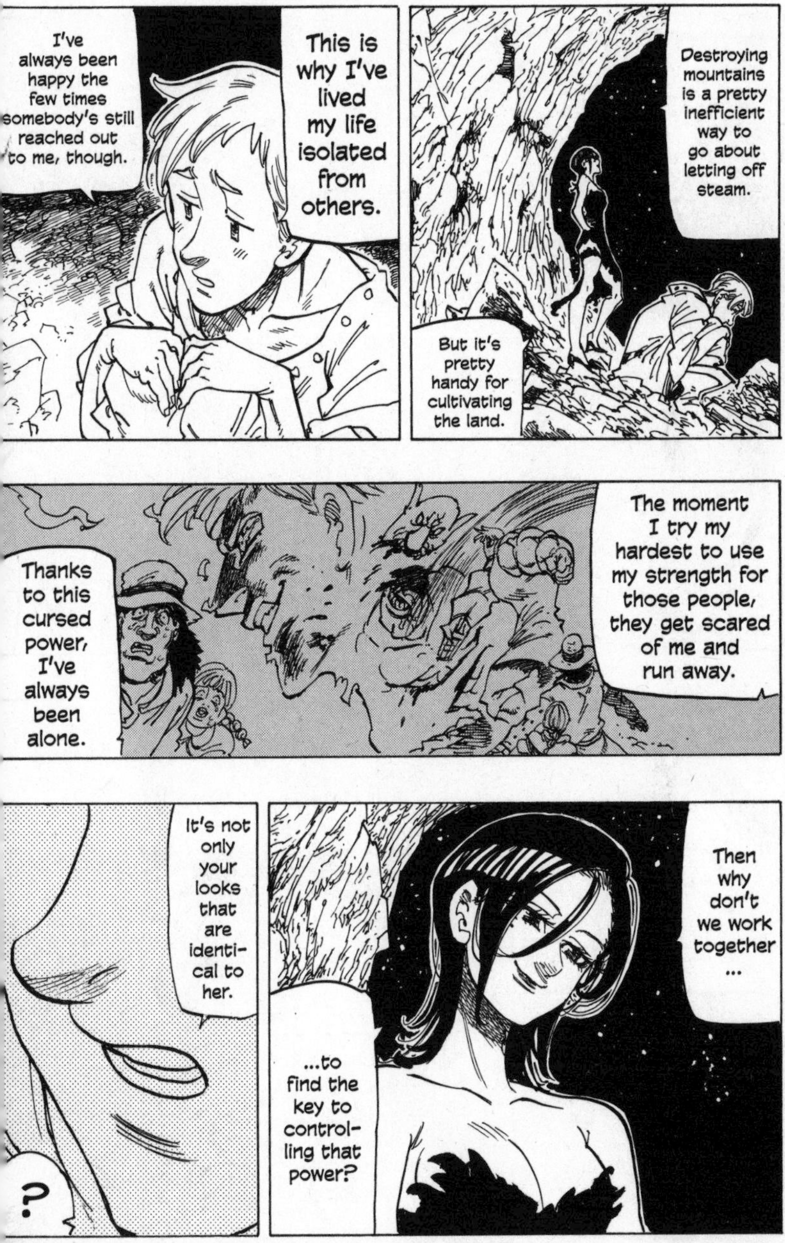
Destroying mountains is a pretty inefficient way to go about letting off steam.
But it's pretty handy for cultivating the land.
This is why I've lived my life isolated from others.
I've always been happy the few times somebody's still reached out to me, though.
The moment I try my hardest to use my strength for those people, they get scared of me and run away.
Thanks to this cursed power, I've always been alone.
Then why don't we work together...
...to find the key to controlling that power?
It's not only your looks that are identical to her.
?

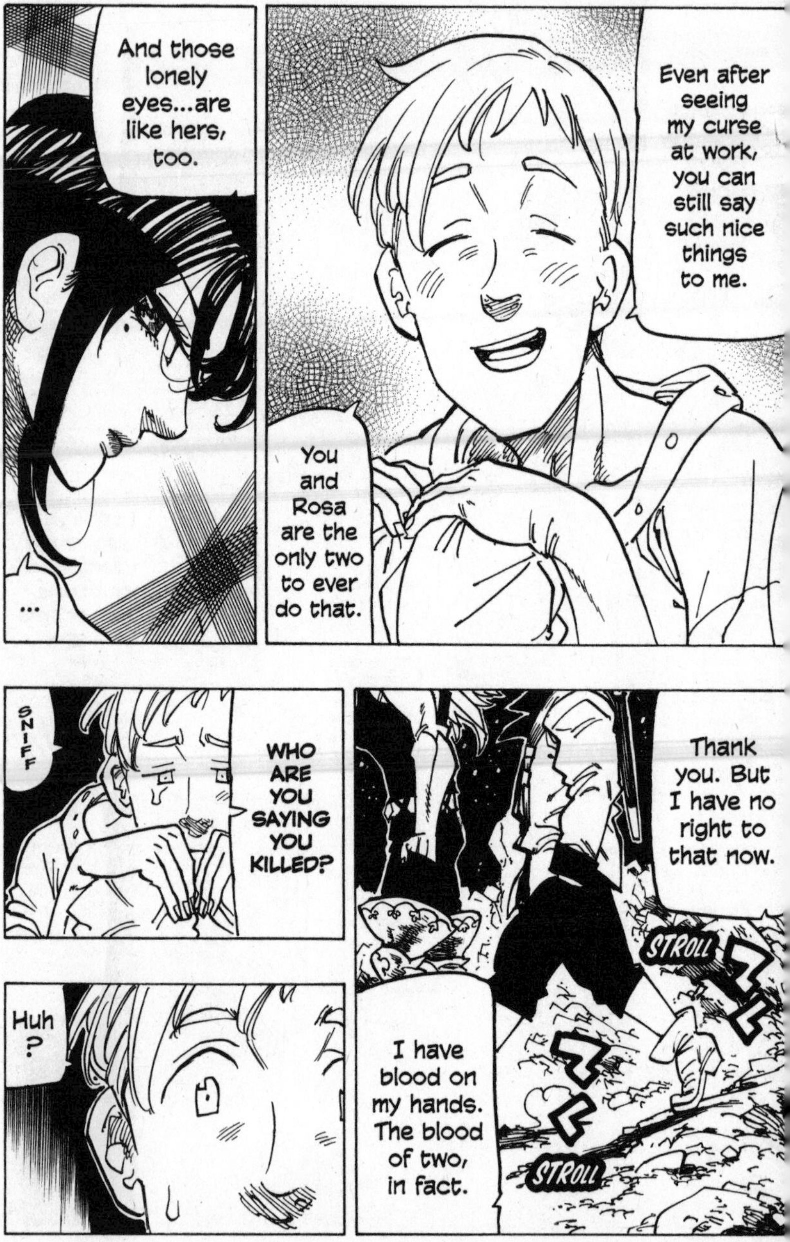
Even after seeing my curse at work, you can still say such nice things to me.
You and Rosa are the only two to ever do that.
And those lonely eyes...are like hers, too.
...
Thank you. But I have no right to that now.
STROLL
I have blood on my hands. The blood of two, in fact.
STROLL
SNIFF
WHO ARE YOU SAYING YOU KILLED?
Huh?

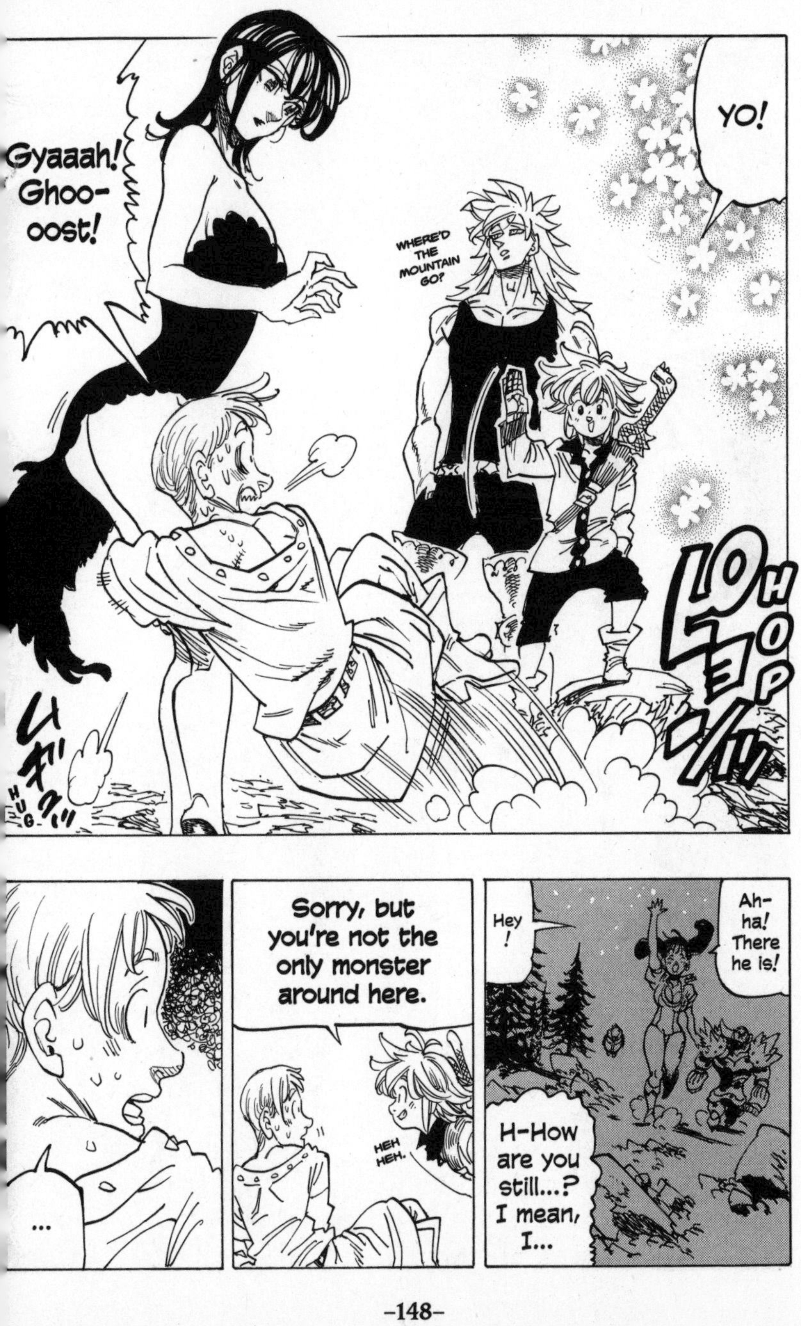
YO!
WHERE'D THE MOUNTAIN GO?
Gyaaah! Ghoo-oost!
HOP
HUG
Ah-ha! There he is!
Hey!
H-How are you still...? I mean, I...
Sorry, but you're not the only monster around here.
HEH HEH.
...

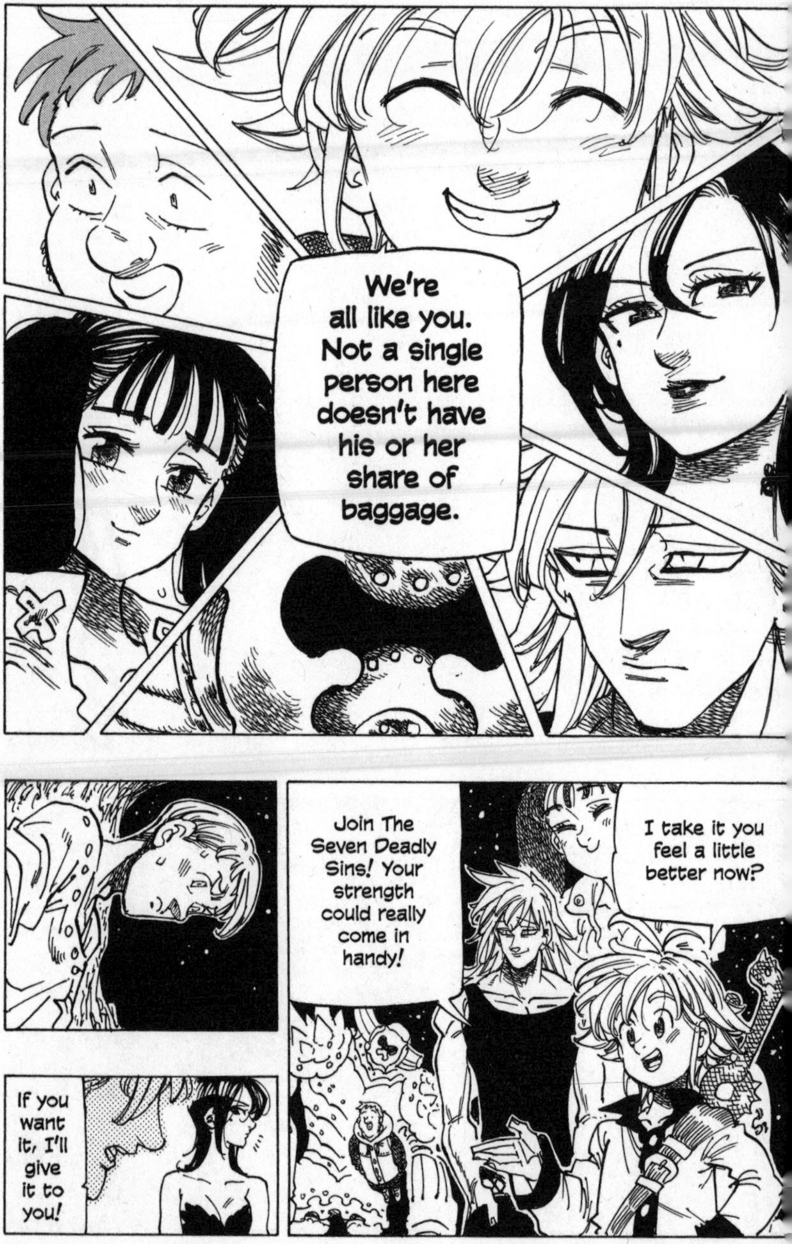

We're all like you. Not a single person here doesn't have his or her share of baggage.
I take it you feel a little better now?
Join The Seven Deadly Sins! Your strength could really come in handy!
If you want it, I'll give it to you!

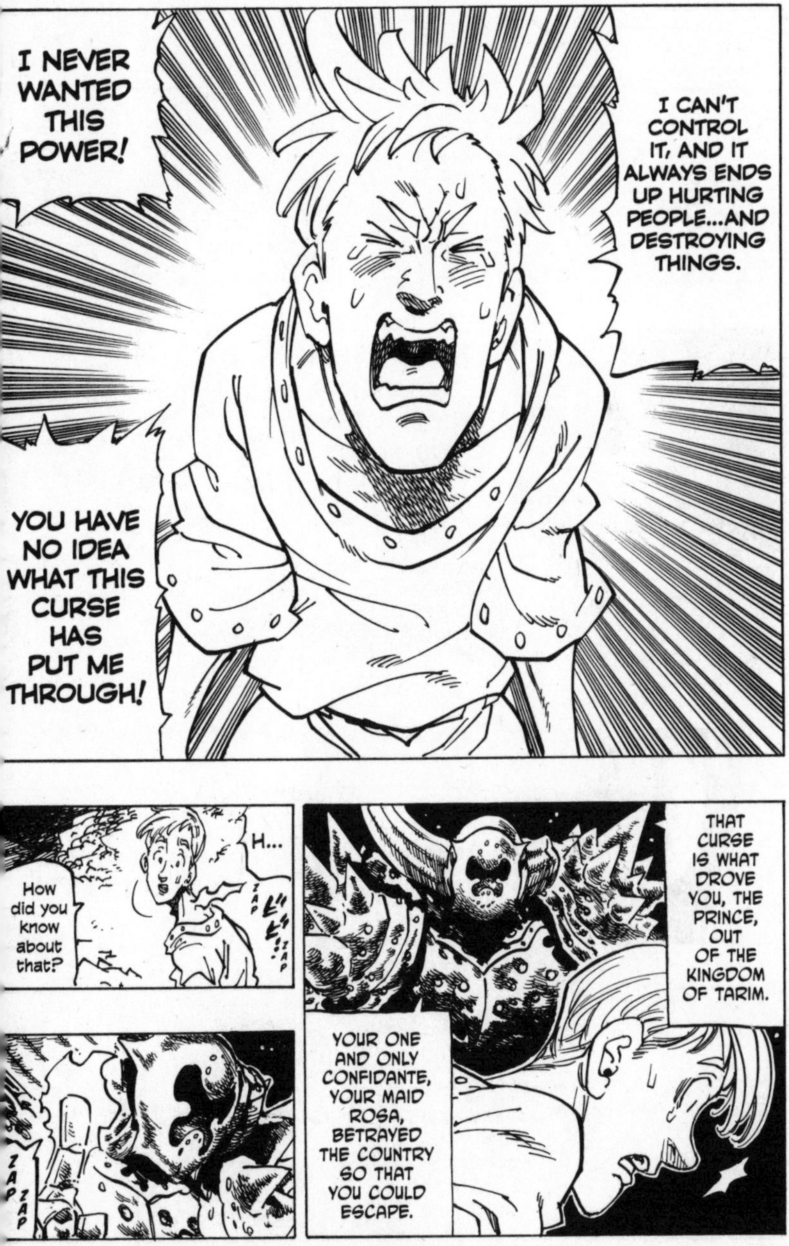
I CAN'T CONTROL IT, AND IT ALWAYS ENDS UP HURTING PEOPLE...AND DESTROYING THINGS.
I NEVER WANTED THIS POWER!
YOU HAVE NO IDEA WHAT THIS CURSE HAS PUT ME THROUGH!
THAT CURSE IS WHAT DROVE YOU, THE PRINCE, OUT OF THE KINGDOM OF TARIM.
YOUR ONE AND ONLY CONFIDANTE, YOUR MAID ROSA, BETRAYED THE COUNTRY SO THAT YOU COULD ESCAPE.
H...
ZAP
ZAP
How did you know about that?
ZAP
ZAP

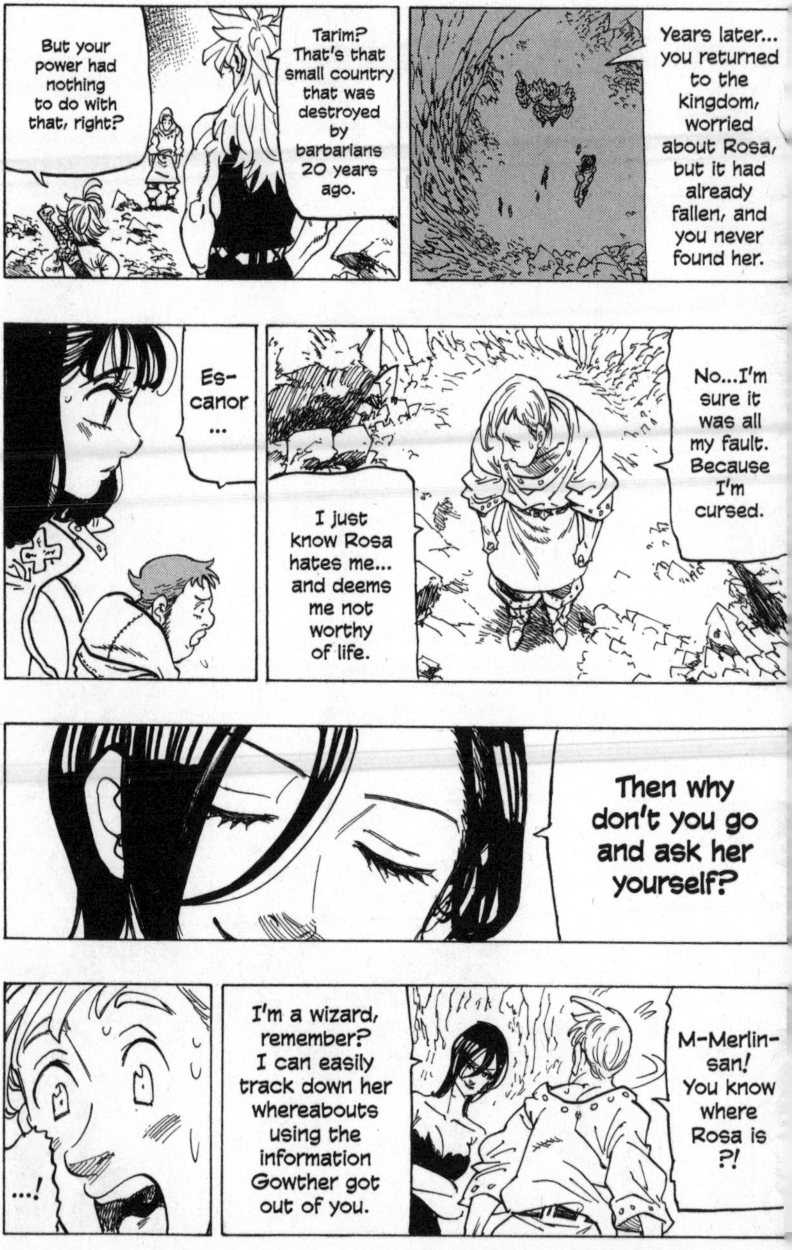
Years later... you returned to the kingdom, worried about Rosa, but it had already fallen, and you never found her.
Tarim? That's that small country that was destroyed by barbarians 20 years ago.
But your power had nothing to do with that, right?
No...I'm sure it was all my fault. Because I'm cursed.
I just know Rosa hates me... and deems me not worthy of life.
Es-canor ...
Then why don't you go and ask her yourself?
M-Merlin-san! You know where Rosa is ?!
I'm a wizard, remember? I can easily track down her whereabouts using the information Gowther got out of you.
...!

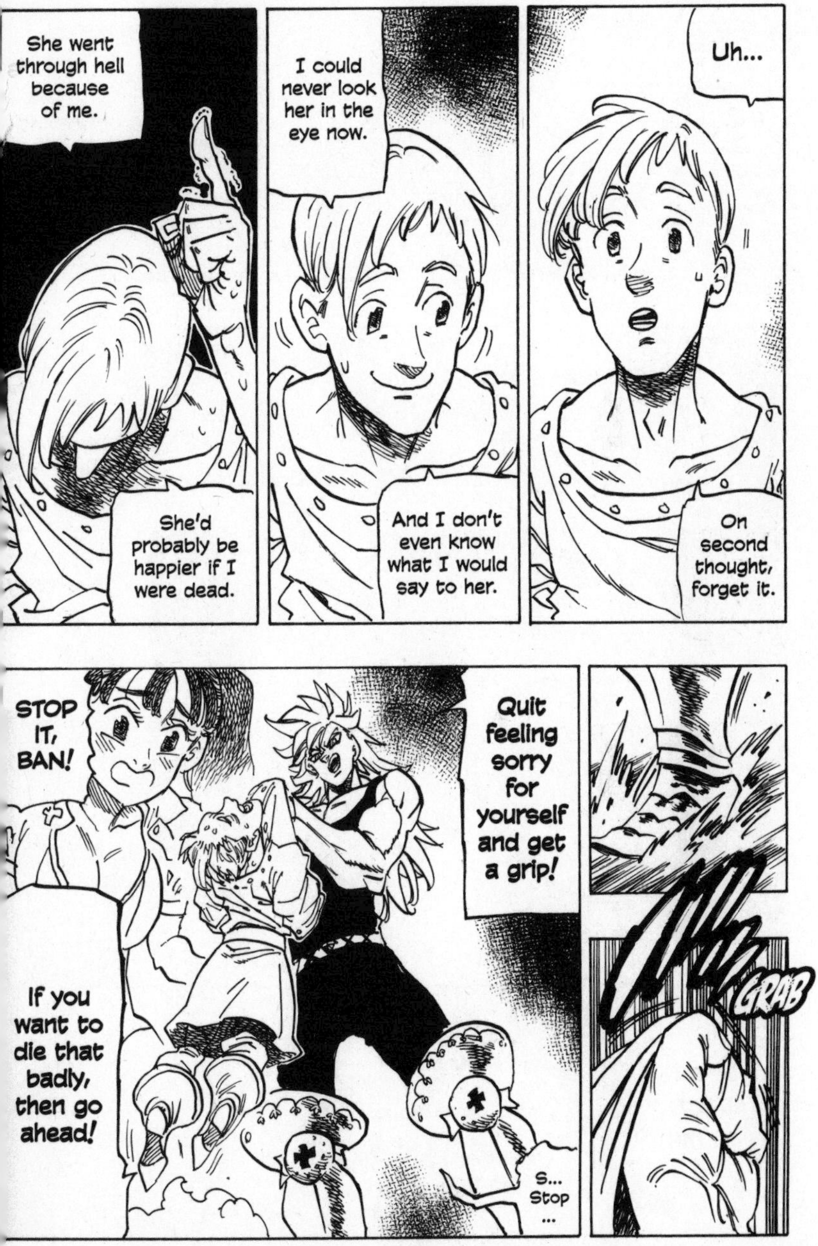
Uh...
On second thought, forget it.
I could never look her in the eye now.
And I don't even know what I would say to her.
She went through hell because of me.
She'd probably be happier if I were dead.
GRAB
Quit feeling sorry for yourself and get a grip!
STOP IT, BAN!
If you want to die that badly, then go ahead!
S... Stop ...

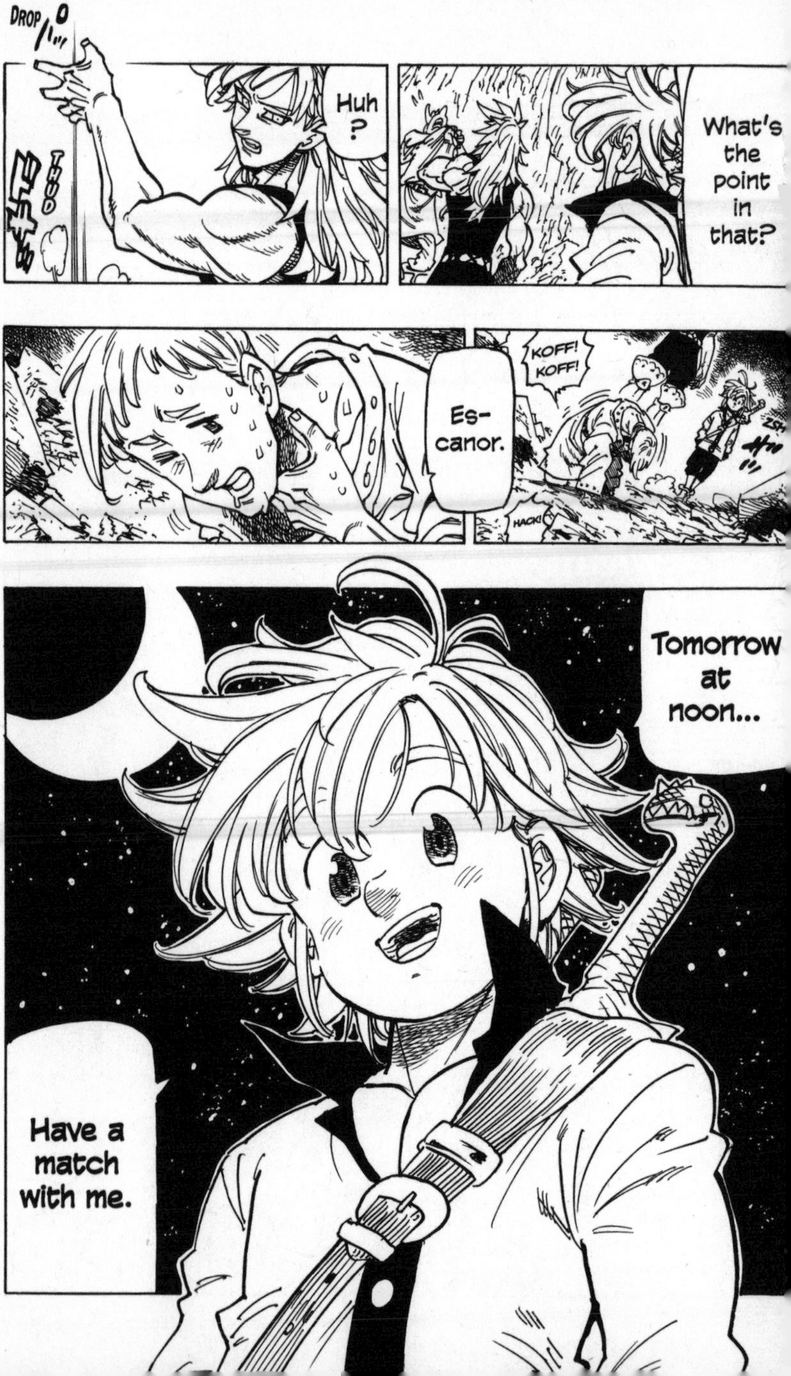
What's the point in that?
Huh?
DROP
THUD
KOFF! KOFF!
ZSH
HACK!
Es-canor.
Tomorrow at noon...
Have a match with me.

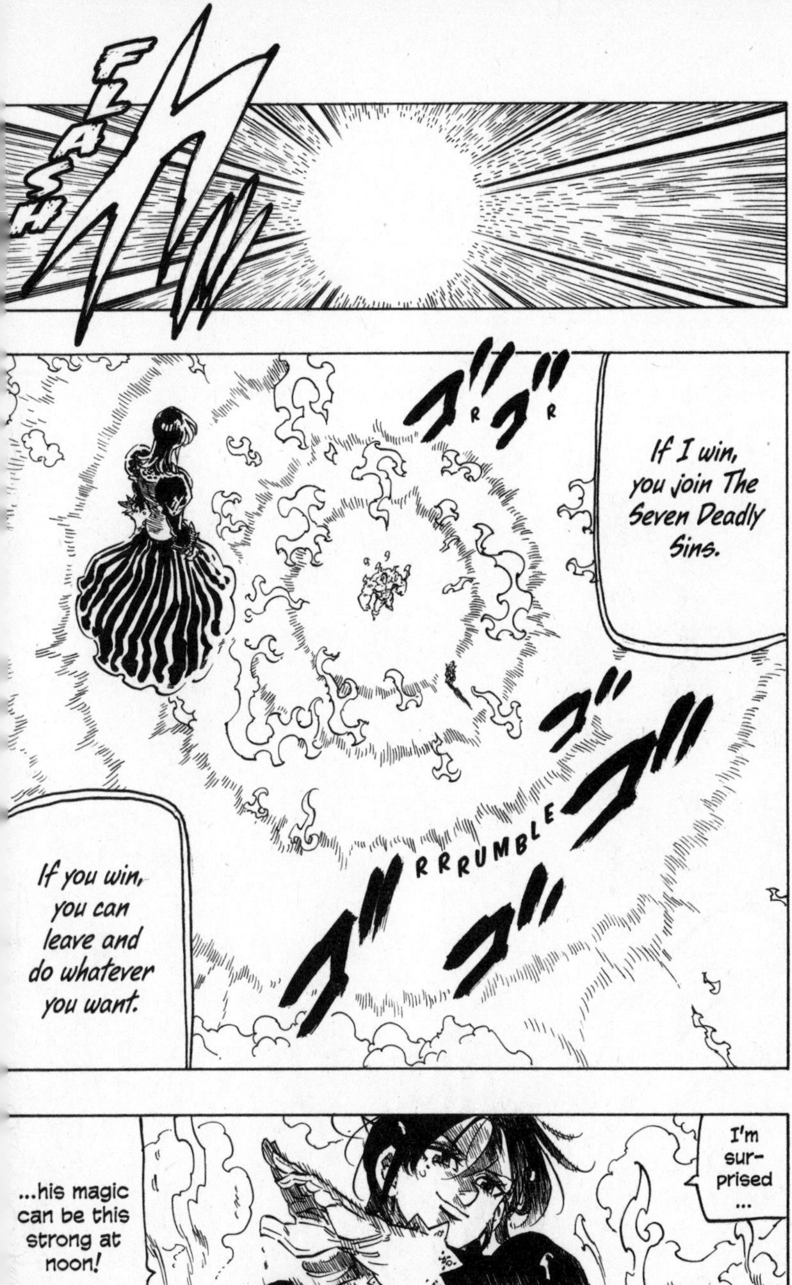
FLASH
If I win, you join The Seven Deadly Sins.
RRRUMBLE
If you win, you can leave and do whatever you want.
I'm sur-prised...
...his magic can be this strong at noon!

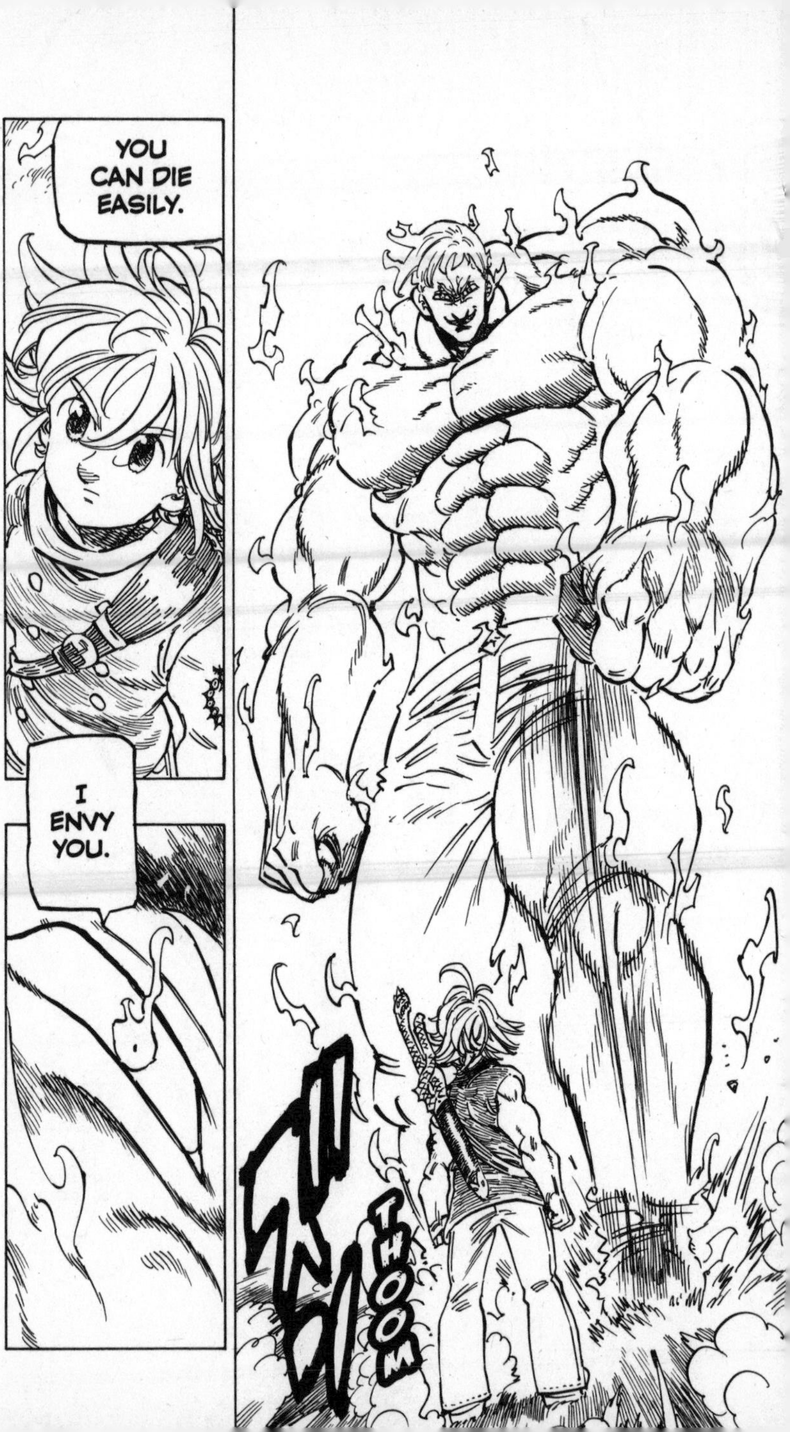
THOOM
YOU CAN DIE EASILY.
I ENVY YOU.

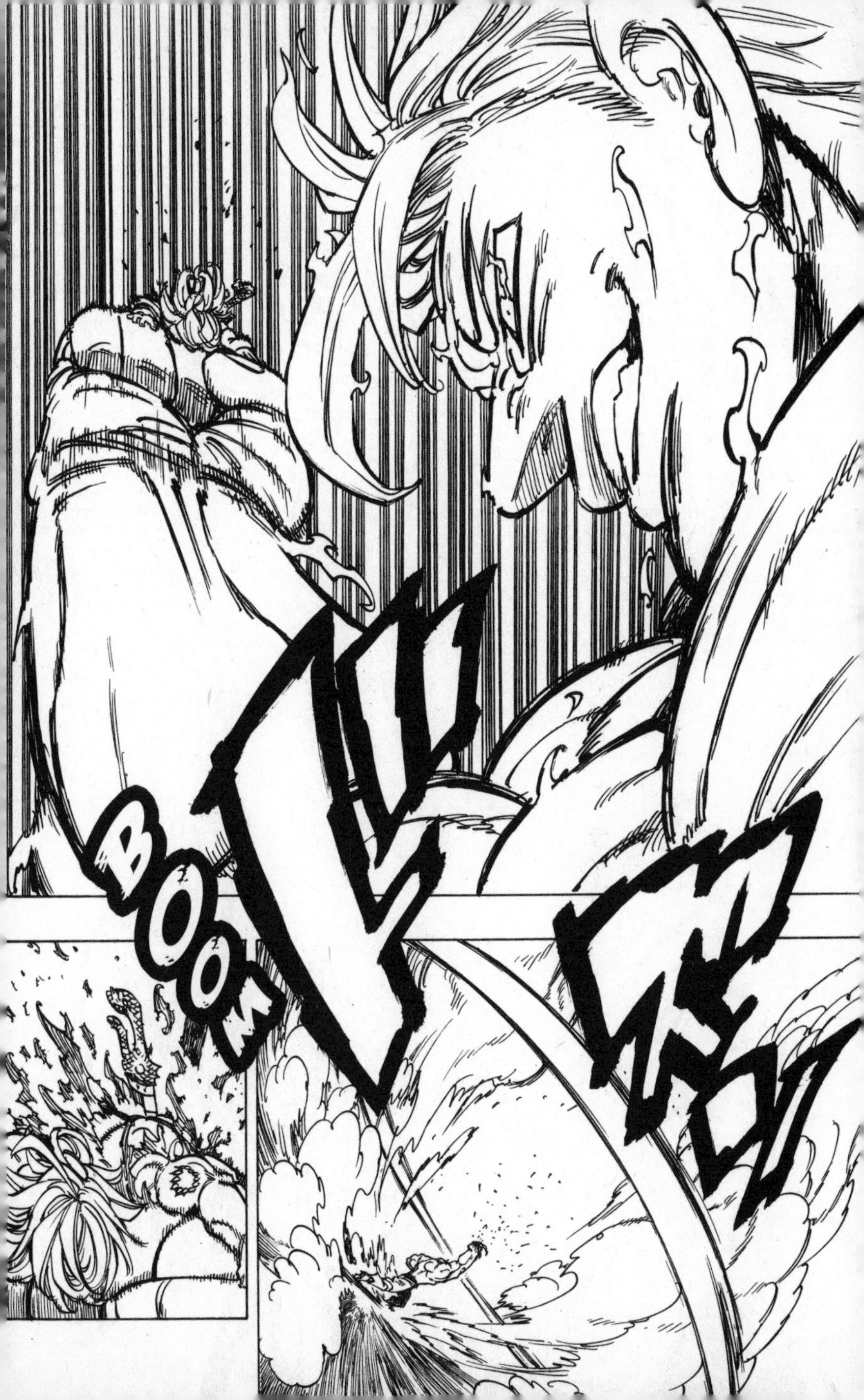
BOOM

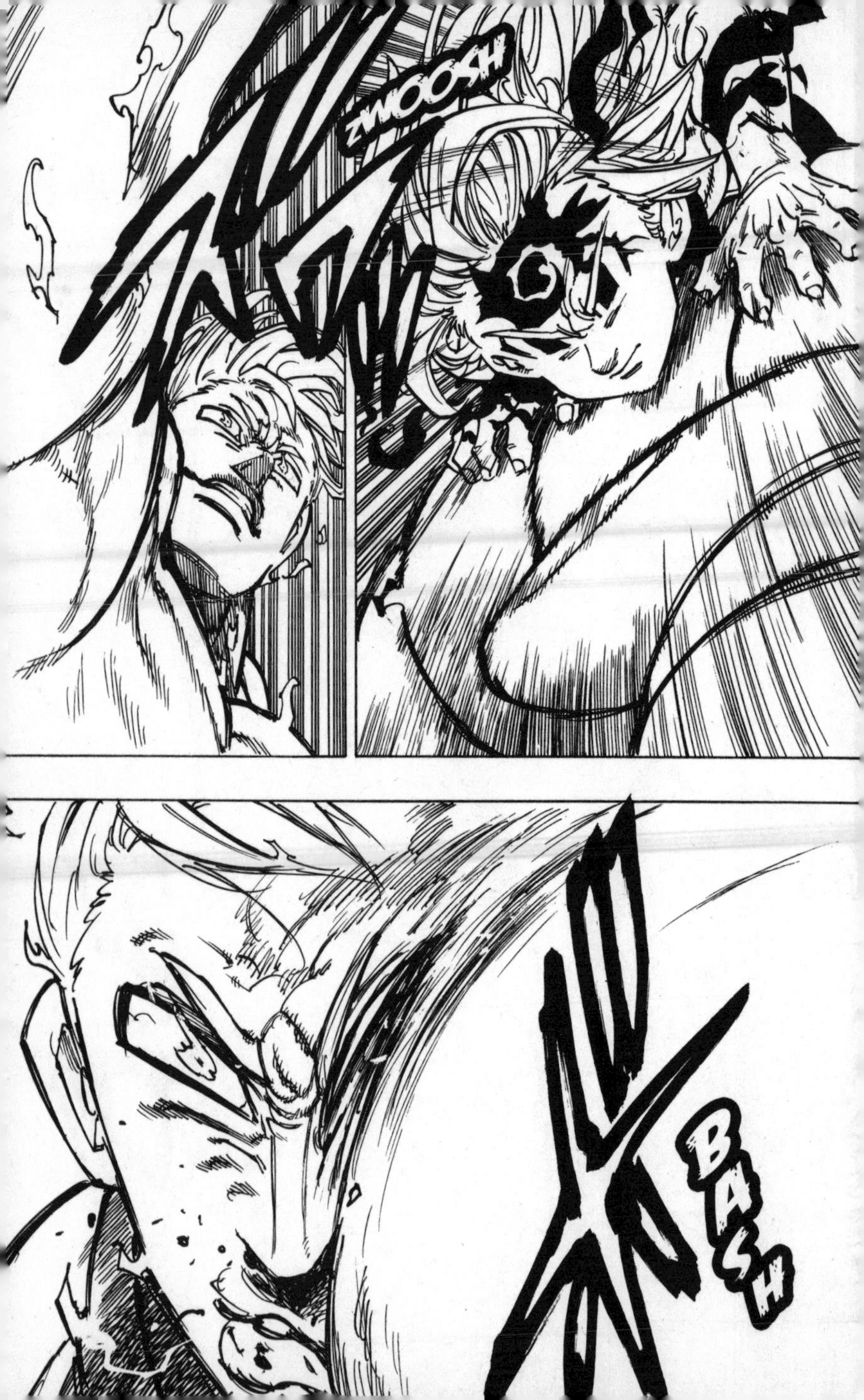
ZWOOSH
BASH

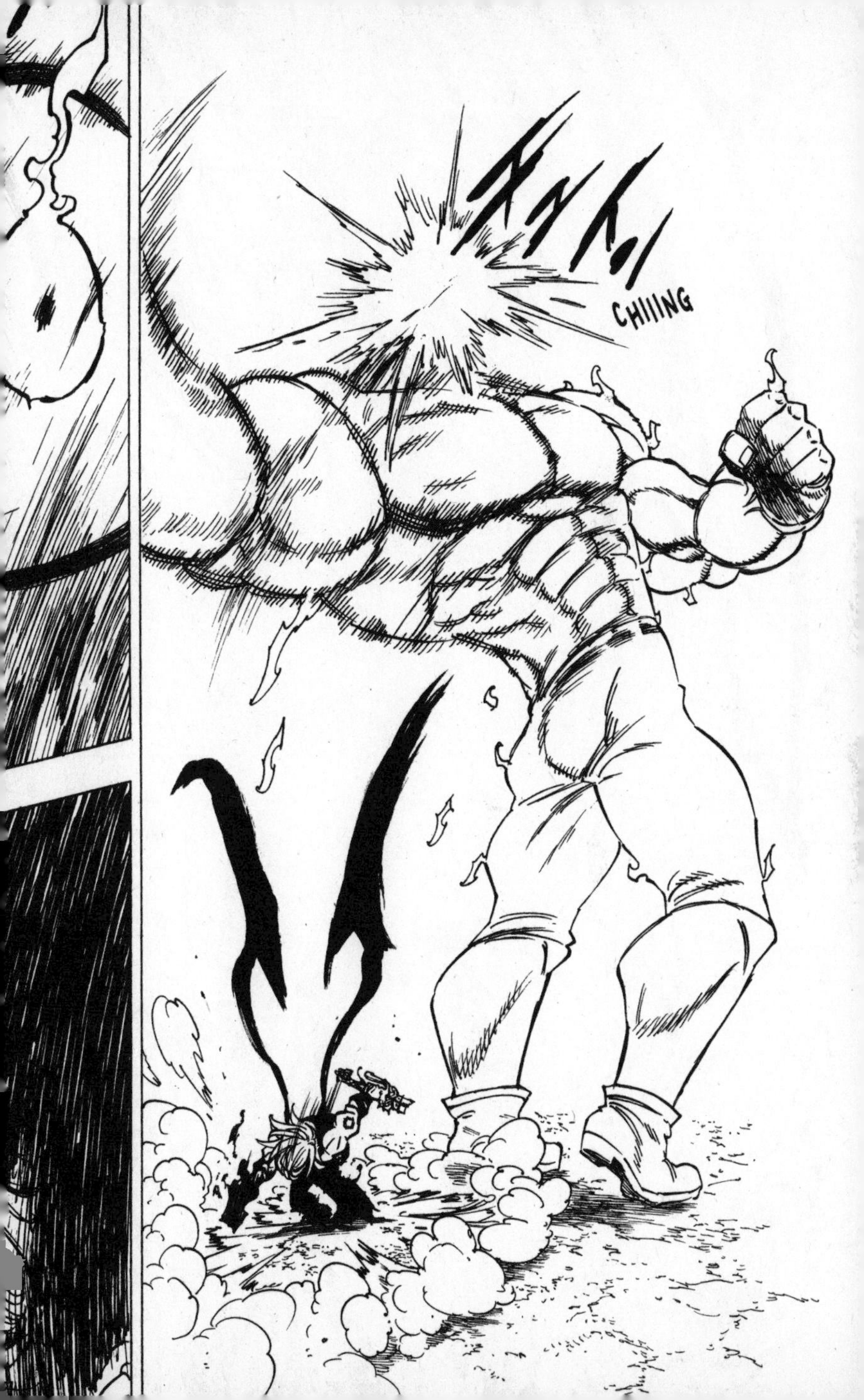
CHIIING

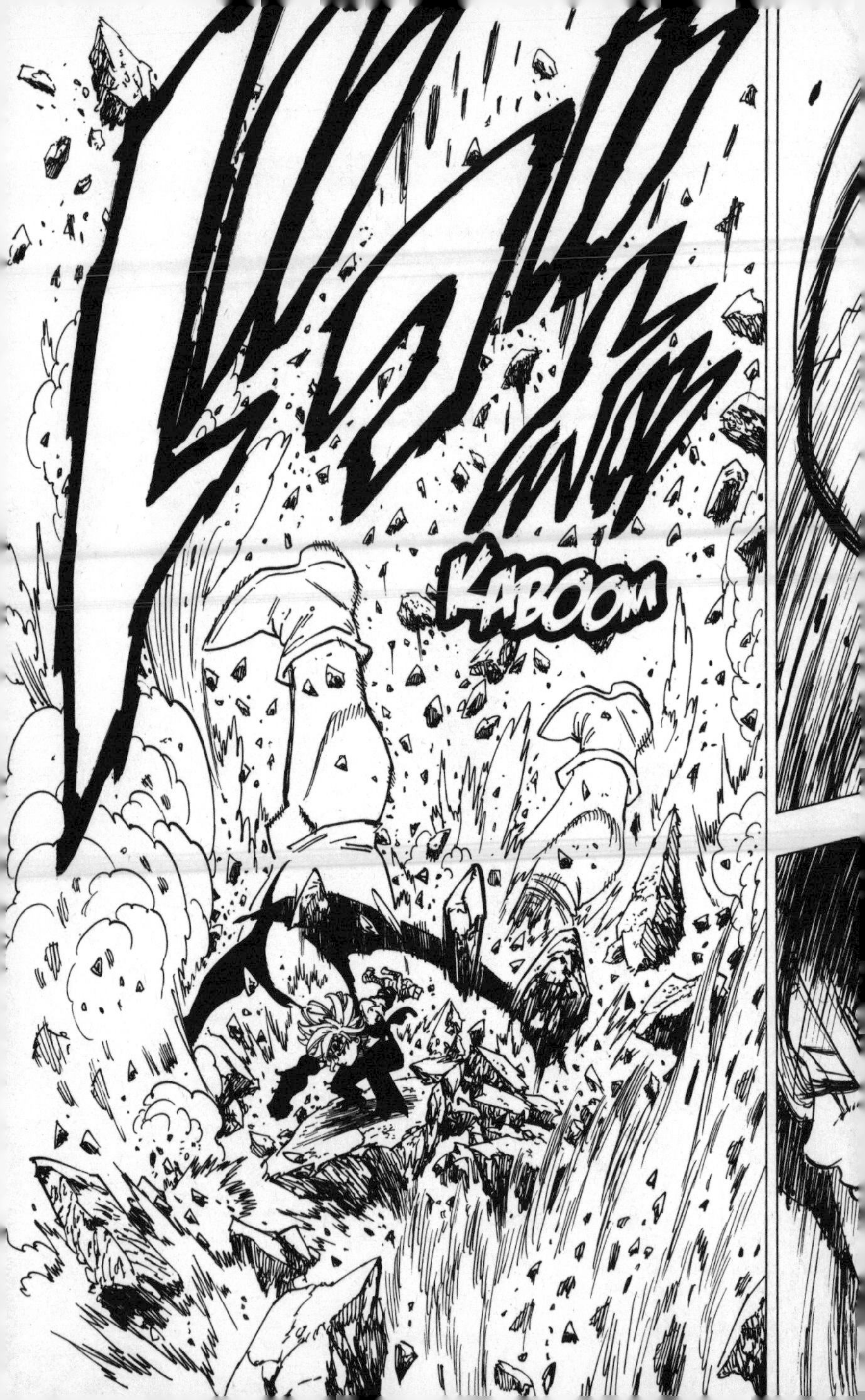
KABOOM

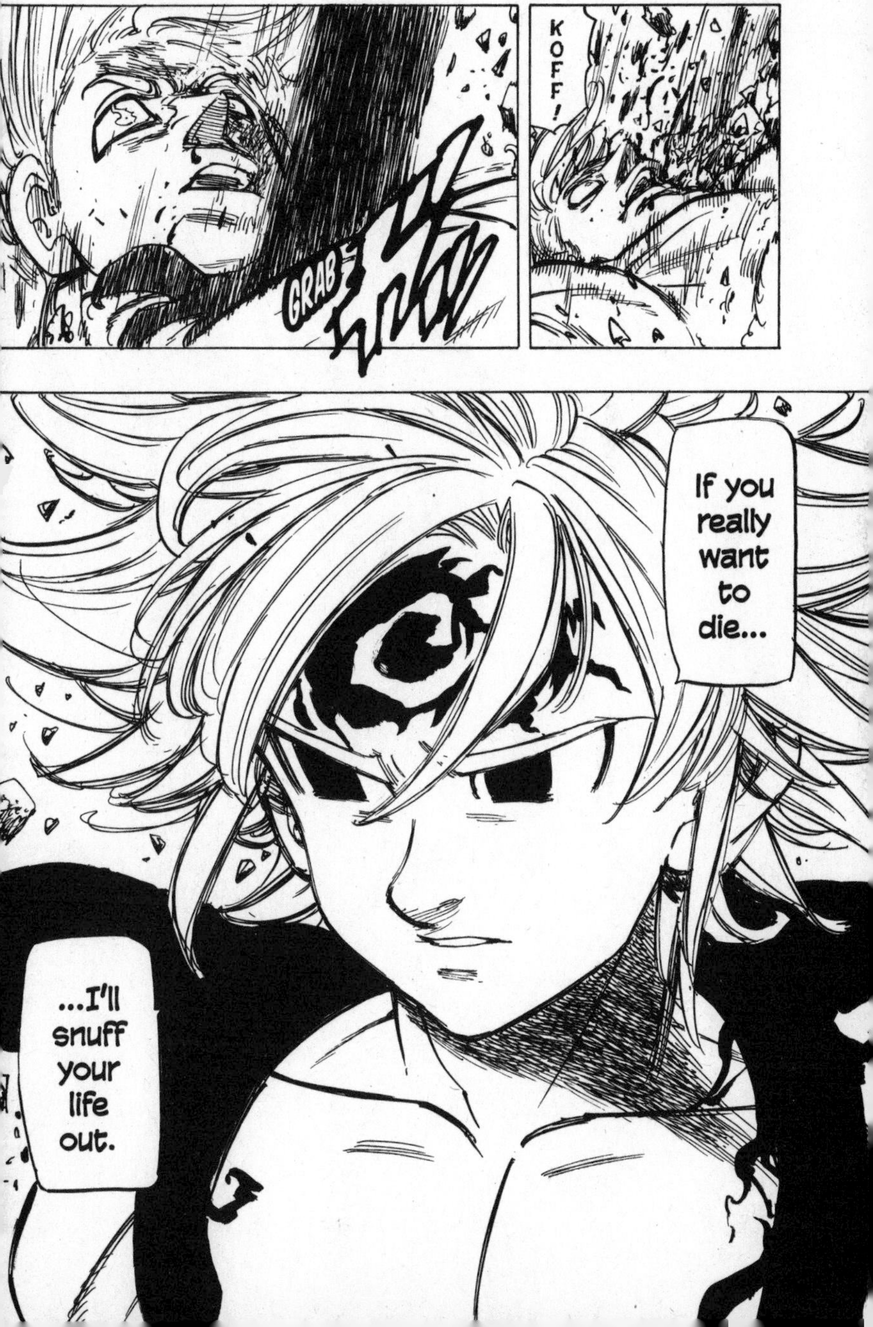
KOFF!
GRAB
If you really want to die...
...I'll snuff your life out.

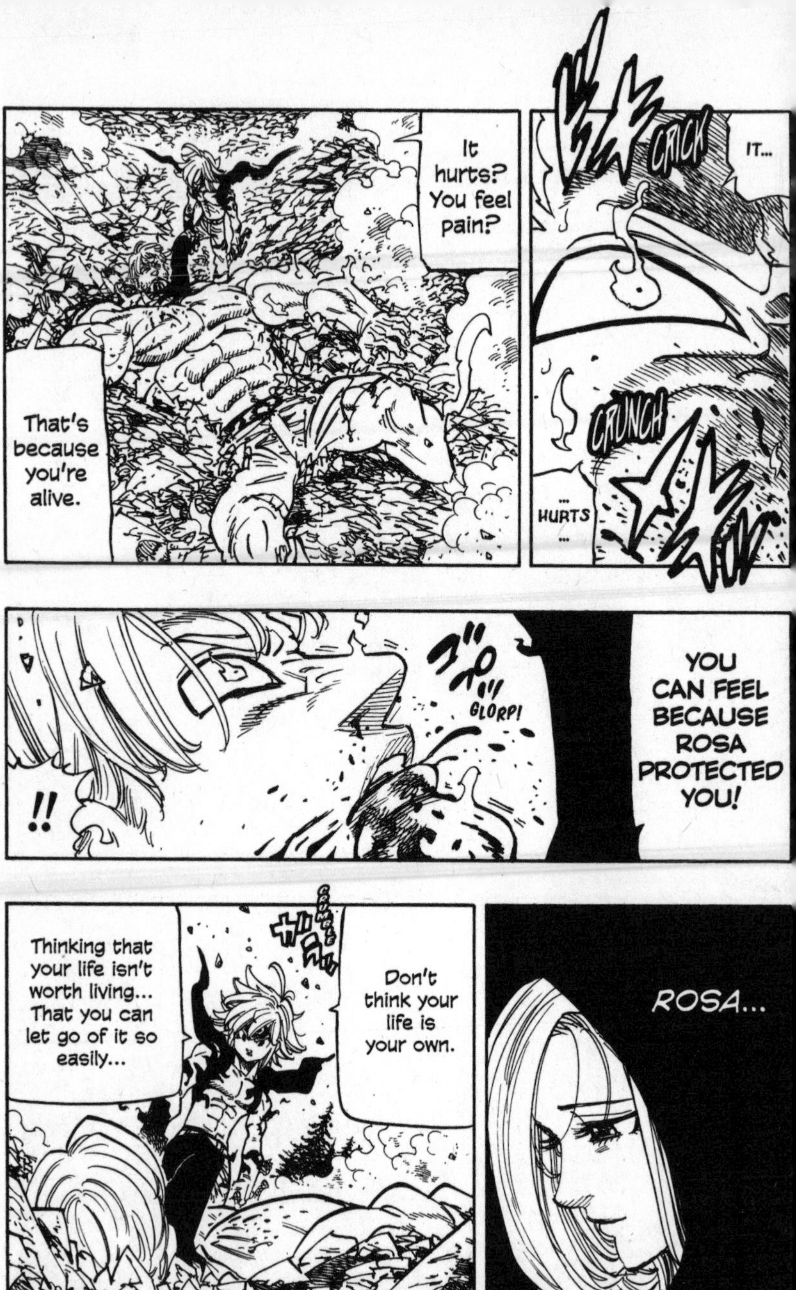
IT...
CRICK
CRUNCH
...HURTS...
It hurts? You feel pain?
That's because you're alive.
YOU CAN FEEL BECAUSE ROSA PROTECTED YOU!
GLORP!
!!
ROSA...
CRUMBLE
Don't think your life is your own.
Thinking that your life isn't worth living... That you can let go of it so easily...

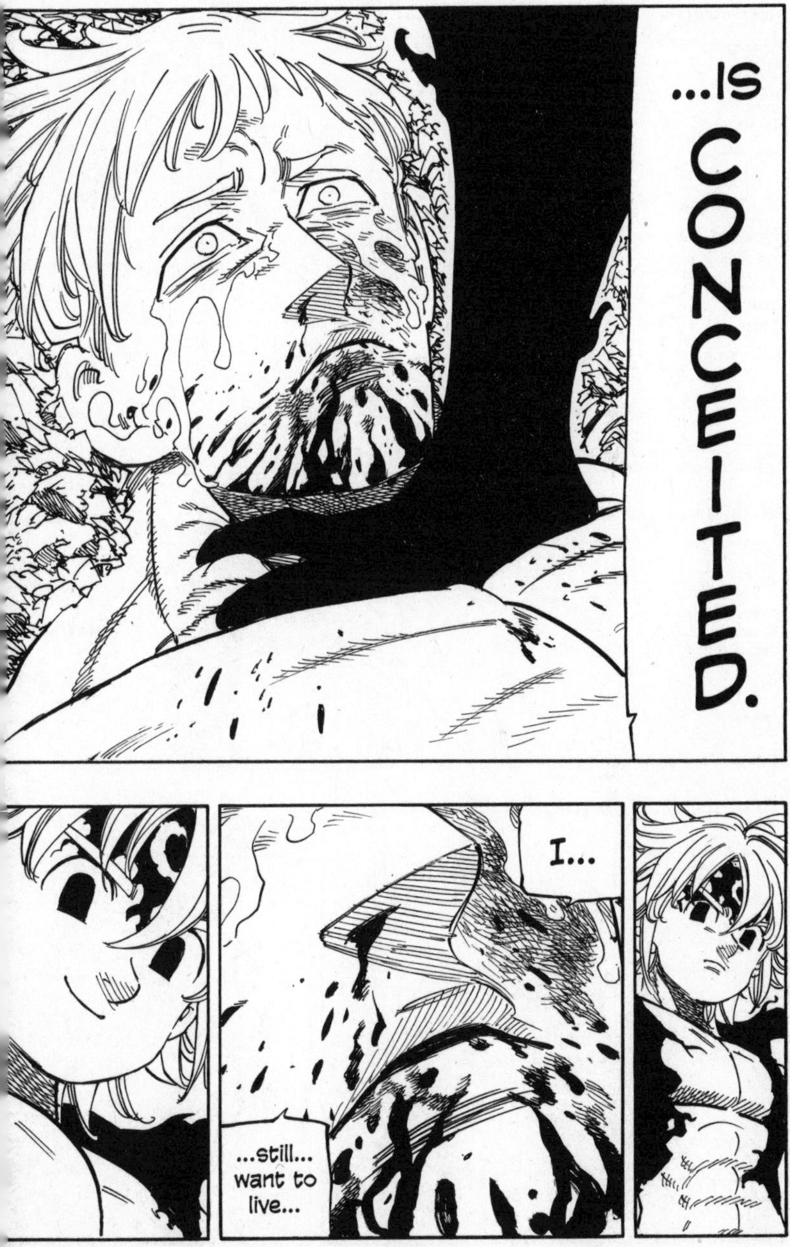
...IS CONCEITED.
I...
...still... want to live...

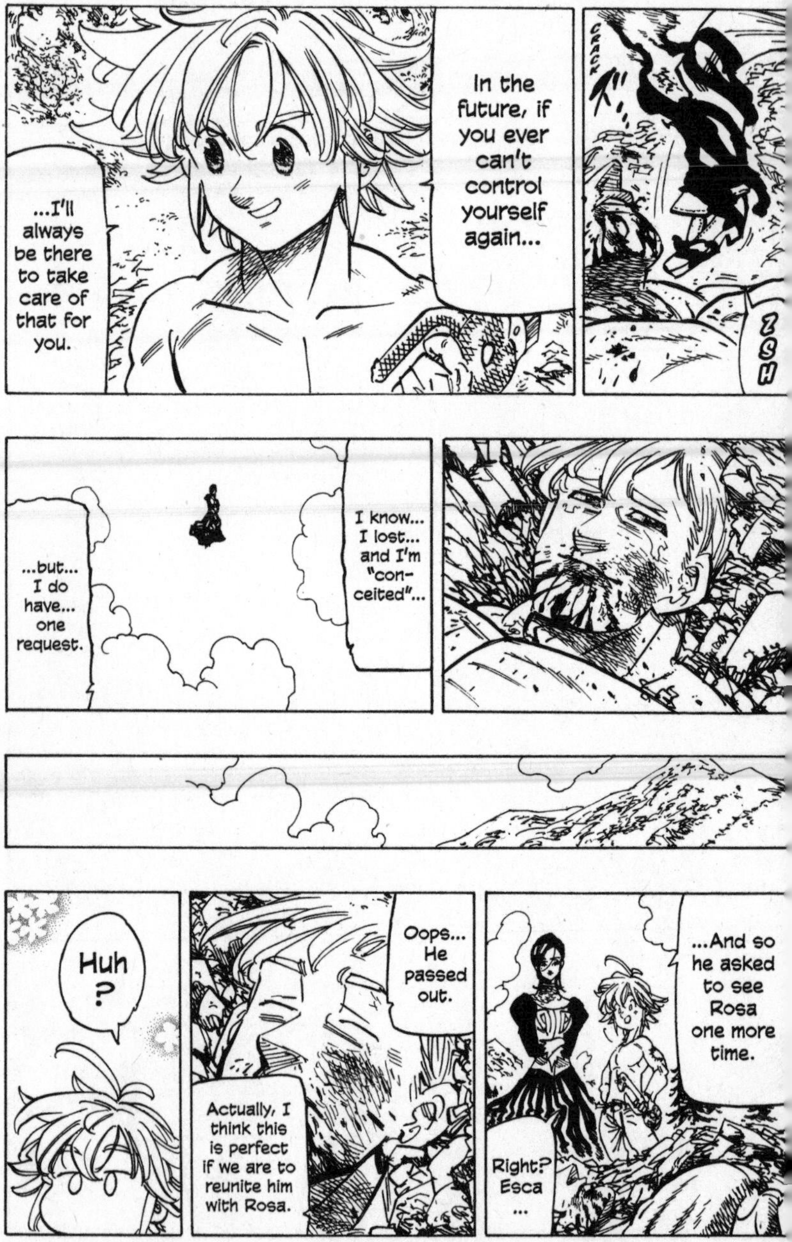
CRACK
ZSH
In the future, if you ever can't control yourself again...
...I'll always be there to take care of that for you.
I know... I lost... and I'm "conceited"...
...but... I do have... one request.
...And so he asked to see Rosa one more time.
Right? Esca ...
Oops... He passed out.
Actually, I think this is perfect if we are to reunite him with Rosa.
Huh ?

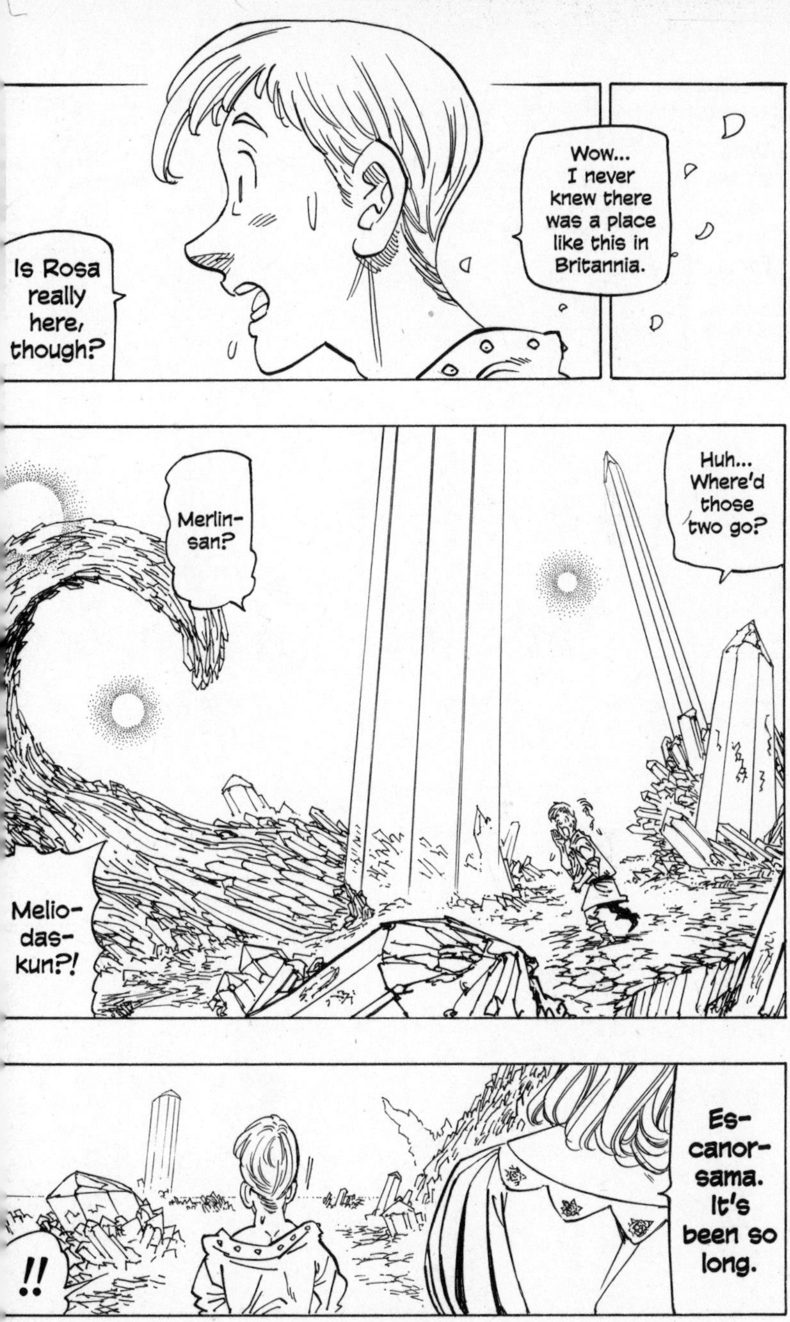
Wow... I never knew there was a place like this in Britannia.
Is Rosa really here, though?
Huh... Where'd those two go?
Merlin-san?
Melio-das-kun?!
Es-canor-sama. It's been so long.
!!

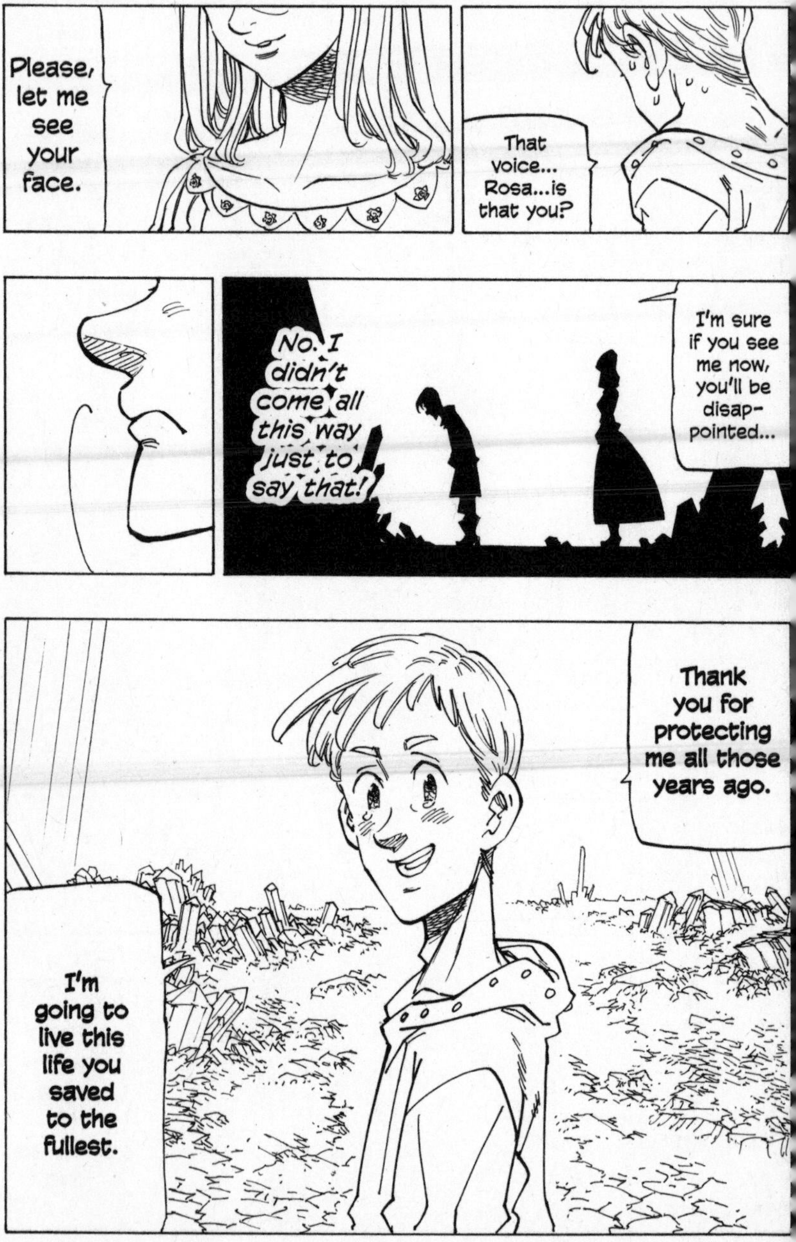
That voice... Rosa...is that you?
Please, let me see your face.
I'm sure if you see me now, you'll be disap-pointed...
No. I didn't come all this way just to say that!
Thank you for protecting me all those years ago.
I'm going to live this life you saved to the fullest.

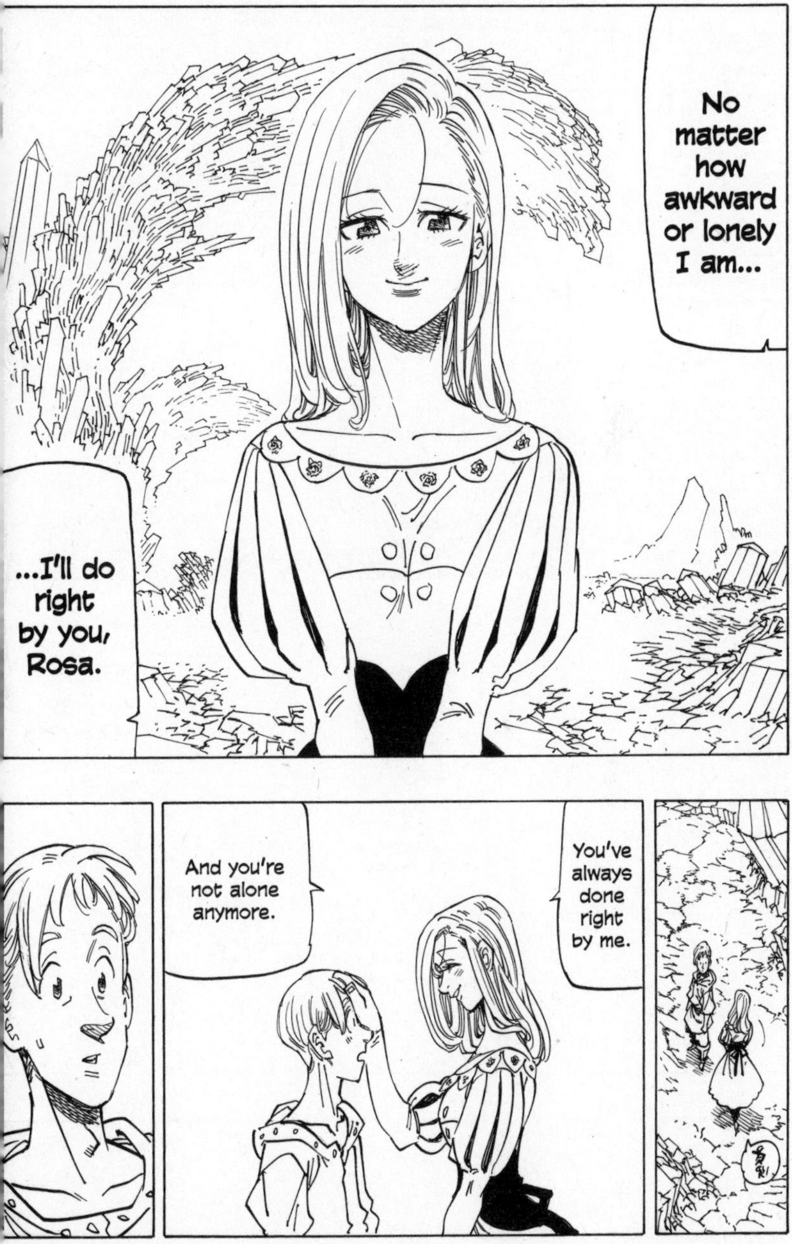
No matter how awkward or lonely I am...
...I'll do right by you, Rosa.
You've always done right by me.
And you're not alone anymore.

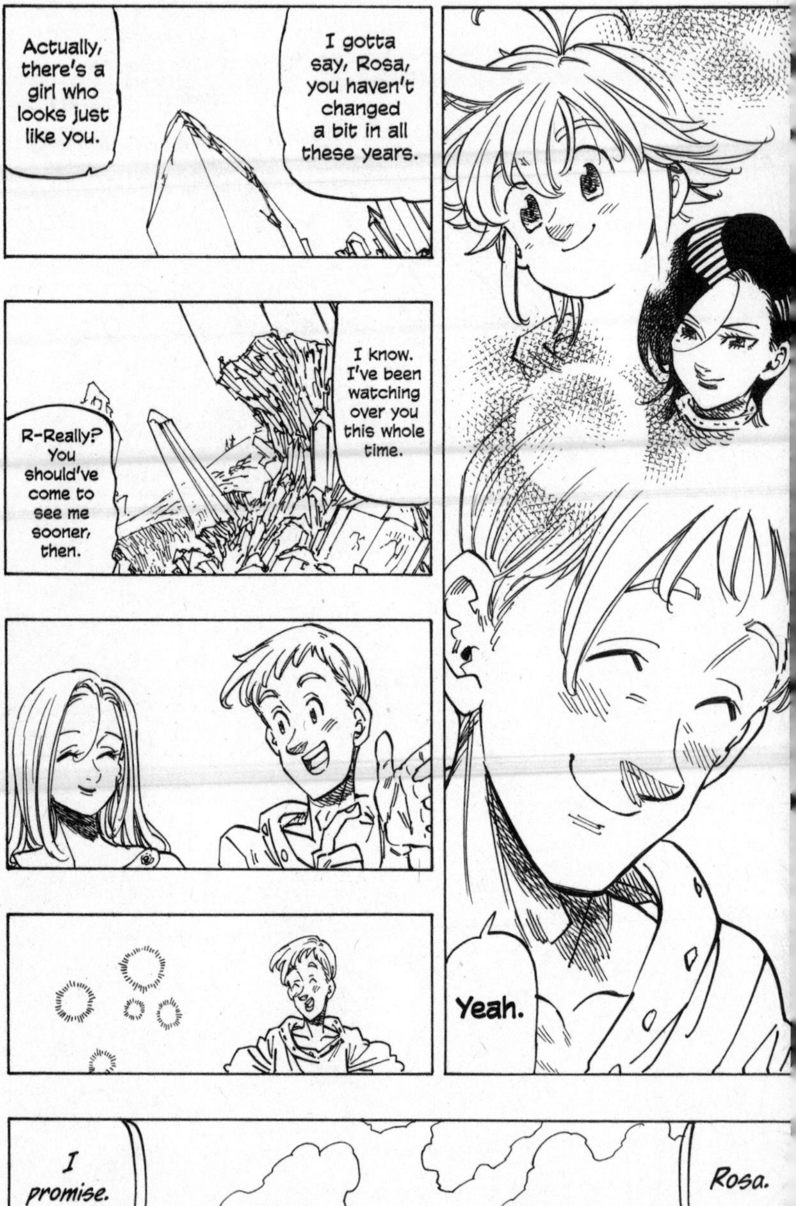
Yeah.
I gotta say, Rosa, you haven't changed a bit in all these years.
Actually, there's a girl who looks just like you.
I know. I've been watching over you this whole time.
R-Really? You should've come to see me sooner, then.
Rosa.
I promise.

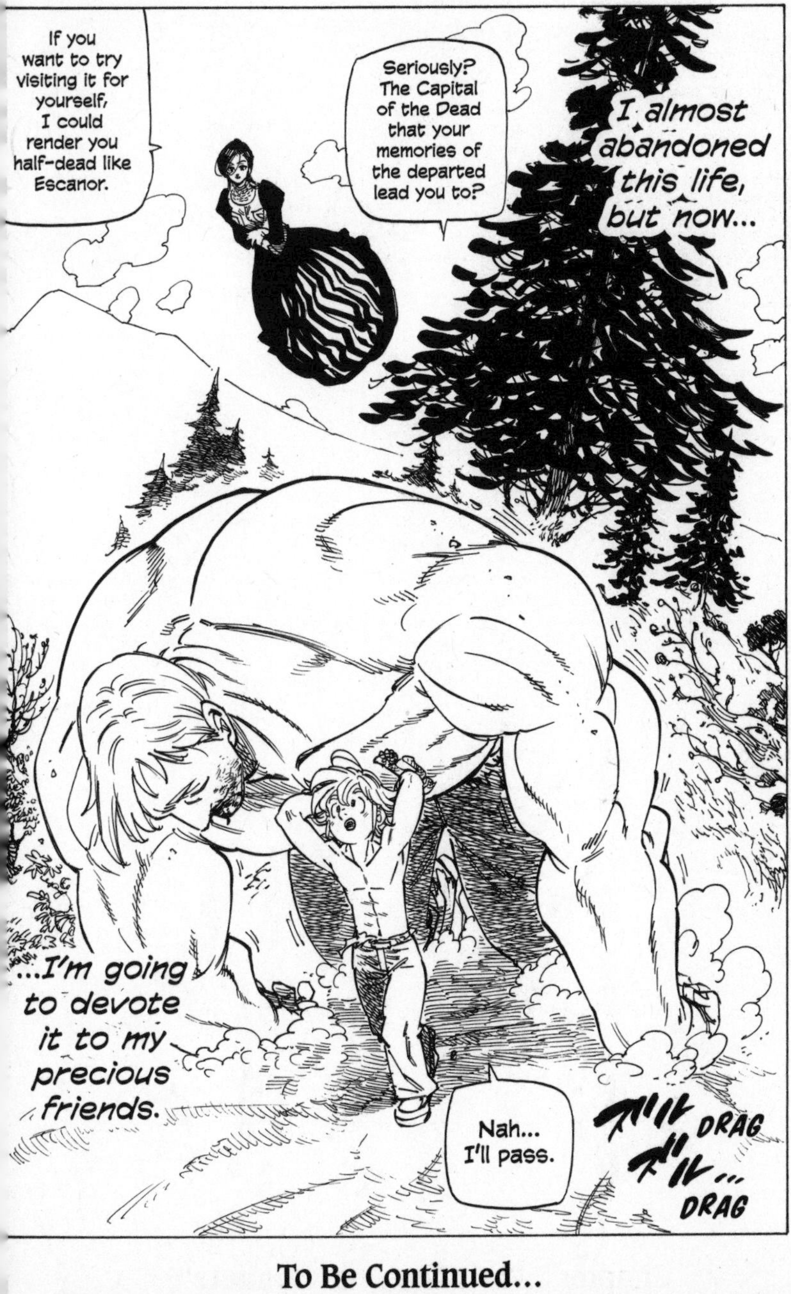
I almost abandoned this life, but now...
Seriously? The Capital of the Dead that your memories of the departed lead you to?
If you want to try visiting it for yourself, I could render you half-dead like Escanor.
DRAG DRAG
Nah... I'll pass.
...I'm going to devote it to my precious friends.

To Be Continued...

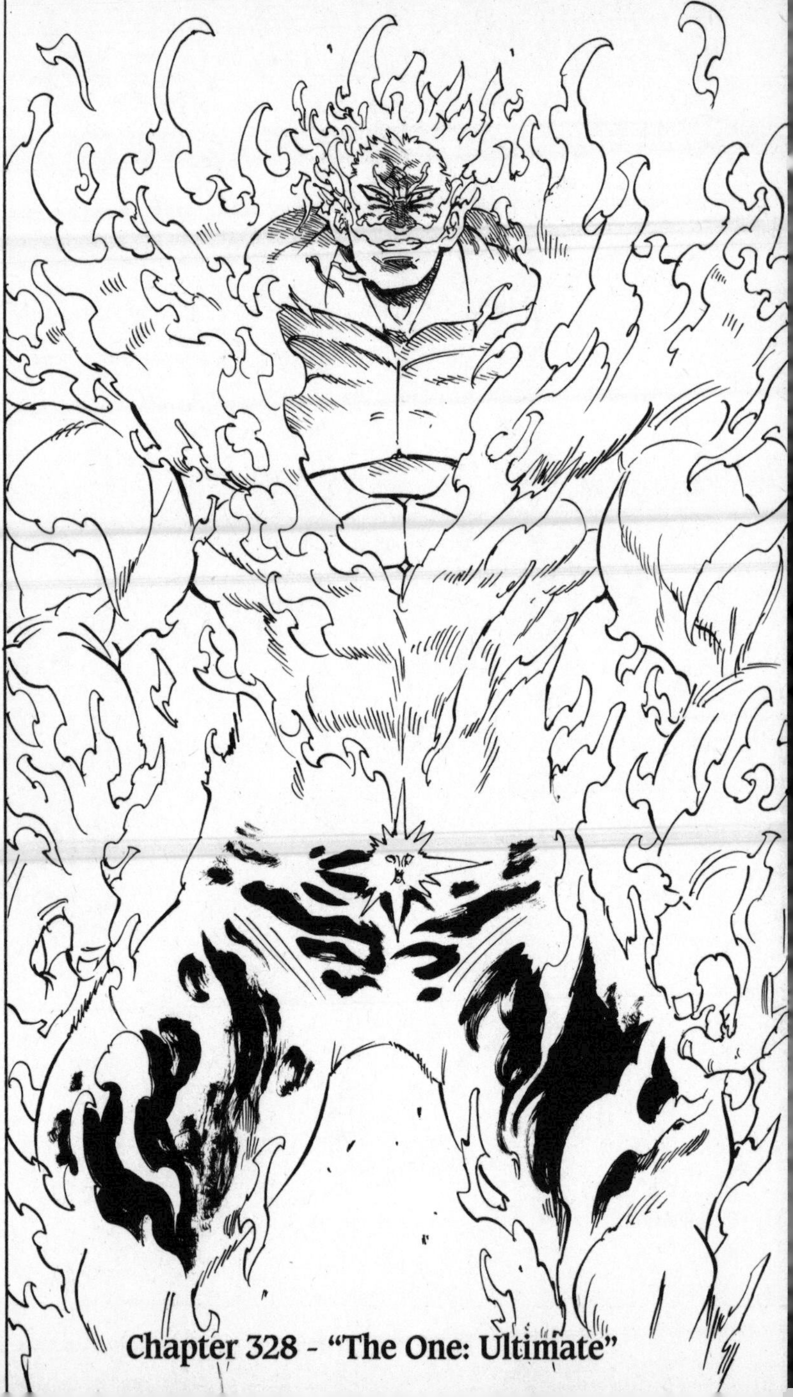

Chapter 328 - "The One: Ultimate"

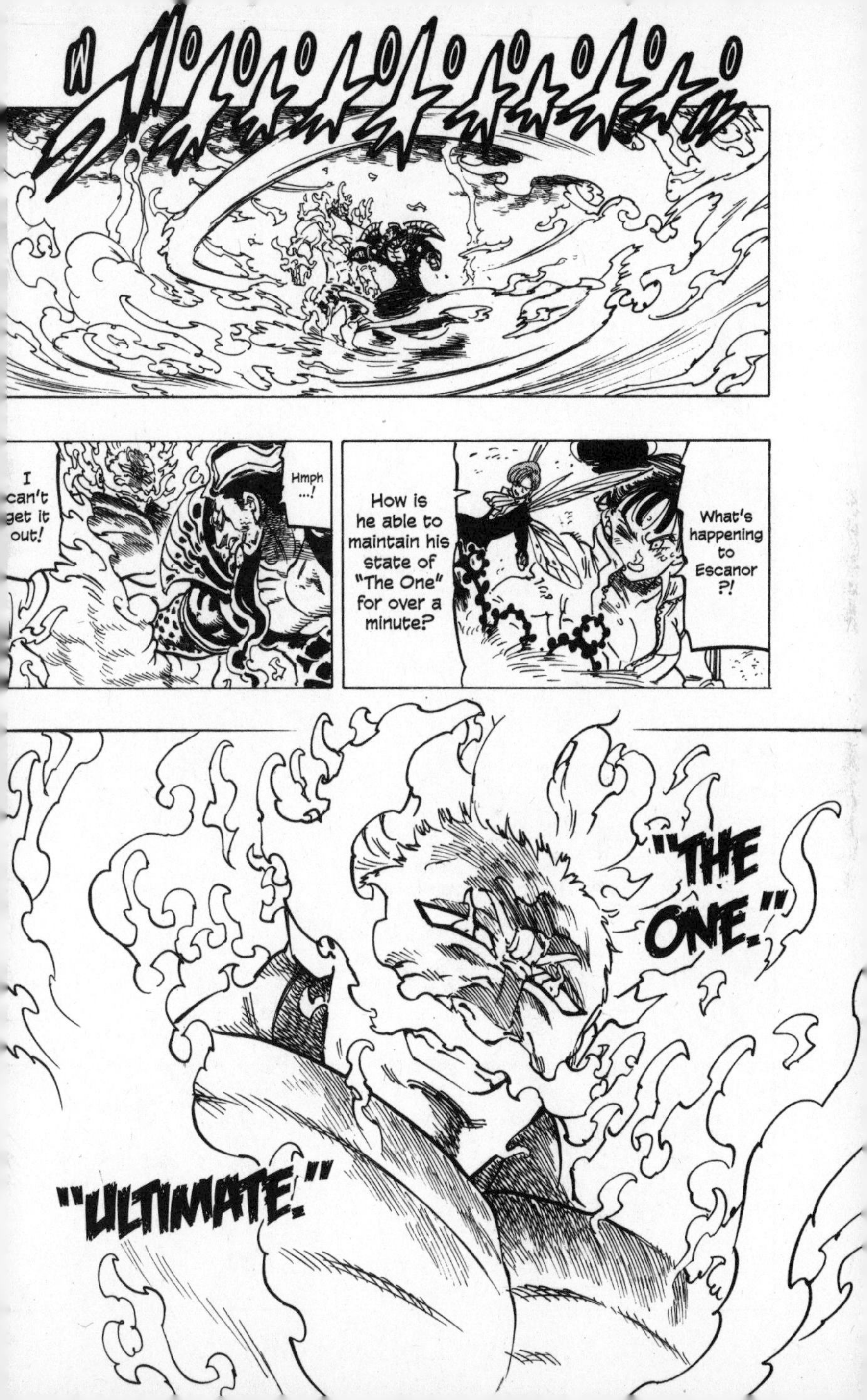
What's happening to Escanor?!
How is he able to maintain his state of "The One" for over a minute?
Hmph ...!
I can't get it out!
"THE ONE."
"ULTIMATE."

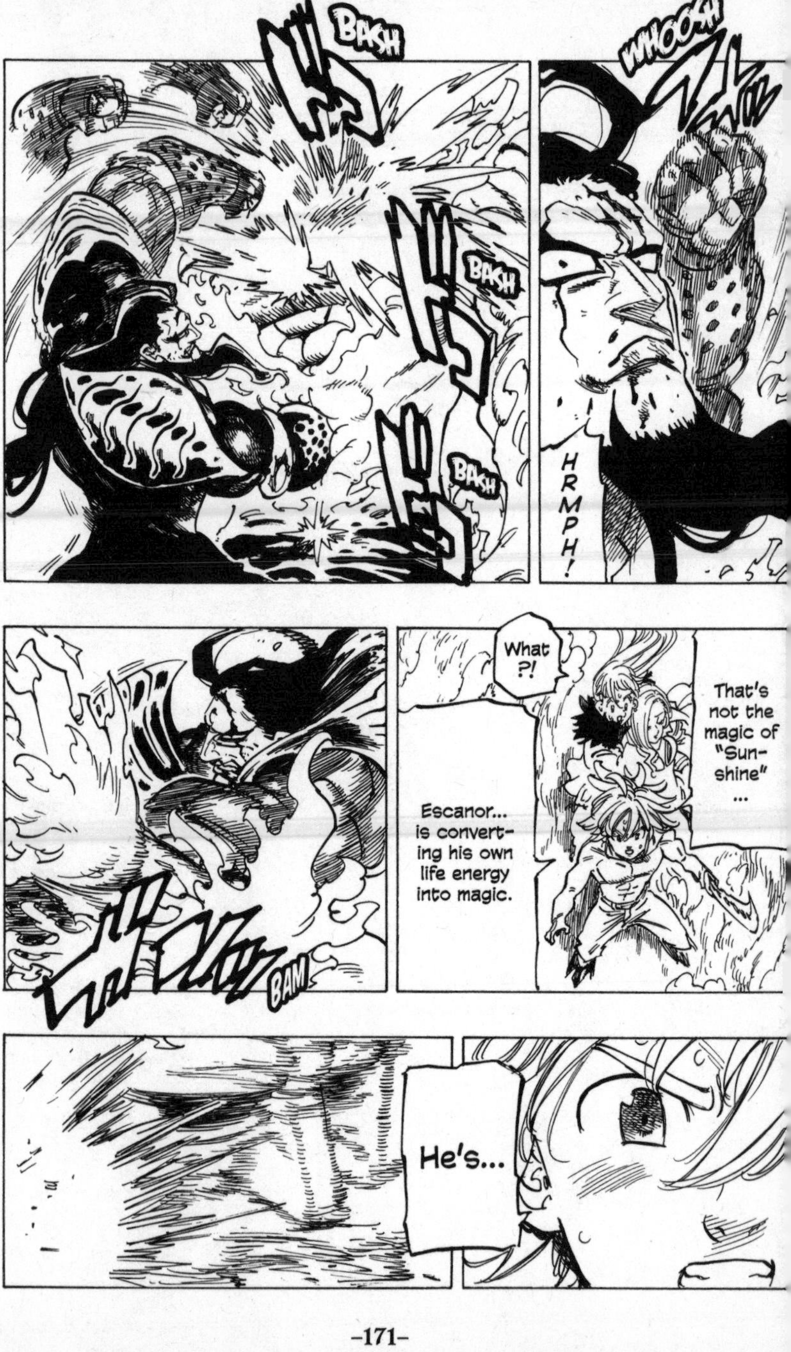
WHOOSH
HRMPH!
BASH
BASH
BASH
That's not the magic of "Sunshine"...
What?!
Escanor... is converting his own life energy into magic.
BAM
He's...

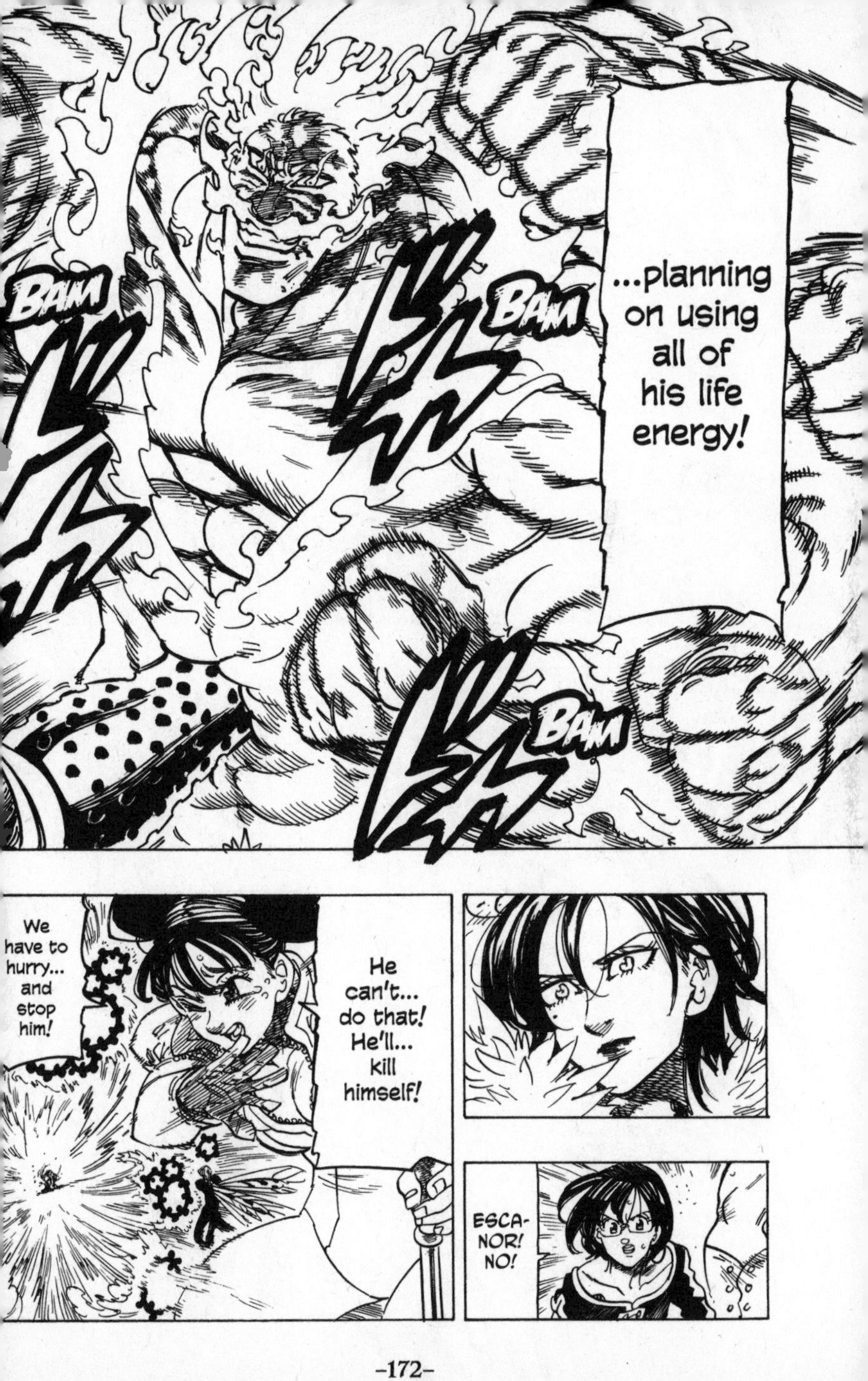
...planning on using all of his life energy!
BAM
BAM
BAM
ESCA-NOR! NO!
He can't... do that! He'll... kill himself!
We have to hurry... and stop him!

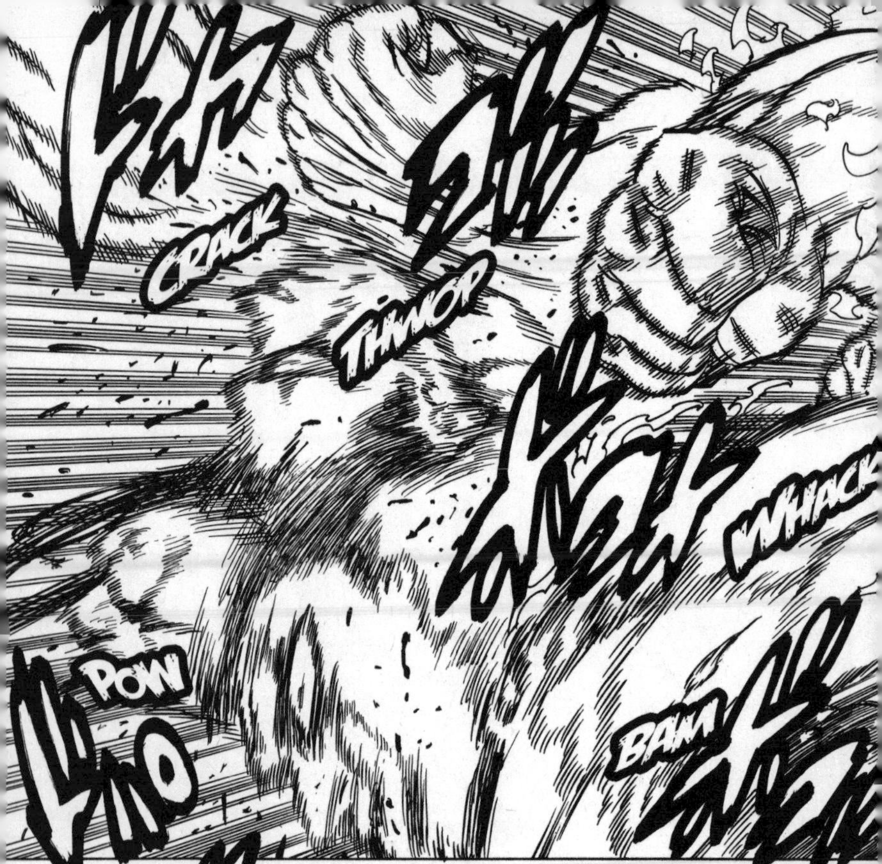
WHACK
THWOP
CRACK
BAM
POW
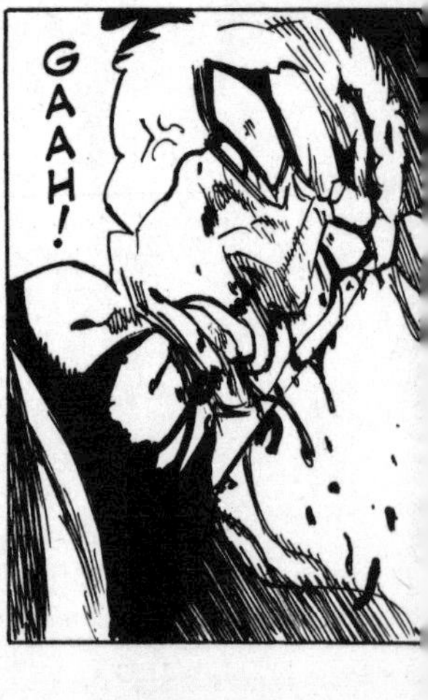
GAAH!
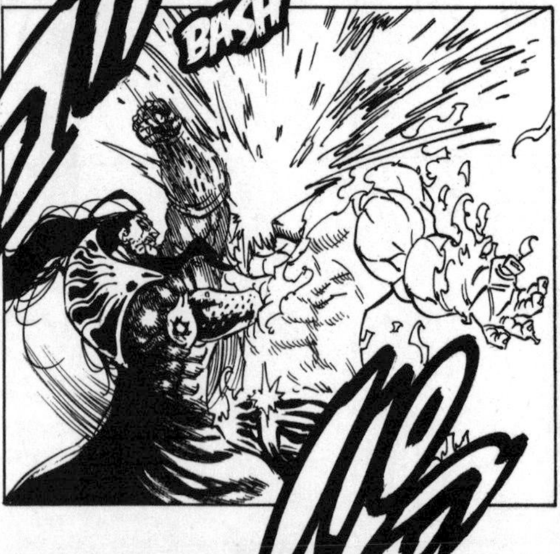
BASH

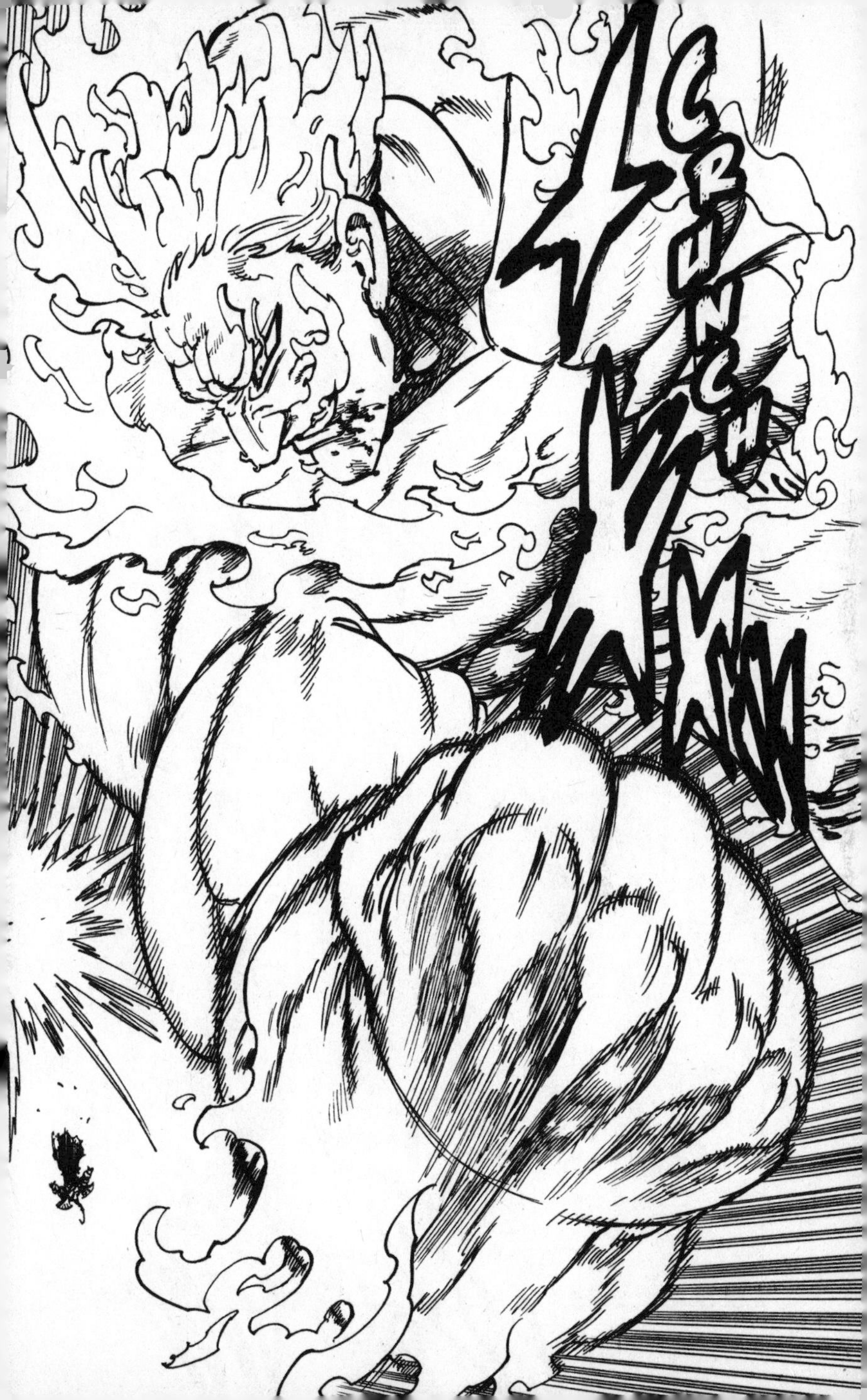
CRUNCH

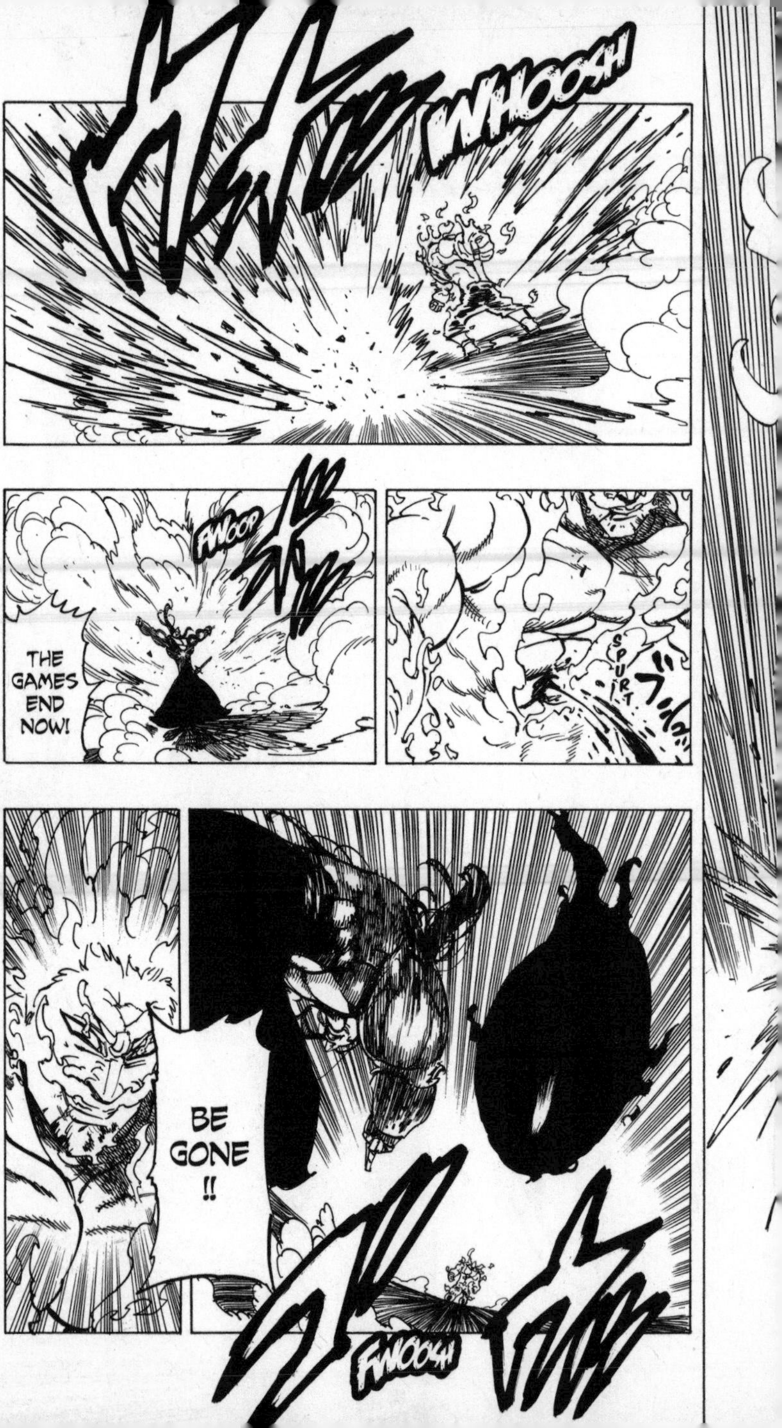
WHOOSH
SPURT
FWOOP
THE GAMES END NOW!
FWOOSH
BE GONE!!

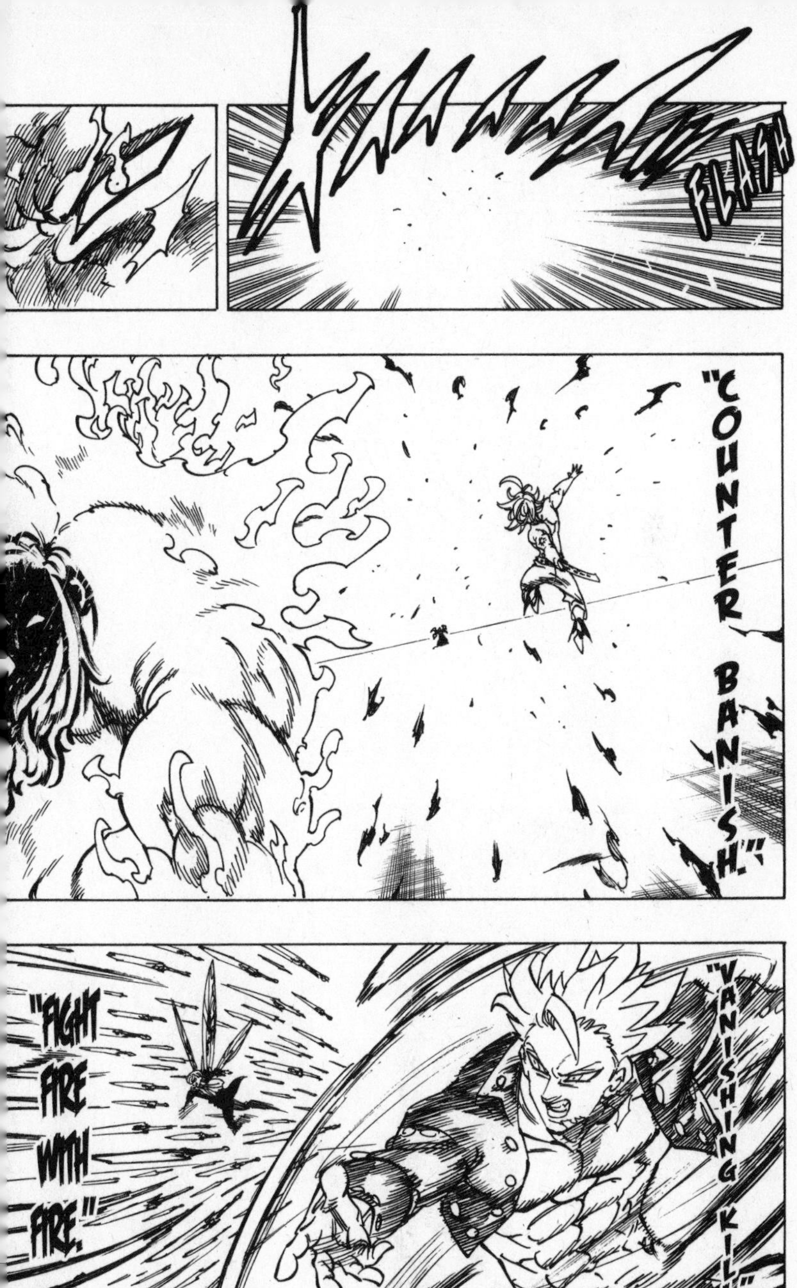
FLASH
"COUNTER BANISH."
"VANISHING KILL."
"FIGHT FIRE WITH FIRE."

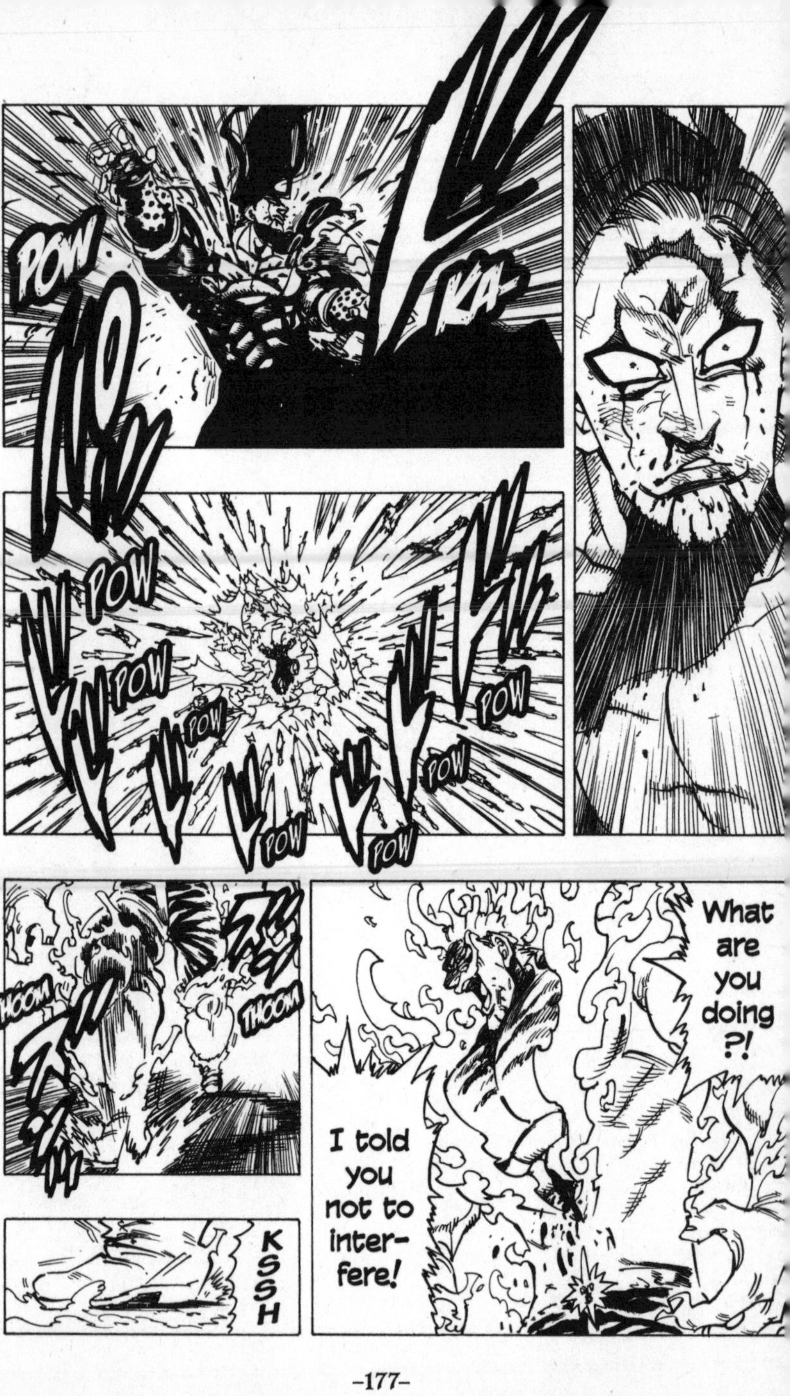
KA-
POW
POW
POW
POW
POW
POW
POW
POW
What are you doing?!
I told you not to interfere!
THOOM
THOOM
KSSH

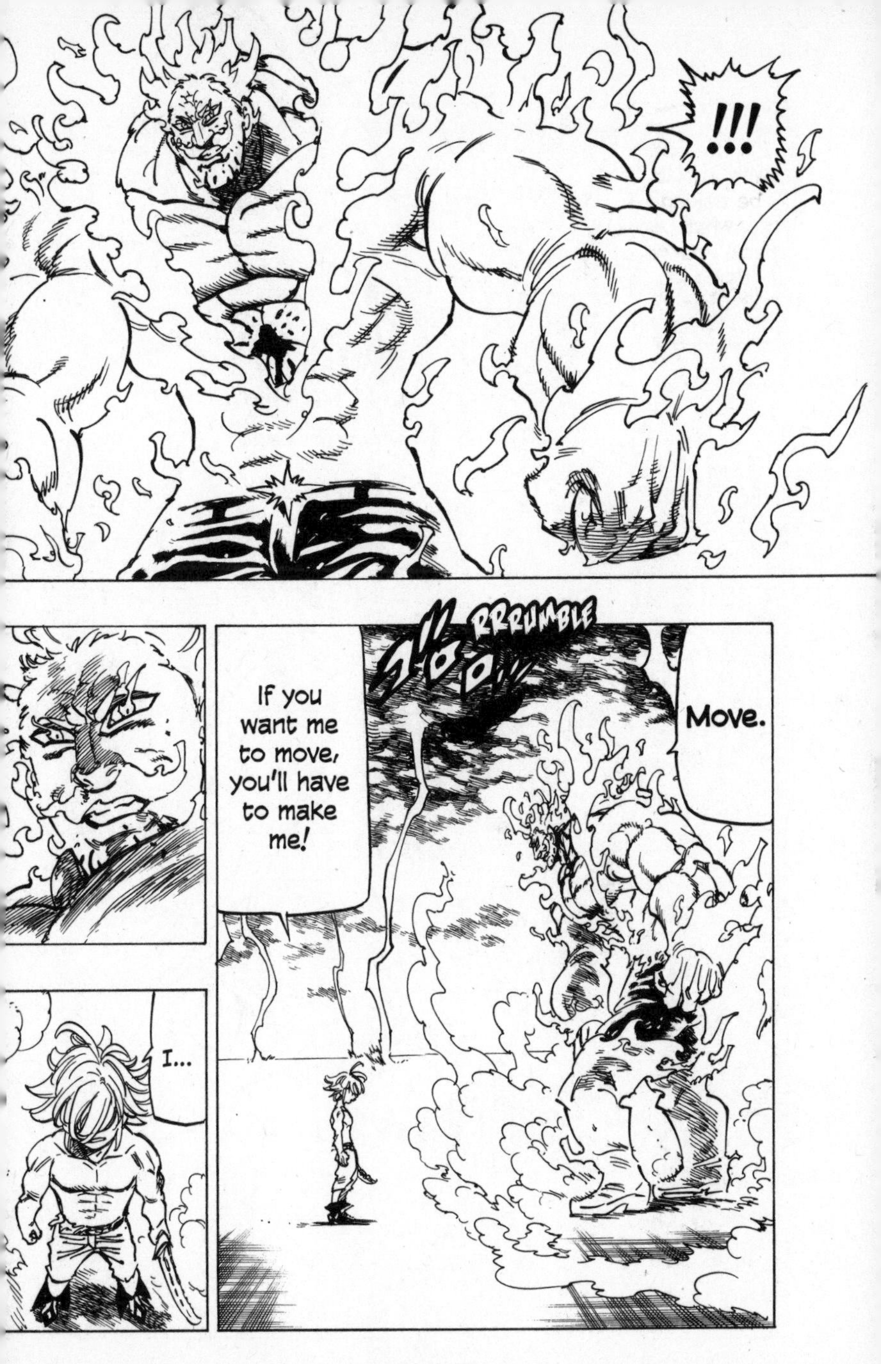
!!!
RRRUMBLE
Move.
If you want me to move, you'll have to make me!
I...

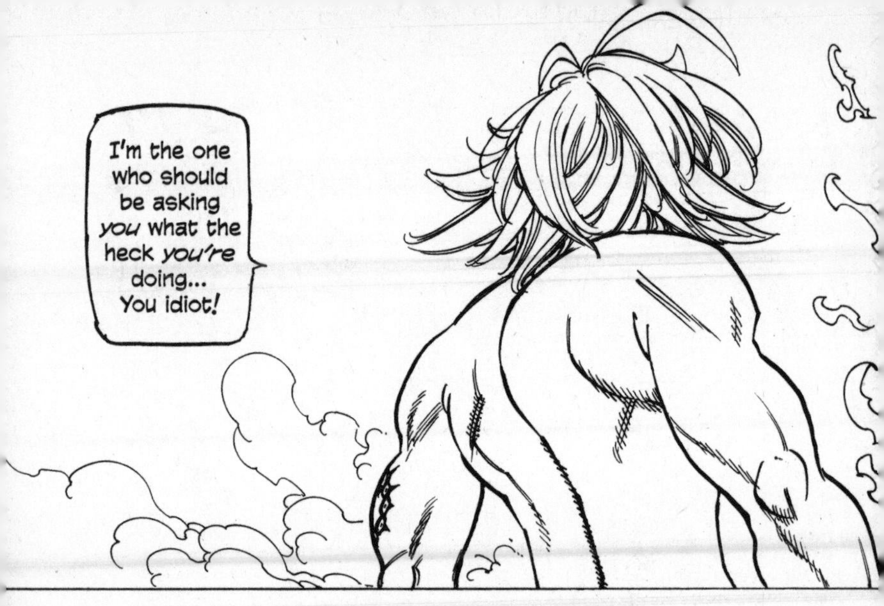
I'm the one who should be asking *you* what the heck *you're* doing... You idiot!
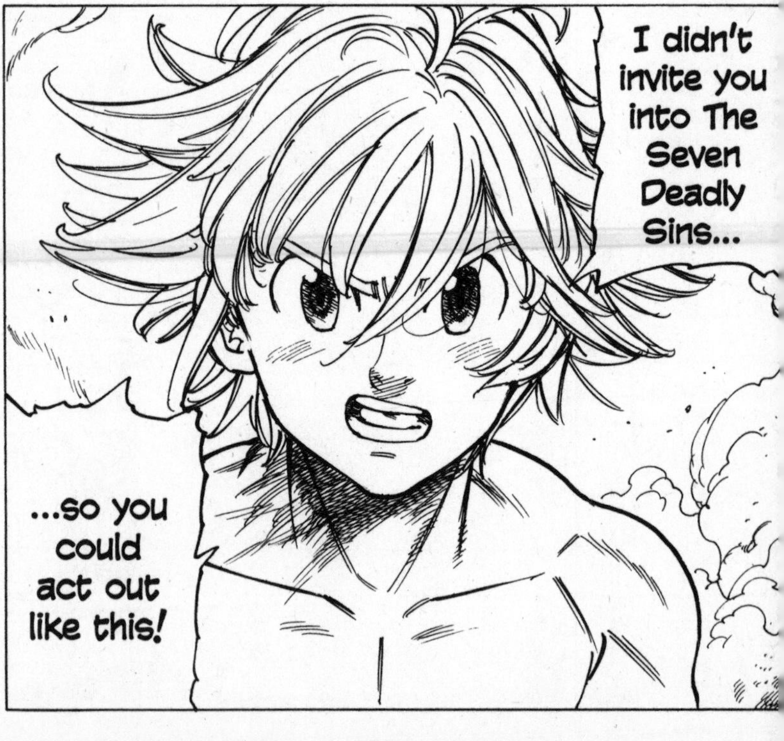
I didn't invite you into The Seven Deadly Sins...
...so you could act out like this!

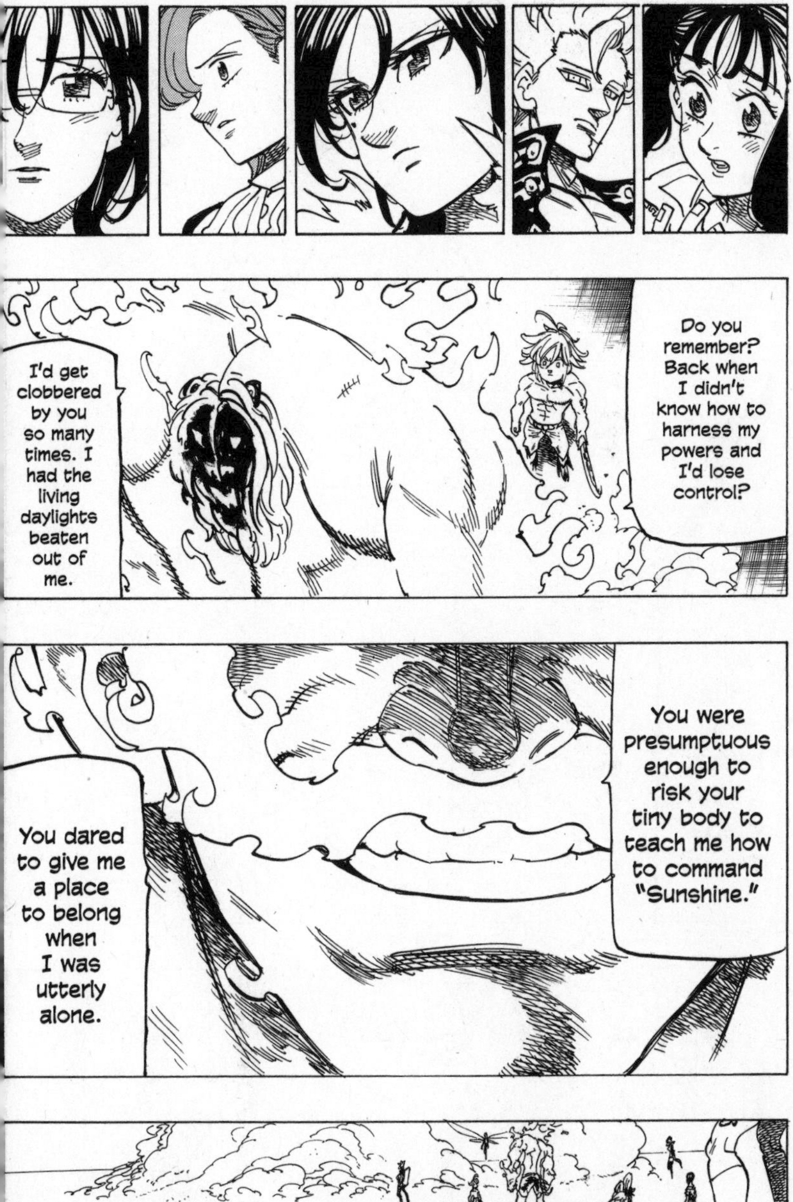
Do you remember? Back when I didn't know how to harness my powers and I'd lose control?
I'd get clobbered by you so many times. I had the living daylights beaten out of me.
You were presumptuous enough to risk your tiny body to teach me how to command "Sunshine."
You dared to give me a place to belong when I was utterly alone.

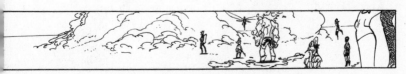

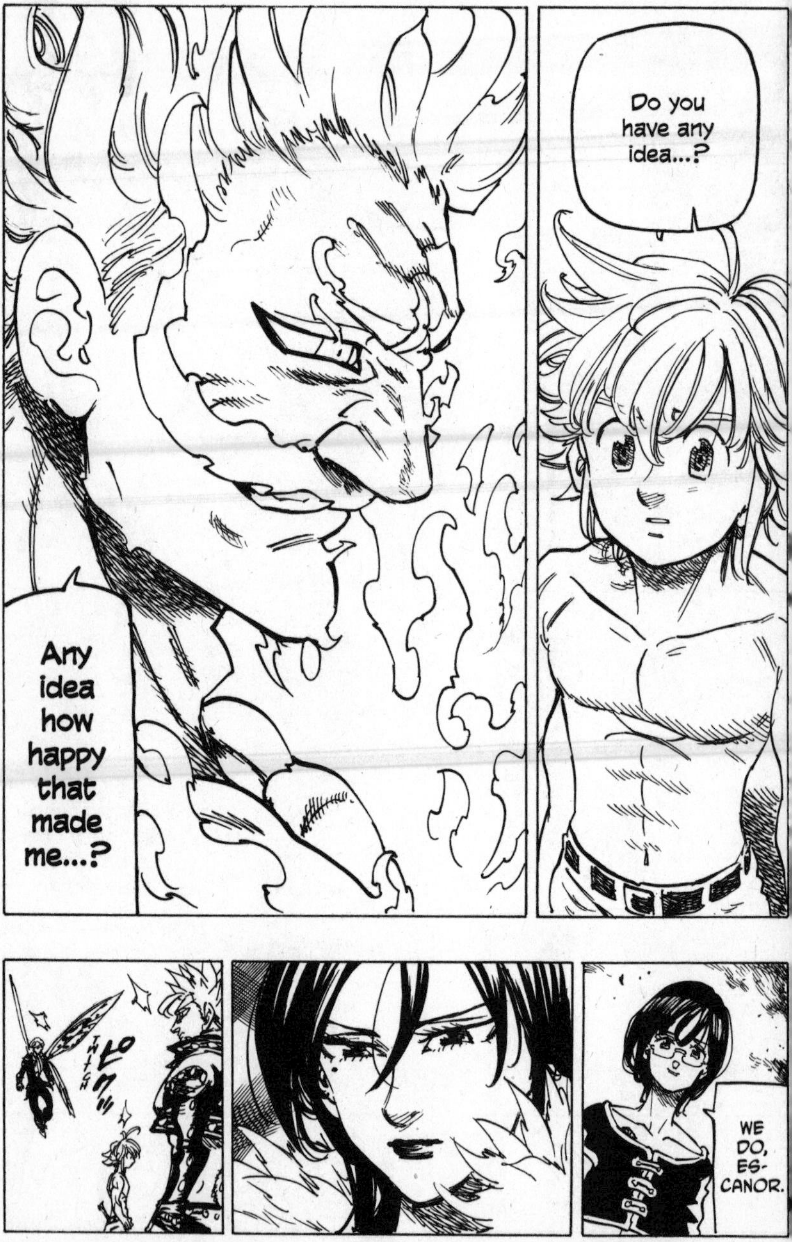
Do you have any idea...?
Any idea how happy that made me...?
WE DO, ES- CANOR.
TWITCH

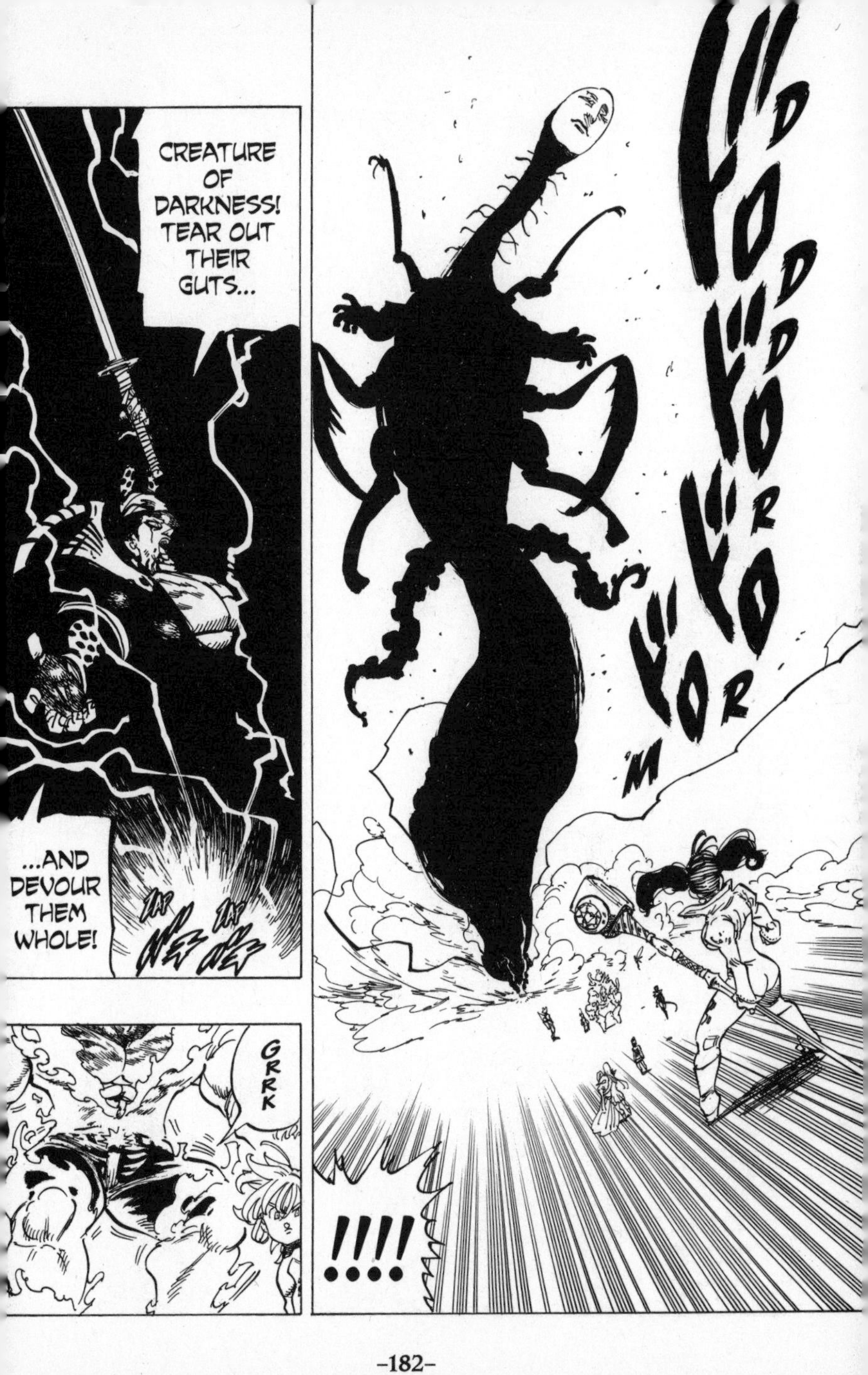
!!!!
CREATURE OF DARKNESS! TEAR OUT THEIR GUTS...
...AND DEVOUR THEM WHOLE!
TAP
TAP
GRRK

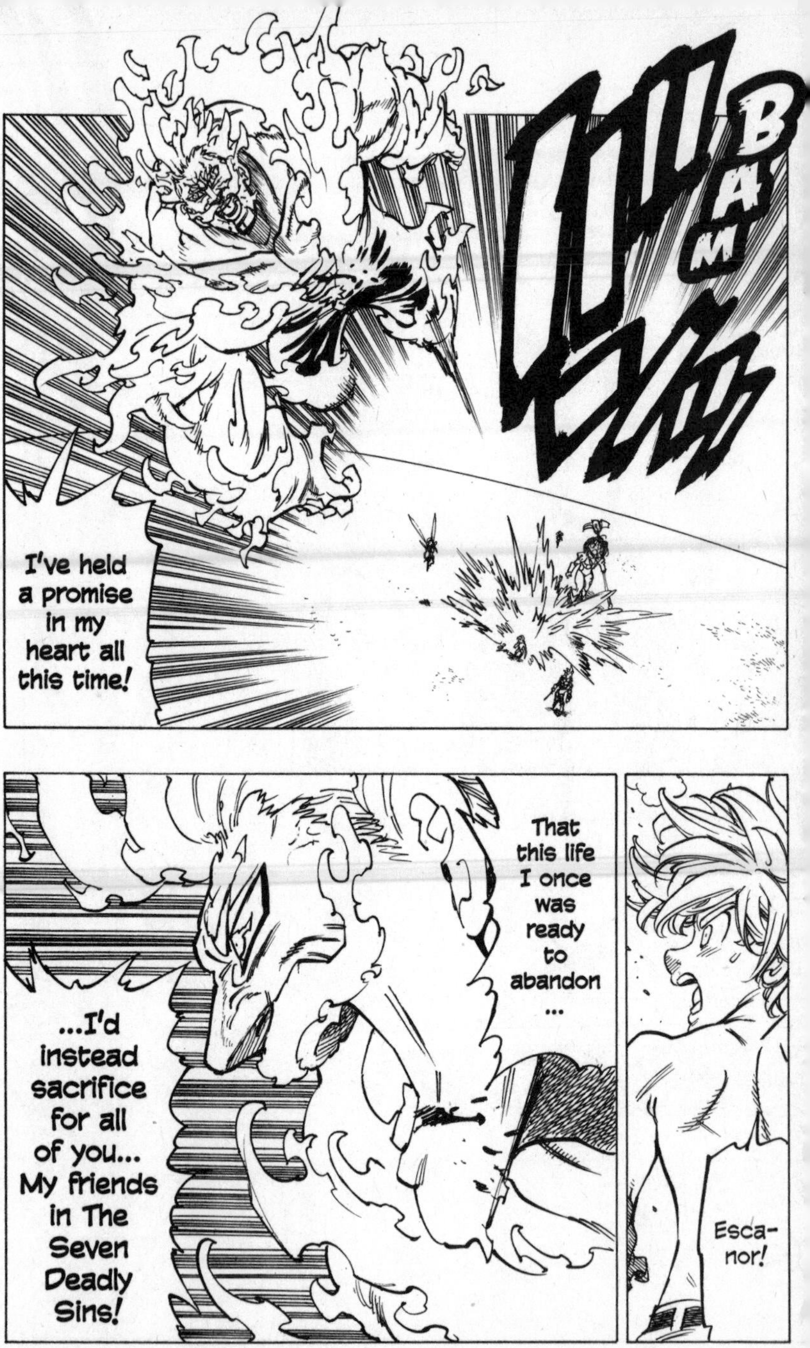
BAM
I've held a promise in my heart all this time!
Esca-nor!
That this life I once was ready to abandon...
...I'd instead sacrifice for all of you... My friends in The Seven Deadly Sins!

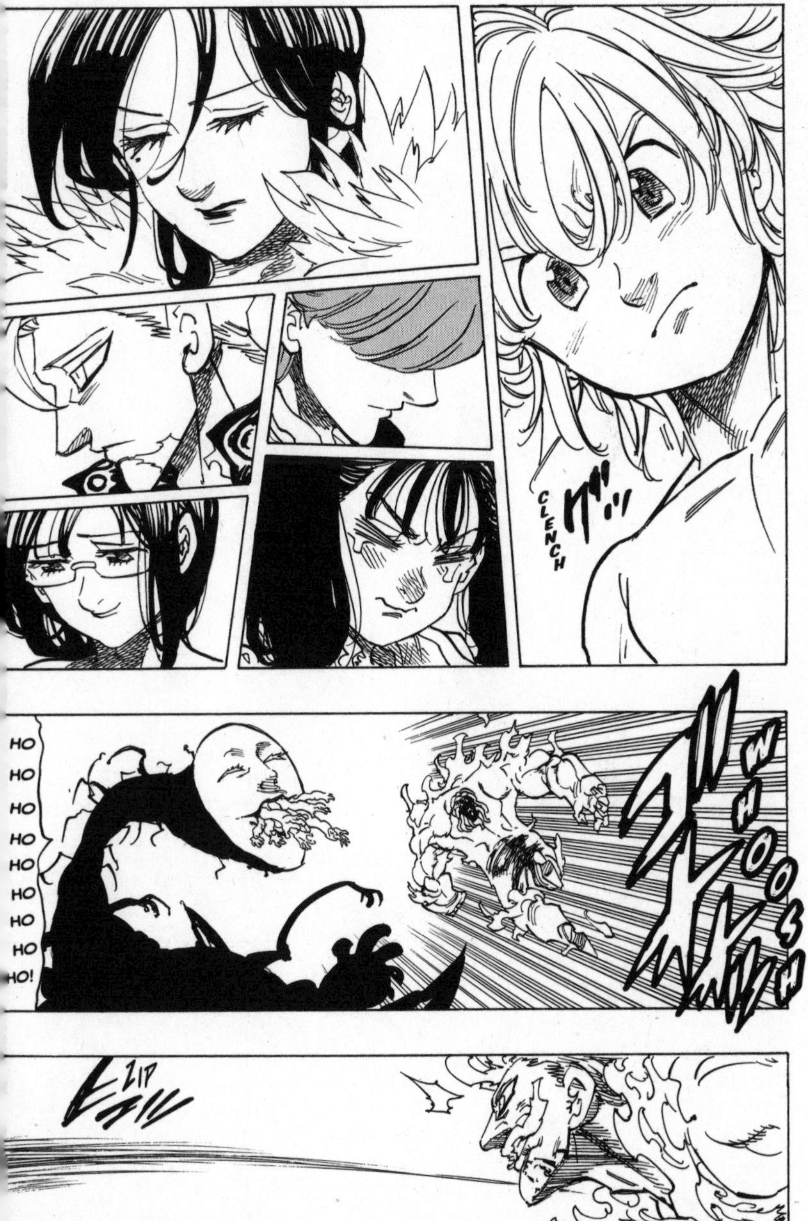
CLENCH
WHOOSH
HO HO HO HO HO HO HO HO HO!
ZIP

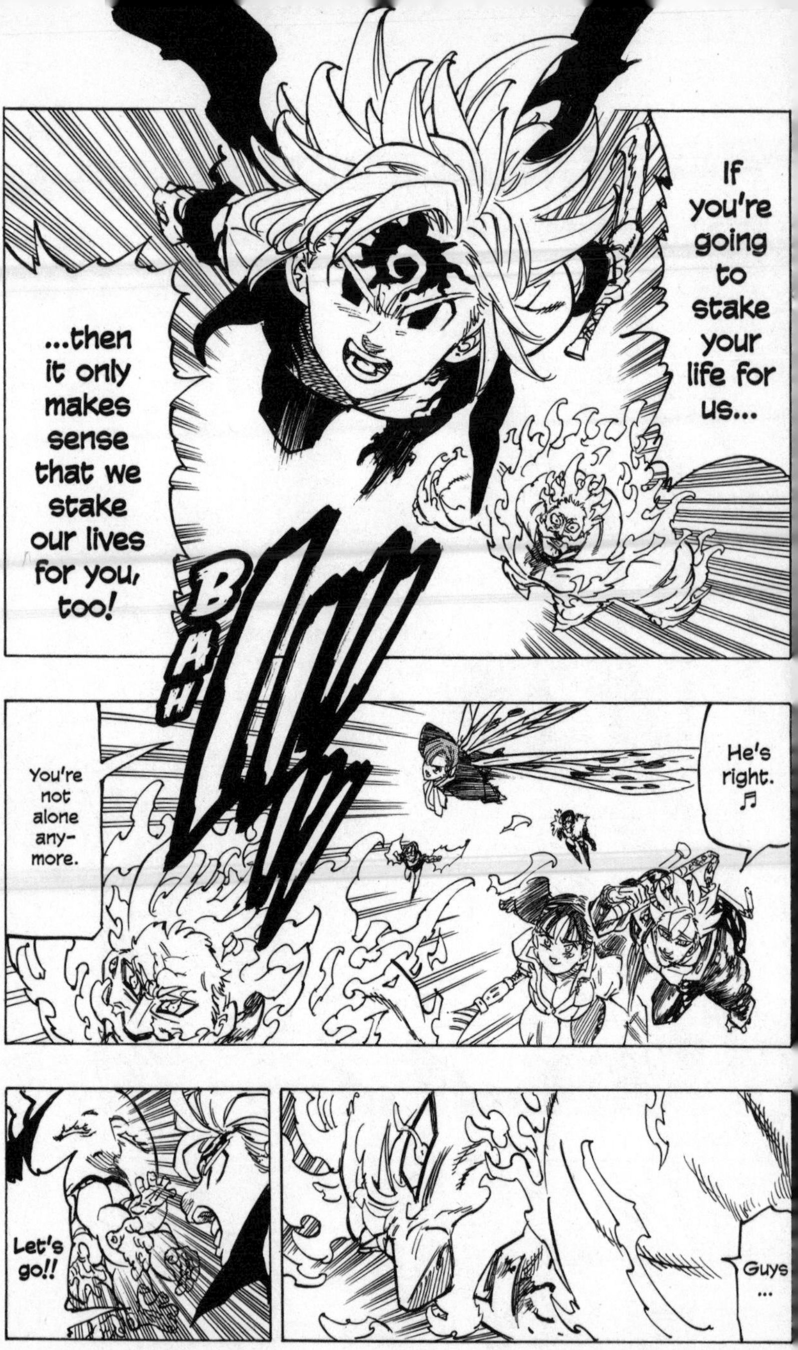

If you're going to stake your life for us...
...then it only makes sense that we stake our lives for you, too!
BAH
He's right. ♬
You're not alone any-more.
Guys ...
Let's go!!

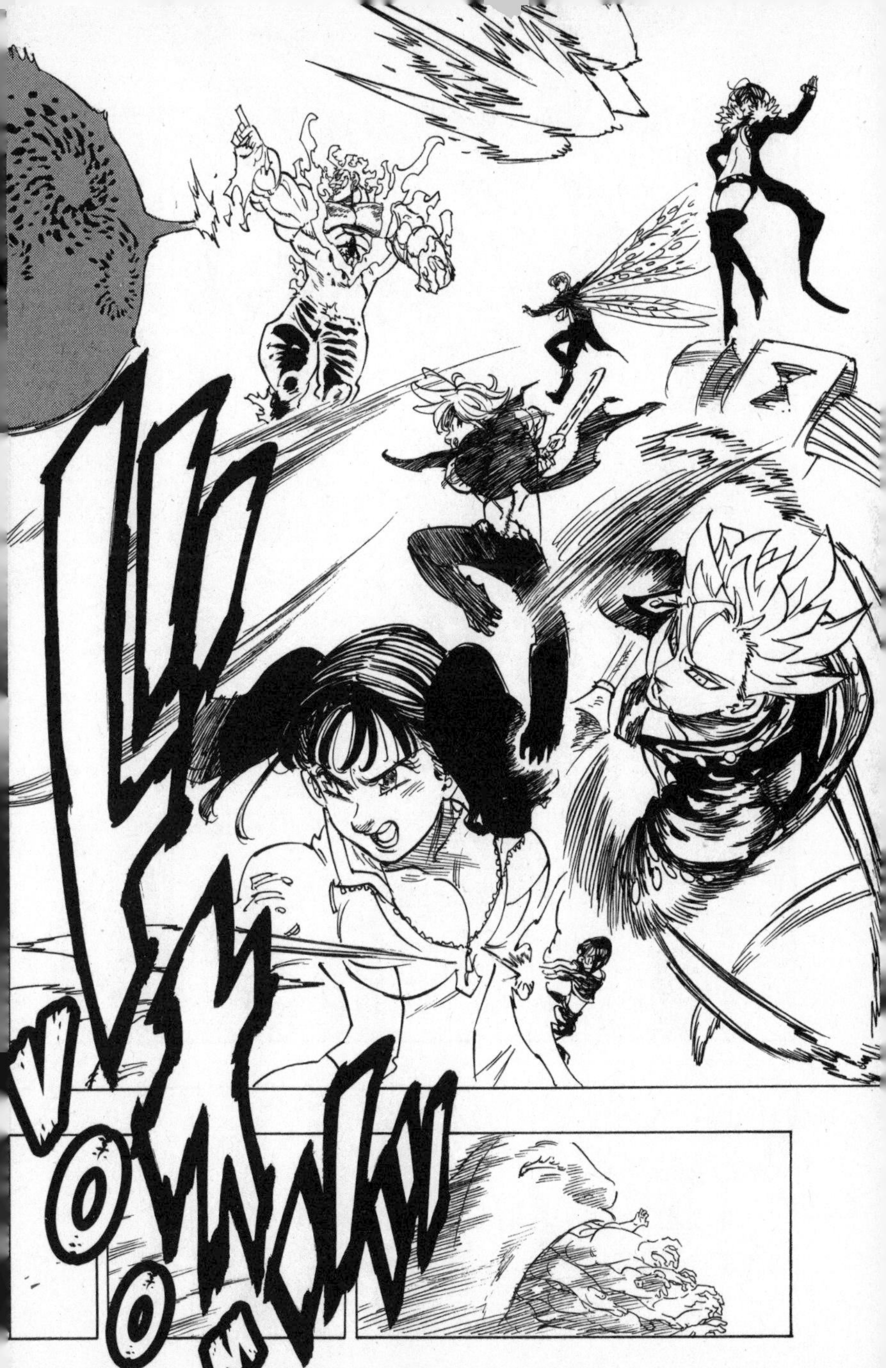
VOOM

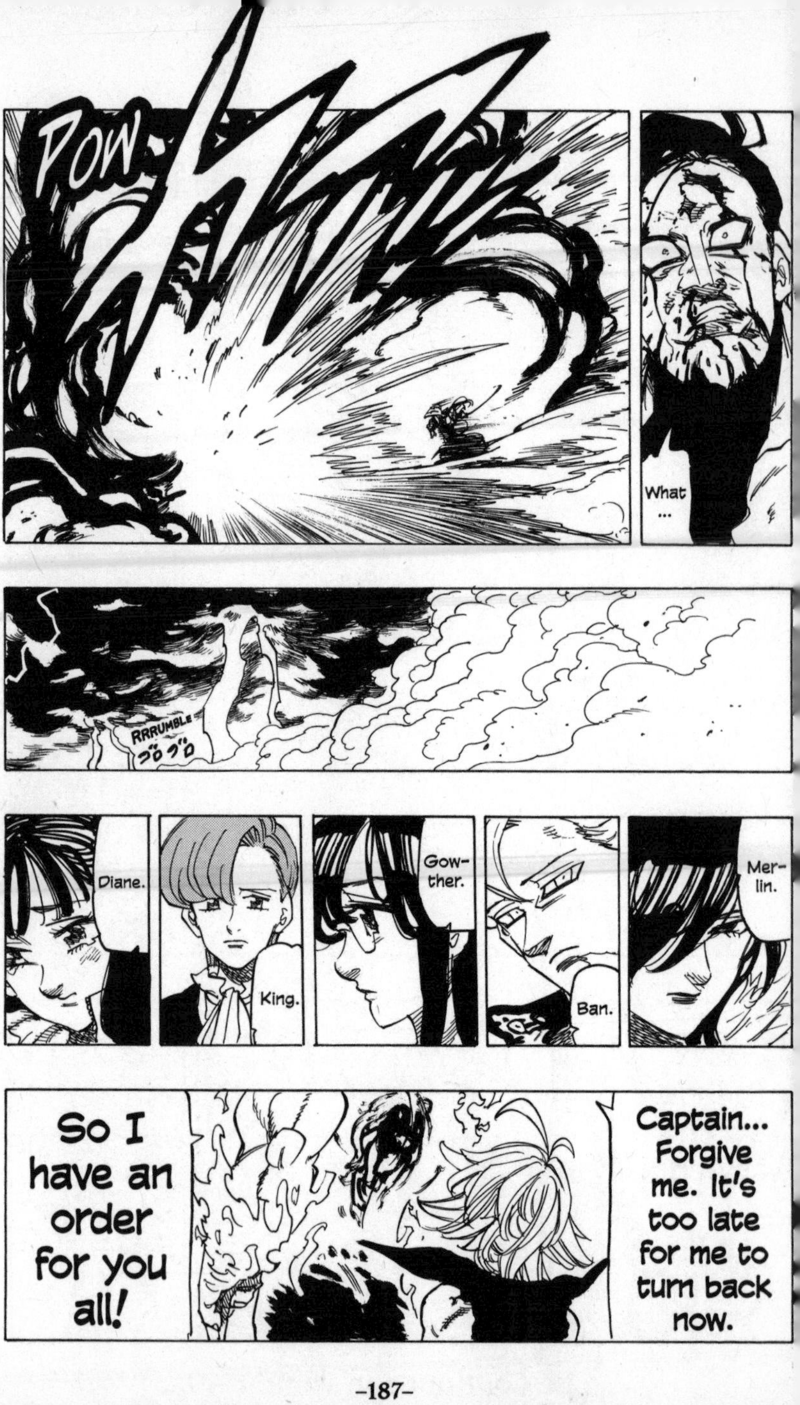
What ...
POW
RRRUMBLE
ゴロゴロ
Mer-lin.
Ban.
Gow-ther.
King.
Diane.
Captain... Forgive me. It's too late for me to turn back now.
So I have an order for you all!

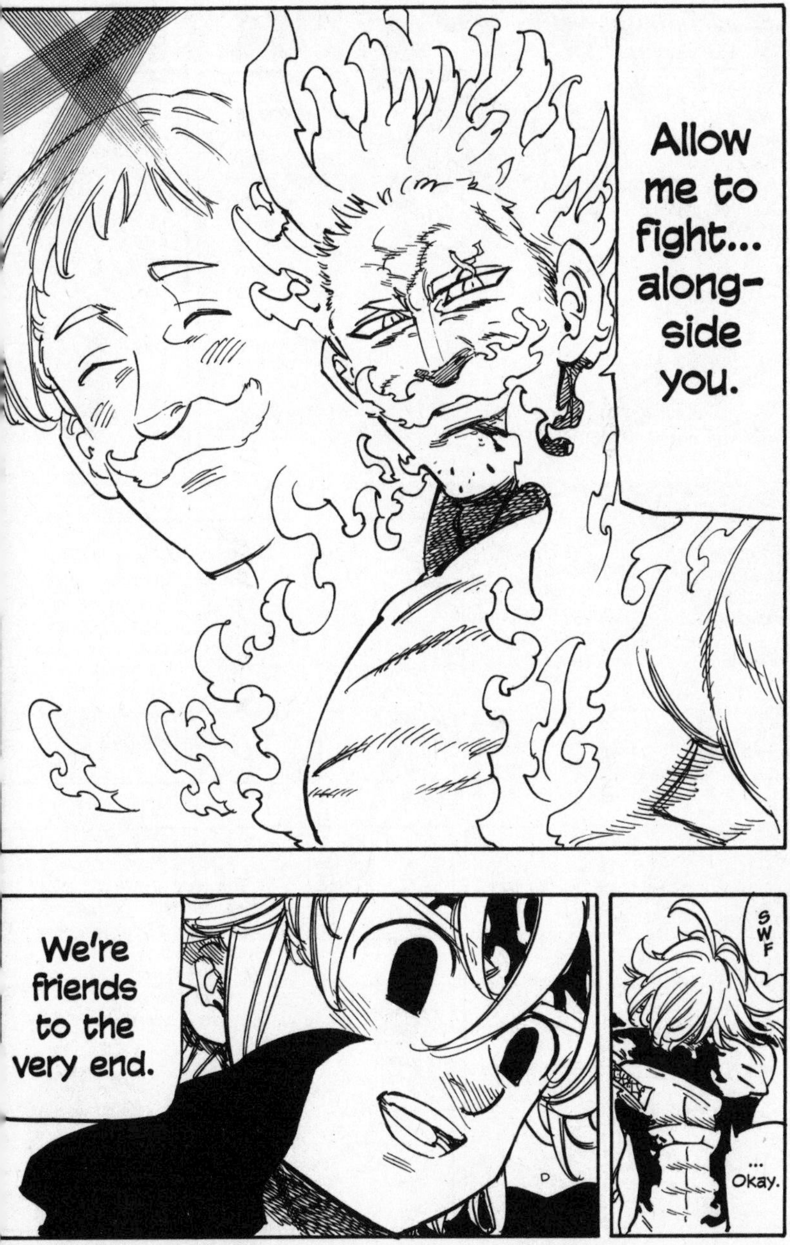
Allow me to fight... along-side you.
SWF
...Okay.
We're friends to the very end.

To Be Continued in volume 40...

Is the final volume of *The Seven Deadly Sins* near? A Special Essay.

40% Fiction

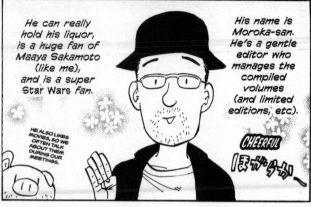

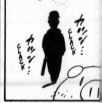

"The Seven Deadly Sins" has one more editor besides the wicked Toshi and sweet potato liquor-loving Y-moto.
CLACK
CLACK
His name is Moroka-san. He's a gentle editor who manages the compiled volumes (and limited editions, etc).
CHEERFUL
He can really hold his liquor, is a huge fan of Maaya Sakamoto (like me), and is a super Star Wars fan.
HE ALSO LIKES MOVIES, SO WE OFTEN TALK ABOUT THEM DURING OUR MEETINGS.
But what Moroka-san loves more passionately than anything is the professional Baseball Team XXX (the red guys).
RAAAWR!
DON'T LET XXX BEAT YOU!!!
And the notebook he rarely uses is, of course, XXX. He's a warrior who often goes to the baseball field!
On days when that team wins, he'll have the aura of a Buddha. On days when they lose, he's as belligerent as a rakshasa.
※ VISUALIZATION
For the record, I'm not a fan of any one team in particular, but for some reason the work clothes (t-shirts) my wife buys me are only XXX, so sometimes...
HM? COULD THAT BE Y-MOTO-KUN?
THANKS...
Here!
POTATO
You'd better not wear that t-shirt when you go to see Moroka-san tomorrow!
Eep...
GULP

THE END

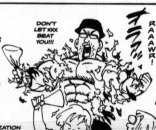

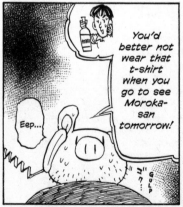

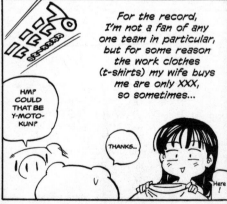

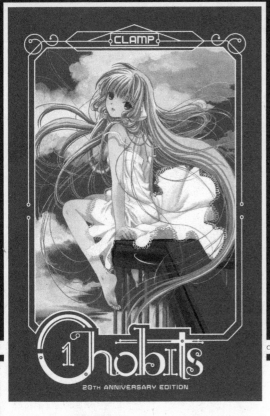

The boys are back, in 400-page hardcovers that are as pretty and badass as they are!

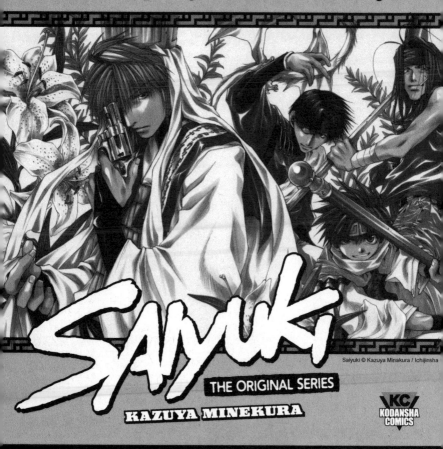

Saiyuki © Kazuya Minakura / Ichijinsha

SAIYUKI
THE ORIGINAL SERIES
KAZUYA MINEKURA

KC KODANSHA COMICS

The Seven Deadly Sins 39 is a work
places, and incidents are the produ
or are used fictitiously. Any resembla
persons, living or dead, is

A Kodansha Comics Trade

Published in the United States by Kodansha Comics, an imprint of
Kodansha USA Publishing, LLC, New York.

Publication rights for this English edition arranged through
Kodansha Ltd., Tokyo.

First published in Japan in 2019 by Kodansha Ltd., Tokyo
as *Nanatsu no taizai*, volume 39.

ISBN 978-1-64651-003-0

Original cover design by Ayumi Kaneko (hive & co., Ltd.)

Printed in the United States of America.

www.kodanshacomics.com

9 8 7 6 5 4 3 2 1
Translation: Christine Dashiell
Lettering: James Dashiell
Editing: Tiff Ferentini
Kodansha Comics edition cover design by Phil Balsman

KC
KODANSHA
COMICS

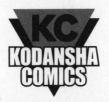

Publisher: Kiichiro Sugawara

Director of publishing services: Ben Applegate
Associate director of operations: Stephen Pakula
Publishing services managing editor: Noelle Webster
Assistant production manager: Emi Lotto, Angela Zurlo